Strengthening Competitiveness in Bangladesh—Thematic Assessment

DIRECTIONS IN DEVELOPMENT
Trade

Strengthening Competitiveness in Bangladesh—Thematic Assessment

A Diagnostic Trade Integration Study

Sanjay Kathuria and Mariem Mezghenni Malouche, Editors

 WORLD BANK GROUP

ISBN (paper): 978-1-4648-0898-2
ISBN (electronic): 978-1-4648-0899-9
DOI: 10.1596/978-1-4648-0898-2

Cover photo: © Mariem Mezghenni Malouche/World Bank; further permission required for reuse.
Cover design: Debra Naylor, Naylor Design, Washington, DC.

Library of Congress Cataloging-in-Publication Data has been requested.

Contents

Figures

Tables

Foreword

Bangladesh can be justly proud of its track record in reducing poverty and achieving progress on key human development indicators, such as child mortality, school enrollment, and female empowerment, to name a few. In mid-2015, reflecting a decade of robust growth, the World Bank reclassified Bangladesh from "low income" to "lower-middle-income."

Over the next decade, the most important development challenge for Bangladesh will be to provide more and better jobs to its workers, as more than 20 million people join the labor force.

Achieving this goal will require Bangladesh to connect more deeply to the world market for garments and other labor-intensive products. Opportunities exist, particularly as wages continue to rise in China, gradually reducing China's dominance in labor-intensive manufacturing.

To benefit fully from international demand and emerging opportunities for export-based job creation, Bangladesh will need to craft a proactive strategy.

This comprehensive report lays out a path for doing so. It covers a lot of ground, including trade policy and institutions, logistics and infrastructure, and finance and foreign direct investment. It also anchors that thematic work in detailed studies of different sectors, such as shipbuilding, non-leather footwear, jute products, garments/polo shirts, bicycles, information technology, services, and pharmaceuticals.

We are confident that the depth and breadth of the report, combined with the high quality of its analysis, will contribute to the development debate in Bangladesh. In addition, policy makers and development partners will find a possible reform agenda, focused on areas critical to Bangladesh's development that they can support.

The World Bank Group is already supporting the Government of Bangladesh in a broad range of areas related to private sector development, and, following the guidance of this report, expects to deepen this engagement, centering around job creation and trade and competitiveness.

We are grateful to the Government of Bangladesh for entrusting the World Bank Group to carry out this important diagnostic work, and to the Enhanced

Integrated Framework Secretariat at the World Trade Organization for funding and other substantive support.

Qimiao Fan
Country Director for Bangladesh,
   Bhutan, and Nepal
The World Bank Group

Anabel Gonzalez
Senior Director
Trade and Competitiveness Global
   Practice
The World Bank Group

Acknowledgments

This Diagnostic Trade Integration Study (DTIS) has been prepared in response to a request from the Government of Bangladesh under the Enhanced Integrated Framework (EIF) for Trade Related Technical Assistance to Least Developed Countries. The EIF is a multi-donor program that supports the least developed countries in becoming more active players in the global trading system by helping them tackle supply-side constraints to trade. The ultimate objective of the study is to build the foundation for accelerated growth by enhancing the integration of the economy of Bangladesh into regional and global markets.

The World Bank thanks the Government of Bangladesh for placing its confidence in the World Bank to conduct this study. The main counterpart for the DTIS is the World Trade Organization (WTO) Cell in the Ministry of Commerce of Bangladesh. The European Union is the donor facilitator, which means it is taking the lead in mobilizing resources to fund the identified actions. The Government of Bangladesh has displayed strong ownership of the task, initiating its preparation and forming a National Steering Committee with concerned ministries, local think tanks, and the private sector to provide guidance to the work. The government's views and comments have been reflected at all stages of the report, from the Concept Note stage to the final Action Matrix. The team particularly thanks Mr. Amitava Chakraborty, Director General (Additional Secretary), WTO Cell, and the team in the WTO Cell, Ministry of Commerce, including Mr. Nesar Ahmed (Director, WTO Cell), Dr. Md. Moniruzzaman (Director, WTO Cell), Mr. Mohammad Zakir Hossain (Deputy Director, WTO Cell), and Mr. Mohammad Mashooqur Rahman Sikder (Deputy Director, WTO Cell).

Development partners, think tanks, the private sector, and other stakeholders have been consulted regularly at different stages in the preparation of the DTIS. Their views have been solicited through consultative workshops and one-on-one meetings. As an example, the team organized a consultative workshop with business leaders, development partners, government, academia, and researchers in June 2010. One-on-one meetings were also held with a number of individuals. The team organized two interim consultative workshops in December 2012. A two-day validation workshop was organized jointly by the WTO Cell, Ministry of Commerce, and the World Bank on October 22–23, 2013, in Dhaka.

The prioritized recommendations of the Action Matrix were discussed in the validation workshop. The team has benefited from consultations with Dr. Mirza Azizul Islam (Former Adviser to the Government of Bangladesh, Ministry of Finance); Dr. Md. Mozibur Rahman (CEO, Bangladesh Foreign Trade Institute [BFTI]); Dr. Mostafa Abid Khan (Director, BFTI); Dr. M. K. Mujeri (Director General, Bangladesh Institute of Development Studies); and Dr. Zaidi Sattar, Dr. Sadiq Ahmed, and Dr. Ahsan Mansur (Policy Research Institute (PRI), Bangladesh).

The report has been prepared by a core World Bank team led by Sanjay Kathuria (Lead Economist) and Mariem Mezghenni Malouche (Senior Economist) and including Nadeem Rizwan (then Research Analyst and now Ph.D candidate at North Carolina State University). The contributing team included several World Bank Group staff and consultants, including Charles Kunaka (Senior Trade Specialist, World Bank); Peter Kusek (Senior Investment Policy Officer, IFC); Michael Friss Jensen, Olivier Cadot, Nihal Pitigala, Hugh Baylis, Zaidi Sattar, and PRI Bangladesh; Dr. Selim Raihan (Dhaka University); Kay Dausendschoen (FutureShip); Glenn Surabian and Yasuo Konishi (Global Development Solutions); and Atdhe Veliu. Support was also received from Martha Denisse Pierola (Economist), Jose Daniel Reyes (Economist), Mohammad Anis (Energy Specialist), Iffath Sharif (Senior Economist), Ayesha Vawda (Senior Education Specialist), Tanya Primiani (Investment Policy Officer, IFC), and Sanjana Zaman (Research Analyst). The team thanks the development partners for their comments and cooperation. The team acknowledges comments received from World Bank Group colleagues, including peer reviewers Ndiame Diop (Lead Economist, MNSED), Philip Schuler (Senior Economist, AFTP1), Vincent Palmade (Lead Economist, SASFP), and Reynaldo Bench (Senior Port Specialist, TWITR); Salman Zaidi (Lead Economist); Zahid Hussain (Lead Economist); Vinaya Swaroop (Sector Manager, SASEP); Gladys Lopez-Acevedo (Lead Economist); Martin Maxwell Norman (Senior Private Sector Development Specialist); Manju Haththotuwa (Senior Private Sector Development Specialist); Arbind Modi (Principal Operations Officer, IFC); Sherif Muhtaseb (Senior Operations Officer, IFC); Hosna Ferdous Sumi (Associate Operations Officer, IFC); Raihana Rabbany (Consultant, IFC); Rodrigo Cubero and Seng Guan Toh (IMF); and Sadiq Ahmad and Zaidi Sattar (PRI). Mariem Mezghenni Malouche, Lalita Moorty, and Md. Abul Basher led the initial preparation of the concept note for the report. The team thanks Mehar Akhtar Khan and Kamrun Nahar Chowdhury for support with desktop publishing, logistics, and organizing the workshops in Dhaka. Rita Soni and Muhammad Shafiq helped with contracting and Sandra Gain and Michael Alwan edited the report. The team also thanks colleagues in the International Finance Corporation (in particular, Masrur Reaz and Paramita Dasgupta) for supporting a number of the sector studies, which greatly helped to increase the coverage of the DTIS, and Christine Kraus, Chief Coordinator for the Enhanced Integrated Framework at the World Trade Organization. Colleagues in the Trade and Competitiveness Global Practice (including Masrur Reaz,

Nusrat Nahid Babi, and Victoria Dimple Penheiro) have been a key part of the team that is engaging in post-DTIS engagement with the Government. Finally, the team acknowledges the support of the World Bank management team led by the former Country Directors Johannes Zutt and Ellen Goldstein throughout the process of preparation.

About the Authors

Sanjay Kathuria is Lead Economist in the World Bank's South Asia Regional Cooperation and Integration Unit, based in Washington, DC. Until August 2012, he was the World Bank's Lead Economist for Bangladesh, based in Dhaka. In 23 years at the World Bank, he has worked in the South Asia Region, as well as in the Latin America and the Caribbean and Europe and Central Asia regions. Prior to joining the World Bank, he was a Fellow at the Indian Council for Research on International Economic Relations in New Delhi. He graduated from St. Stephen's College and he received his master's from the Delhi School of Economics and his PhD from Oxford University. His research interests include economic growth, economic integration, international trade and trade policy, competitiveness, technology development, fiscal policy, and financial sector development. He has published several books and academic and popular articles on those topics. Recent books and report credits include coauthor of *Consolidating and Accelerating Exports in Bangladesh* (World Bank, 2012); lead author of *Macedonia, FYR: Moving to Faster and More Inclusive Growth: A Country Economic Memorandum* (World Bank, 2009); and editor of *Western Balkan Integration and the EU: An Agenda for Growth and Development* (World Bank, 2008).

Mariem Mezghenni Malouche is a Senior Economist at the World Bank in Washington, D.C. Her areas of interest include trade and competitiveness, economic integration, trade policy, nontariff measures, export diversification, trade finance, and diaspora. She joined the World Bank in 2004 as an economist in the Middle East and North Africa (MENA) Region and later the International Trade department. She earned a PhD in international economics from Université Paris-Dauphine, France, and a master's degree in business from University of Tunis III with highest honors. She is a coauthor of *Streamlining Non-Tariff Measures: A Toolkit for Policy Makers* (World Bank, 2012); coeditor of *Non-Tariff Measures: A Fresh Look at Trade Policy's New Frontier*; and coeditor of *Trade Finance during the Great Trade Collapse* (World Bank, 2011). She has participated in and contributed to a number of country-level policy dialogues, development policy loans, and reports in the Middle East and North Africa, South Asia, and Sub-Saharan Africa regions, notably in Bangladesh, Kazakhstan, Lao PDR, Libya, Mauritius, Morocco, and Tunisia.

Hugh Baylis is a trade finance expert who has held various positions in international organizations and private sector banks. He was senior advisor at the International Finance Corporation where he established and managed the Global Trade Finance Program (GTFP) providing trade support to banks in developing countries. He also established similar programs at the Asian Development Bank and at the European Bank for Reconstruction and Development. Prior to that, he held senior positions at Chase Manhattan Bank New York and at Continental Bank of Chicago in Paris and Madrid.

Olivier Cadot is a professor of international economics and director of the Institute of Applied Economics at the University of Lausanne. Prior to taking up his position at Lausanne, he was Associate Professor of Economics at INSEAD. He has held visiting appointments at various universities in the U.S. and France. He was a Senior Economist in the World Bank's Trade Department between 2009 and 2011 and has advised the European Commission and the governments of France and the Swiss Confederation on trade policy matters. He was elected best teacher of the year at the Faculty of Business and Economics (HEC) at the University of Lausanne and was nominated three times for the Outstanding Teacher Award at INSEAD. He has published numerous scholarly papers on international trade and economic development.

Julien Gourdon is an Economist at the Organisation for Economic Co-operation and Development (OECD), Paris. He holds a PhD in economics from Université d'Auvergne (CERDI), Clermont-Ferrand. He specializes in international trade and development economics; his main topics of interest are trade policies, exports competitiveness, trade and income inequalities, and the impact evaluation of trade assistance projects. Formerly, he was Economist at Centre d'Etudes Prospectives et d'Informations Internationales (CEPII) from 2011 to 2014 and at the World Bank from 2006 to 2011.

Michael Friis Jensen holds a PhD in development economics from the University of Copenhagen. In his PhD he worked on quality standards in the Kenyan fresh produce industry and on the World Trade Organization's Sanitary and Phytosanitary (SPS) and Technical Barriers to Trade (TBT) agreements. He has 19 years of professional experience since graduation with a MSc in agricultural economics in 1997. He was a researcher at the Danish Institute for International Studies (DIIS) from 2004 to 2007 and from 2009 to 2010 and a senior economist at the World Bank, where he led the work on quality and standards at the International Trade Department, from 2007 to 2009. Since 2010, he has worked as a consultant on issues related to quality and standards and trade policy.

Charles Kunaka is a Senior Trade Specialist in the Trade and Competitiveness Global Practice of the World Bank. He has over 20 years of experience working on logistics and trade corridors. He works on World Bank investment operations on trade and transport facilitation in the Africa and South Asia regions and is involved in knowledge and technical assistance work in all regions of the Bank. He has published extensively on various aspects of transport services and trade corridors. He first joined the Bank in 2006 in the Africa Transport unit working on the Sub-Saharan Africa Transport Policy Program; before that, he was a senior transport specialist at the Southern African Development Community. He holds a PhD in transport economics and policy from University College London in the United Kingdom.

Peter Kusek is a Senior Investment Policy Officer in the World Bank Group's Trade and Competitiveness Global Practice, advising client governments on business environment reforms. He specializes in foreign direct investment regulation and administrative practices. He also leads the investment climate analytics program. Prior to joining the World Bank Group, Peter worked on small-enterprise development in Bangladesh, on microfinance in Tanzania, and at the Ministry of Finance of the Czech Republic. He was also program manager at the Center for Strategic and International Studies, a Washington-based foreign and security policy think tank. Peter holds a master's degree in economic policy and international development from Princeton University's Woodrow Wilson School of Public and International Affairs.

Martha Denisse Pierola is a Senior Economist in the Integration and Trade Sector of the Inter-American Development Bank (IDB). She has published papers on export growth and exporter dynamics and co-created the Exporter Dynamics Database. Her current research studies the origin of large exporters and their contribution to growth and diversification, and the impact of China's rise on productivity in Latin America's manufacturing sector. She has also worked on regionalism and trade costs. Before joining the IDB, she worked as an economist for the World Bank and the Peruvian Government and also consulted for the private sector and other international organizations. She has a PhD in international economics from the Graduate Institute of International Studies and a master's degree in international law and economics from the World Trade Institute.

Nihal Pitigala is an economist with over 20 years of experience in trade and development. He has published a number of peer-reviewed articles on South Asia regional trade, trade policy, and global value chains. At the World Bank, he has supported both research (Development Economics Research Group) and operational work (PREM Trade Group). He has written a number of policy papers on trade policy and conducted advisory work across Asia and Africa. He also helped to develop the World Bank Group Trade Strategy launched in 2011. Prior to consulting at the World Bank, he served as an economic advisor to the Board of Investment in Sri Lanka. He holds a PhD in economics (trade) from the University of Sussex.

Jose Daniel Reyes is a Senior Economist in the Investment Climate Unit of the Trade and Competitiveness Global Practice at the World Bank. He has several years of research and professional experience, working on issues of trade policy, competitiveness, and globalization. His recent policy work focuses on supporting developing countries in streamlining nontariff measures, on the representation of big trade data to inform policy making, on and firm-level dynamics. Prior to joining the World Bank, Daniel worked for the IDB and for the Colombian government monitoring country performance in the Latin American region. He has worked on trade and competitiveness issues in Central America, Africa, Europe, and Asia. He holds a PhD in economics from Georgetown University.

Nadeem Rizwan is a development professional with more than 8 years of experience. He worked in the World Bank Dhaka office in Bangladesh as a Research Analyst in the Macroeconomics and Fiscal Management unit for more than five years. He has contributed to numerous World Bank reports on Bangladesh (including the Diagnostic Trade Integration Study) on trade, remittances, and issues related to economic growth. Prior to joining the Bank, Nadeem worked as Senior Business Consultant in Katalyst where he developed expertise on agricultural value chains and agriculture market systems development. Nadeem holds an MA in economics from University of Alberta, Canada and an MBA from Institute of Business Administration, University of Dhaka, Bangladesh. He is currently pursuing a PhD in Economics in the North Carolina State University in the U.S.

Zaidi Sattar is Chairman, Policy Research Institute of Bangladesh (PRI). He was educated at Boston University and is recognized as a leading expert on trade and industrial policy issues in Bangladesh. Dr. Sattar was a core team member drafting the Seventh Five Year Plan (2016–20), Sixth Five Year Plan (2011–15) and the Perspective Plan (2010–21) of Bangladesh. He was task leader and co-author of two seminal World Bank publications, *Trade Policies in South Asia: An Overview* (2004) and *Studies in India-Bangladesh Trade* (2006). From 1984 to 1992 he taught economics at the Catholic University of America in Washington, DC. Earlier, he was a member of the elite Civil Service of Pakistan and Bangladesh (1969–83), having served in different ministries and districts in Pakistan and Bangladesh.

Abbreviations

AEO	Authorized Economic Operator
AGOA	African Growth and Opportunity Act
APEC	Asia-Pacific Economic Cooperation
APTA	Asia-Pacific Trade Agreement
ASEAN	Association of Southeast Asian Nations
BB	Bangladesh Bank
BEPZA	Bangladesh Export Processing Zones Authority
BEST	Better Work and Standards
BFTI	Bangladesh Foreign Trade Institute
BIDS	Bangladesh Institute of Development Studies
BOI	Board of Investment
BQSP	Bangladesh Quality Support Program
BSTI	Bangladesh Standards and Testing Institution
BTB	back-to-back
BTC	Bangladesh Tariff Commission
BUILD	Business Initiative Leading Development
BWH	bonded warehouses
CBTPA	Caribbean Basin Trade Promotion Act
CD	customs duty
CGE	computable general equilibrium
CIF	cost, insurance, and freight
CPD	Centre for Policy Dialogue
CRR	centralized risk registry
DCC	Dhaka-Chittagong Corridor
DTIS	Diagnostic Trade Integration Study
EBA	Everything But Arms
EPA	export promotion agency
EPB	Export Promotion Bureau
EPZ	Export Processing Zone

ERP	effective rate of protection
EU	European Union
FAO	Food and Agricultural Organization of the United Nations
FBCCI	Federation of Bangladesh Chambers of Commerce and Industry
FDI	foreign direct investment
FOB	free on board
FPIPPA	Foreign Private Investment Promotion and Protection Act
FTA	Free Trade Agreement
FY	fiscal year
GDP	gross domestic product
GHERS	Greater Harvest and Economic Returns from Shrimp
GSP	Generalized System of Preferences
GTSF	Global Trade Supplier Finance
HACCP	hazard analysis and critical control points
HS	Harmonized System
ICD	inland container depot
ICT	information and communications technology
IFC	International Finance Corporation
IMF	International Monetary Fund
IT	information technology
ITC	International Trade Centre
ITES	information technology-enabled services
IWT	inland waterways transport
L/C	letter of credit
LMIC	low- and middle-income countries
MFN	most favored nation
MOC	Ministry of Commerce
MOF	Ministry of Finance
MRA	Mutual Recognition Agreement
NABL	National Accreditation Board for Testing and Calibration Laboratories (India)
NAFTA	North American Free Trade Agreement
NBR	National Board of Revenue
NIPFP	National Institute of Public Finance and Policy (India)
NPR	nominal protection rate
NSBs	national standardization bodies
NTB	nontariff barrier
NTM	nontariff measure
OECD	Organisation for Economic Co-operation and Development

OTRI	Overall Trade Restrictiveness Index
OTS	Operative Tariff Schedules
PFF	Public Finance Foundation
PRI	Policy Research Institute
PSI	preshipment inspection
RCA	revealed comparative advantage
RD	regulatory duty
RMG	ready-made garment
SAFTA	South Asian Free Trade Area
SBW	Special Bonded Warehouses
SD	supplementary duty
SITC	Standard International Trade Classification
SME	small and medium enterprises
SPS	sanitary and phytosanitary standards
TBT	technical barriers to trade; Agreement on Technical Barriers to Trade (WTO)
TCI	Trade Complementarity Index
TEU	20-foot equivalent container unit
TIR	Transports Internationaux Routiers (International Road Transport)
TTRI	Tariff Trade Restrictiveness Index
UN	United Nations
UNCTAD	United Nations Conference on Trade and Development
UNIDO	United Nations Industrial Development Organization
USAID	U.S. Agency for International Development
VAT	value-added tax
WBI	World Bank Institute
WCO	World Customs Organization
WTO	World Trade Organization

Government fiscal year
July 1–June 30

Current equivalents
Currency unit = Bangladesh taka (Tk)
US$1 = Tk 78.4 (March 2016)

Key Messages

Bangladesh's ambition is to build on its solid growth and poverty reduction achievements and accelerate growth to become a middle-income country by 2021, continue its high pace of poverty reduction, and share prosperity more widely among its citizens.

One of the country's greatest development challenges is to provide gainful employment to the more than two million people who will join the labor force each year over the next decade. Moreover, only 58.1 million of the country's 103.3 million working-age people are employed. Bangladesh needs to use its labor endowment even more intensively to increase growth and, in turn, absorb the additional labor.

The Commission on Growth and Development (2008) suggests that all 13 country cases of sustained high growth over the postwar period were marked by full exploitation of the knowledge, resources, and deep and elastic demand that the global economy offered. Bangladesh will need to do the same and exploit the international market more intensively, building on the pivotal role that exports have already played in providing gainful employment and access to imports.

Bangladesh's exports have exhibited strong growth and doubled their world market share between 1995 and 2012, owing to success in garments, catering largely to the European Union and the United States. Since 2009, Bangladesh has become the world's second largest garment exporter, making it unique among least developed countries (LDCs) in its high share of manufactures in total exports, which reached 90.5 percent in 2013, compared with about 26.2 percent for LDCs.

Garment exports can continue to grow in existing and newer markets. Newer products will emerge more slowly. Thus, more rapid export growth will initially rely on capturing higher market shares in Bangladesh's existing strengths, that is, basic garments, in current markets and penetrating newer and dynamic markets, such as China, India, and Japan, and the countries of the Association of Southeast Asian Nations (ASEAN). In addition, many firms are starting to produce higher-value garments and this will expand the target market for Bangladesh. Other products are emerging, such as jute goods, footwear, seafood, and information technology enabled services (ITES), and some of these may over time become part of a larger product cluster.

1. To achieve the above and sustain and accelerate export growth will require actions centered around four pillars. The first pillar is *breaking into new markets* through (a) better trade logistics to reduce delivery lags, as world markets become more competitive and newer products demand shorter lead times, to generate new sources of competitiveness and thereby enable market diversification, and (b) better exploitation of regional trading opportunities in nearby growing and dynamic markets, especially East Asia and South Asia. The second pillar is *breaking into new products* through (a) more neutral and rational trade policy and taxation and bonded warehouse schemes; (b) concerted efforts to spur domestic investment and attract foreign direct investment, to contribute to export promotion and diversification, including by easing the energy and land constraints; and (c) strategic development and promotion of services trade. The third pillar is *improving worker and consumer welfare* by (a) improving skills and literacy, (b) implementing labor and work safety guidelines, and (c) making safety nets more effective in dealing with trade shocks. The fourth pillar is *building a supportive environment*, including (a) sustaining sound macroeconomic fundamentals and (b) strengthening the institutional capacity for strategic policy making aimed at the objective of international competitiveness to help bring focus and coherence to the government's reform efforts.

Detailed studies of a number of growing export sectors confirmed the cross-cutting findings highlighted above and added other, sector-specific issues. In shipbuilding, enforcement of standards for domestic ships would help bring the domestic and export market segments closer and help exporting yards to achieve better scale economies. More credible enforcement of standards in pharmaceuticals would help people's health and reduce the disincentives of firms, including foreign firms that practice self-enforcement. Training to upgrade skills is a critical need in many sectors, including shipbuilding, ITES, and bicycles. Foreign direct investment (FDI) could play a much larger role in many sectors, especially those with technology upgrading needs, such as pharmaceuticals, bicycles, and shipbuilding. Improvements in access to finance and easing of Bangladesh Bank-monitored current account transactions would relieve constraints across all sectors. Additional submarine cables would help the reliability of Internet services for the ITES sector.

A neutral trade policy needs to be defined by consumer interests, not just the interests of domestic producers and exporters. Currently, distortions affect critical areas that affect consumer welfare, such as medicines and consumer products, and producer interests have tended to dominate over consumer interests. For example, allowing trade and FDI in drug supply would enhance the choices and quality of medicines and enable a more effective health strategy. In addition, societal demands for better regulation of imports to address an expanding array of issues, such as public safety, food safety, and plant and animal health, will increase and this will need to be done in a credible and efficient manner that respects the balance between safety and access to a variety of imports.

Strengthening Competitiveness in Bangladesh—Thematic Assessment
http://dx.doi.org/10.1596/978-1-4648-0898-2

Trade regime signals are critical for defining domestic production structures and shaping labor and capital usage. Bangladesh needs to increase the share of labor-intensive manufacturing in its gross domestic product (GDP) and a stronger export orientation will play a critical role here. Increasing basic skills will be critical—for Bangladesh to remain competitive in exports, improve worker productivity, and enable sustainable wage increases. For skill flows, development of cognitive and noncognitive skills through a focus on the quality of primary and secondary education, along with industry-specific skills, will bring immense dividends.

An example of outward orientation would be the following. If it were to capture 20 percent of China's current garment exports, Bangladesh's total exports would more than double, increasing by US$29 billion, and, based on current parameters, create 5.4 million new jobs and 13.5 million new indirect jobs. These would be virtually enough to absorb all new entrants into the labor force over the next decade.

With the implementation of the four-pillar agenda, a virtuous circle of export-led growth can be put in place, with multiple sources of strength. This will help improve the overall competitiveness of the economy and provide sources of strength other than low wages.

The ultimate goal of export-led growth is poverty reduction and the enhanced welfare of Bangladesh's citizens. Rapidly growing exports and the millions of new jobs accompanying them, along with skill upgrading, will increase productivity and wages, which over the long term is the only sustainable way to improve living standards. It will also begin a discourse to move beyond wage-based competitiveness. Improving skills will allow the effective participation of people in growth. Improving labor standards and worker safety is also part of this agenda and, in the wake of recent tragic incidents in the garment sector, has become a part of the preconditions for garment exports.

Bangladesh is well placed to take on some its strongest development challenges, provided it displays the right leadership. Its track record on growth and employment is strong. To grow faster, absorb more labor, and continue its pace of poverty reduction, the country will need to build on that record and improve on it. The good news is that a number of reforms are relatively low-hanging fruits, may be implemented in the short to medium term, and can bring large payoffs.

The example of Vietnam shows that accelerated, export-oriented development is possible, even in the context of the current global environment. Vietnam moved from being one of the poorest countries in the world to a lower-middle-income one in the space of 25 years, with FDI and trade playing a dominant role in the economy. Vietnam's exports and imports each form 90 percent of GDP and, with 88 million people compared with Bangladesh's 150 million, Vietnam exports four times as much as Bangladesh today.

Bangladesh will need strong leadership to support its multisector competitiveness agenda. In many cases, it will require taking on strong domestic interests that may not welcome competition, either through imports or FDI. In other cases, it will require cohesion and coordination between different ministries or departments, such as the National Board of Revenue; the Ministries of Commerce, Finance, and Industry; the Roads Division, and so on. If Bangladesh's Vision 2021 goals are to be achieved, this leadership has to be exercised.

Reference

Commission on Growth and Development. 2008. *Strategies for Sustained Growth and Inclusive Development*. Washington, DC: World Bank.

CHAPTER 1

Bangladesh's Trade Performance

Sanjay Kathuria, Mariem Mezghenni Malouche,
Martha Denisse Pierola, and Jose Daniel Reyes

Introduction

The Government of Bangladesh recognizes that export-led growth and a broadening of the export structure are pivotal to the country's growth ambitions. In the Sixth Five-Year Plan, trade is considered a strong source for accelerating growth and providing high productivity and high-income jobs. The government recognizes that a dynamic manufacturing sector will benefit from greater outward orientation, particularly based on the experiences of other successful Asian exporters, such as China, India, the Republic of Korea, Thailand, and Vietnam. The government has emphasized product and market diversification and regional and global integration. The Sixth Five-Year Plan projects "…the share of exports in relation to gross domestic product (GDP) to rise by 7.7 percentage points to 23.9 percent of GDP by the end of the Sixth Five-Year Plan, reflecting a leading role that export sector is envisaged to play in increasing domestic activity" (Government of Bangladesh 2011, 86).

This chapter describes the trade performance of Bangladesh at the macro and micro levels for goods and services. The analysis of the basic orientation of trade is crucial to judge the extent to which a country's trade structure is conducive to future growth. The analysis of trade performance at the aggregate and sector levels is complemented by a micro analysis based on detailed firm-level data from customs, in the trade outcomes analysis. The analysis uses the decomposition of the margins of trade growth as a framework for exploring trade competitiveness and analyzes the *level, growth, and market share* performance of existing exports (the intensive margin), as well as the *market share* performance of new exports.

Complementing more aggregate assessments with firm-level data can lead to improved understanding about competitiveness. Firms are heterogeneous in characteristics and performance. Moreover, important changes in production models are taking place worldwide, which are deeply affecting economies' transmission mechanisms, domestically and internationally. Macro aggregations miss the critical features and effects of firm heterogeneity on the macro-economy. After briefly describing the overall external environment in Bangladesh, the chapter provides a thorough analysis of merchandise trade performance, including that based on customs transactions data. It then presents the performance of services exports.

The analysis highlights the following: (a) the heavy sector and market concentration of exports; (b) the potential to improve trade performance by penetrating new markets and exporting new products, as the low entry and exit rates of firms suggests competitiveness challenges likely driven by weaknesses in the general export environment; and (c) untapped potential in services exports despite a noticeable increase in services exports, driven by the growth in communications services and other business services (including engineering, consulting, and other professional services), which reflects Bangladesh's large pool of labor and growing opportunities in emerging services, such as skill-intensive and professional services. Overall, the analysis suggests that there is potential to intensify exports based on the existing factor endowment (a large pool of unskilled labor); that is, existing exports can grow significantly in current and new markets. The data suggest that Bangladesh will have to work harder to produce another large, labor-intensive cluster like garments, but its export presence in a wide variety of manufactured products indicates that it is possible, with the right supporting environment and with skill upgrading.

Bangladesh's Macroeconomic Performance

Bangladesh has posted robust and resilient economic performance over the past decade, accompanied by a sustained decline in poverty. Real GDP grew at a healthy rate of around 6 percent per year (table 1.1) over the past decade, accelerating by a percentage point compared with the previous decade. GDP growth was remarkably stable, with a low standard deviation of 0.7 percent during this decade (half of what it was a decade earlier). This robust growth was accompanied by a uniform and steady decline in poverty headcount rates between 2000 (48.9 percent) and 2010 (31.5 percent) and a continuous decline in the number of poor people—from nearly 63 million in 2000 to 47 million in 2010, despite a growing population.

Economic growth has accelerated largely since the 1990s, because of the accumulation of physical capital, increase in the size of the labor force, and, to a much smaller extent, increase in total factor productivity.[1] Underpinning this were several economic reforms: sound macroeconomic management; targeted trade policy reforms that enabled the garments sector to thrive and similarly focused policies that facilitated takeoffs in other sectors, such as frozen foods in European markets; import and financial sector liberalization, and investment in human development and social protection. Remittances and garment exports were the twin drivers of growth in the economy—remittances through their effect on consumption and construction as well as easing the foreign exchange constraint and garment exports through providing sustained direct and indirect employment for millions of workers in garments, input and ancillary suppliers,

Table 1.1 Key Macroeconomic Indicators, FY2006–FY2014

Indicator	FY2006	FY2007	FY2008	FY2009	FY2010	FY2011	FY2012	FY2013	FY2014
Output and prices									
Real GDP growth (%)	6.7	7.1	6.0	5.0	5.6	6.5	6.5	6.0	6.1
Gross investment (% GDP)	26.1	26.2	26.2	26.2	26.2	27.4	28.3	28.4	28.7
CPI inflation (average)	—	9.4	12.3	7.6	6.8	10.9	8.7	6.8	7.3
External accounts									
Exports (US$ millions)	10,526	12,178	14,111	15,565	16,205	22,924	24,288	27,018	30,177
Annual % change	21.6	15.7	15.9	10.3	4.1	41.5	5.9	11.2	11.7
Garments/total exports (%)	75.1	75.6	75.8	79.3	77.1	78.1	78.6	79.6	81.2
Imports (US$ millions)	14,746	17,157	21,629	22,507	23,738	33,658	36,985	37,290	40,616
Annual % change	12.2	16.3	26.1	4.0	5.5	41.8	9.9	0.8	8.9
Remittances (US$ millions)	4,802	5,979	7,915	9,689	10,987	11,650	12,843	14,456	14,228
Annual % change	24.8	24.5	32.4	22.4	13.4	6.0	10.2	12.6	−1.6
Current account balance (% GDP)	1.1	1.2	0.7	2.4	3.2	0.7	−0.3	1.6	0.9
Gross official reserves (US$ millions)	3,484	5,077	6,151	7,471	10,750	10,912	10,325	15,315	18,248
Gross official reserves (months of GNFS imports)	2.8	3.4	3.4	3.7	5.1	3.9	3.3	4.7	5.4

Sources: Bangladesh Bureau of Statistics, Bangladesh Bank, Export Promotion Bureau, Ministry of Finance, International Monetary Fund, and World Bank estimates.

Note: — = not available; FY = fiscal year; CPI = consumer price index; GDP = gross domestic product; GNFS = goods and non-factor services.

and so forth. The manufacturing sector has been the largest single contributor to growth in the past two decades. As a result, the share of manufacturing in total GDP increased from 9.8 percent in fiscal year (FY) 1980 to 18.7 percent in FY2014. Modest investment rates notwithstanding, capital deepening in agriculture and industry played an important role.

Bangladesh has also proven to be relatively resilient to global economic shocks. Its growth continued to be resilient despite several external shocks that slowed exports, remittances, and investment growth, including the end of the Agreement on Textile and Clothing in 2005 and the 2008–09 global financial crisis, thanks largely to strong fundamentals at the onset of the crisis, relatively underdeveloped and insulated financial markets, and preemptive policy response. However, while slow growth in Europe and the United States, the country's two main export markets, put strains on Bangladesh's export growth, exports have recovered and grown at a reasonable pace.

The current account and balance of payments have been stable, thanks to remittances. Bangladesh relies heavily on imports for capital goods, oil, intermediates, and a variety of consumer goods. Exports are not sufficient to pay for all imports, but the current account has been positive since FY2006, owing to growing remittances, which have proved critical to the stability of the balance of payments. Despite some concerns in FY2011 and FY2012 about oil imports and their impact on the balance of payments, the external sector has by and large been stable over the years. Reserves grew and stood at more than five months of goods and services imports in FY2014. Macroeconomic pressures that had developed on account of energy subsidies have also eased, supported by more restrained fiscal and monetary policies.[2]

However, despite the stable macroeconomic situation, institutional weaknesses and several vulnerabilities loom large and pose challenges for macroeconomic management. Political uncertainty, together with frequent general strikes and associated violence, has added to the longstanding energy and infrastructure deficits in dampening investment, posing a nontrivial threat to sustaining the recent average 6 percent growth, let alone raising it to 7 percent in the near future. Moreover, deep-rooted weaknesses in institutional capacity underlie the failure to speed up implementation of top priority infrastructure projects and are not easily addressed.

Bangladesh's near- and medium-term macroeconomic outlook is subject to several vulnerabilities.[3] A resumption of political violence or heightened uncertainty would adversely impact investment, growth, and inflation. Continued weakness in the banking sector, in particular at the state-owned banks, could undermine credit and growth prospects and affect fiscal sustainability, as would a failure to launch the new VAT. On the external side, a protracted slowdown in the European Union (Bangladesh's main export destination) could hurt exports. Moreover, the outlook for remittances is uncertain: while worker outflows have recovered, persistent low oil prices could eventually affect investment and employment in key host countries. While previous oil price shocks had limited and short-lived effects on remittances, the current more pronounced and prolonged decline, coupled with fiscal tightening in many oil-exporting countries, is likely to hurt migrant worker earnings and consequently remittances. From a broader perspective, natural disasters and global climate change pose major risks for Bangladesh. Linkages with large emerging market economies and international financial markets remain limited, cushioning against potential shocks from these sources.

Bangladesh's export growth has been impressive since the early 1990s, and it has been accompanied by reduced distortions in trade policy. Although Bangladesh is still a least developed country (LDC), it has an unusually high share of manufactured exports in its export basket (90.5 percent in 2013) relative to its income level, which illustrates its strengths in mass manufacturing and labor availability. Economic growth has been associated with greater trade openness over the past two decades. As measured by the ratio of exports plus imports to GDP, openness has increased from 18 percent on average in the 1980s to 35 percent in the 2000s (figure 1.1). A reduction in trade policy distortions has helped Bangladesh's export competitiveness to a significant extent.

Primarily owing to the emergence of a dynamic ready-made garments (RMG) industry, Bangladesh doubled its world market trade share, from 0.08 percent in 1995 to 0.16 percent in 2011. Its overall exports grew on average by 11.2 percent from 2000/01 to 2009/10. During 2005–10, Bangladesh gained world market share in most of its top 25 export products (figure 1.2). Exports remained strong during the 2008–09 crisis, owing to the so-called Walmart effect, driven by low-value garment exports.

Figure 1.1 Trade Openness in Bangladesh and Comparators, Measured by Exports and Imports as a Share of GDP

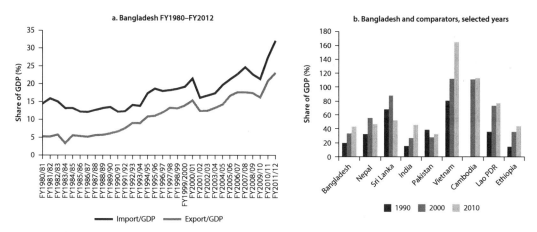

Source: Calculations based on Export Promotion Bureau and World Development Indicators data.
Note: GDP = gross domestic product.

Figure 1.2 Growing Share of Bangladesh's Top 25 Exports in World Markets, 2005–10

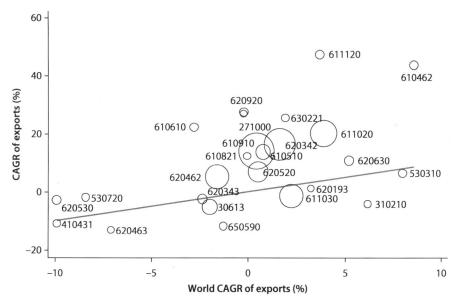

Source: Calculations based on United Nations Comtrade data.
Note: Products are identified by six-digit Harmonized System (HS) codes. The bubbles in the figure are relative to the importance of the product in the Bangladesh export basket, and the straight line shows the points at which world and Bangladesh growth rates are the same. CAGR = compound annual growth rate.

Bangladesh has scope to diversify its exports and increase the contribution of trade in growth and poverty reduction. Although growing over time, the role of trade in the overall economy is still low. Imports were 21 percent of GDP, while exports were 17.4 percent of GDP in FY2014. Exports lack diversity, with garments accounting for four-fifths of total exports. Bangladesh is sometimes

Strengthening Competitiveness in Bangladesh—Thematic Assessment
http://dx.doi.org/10.1596/978-1-4648-0898-2

referred to as a "mono-product" export basket. Market concentration is also high. More important, there are concerns whether physical and institutional infrastructure as well as skill availability can keep pace with the desired growth rate of Bangladesh's exports. And trade policy has not been used in a deliberate way to enhance consumer welfare or promote export competitiveness in general. Neither has it been mainstreamed as a critical policy for long-term growth.

Bangladesh's Performance in Goods Trade

Bangladesh's export portfolio has been dominated by RMG, knitwear and woven garments in particular. In FY2013, RMG represented 79.7 percent of total exports (figure 1.3) and most of the growth has come from the RMG sector over the years. Within the RMG sector, the knitwear sector has grown at 18.4 percent over 2001–10; woven garments during the same period grew at 7.2 percent. The main reason for this difference is that EU rules of origin required a "double transformation" from yarn to fabric and from fabric to garment to be eligible for lower duties under the Generalized System of Preferences (GSP). These rules of origin benefitted the knitwear industry, which was more likely to meet the required local content. Domestic value addition in knitwear is about 75 percent, thanks to strong backward linkages to spinning factories, with local factories supplying about 90 percent of the total fabric required. By contrast, only about 16 percent of the woven exports to the European Union qualified for the GSP facility because imported fabric typically accounted for 60 percent of the output price. However, effective January 2011, the European Union's rules of origin have been

Figure 1.3 Bangladesh's Top Export Products, FY2013
percent of total exports

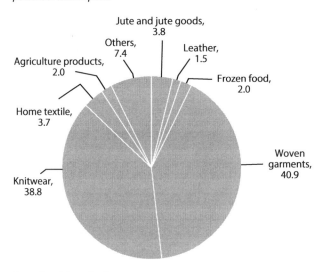

Source: Export Promotion Bureau.

relaxed, which has already improved the performance of woven garments (see chapter 3 on market access for a discussion of GSP). In the following two years, 2011–13, woven garments exports grew at a rate of 15 percent, while knitwear growth was barely 6 percent.

The concentration in garments still appears to be almost unique to Bangladesh among many peer countries. Figure 1.4 shows that between 2000 and 2012, this concentration increased further: the share of garments in Bangladesh's exports rose from 77 to 84 percent. In other countries, such as Lesotho and Pakistan, where per capita incomes grew slower than Bangladesh's over 2000–12, the reliance on garments declined substantially (Sri Lanka is an exception to this trend). In high-growth countries, such as China, Vietnam, and India, the relative reliance on garments has been declining even faster.

Concentration of export markets and products is high. Bangladesh's exports are heavily concentrated at the sector level and even at the product level, where five products account for more than 50 percent of sales in the U.S. and EU markets.[4] Twenty-one of the top 25 products are clothing articles. In general, product concentration in Bangladesh is much higher than in comparators (figure 1.5 shows the number of products exported by countries). Similarly, in terms of markets, the European Union and the United States together account for about two-thirds of the country's total exports. Despite Bangladesh's fortunate location between the world's fastest-growing and potentially largest economies, the shares of China, India, and the Association of Southeast Asian Nations (ASEAN) in Bangladesh's exports are only 2.5, 1.5, and 1.5 percent, respectively.

Figure 1.4 Ready-Made Garments as a Share of Total Merchandise Exports, Bangladesh and Other Major Garment-Exporting Countries, 2000 and 2012

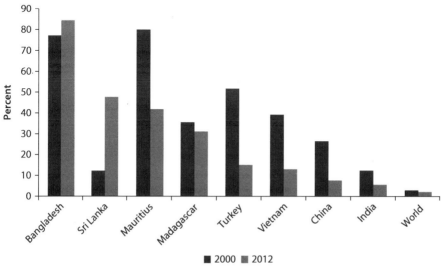

Source: UN Comtrade database.

Strengthening Competitiveness in Bangladesh—Thematic Assessment
http://dx.doi.org/10.1596/978-1-4648-0898-2

Figure 1.5 Number of Exported Products, Bangladesh and Comparators, 2011

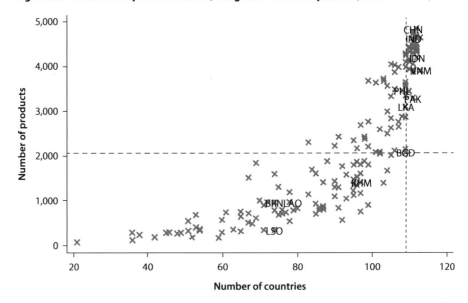

Source: World Bank staff.
Note: The "x" markers represent particular countries. Bangladesh is at the intersection of the dotted lines.

Bangladesh is not making the most of the growth of the Asian giants. Exports have been boosted by duty-free access to Australia, Canada, China, the European Union, Japan, and Norway. In June 2013, the United States suspended the GSP facility provided to Bangladesh. However, the GSP facility did not provide duty-free access for some of Bangladesh's key exports, and only a few goods qualified under the U.S. GSP. Only 0.62 percent of the country's goods exported to the United States qualified under this system (WTO 2012). As a result, import duties on Bangladesh's exports to the United States amounted to US$824 million in 2014.[5] At present, 96 percent of Bangladesh's exports to the United States consist of RMG and textile products, which are bought by retail groups such as Walmart, Gap, and Target.

However, garments are not a single category of exports; if garments are treated separately, Bangladesh is actually more diversified than most comparators. As highlighted in Cadot, Carrère, and Strauss-Kahn (2011), export concentration follows a U-shape path as a function of the level of development (as measured by purchasing power parity (PPP) income per capita in constant 2005 U.S. dollars). Poor countries start out concentrated, then diversify, and then—beyond about the PPP level of US$25,000—re-concentrate. As shown by Theil's concentration index in figure 1.6,[6] Bangladesh's exports have been de-concentrating—diversifying—rapidly over the years, so that the country is now clearly below the regression curve describing the average concentration at each level of income. Bangladesh exports a range of garment products, whereas many countries at the same level of income export a single primary product. T-shirts, trousers, and swimsuits (all garments) are

Figure 1.6 Export Concentration, Bangladesh and Comparators

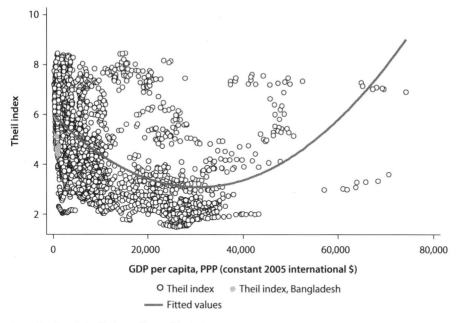

Source: Data from Cadot, Carrère, and Strauss-Kahn 2011.
Note: Calculations use UN Comtrade mirrored export data. Concentration is measured by Theil's index at HS6. GDP = gross domestic product; PPP = purchasing power parity.

the same type of export, but they represent a type of diversification, as their prices are imperfectly correlated (for instance, knitwear and woven garments are typically not the same product). Thus, the concentration in a range of products all belonging to the RMG category does not expose Bangladesh to the single-price fluctuations that exporters of primary products face.

Bangladesh's export patterns have changed little over time, indicating a lack of dynamic churning. First, the same products have dominated the market over the decade. This is a striking difference compared with more vibrant economies, for which the top five products are seldom the same over a decade, with a substantial churning of top export earners over time. For example, in China only one of the top five products in 1998 was still among the top five in 2008. Second, Bangladesh has low export growth of old products in new markets. The decomposition of Bangladesh's export growth between the intensive and extensive margins shows that this is mostly explained by an increase in exports of old products in old markets. The contribution of this component in Bangladesh is particularly high compared with peer countries.

Persistent Low Sophistication of Exports

The sophistication of Bangladesh's export basket has also stagnated over time. The level of sophistication of products appears to matter for economic growth. According to Hausmann, Hwang, and Rodrik (2007), countries that have a more sophisticated export basket enjoy accelerated subsequent growth while those

with a less sophisticated export basket tend to lag behind. The data for
Bangladesh and selected peer countries show that the sophistication of
Bangladesh's export basket is comparable to that of Pakistan, despite Bangladesh's
lower per capita income (figure 1.7). However, Bangladesh's sophistication stagnated between 2002 and 2008, whereas India's and China's have increased over
time. According to Lall's (2000) classification, Bangladesh's exports are heavily
concentrated in the low-tech space, representing more than 90 percent of total
exports of goods (other LDCs export primary and resource-based products).
This reflects the concentration of Bangladesh's exports at the lower end of the
textiles and clothing sector, despite the sector being differentiated. An assessment
of the relative quality (relative unit values) of textile exports to the European
Union shows that Bangladesh's increased market share in the EU market is

Figure 1.7 Export Sophistication, Bangladesh and Comparators

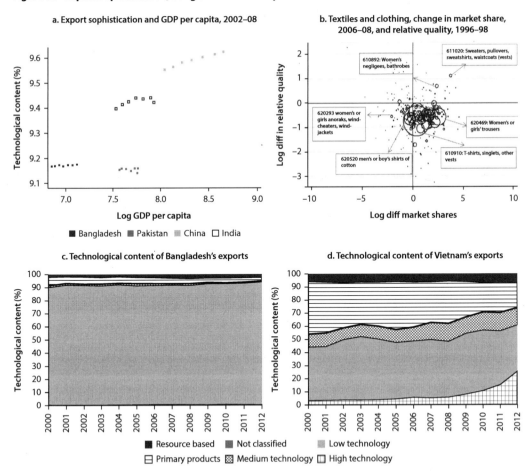

Source: World Bank data.
Note: EXPY is a measure of the level of sophistication of the export basket of a given country (see Hausmann, Hwang, and Rodrik 2007). Panel b
shows market shares and relative quality from the average in 1996–1998 to the average in 2006–08. Circles in panel b represent products defined
at 6-digit HS codes. GDP = gross domestic product.

associated with a decrease in the average unit price of products relative to the unit prices other exporters charge for the same type of products. Vietnam, another leading garment exporter, has been able to increase significantly its share of high-tech exports since the mid-2000s (figure 1.7, panel d, and box 1.1).

Nonetheless, there appears to be diversification potential in different goods, but despite starts, Bangladesh has not yet achieved scale in products other than garments. The product space literature confirms that Bangladesh's strengths are

---

Box 1.1 Vietnam Has Increased Its Export Basket Sophistication and Market Diversification

Vietnam has consolidated its labor-intensive manufacturing exports while increasing the share of high-tech products. Vietnam's traditional labor-intensive manufacturing exports, such as garments, footwear, and furniture, continue to sustain rapid growth. A noteworthy addition to the export basket has been the exports of high-tech and high-value products (for example, cell phones and parts, computers, electronics and accessories, automobile parts) that emerged as the largest and fastest growing export items in 2012. Vietnam exported US$12.7 billion worth of cell phones and accessories in 2012, compared with US$3.7 billion of rice, US$6.1 billion of seafood, and US$7.3 billion of footwear. In 2013, exports of cell phones and accessories were expected to exceed US$18 billion, overtaking garments as the largest export item from Vietnam.

Vietnam's top three markets represent less than 50 percent of export markets. Vietnam's top three export markets in 2012 were Europe, the United States, and Japan, accounting for 46 percent of its exports, down from 49 percent in 2002. The modest decline in the share of exports going to advanced countries has been captured by its neighbors, namely China and Association of Southeast Asian Nations (ASEAN) countries. Given that South-South trade is increasing at 1.5 times the rate of growth of North-South trade, it is important for Vietnam to continue to diversify its export destinations and explore new markets in Africa, South Asia, and Latin America.

The composition of Vietnam's imports has changed, largely reflecting the changes in its exports basket and the move to a more high-tech, industrial landscape. The share of machinery and equipment, petroleum products, textile materials, plastics, and motor vehicles in total import value has gradually fallen, while the share of high-tech intermediate products has increased nearly five times—from 3 percent of the total import bill in 2002 to 16 percent in 2012. The share of many other items—such as agricultural materials, metals, and chemicals—in total imports has remained unchanged in the past decade.

Vietnam's imports from China have significantly increased, while shares of other countries in the import bill have commensurately declined. Vietnam imported 25 percent of its import needs from China in 2012, compared with only 11 percent in 2002. This trend is similar to what is observed in many other low- and middle-income countries, where China has gradually displaced advanced economies to emerge as their primary trading partner. This process has been facilitated by growing intra-enterprise trade by multinational companies, a dramatic decline in logistics costs, and the increasing move to form efficient global supply chains. The rise of

box continues next page

Box 1.1 Vietnam Has Increased Its Export Basket Sophistication and Market Diversification
(continued)

China's share in Vietnam's imports has meant a smaller share for most other countries, mostly Japan, the European Union, and ASEAN countries.

Political and economic reforms (Doi Moi) launched in 1986 have transformed Vietnam from one of the poorest countries in the world, with per capita income below US$100, to a lower-middle-income country within a quarter of a century, with per capita income of US$1,130 by the end of 2010. The ratio of the population in poverty fell from 58 percent in 1993 to 14.5 percent in 2008, and most indicators of welfare have improved. Vietnam has already attained five of its 10 original Millennium Development Goal targets and is well on the way to attaining two more by 2015.

Vietnam's success story was driven by economic and social transformation from a centrally planned to a more market-oriented economy. Vietnam, like China, started with de-collectivizing land use and adopted a gradualist approach to reforms in the state-owned sector, at the same time as it opened up to foreign trade and investment. Vietnam's trade- and foreign direct investment–friendly policies since the introduction of reforms have made a noteworthy contribution to its success in export development. At the same time, the termination of the U.S. embargo in 1992 and the enactment of the United States–Vietnam bilateral trade agreement in 2000 contributed to accelerating Vietnam's integration into the world market. Today, Vietnam is a much more open economy, with total trade (exports plus imports) growing to 160 percent of gross domestic product in 2010, compared with merely 19 percent 20 years ago. Productivity increase has been an important source of Vietnam's economic growth, along with capital accumulation and labor input increases. The Socio-Economic Development Strategy 2011–20 defines three "breakthrough areas": (a) promoting human resources and skills development (particularly skills for modern industry and innovation), (b) improving market institutions, and (c) developing infrastructure. The overall goal is for Vietnam to lay the foundations for a modern, industrialized society by 2020.

Source: World Bank 2013.

---

still centered on the garments and footwear cluster and exports of bicycles and ships, for example, are in the periphery. Although a number of export products have emerged and some, such as jute products and frozen foods, have become quite large, the dominance of garments continues, with their share of total exports going up further, from 74.2 to 81.2 percent between FY2005 and FY2014. Moreover, even a large, labor-intensive cluster has not yet emerged: jute goods were 2.3 percent and leather 1.7 percent of total exports in FY2014. However, because footwear is in the dominant cluster, the product space literature would suggest that it could grow. By contrast, Vietnam seems to have been able to consolidate its garment exports and increase the share of higher value products (box 1.1).

Bangladesh has reinforced its revealed comparative advantage (RCA) in garments, located at the periphery of the forest. Figure 1.8 shows the product space for Bangladesh in 1990 and 2010, indicating the sectors in which

Figure 1.8 What Bangladesh, Sri Lanka, and Vietnam Export: Product Space, 1990 and 2010

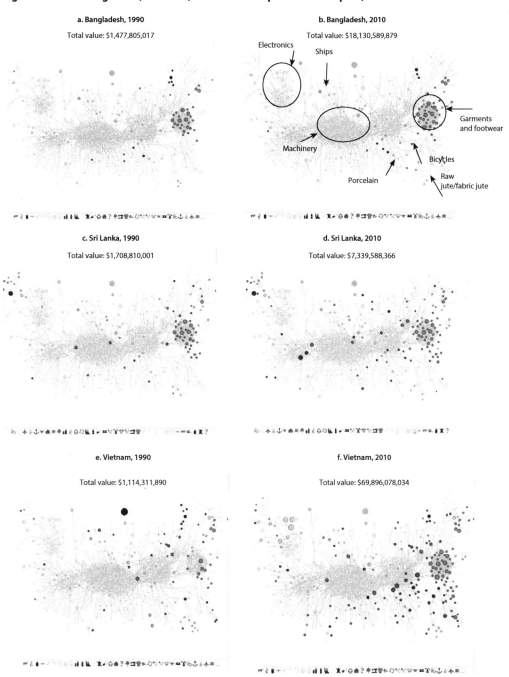

a. Bangladesh, 1990

Total value: $1,477,805,017

b. Bangladesh, 2010

Total value: $18,130,589,879

Electronics

Ships

Machinery

Porcelain

Bicycles

Raw jute/fabric jute

Garments and footwear

c. Sri Lanka, 1990

Total value: $1,708,810,001

d. Sri Lanka, 2010

Total value: $7,339,588,366

e. Vietnam, 1990

Total value: $1,114,311,890

f. Vietnam, 2010

Total value: $69,896,078,034

Source: World Bank staff, generated from http://atlas.media.mit.edu/.
Note: Colors indicate different sectors; outlined circles indicate exports with revealed comparative advantage greater than 1.

Strengthening Competitiveness in Bangladesh—Thematic Assessment
http://dx.doi.org/10.1596/978-1-4648-0898-2

Bangladesh has acquired or lost RCA[7] over time (outlined and colored dots indicate exports with an RCA higher than 1). The figure provides a glimpse of the pace of structural transformation in the economy. Bangladesh's product space of 1990 is relatively similar to its 2010 one, with not much movement along the product space (for example, from garments to machinery or electronics, which are more knowledge intensive). Bangladesh did increase the number of products (defined at SITC four digits) with RCA higher than 1 from 47 in 1990 to 65 in 2010, mostly garment and textile products.

The location of garments at the periphery of the product space indicates that moving to another sector would require different capabilities than those used for garments. Interestingly, the two products with the highest RCAs are processed raw jute and woven jute. The product space for Vietnam reveals how it has caught up with and surpassed Bangladesh over the same period. Starting with around the same level of exports as Bangladesh in 1990, Vietnam exported four times more than Bangladesh in 2010. Vietnam expanded its garment exports, but also built capabilities in new products, such as electric wire, furniture, electronics, and machinery. Sri Lanka, another garment exporter in the region, was able to maintain its competitiveness in garments and strengthen its global competitiveness in chemicals and medical instruments, as well as foodstuffs. Malaysia was able to diversify away from garments over the same period and improved its competitiveness in electronics, chemicals and medical instruments, and machinery, a denser area of the forest.

For Bangladesh, South-South trade provides some opportunities for export diversification. Bangladesh currently exports standard products that can easily be sold in other emerging countries that have more dynamic and growing economies and middle classes. Moreover, Bangladeshi locally produced goods, even those that would not meet the requirements of high-income countries with stringent standards, could be exported more easily to neighboring countries with similar consumer habits. In fact, Bangladesh's exports to other low-income countries are more diversified than its exports to high-income countries. This is shown in figure 1.9, which plots the average factor intensity of Bangladesh's exports per destination country against the destination country's income level. There is much more factor variation at low income levels than at high income levels, indicating more variety in the factor content of Bangladesh's exports to low-income countries. Moreover, gravity estimates suggest the existence of untapped potential to increase exports to large and proximate markets, such as China, India, and Pakistan.[8] The respective shares of China, India, and ASEAN in Bangladesh's total exports are 2.5, 1.5, and 1.5 percent, respectively.

Garments Can Still Drive Future Growth

The garments sector can continue to grow for the following reasons. First, international experience suggests that there is an income threshold before per capita garment exports start to decline. The threshold could come at a per capita income level between US$1,500 and US$2,000 (in constant 2000 U.S. dollars). Bangladesh appears to have some distance to traverse before hitting this threshold. It could

Figure 1.9 Average Factor Intensities of Bangladesh's Exports, by Income of Destination Country, 2011

a. Capital intensity **b. Human capital intensity**

Source: Calculations based on UNCTAD's revealed factor intensity database and UN Comtrade (mirrored data).
Note: In panel a, the vertical axis measures the average capital intensity of Bangladesh's exports, in thousands of U.S. dollars per worker, by destination country, whereas the horizontal axis measures the income level of destination countries, in thousands of U.S. dollars per capita. In panel b, the vertical axis measures the average human capital intensity of Bangladesh's exports, in average years of schooling per worker. The horizontal axis is the same as in panel a. BD = Bangladesh; GDP = gross domestic product; UNCTAD = United Nations Conference on Trade and Development.

Figure 1.10 Per Capita Income Threshold for Export of Garments

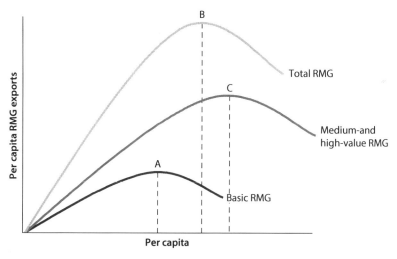

Source: World Bank 2012a.

continue to grow in basic garments, its core strength, and then sustain garment growth by moving to medium- and higher-end garments. This is represented in figure 1.10: per capita garment export growth is sustained by moving away from basic garments and the decline in per capita *basic* garments exports (point A) must occur before the overall decline in per capita garment exports (point B) (see World Bank 2012a for details). Second, recent research shows that growth of firms within a sector generates externalities for other firms in recognition, information, and access to credit (Cadot, Carrère, and Strauss-Kahn 2011). This "brand recognition" and sector synergies for Bangladesh in garments will help it to reinforce its growing dominance in the sector, wherein growth could come through quality upgrading and backward or forward linkages. Third, there is the search for other production destinations as China's growth in wages leads to its gradual shift away from very labor-intensive production. Bangladesh, already the second largest RMG exporter in the world, with 4.8 percent of the market, continues to grow and there are signs that Japanese retailers, which have hitherto mostly sourced from China and Vietnam, are starting to source more of their textiles and garments from Bangladesh (WTO 2012). All this implies that continued garment growth is sustainable in the foreseeable future, including through "vertical diversification" to allow Bangladesh to slowly move away from low-end positioning and allow greater increases in unit values (Lopez-Acevedo and Robertson 2012). In turn, the increase in unit values will allow wage increases, which could contribute to the domestic economy's diversification through demand effects.

However, labor issues (such as wages, workplace safety, and compliance with labor standards) could generate major reputational risk for Bangladesh's overall garment exports and will need to be carefully managed. Labor standards and safety issues can affect future exports and Bangladesh's overall reputation in the exporting sector. Concerns were heightened following a series of fatal incidents, and the government has been pressured to take a number of measures to improve workers' safety. International buyers and governments have also reacted strongly to these events (box 1.2). The United States suspended GSP trade privileges for Bangladesh over concerns about safety problems and labor rights violations in the garment industry on June 27, 2013. Whatever measures the government will implement under domestic and international pressure, the important issue will be enforcement and commitment to ensure better and safer practices. Continued improvement in labor conditions in the garments sector, in coordination with international business and development partners, would be important. The aim would be to ensure workers' safety, improve consumers' welfare, and maximize the demographic dividend.

Box 1.2 Rana Plaza Momentum for Reforms: Implementation Will Be Key

The fallout from the April 24, 2013, collapse of the eight-story Rana Plaza multipurpose building in Savar, Dhaka, has had domestic and international repercussions. The death toll exceeded 1,100, mostly female garment workers who worked on the upper floors of the building in several garment factories supplying about 30 Western clothing retailers. Analysis suggests that the building was not built to code; was not fit to sustain the additional weight of the three highest floors, which were added after the original building was built; and was not suited to carry the weight of people and equipment that a garment factory requires or to withstand the vibrations of the back-up generators that were installed in the upper-floor factories. A few people have been jailed for complicity in this situation, including the building owner and

box continues next page

Box 1.2 Rana Plaza Momentum for Reforms: Implementation Will Be Key *(continued)*

some factory owners (who urged factory workers to return to their workplaces a day after large cracks were found in the building and a structural engineer pronounced the building to be unfit for use), and others have been suspended, including public officials who authorized the building's construction.

In the meantime, international clothing retailers that source products in Bangladesh as well as the European Union are paying more attention to ensure safety compliance and improve supply chain transparency. The Accord on Fire and Building Safety (http://bangladeshaccord .org), consisting of more than 190 global apparel brands (mostly European), has agreed on a legally binding plan to inspect Bangladeshi garment factories that supply the companies, and publicly disclose the names of these factories as well as inspection reports and agreed reme- diation measures. As of September 2014, 1,103 factories had been inspected, resulting in the highlighting of 52,605 safety issues. The brands also agreed on 500 corrective action plans (CAPs) with the factory owners. The inspection reports and CAPs are being published online.

A group of 26 American retailers, which have formed the Alliance for Bangladesh Worker Safety, announced a nonbinding five-year initiative, developed with the help of the Bipartisan Policy Center. This initiative seeks to improve factory safety in the Bangladeshi garment indus- try by inspecting 100 percent of Alliance member factories,[a] developing common safety stan- dards, sharing inspection results transparently, and ensuring that all alliance factories actively support the democratic election and successful operation of Worker Participation Committees in each factory. As of March 2015, the Alliance had conducted initial inspections of 580 facto- ries (100 percent), of which 19 have been partially or fully closed. Almost 300 CAPs have been finalized with the factories. The Alliance plans to complete final inspection (after implementa- tion of remediation measures) of all these factories by July 2017.

As initial inspection of all the factories has been completed, international buyers can move toward implementation of remediation measures and coordinate among themselves while doing so, to help minimize additional burden and the possibility of remediation fatigue among factory owners. Financing of the remedial work is also becoming a growing concern, as in some cases buyers are allegedly not getting involved as promised.

Although Bangladesh is still considered the leading apparel sourcing destination alterna- tive to China, its popularity as a top destination for sourcing in the next five years dropped after the Rana Plaza incident, leading to order cancellations of around US$110 million from 37 factories, according to a newspaper report.[b] The potential impact on Bangladesh's garment industry, which accounts for almost 80 percent of export earnings, and therefore on gross domestic product, could be significant. Under pressure to respond to the Savar tragedy, the Government of Bangladesh has made considerable progress in improving labor safety and working conditions by amending the Labor Law, revising the minimum wage for garment workers from Tk 3,000 (US$38) to Tk 5,300 (US$68), and strengthening the labor inspection system. The government has also inspected 282 factories that are not under the purview of the Western initiatives. Although there is progress in improving workplace compliance, more needs to be done to fulfill the commitment of raising it to international standards.

a. Nandita Bose, "Insight: Inspection Intensifies Bangladesh Garment Industry's Woes," Reuters via *The Bangladesh Chronicle*, June 27, 2014.
b. Ibrahim Hossain Ovi, "Safety Compliance a Make or Break for Many Garment Factories," *The Dhaka Tribune*, April 30, 2014.

Dependence on Imports

For low- and middle-income countries, exports are not only important for their well-established static and dynamic gains (scale economies, competition, knowledge transfer, and so forth). Exports are also a main source of the foreign currency that is necessary to finance imports of capital goods and other inputs. Indeed, the gains to trade are as much derived from imports as from exports—openness to imports also acts as a disciplining force on domestic markets, leading to lower cost, higher quality inputs and intermediate goods for producers. Access to a variety of products also encourages innovation and technological change. The smooth flow of imports is particularly critical for exporters who need to be competitive globally and are constantly competing with other players. Imports need to flow smoothly to support the import needs of the export sectors and the needs of the domestic population. Imports benefit consumers by decreasing prices and increasing product variety. Services imports have also become a pillar of countries' export competitiveness agenda by making services, as inputs to industry, more efficient and cost-effective.

Bangladesh imports critical and necessary inputs. A large share of imports is geared toward the export sector. About 50 percent of imports are from the category Consumer and Intermediate Goods, of which about 80 percent are intermediate goods (30 percent petroleum) (figures 1.11 and 1.12). Consumer goods represent no more than 20 percent of total imports, partly reflecting a protected consumer domestic market (see chapter 2 on trade policy). Capital goods

Figure 1.11 Bangladesh's Imports by Broad Category, 1990/91 to 2010/11

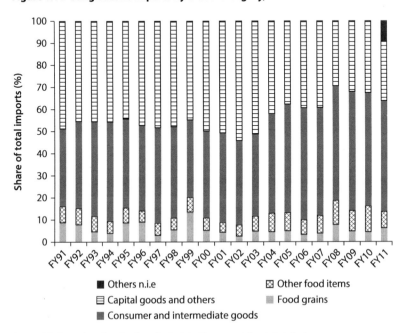

Source: Calculations based on data from the Statistics Department, Bangladesh Bank.

Figure 1.12 Bangladesh's Imports of Consumer and Intermediate Goods, 2011

percent of total imports

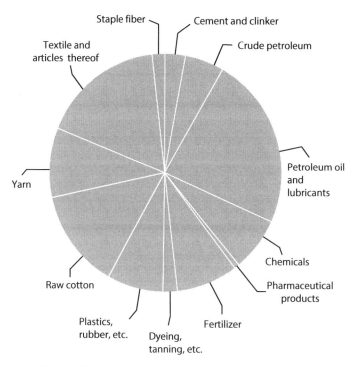

Source: Calculations based on data from the Statistics Department, Bangladesh Bank.

represented a third of imports in 2011. Although the share of machinery has declined over time, the share of iron and steel and "other capital goods" has increased in recent years. Even as exports have risen significantly, imports have been rising even faster, resulting in a chronic and widening trade deficit that has been offset by strong remittance inflows from Bangladeshi workers overseas.

Bangladesh depends on Asia for much of its imports. In 2010/11, Asia's share in Bangladesh's total goods imports was 64.4 percent, including China (17.6 percent), India (13.6 percent), Singapore and Japan (nearly 4 percent each), and other Asian countries (24 percent). Imports from the European Union and North America combined accounted for only 14.7 percent of the total value of imports.

Exporting Firms' Performance and Dynamics

The trade outcomes analysis uses the decomposition of the margins of trade growth as a framework for exploring trade competitiveness, as outlined in figure 1.13. The analysis is based on firm-level customs transaction data analysis and sheds light on firm-level dynamics. The analysis focuses on three main aspects: (a) exporters' characteristics: average size, number of products exported,

Figure 1.13 Decomposition of Export Growth—A Framework for Measuring Trade Competitiveness

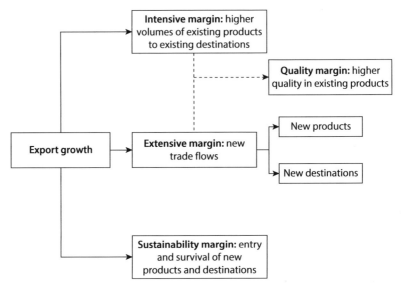

Source: Reis and Farole 2012.

number of markets covered, and so forth; (b) exporters' dynamics and survival: entry, exit, and survival rates; and (c) exporters' growth patterns: exporters' average growth rates by industry and market, growth in exports of "new" versus "old" products or markets, and so forth. The analysis uses a World Bank data set to compare exporters in Bangladesh with those in more than 45 low- and middle-income countries. Firm level results may sometimes seem inconsistent with broader published data, but this is not the case. For example, even if on average Bangladeshi firms export to more destinations than, say, country X, this is consistent with country X overall exporting to more countries (firms could have non-overlapping exporting destinations) and having a more diversified market base.

The Bangladesh database includes 7,305 exporting firms on average with an average export level per exporter of US$2.5 million over 2008–11 (table 1.2). By comparison, Cambodia, a smaller economy, had an average 618 exporters over 2008–09, with average exports of US$5.2 million per exporter. Chile had a comparable number of exporters, 7,314, exporting US$8.3 million on average per exporter. Bangladesh has experienced growth in the extensive (number of exporters) and the intensive (average exporter size) margins. However, while the Bangladeshi exporter base has grown at a relatively steady pace (especially in the most recent years), average exporter size displayed faster growth over the period 2005–11.

Many Bangladeshi exporting firms export several products. Exporting firms in Bangladesh export on average about four products to four markets (figure 1.14).[9]

Table 1.2 Key Descriptive Statistics on Exporters in Bangladesh and Comparators

annual averages

Country	Period	Number of exporters	Number of entrants	Average exporter size	Median exporter size	Share top 1% exporters	Ave. No. Prod. per exporter	Avg. No. Dest. per exporter	Entry rate	Exit rate	1st-year survival rate
Bangladesh	2008–2011	7,305	1,924	2,484,106	280,915	21%	4.33	4.09	26%	22%	59%
Cambodia	2008–2009	618	201	5,158,033	498,441	15%	7.53	5.10	32%	30%	56%
Ethiopia	2010–2012	2,041	657	1,139,086	107,904	33%	3.41	2.32	33%	36%	51%
Lesotho	2012	1,486	—	980,655	1,348	75%	6.66	1.40	—	—	—
Nepal	2010–2011	2,231	606	395,277	32,987	47%	3.19	2.53	27%	25%	—
Pakistan	2008–2010	15,628	4,035	1,201,998	61,540	41%	5.13	3.26	26%	24%	56%
Romania	2008–2011	10,530	3,343	4,357,966	233,239	53%	7.22	2.95	32%	29%	49%
Turkey	2008–2010	46,999	13,826	2,278,580	117,831	—	10.18	4.11	29%	28%	55%

Source: Cebeci et al. 2012.

Note: — = not available.

Figure 1.14 Diversification of Bangladeshi Exporting Firms, 2008–12

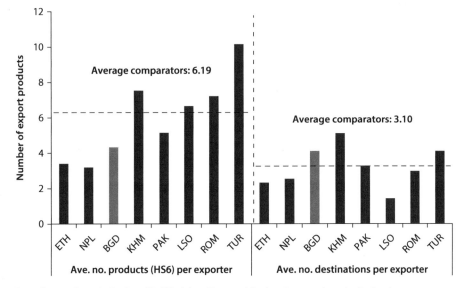

Source: Exporter Dynamics Database, World Bank (http://econ.worldbank.org/exporter-dynamics-database).
Note: Countries sorted by gross domestic product per capita. BGD = Bangladesh; ETH = Ethiopia; KHM = Cambodia; LSO = Lesotho; NPL = Nepal; PAK = Pakistan; ROM = Romania; TUR = Turkey.

Figure 1.15 Firm-Level Concentration across Bangladeshi Products and Destinations, 2011

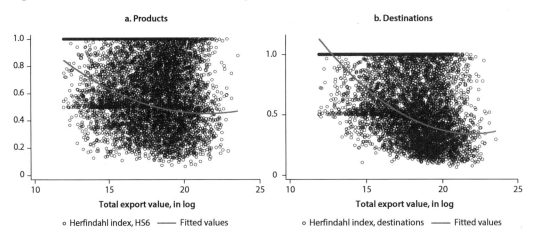

Source: Calculations based on Bangladesh National Board of Revenue data.
Note: The horizontal axis measures the log of a firm's total export sales in 2011, in Bangladeshi taka (ranging up to 10 billion, or about US$120 million). The vertical axis measures the Herfindahl index of concentration across HS6 products (panel a) and destinations (panel b). The Herfindahl index is the sum of the squares of product or destination shares. It is equal to one for single-product or single-destination firms.

Many Bangladeshi exporting firms grow and diversify across products and destinations, although other firms of all sizes remain focused, often on a single product or single destination (figure 1.15). Market diversification increased between 2005 and 2011. From serving about three markets on average in 2005, the average exporter in Bangladesh served about four markets in 2011. Bangladesh also shows one of the smallest differences between average and median size of exporters, indicating a less skewed (more even) size distribution of exporters. The skewness in the exporter size distribution in Bangladesh is, however, increasing over time (a large difference indicates that one very large exporter or a group of very large exporters coexists with a mass of very small exporters).

The decomposition of Bangladesh's export growth between the intensive and extensive margins shows that most of the export growth is explained by the increase of exports of old products in old markets, as in most countries (table 1.3). The contribution of this component in Bangladesh is particularly high compared with peer countries. Bangladesh's performance is more modest when it comes to growth of old products in new markets or growth of new products in old and new markets, reinforcing the observation of sluggish export diversification across products and markets. However, relatively speaking, old products do better in new markets compared with newer products emerging in either old or new markets.

Analysis of exporters from 38 low- and middle-income countries available in the Exporter Dynamics Database (box 1.3) indicates that total exports are often dominated by large, multiproduct, multi-destination exporters, but these form

Table 1.3 Comparative Decomposition of Export Growth, 2008–12

Margin	Components of export growth	BGD	IND	PAK	LKA
Intensive margin	Increase of old products in old markets	263.2	100.6	110.4	120.1
	Decrease of old products in old markets	−159.9	−58.1	−70.4	−83.4
	Extinction of exports of existing products to existing markets	−29.9	−19.2	−33.2	−24.5
Extensive margin	Increase of new products in new markets	0.1	0.0	0.1	0.0
	Increase of new products in old markets	5.6	0.0	1.7	5.4
	Increase of old products in new markets	20.9	10.0	24.8	15.6

Source: World Bank calculations.
Note: The decomposition is first computed on a year-by-year basis over 2008–12 and then averaged for the period. BGD = Bangladesh; IND = India; LKA = Sri Lanka; PAK = Pakistan.

Box 1.3 Exporter Dynamics Database

The Exporter Dynamics Database includes exporter characteristics and measures of exporter growth based on firm-level customs information from 38 low- and middle-income countries and 7 high-income countries, primarily for the period 2003 to 2010. Pooling across the data sets for all countries allows 15 million unique observations at the levels of country, firm, product, destination, and year. This raw data set is used to construct the database.

The measures are available at different levels of aggregation, including country-year, country-year-product, and country-year-destination. Several new stylized facts about exporter behavior across countries emerge from the database: (a) Larger or more developed economies have more exporters, larger and more diversified exporters, and lower entry and exit rates than

box continues next page

Box 1.3 Exporter Dynamics Database *(continued)*

smaller or low- and middle-income economies; (b) in the short run, expansions along the
intensive margin (exporter size) contribute more to export growth than expansions along the
extensive margin (number of exporters); (c) exit rates are highly correlated with entry rates and
both are negatively correlated with survival rates, average exporter size, and diversification;
and (d) the number of exporters and the entry and exit rates in a country-product group are
partially driven by country and product-group effects; however, the average size of exporters
in a country-product group is not.

Although the first three facts can be explained by models incorporating firm heterogeneity
and uncertainty, the fourth fact is more difficult to explain with existing models. Several findings are confirmed in this database, including the importance of large multiproduct firms. The
database can be a valuable tool to improve understanding of the micro foundations of export
growth, by providing new insights about exporter characteristics and dynamics.

The figures included in this chapter (figures 1.14–1.17) contain information for some countries that are not included in the first version of the database (Ethiopia, Lesotho, Nepal, and
Romania). The information for these countries was added and released as part of the second
(expanded) version of the database (January 2014).

Source: Cebeci et al. 2012.

---

a small share of the number of exporters. In particular, exporters selling more
than four products to more than four markets account for 60 percent of exports
on average (64 percent in Bangladesh), but only for 13 percent of the number
of exporters, on average, across all countries. The latter numbers vary from
about 3.5 percent in Albania and Botswana to 21.5 percent in South Africa,
22.4 percent in Bangladesh, and 29.4 percent in Cambodia (Cebeci et al. 2012).

Firms exporting fewer products are the largest exporters. Diversification has
not necessarily been an engine of fast growth for Bangladeshi firms, as large
export surges (20-fold or more export sales growth over a five-year period)
tend to be associated with single-product or at least heavily concentrated firms.
Figure 1.16 shows that single-product firms (the first bar in the graph) saw their
exports multiply, on average, by 10 over the five-year period between 2006/07
and 2010/11. Firms with two products performed well, but their growth was just
over twofold. Average growth reduced as the number of products rose, reaching
14 percent (cumulatively over the five-year period) for firms with 30 products.[10]
This trend is common across countries, with expansions along the intensive margin (increases in the average exporter size) contributing more to export growth
in the short run than expansions along the extensive margin (increases in the
number of exporters). This evidence supports a trade model with heterogeneous
firms along the lines of Melitz (2003), where entrants into export markets tend
to be marginal firms that have little impact on total exports. Moreover, firms face
fixed costs to export each product and serve each market. Only more capable
firms are able to generate variable profits to cover those fixed costs and thus supply a wider range of products to each market.

Figure 1.16 Growth Factor of Bangladeshi Firms as a Function of Number of Products

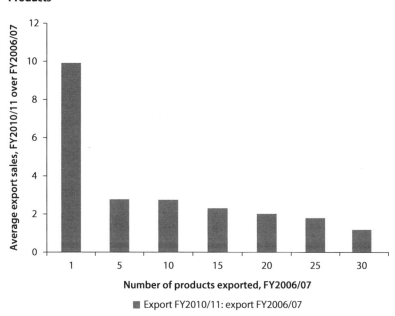

Source: Calculations based on Bangladesh National Board of Revenue data.
Note: Bar height measures the ratio of average export sales in FY2010/11 over FY2006/07 (two-year averaging after converting National Board of Revenue data to calendar year format was used to reduce the incidence of misreporting). Growth is in taka, which depreciated by 5 percent relative to the U.S. dollar over the period.

Few new exporting firms are entering the market in Bangladesh, given the country's level of income. The entry and exit rates in Bangladesh are below 25 percent, much lower than the average and median for low- and middle-income countries at around 37 percent (figure 1.17). Entry rates range from 22 percent in Brazil to more than 50 percent in Malawi and the Republic of Yemen, while exit rates range from 22 percent in Bangladesh to 61 percent in Malawi. Less churning usually takes place in more sophisticated export markets, where there are a lot of firms that sell a wider range of goods to more markets (Cebeci et al. 2012).

Average entry rates in Bangladesh (26 percent) are lower than those observed on average in comparator countries (figure 1.17).[11] This pattern is surprising considering recent evidence that shows that relatively lower churning in exporting is normally observed in larger and more developed economies (Cebeci et al. 2012).[12] However, the lower churning observed in Bangladesh may reflect the maturity and concentration observed in its garments sector.

Related to lack of churn is the survival rate of entrants in the first year in Bangladesh, which is better than in competing countries. Survival rates of new entrants into export markets have no clear correlation with the level of development (Cebeci et al. 2012). The better survival rate reflects the larger number of survivors among the entrants coupled with the lower rate of new entry (figure 1.17). First-year survival rates of new exporters vary between

Figure 1.17 Dynamics of Bangladeshi Exporters and Comparators, 2008–12

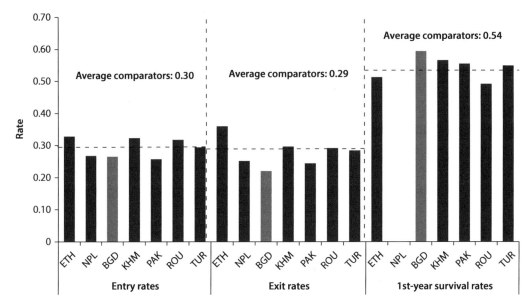

Source: World Bank Exporter Dynamics Database (http://econ.worldbank.org/exporter-dynamics-database).
Note: Countries sorted by gross domestic product per capita (descending order). BGD = Bangladesh; ETH = Ethiopia; KHM = Cambodia;
NPL = Nepal; PAK = Pakistan; ROU = Romania; TUR = Turkey.

23 percent in Cameroon and 61 percent in Bangladesh. The low survival rates across countries suggest an extremely high attrition rate of new entrants after just one year in export markets, particularly in Africa. However, that is not a defining characteristic of less-developed countries because high attrition rates of new entrants are also observed in Spain and Estonia.

Given the distribution of exporter size, an export promotion program targeting small and medium enterprises (SMEs) is unlikely to change the country's aggregate export performance. The distribution of total export values across Bangladesh's export firms is also very concentrated, with the top 1 percent and the top 5 percent accounting for more than a quarter and more than half of total exports, respectively, in 2008–11.[13] However, this applies to most of the countries for which data are available, and Bangladesh has in fact a more even distribution of exporters by size than some comparator countries. The distribution of exporter size in Bangladesh implies that the effect of export promotion schemes targeting small exporters will not have a significant impact on overall export performance.[14] A reasonable objective for such a program would be to nurture "export entrepreneurs" (such as potential exporters), some of whom may, over the long run, turn small-scale success into a large-scale business. Export promotion can be used as a tool to help reorient Bangladeshi exporters to faster growing markets, as recent research suggests that export promotion agencies are typically better at promoting entry into new markets than any other form of export expansion (Cadot, Carrère, and Strauss-Kahn 2011).

Figure 1.18 Linking Trade Outcome Categories to Competitiveness Challenges

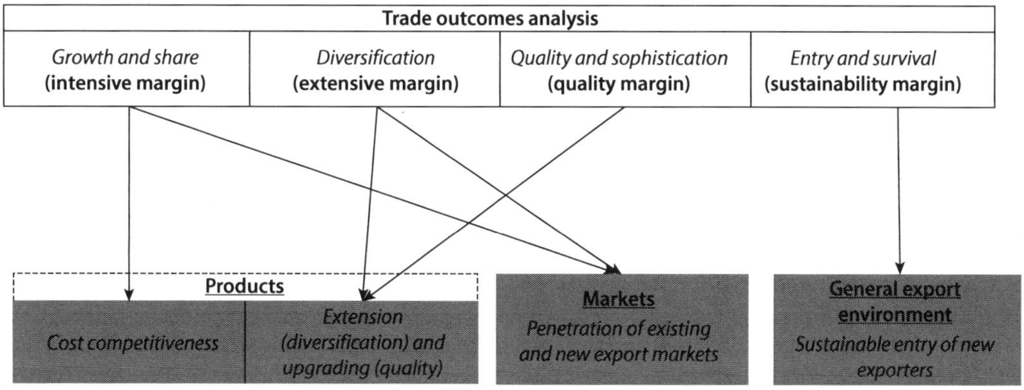

Source: Reis and Farole 2012.

Linking the analysis with the competitiveness challenges described in figure 1.18 suggests that there is important potential to improve trade performance at the extensive margin by essentially penetrating new markets and exporting new products, through diversification and quality upgrading. Bangladesh's low entry and exit rates suggest that competitiveness challenges most likely are driven by weaknesses in the general export environment. Overall, the analysis suggests that there is potential to intensify exports based on the existing factor endowment (large pool of unskilled labor)—that is, existing exports can grow significantly in current and new markets. The data suggest that Bangladesh will have to work harder to produce another large, labor-intensive cluster like garments, but its export presence in a wide variety of manufactured products indicates that it is possible, with the right supporting environment and with skill upgrading.

Bangladesh's Trade in Services

Trade in services, particularly business services, has become a dynamic component of trade as well as another source of export diversification in low- and middle-income countries. During 2000–07, trade in services grew as fast as trade in goods, at an average rate of 12 percent per year. India's success is well known: exports of software and business process services account for approximately 33 percent of India's total exports. Brazil, Costa Rica, and Uruguay export professional and information technology–related services; Mexico exports communications and distribution services; and Chile exports distribution and transportation services. African countries are also participating. Kenya, Morocco, South Africa, and Tunisia provide professional services to Europe; the Arab Republic of Egypt has developed a world-class call center sector. Health services are successfully exported by the Philippines and Thailand.

Bangladesh's services exports have trebled over the past decade, from a little over US$800 million in 2000 to around US$2.4 billion in 2010.[15] As highlighted in table 1.4, the contribution of traditional services such as transport and travel has declined over the decades from around 50 percent to about 20 percent of total services exports. The contribution of other services—in particular, communications, other business services, and, to some extent, computer and information services—has grown over this period. In value terms, other business services constitute the largest segment within other services. They grew almost six-fold in value and increased their share in total services exports by around a third between 2000 and 2010. Likewise, communications services grew more than tenfold in value terms over this period. Bangladesh's move toward new services reflects partial liberalization of subsectors such as information and communications services and business services and the country's comparative advantage in labor-based services. The growth in communications services exports reflects the impact of deregulation in services such as telecommunications. The growth in other business services (including engineering, consulting, and other professional services) reflects Bangladesh's large pool of labor and growing opportunities in emerging services such as skill-intensive and professional services.

Bangladesh's low growth in tourism exports and poor ranking in this segment are noteworthy. It suggests constraints related to infrastructure and connectivity as well as possible lack of focus on developing this sector for exports. The low value of computer and information services exports (the relatively fast growth over 2000–10 was due to a low base value) is also striking, given the growing demand for software services in the global market and the emergence of other LDC exporters of computer services. It suggests that Bangladesh, notwithstanding its potential in labor-based and skill-intensive business services, has not been able to leverage its potential in this segment and could be facing competition from other low-cost LDC exporters of information technology (IT) and IT-enabled services.

Table 1.4 Value and Share of Exports by Service Subsectors, Bangladesh, Selected Years
value, US$ millions; share, %

Subsector	2000		2005		2010	
	Value	Share	Value	Share	Value	Share
Commercial services	283.192	100.00	474.21	100.00	1,209.41	100.00
Transport	91.368	32.26	113.009	23.83	173.591	14.35
Travel	50.421	17.80	70.009	14.76	81.221	6.72
Other commercial services	141.403	49.93	291.192	61.41	954.598	78.93
Communications	21.532	7.60	23.906	5.04	277.67	22.96
Construction	0.194	0.07	14.156	2.99	6.909	0.57
Insurance	3.513	1.24	5.027	1.06	6.841	0.57
Financial services	13.083	4.62	17.972	3.79	40.841	3.38
Computer and information	3.243	1.15	18.713	3.95	37.756	3.12
Royalties and license fees	0.058	0.02	0.261	0.06	0.517	0.04
Other business services	99.253	35.05	210.013	44.29	582.147	48.13
Personal, cultural, and recreational services	0.527	0.19	1.144	0.24	1.925	0.16

Source: UNCTADstat database; http://unctadstat.unctad.org/.
Note: Shares calculated after excluding government services not included elsewhere.

Bangladesh's services imports have registered a considerable increase over the past decade, from US$1.6 billion in 2000 to US$4.4 billion in 2010. Traditional services imports have increased; for example, transport services imports more than tripled from US$1 billion in 2000 to US$3.4 billion in 2010, and its share of total services imports increased from 66 percent to over 83 percent over this period (table 1.5).[16] The growing dependence on imports of transport services in part reflects demand from the RMG sector and Bangladesh's reliance on foreign transport carriers, given the country's capacity constraints in transport and logistics. There has also been a more than trebling of imports of other business services in value terms, reflecting the growing importance of these supporting services to the economy. However, both in value and share, transport services dwarf all other segments.

Bangladesh has had a persistent trade deficit in services, which has grown from around US$800 million to nearly US$2 billion in the past decade. This deficit is concentrated in traditional services such as transport and travel; there is a positive trade balance in other commercial services, on account of emerging segments such as communications and other business services. In global rankings of countries, Bangladesh ranks at 107 as a service exporter, although its rank is higher in the case of "other commercial services" exports, owing to the category of other business services (table 1.4). Bangladesh ranks among the top 100 service-importing countries, primarily because of its import dependence in transport services.

These service trade figures clearly highlight two important points: First, Bangladesh is potentially more competitive in nontraditional services that rely on information and communications technology and on the availability of competitive labor, in services that have been liberalized (although the potential in

Table 1.5 Value and Share of Imports for Service Subsectors, Bangladesh, Selected Years
value, US$ millions; share, %

Subsector	2000		2005		2010	
	Value	Share	Value	Share	Value	Share
Commercial services	1,523.35	100.00	2,011.36	100.00	4,128.30	100.00
Transport	1,012.76	66.48	1,544.73	76.80	3,440.64	83.34
Travel	289.91	19.03	136.27	6.77	260.60	6.31
Other commercial services	220.68	14.49	330.36	16.42	427.06	10.34
Communications	7.39	0.48	20.62	1.03	20.23	0.49
Construction	2.15	0.14	1.07	0.05	6.29	0.15
Insurance	91.07	5.98	150.65	7.49	26.32	0.64
Financial services	30.75	2.02	13.27	0.66	45.35	1.10
Computer and information	1.52	0.10	4.26	0.21	5.42	0.13
Royalties and license fees	4.42	0.29	2.75	0.14	17.64	0.43
Other business services	83.29	5.47	137.72	6.85	305.70	7.40
Personal, cultural, and recreational services	0.10	0.01	0.03	0.00	0.13	0.00

Source: UNCTADstat database; http://unctadstat.unctad.org/.
Note: Shares calculated after excluding government services not included elsewhere.

Strengthening Competitiveness in Bangladesh—Thematic Assessment
http://dx.doi.org/10.1596/978-1-4648-0898-2

computer and information services appears to be unrealized so far). Second, at present, Bangladesh appears to be less competitive in traditional services such as transport and travel. One reason is because infrastructure availability and supply capacity are critical for delivery of these services. Furthermore, there is need for further liberalization and policy reforms or for greater policy thrust to promote exports (as argued in various studies regarding the country's infrastructure and logistics services sectors, as well as in this chapter). The growth trends in different services segments similarly confirm the growing and likely potential in some emerging services.

The RCA indices from the UNCTADstat database for Bangladesh's services exports also highlight that the country is relatively competitive in communications and other business services. The latter have RCAs of 1 or more, while RCAs for transport and travel services have consistently been less than 1 and declined over the past few years (table 1.6). The RCA values as well as the shifts in composition of the services export basket suggest that Bangladesh's traditional exports are affected by domestic constraints arising from inadequate infrastructure and lack of supportive policies. The decline in the RCA value for computer and information services, notwithstanding the skill-intensive nature of this segment, is noteworthy, especially against the much higher RCAs for other business services and communications services. As noted earlier, these RCAs are indicative of the country's untapped potential in this segment caused by domestic and external factors (see Kathuria and Malouche 2016, chapter 7, on IT-enabled services).

Bangladesh's overall RCA for services exports has been less than 1 and stagnant over the past decade in contrast with its RCA for goods. The country has also registered higher growth in goods as opposed to services exports over the past two decades. This is also reflected at the regional level, where Bangladesh's export performance in goods has been superior to that in services, as is highlighted in figure 1.19. The country's share in world services exports has risen only

Table 1.6 Revealed Comparative Advantage in Bangladeshi Services, Selected Years

Services category	2000	2005	2010
Other business services	1.9169	2.3415	1.9037
Communications services	4.1406	4.9121	10.1303
Transportation	0.6545	0.5509	0.6728
Travel	0.5007	0.3342	0.2634
Financial services	0.5516	0.4356	0.4672
Computer and information services	1.1188	0.6385	0.5342
Construction services	1.5859	0.3002	0.2229
Insurance services	0.6064	0.5641	0.2475
Personal, cultural, and recreational services	0.3334	0.1110	0.1111
Royalties and license fees	0.0092	0.0002	0.0066

Source: UNCTADstat database; http://unctadstat.unctad.org/.

Figure 1.19 Revealed Comparative Advantage for Goods and Services Exports, Bangladesh and South Asia, Selected Years

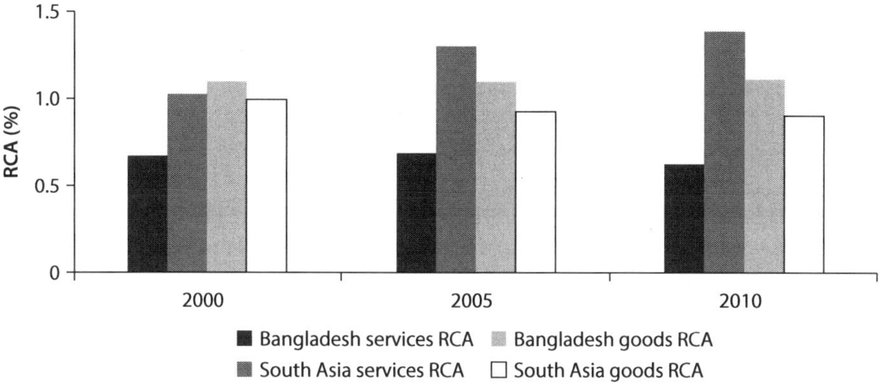

Source: UNCTADstat database; http://unctadstat.unctad.org/.
Note: RCA = revealed comparative advantage.

marginally, from 0.05 percent in 1990 to 0.06 percent in 2010, compared with an increase in its world share of goods exports from 0.05 percent in 1990 to 0.12 percent in 2010. The share of services exports in Bangladesh's total exports has remained at around 11 percent over the past decade, lower than for the other large countries in South Asia, while the share of services imports in its total imports has been in the range of 15–18 percent.

Exports of Labor Services

Bangladesh is an important source of largely semiskilled and unskilled migrant workers to selected countries.[17] Data on overseas employment provided by the Bureau of Manpower Employment and Training of Bangladesh highlight the rising trend in overseas employment of Bangladeshi workers over the past three decades. Overseas employment of Bangladeshi workers increased from around 200,000 workers in 2000 to 600,000 workers in 2012, with female workers constituting about 6.1 percent of all migrant workers in 2012 (figure 1.20). The main destination markets are the Middle East, the United States, the United Kingdom, and Southeast Asia (table 1.7). These also constitute the main source countries for remittances. Saudi Arabia alone accounts for nearly one-third of the total stock of Bangladeshi migrant workers.

Corresponding to the rise in overseas employment, there has also been a considerable increase in remittance inflows, from less than US$1 billion in the 1990s to nearly US$2 billion in 2000 and to more than US$14 billion in 2012 (figure 1.21). The significance of labor services exports is evident from the increase in the share of remittances in Bangladesh's GDP from 4.1 percent in 1999/2000 to 11.1 percent in 2012/13. Bangladesh is ranked eighth among the top 10 remittance recipients in the world (World Bank 2012c). These large inflows of remittances have macroeconomic and developmental implications for

32

Figure 1.20 Overseas Employment of Bangladeshi Workers, 1976–2012

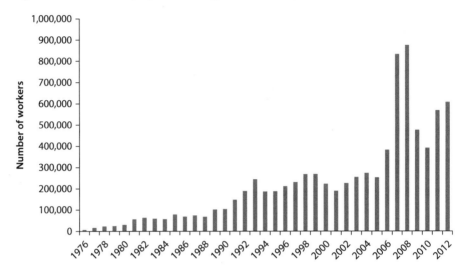

Source: Bureau of Manpower Employment and Training.

Table 1.7 Top 10 Destination Countries for Bangladeshi Migrants, 2000–10

Country	Number of migrants[a]	Share of total migration (%)
Saudi Arabia	2,046,736	31.1
United Arab Emirates	1,542,376	23.5
Malaysia	553,789	8.4
United Kingdom	379,716	5.8
United States	298,067	4.5
Oman	281,105	4.3
Kuwait	260,013	4.0
Singapore	223,677	3.4
Qatar	154,309	2.3
Bahrain	149,698	2.3

Source: Calculated from Bureau of Manpower Employment and Training data.
a. Number of migrants up to June 2010.

Bangladesh's economy (see World Bank 2012b). Studies indicate a strong multiplier effect of remittances in the rural areas of Bangladesh. Effects include increased consumption spending and increased investment in health and education relative to nonmigrant families. In addition, the establishment of enterprises and small businesses by returnee migrants or their family members is generating employment and creating markets for locally produced goods and services (Raihan et al. 2009). Thus, the management of migration and associated remittances is an important issue for Bangladesh.

Bangladesh's mode 4 exports are dominated by low-skilled workers, followed by skilled and semiskilled workers, according to government sources. This movement is mostly in the form of contract labor. Table 1.8 highlights the

Figure 1.21 Remittances Earned by Bangladeshi Migrants, 1976–2012

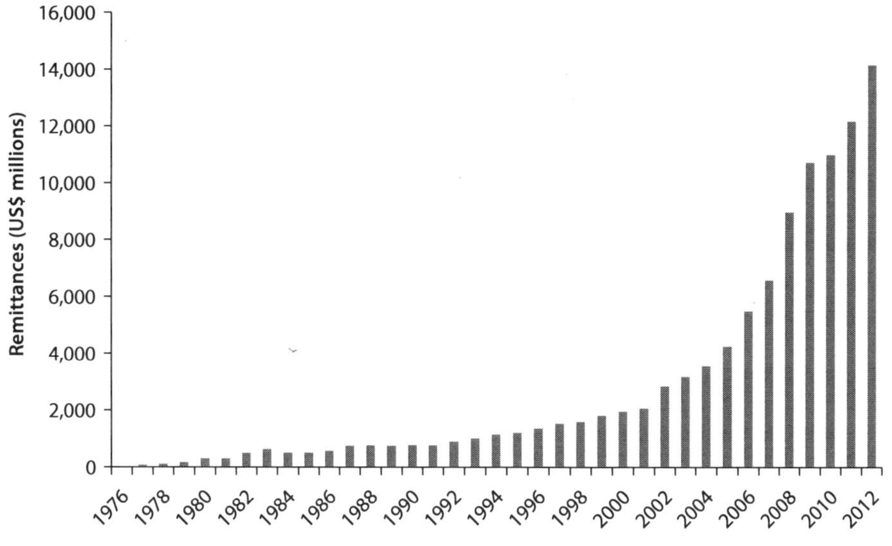

Source: Bureau of Manpower Employment and Training.

Table 1.8 Breakdown of Bangladeshi Overseas Workers by Skill, 1990–2012

Year	Category				Total
	Professional	Skilled	Semiskilled	Low-skilled	
1990	6,004	35,613	20,792	41,405	103,814
2000	5,940	42,742	30,702	109,581	188,965
2005	1,945	113,655	24,546	112,556	252,702
2012[a]	812	209,368	20,498	377,120	607,798

Source: Bureau of Manpower Employment and Training.
a. Number of overseas workers calculated up to December 2012.

categorization of Bangladesh's labor exports by skill. The table highlights the declining trend in professional labor exports and the significant rise in low-skilled labor exports, which are mainly in occupations such as domestic work, construction (masonry), and transport operations and in manual trades such as carpentry, fabrication, welding, and cleaning.

There is also limited skill movement from Bangladesh to English-speaking developed countries such as Australia, the United Kingdom, and the United States. These numbers are quite small in comparison with the large number of low-skilled workers working worldwide, particularly in the Middle East and relative to larger countries in South Asia (figure 1.22 shows that remittances are dominated by Bangladeshis in the Middle East). According to the U.S. Department of Homeland Security data for 2009, there were a mere 389 persons engaged on H-1B visas and 46 on L-1 visas from Bangladesh, even fewer than the number of Sri Lankans working under these categories in the United States (U.S. Department of Homeland Security 2009). Similarly, in the case of the United Kingdom, the

Strengthening Competitiveness in Bangladesh—Thematic Assessment
http://dx.doi.org/10.1596/978-1-4648-0898-2

Figure 1.22 Remittances Earned by Bangladeshi Migrants by Country, 2012

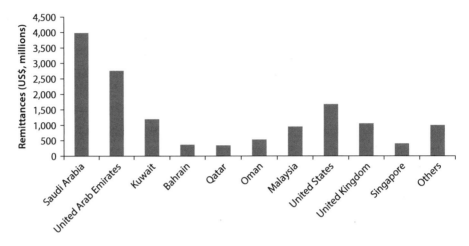

Source: Bangladesh Bank.

number of applications under the Highly Skilled Migrant Program has been quite small, 200 or fewer for most years (Salt and Millar 2006). Overall, the overseas employment data for Bangladesh suggest a comparative advantage in less-skilled labor services exports, a concentration of market access interests in the Middle East, possible domestic and external constraints to increasing professional services exports, as well as a potential to diversify in markets and skill categories.

Conclusion

Bangladesh's exports doubled their world market share between 1995 and 2012, owing to the success in garments, catering largely to the European Union and the United States. Since 2009, Bangladesh has become the world's second largest garment exporter, making it unique among LDCs in its high share of manufactures in total exports.

The analysis suggests that there is great potential to intensify exports based on the existing factor endowment (large pool of unskilled labor), but also the scope to improve factor endowments to diversify, move up the value chain, and produce more sophisticated goods and in a more productive way.

Future export growth will likely rely first on capturing new markets with existing products. Garments can continue to grow in existing and newer markets. Newer products will emerge more slowly. Thus, more rapid export growth will initially rely on capturing higher market shares in Bangladesh's existing strengths, that is, basic garments, in current markets and penetrating newer and dynamic markets such as ASEAN, China, India, and Japan. Other products are emerging, such as jute goods, footwear, seafood, information technology enabled services (ITES), and others, and some of these may over time become part of a larger product cluster.

Bangladesh will need to focus more attention to skills development and workers' welfare. The low level of literacy and years of schooling of the labor force make skill acquisition more difficult. According to the latest World Bank Poverty Assessment (2013), just a third of the primary graduates acquire the numeracy and literacy skills they are expected to master by the time they graduate. Moreover, among the labor force, the percentage of persons having professional education such as engineering and medicine is very small (only 0.17 percent of the labor force has such degrees). Skills are emerging as a major constraint, even in the garments sector, let alone other, more skill-intensive sectors. A World Bank survey of 1,000 garment firms in 2011 found that skills were the major disadvantage if firms located outside Dhaka. High rejection rates in a 2010 United Nations Industrial Development Organization survey also point to low average skills of garment workers. In sectors such as ITES, shipbuilding, and pharmaceuticals, part of this Diagnostic Trade Integration Study, higher skills are in constant demand (World Bank 2012a, 2012b).

Notes

1. For a detailed analysis, see World Bank (2007, 2012b).
2. For details, see IMF (2013), http://www.imf.org/external/pubs/ft/scr/2013/cr13157.pdf.
3. Based on World Bank (2016), Bangladesh Development Update.
4. The products are (a) T-shirts, singlets, and other vests, HS code 6109; (b) jerseys, pullovers, cardigans, and so forth, HS code 6110; (c) men's suits, jackets, trousers, and shorts, HS code 6203; (d) women's suits, jackets, skirts, and shorts, HS code 6204; and (e) men's shirts, HS code 6205.
5. U.S. International Trade Commission database.
6. Theil's concentration index is an alternative to the Gini or Herfindahl indices. It is more flexible in that it can be decomposed into additive group components, a useful property in the context of export diversification.
7. The concept of RCA is defined as Balassa's (1965) measure of relative export performance by country and industry, defined as a country's share of world exports of a good divided by its share of total world exports. The index for country i, good j is $RCA_{ij} = 100(X_{ij}/X_{wj})/(X_{it}/X_{wt})$ where X_{ab} is exports by country a (w = world) of good b (t = total for all goods). An RCA index above 1.0 indicates that a country's share of exports in a sector exceeds the global export share of the same product.
8. In trade, the gravity model presumes that distance (a proxy for actual shipping cost, policy barriers, and informational asymmetry) and mass (GDPs of exporting and importing countries) explain a large share of bilateral trade. Whether a country is under-exporting to a destination country of interest can be gauged by comparing actual export values in a given year with a predicted export value obtained from a regression that controls for the standard gravity variables, such as absolute bilateral distance, GDP, and per capita incomes.
9. Products are defined at a disaggregated level, from customs data.
10. This is not just a convergence effect. A regression controlling for initial export sales still returns a negative and significant coefficient on the initial number of products.

11. The group of comparator countries was selected based on the following criteria: (a) countries in the same geographical region (Nepal and Pakistan), (b) countries with a similar leading sector (Ethiopia), and (c) countries in the Exporter Dynamics Database with a large manufacturing base and high export growth in the past decade (Cambodia, Lesotho, Romania, and Turkey).

12. Trial and error or entry and exit of exporters is less frequent in developed economies where exporting firms are more mature and closer to their steady-state equilibrium (Cebeci et al. 2012).

13. Calculated from firm-level export data collected from the National Board of Revenue.

14. According to a benchmark calculation, an export promotion scheme targeting 1,000 SMEs could hope to raise exports by about US$11.2 million a year.

15. http://unctadstat.unctad.org (accessed April 23, 2012).

16. http://unctadstat.unctad.org (accessed April 23, 2012).

17. See Kathuria and Malouche 2016, chapter 8, on opportunities and challenges for services exports, for a more detailed discussion on export of labor.

References

Balassa, Bela. 1965. "Trade Liberalisation and Revealed Comparative Advantage." *The Manchester School* 33 (2): 99–123.

Cadot, O., C. Carrère, and V. Strauss-Kahn. 2011. "Export Diversification: What's Behind the Hump?" *The Review of Economics and Statistics* 93 (2): 590–605.

Cebeci, T., A. Fernandes, C. Freund, and M. Pierola. 2012. "Exporter Dynamics Database." Policy Research Working Paper 6229, World Bank, Washington, DC.

Government of Bangladesh. 2011. *Sixth Five-Year Plan, FY2011–FY2015*. Planning Commission, Ministry of Planning, Dhaka.

Hausmann, R., J. Hwang, and D. Rodrik. 2007. "What You Export Matters." *Journal of Economic Growth* 12: 1–25.

IMF (International Monetary Fund). 2013. *Bangladesh: Second Review under the Three-Year Arrangement under the Extended Credit Facility and Request for Modification of Performance Criteria*. IMF Country Report 13/157, IMF, Washington, DC.

Kathuria, Sanjay, and Mariem Mezghenni Malouche, eds. 2016. *Attracting Investment in Bangladesh—Sectoral Analyses: A Diagnostic Trade Integration Study*. Directions in Development. Washington, DC: World Bank.

Lall, S. 2000. "The Technological Structure and Performance of Developing Country Manufactured Exports, 1985–1998." Working Paper, Q. E. House, University of Oxford.

Lopez-Acevedo, G., and R. Robertson, eds. 2012. *Sewing Success? Employment, Wages, and Poverty Following the End of the Multi-Fibre Arrangement*. Washington, DC: World Bank.

Melitz, M. J. 2003. "The Impact of Trade on Intra-Industry Reallocations and Aggregate Industry Productivity." *Econometrica* 1: 1695–1725.

Raihan, S., B. H. Khondker, G. Sugiyarto, and S. Jha. 2009. "Remittances and Household Welfare: A Case Study of Bangladesh." Asian Development Bank Economics Working Paper 189, Asian Development Bank, Manila.

Reis, José Guilherme, and Thomas Farole. 2012. *Trade Competitiveness Diagnostic Toolkit.* Washington, DC: World Bank.

Salt, J., and J. Millar. 2006. "Foreign Labour in the United Kingdom: Current Patterns and Trends." Migration Research Unit, University College, London.

U.S. Department of Homeland Security. 2009. *Yearbook of Immigration Statistics Office of Immigration Statistics.* https://www.dhs.gov/xlibrary/assets/statistics/yearbook/2009 /ois_yb_2009.pdf.

World Bank. 2007. "Bangladesh—Strategy for Sustained Growth: Volume 1—Summary Report." Report No. 38289-BD, World Bank, Washington, DC. https://openknowledge .worldbank.org/handle/10986/7765.

———. 2012a. "Consolidating and Accelerating Exports in Bangladesh: A Policy Agenda." Bangladesh Development Series 29, Poverty Reduction and Economic Management Sector, South Asia Region, World Bank, Washington, DC.

———. 2012b. "Bangladesh: Towards Accelerated, Inclusive and Sustainable Growth— Opportunities and Challenges." Report 67991. Poverty Reduction and Economic Management Unit, South Asia Region, World Bank, Washington, DC.

———. 2012c. "Remittances to Developing Countries Will Surpass $400 Billion in 2012." Migration and Development Brief 19, Migration and Remittances Unit, Development Prospects Group, World Bank, Washington, DC. https://openknowledge.worldbank.org /handle/10986/17062.

———. 2013. "Taking Stock: An Update on Vietnam's Recent Economic Developments, July 2013." World Bank, Hanoi, Vietnam. https://openknowledge.worldbank.org /handle/10986/16258.

WTO (World Trade Organization). 2012. *Trade Policy Review: Bangladesh.* Geneva: WTO. https://www.wto.org/english/tratop_e/tpr_e/tp370_e.htm.

CHAPTER 2

Trade Policy, Export Incentives, and Consumer Welfare

Olivier Cadot, Julien Gourdon, Sanjay Kathuria,
Mariem Mezghenni Malouche, and Zaidi Sattar

Introduction

In Bangladesh, the government's development program aims to use trade policy as an instrument for generating export expansion and diversification. The broad trade policy objectives are consistent with the Vision 2021 development strategy, which aims at raising the country's growth rate to 10 percent per year within the next five years. This is to be achieved through an array of policies, including the following:

- Enhanced access to imported capital equipment and raw materials through tailored adjustments to the import regime
- Infant-industry protection for targeted sectors
- Fiscal incentives for users of foreign technology
- Export promotion and encouragement for quality upgrading in the ready-made garments (RMG) sector
- Reinforcement of standardization and quality-control capabilities.

Trade policy has served Bangladesh well so far, resulting in sustained export growth. Dollar exports have doubled over the past six years. Bangladesh is now the second largest exporter of garments and could benefit significantly from China's rising wages and the ongoing move to cheaper garment producers. And Bangladesh has an unusually high share (for its income level) of manufactured exports in its export basket, which illustrates its strengths in mass manufacturing and labor availability. The economy has become increasingly open, fueled by a trade policy environment that is more conducive to exports. Trade policy reform included a substantial scaling down and rationalization of tariffs, major reductions of quantitative restrictions and import licensing, unification of exchange rates, and the move to a managed float exchange rate regime.

Yet, significant inconsistencies stemming from lingering trade protectionism for some industries, along with a focus on revenue targets, raise questions about

Strengthening Competitiveness in Bangladesh—Thematic Assessment
http://dx.doi.org/10.1596/978-1-4648-0898-2

the overall efficacy of trade policy and sustainability of export growth. Trade policy often responds to protectionist pressures, reminiscent of the import-substituting trade regime that prevailed before the 1990s. Revenue or protectionist considerations have usually dominated over trade policy issues. Thus, trade policy in Bangladesh has been skewed, where consumers and export sectors other than garments have not been conscious beneficiaries of such policies. Moreover, in recent years, border taxes have increased, grown more complex, and led to high and varied rates of effective protection. Overall, the trade policy regime has translated into reduced incentives to export and diversify and has led to higher domestic prices.

Trade policy design and implementation are also challenged by lack of coordination among responsible agencies. The principal responsibility of domestic and international trade in Bangladesh rests with the Ministry of Commerce. The Imports and Exports (Control) Act of 1950 empowers the Ministry of Commerce to regulate the import and export of goods and services, which it carries out through a periodic Import Policy Order that encompasses a range of nontariff barriers (such as quotas, import controls, and licensing) and export policy that provides for incentives and other schemes. In addition, the Ministry of Commerce is the focal point for bilateral, multilateral, and regional negotiations and for ensuring Bangladesh's compliance with World Trade Organization (WTO) agreements, including agreements on dumping, safeguards, and countervailing duties. In practice, the Ministry of Finance, through the National Board of Revenue (NBR), takes the lead role in tariff-setting in Bangladesh and the Ministry of Industries also offers a range of incentives under its industrial policy. In reality, trade policy formulation includes fragmented elements that are not necessarily implemented coherently in the pursuit of a common vision (see chapter 4 for a broader discussion on building institutional capacity in Bangladesh).

This chapter discusses the different aspects of trade policy that the government needs to address. We use, among other sources, novel customs transaction data and a detailed firm-level survey of effective protection in 100 firms. The analysis focuses on tariffs and fiscal revenues, nontariff measures, related welfare issues, quality standards, and services trade restrictiveness. The chapter analyzes the extent to which trade policy has been trade and welfare enhancing. This also implies that any protectionist measures should be justified in terms of economy-wide positive spillovers and should also be temporary. Since much of the analysis is comparative, Bangladesh also needs to keep in mind the more harmonized trade policies in export-competing countries, such as Indonesia, Vietnam, and others.

Heavy Border Taxation

This section looks at border taxation, which increases the cost of inputs and intermediate goods, thereby increasing domestic production costs; it also raises the price of consumer goods, hurting the poor and the urban middle-income class. Tariffs and para-tariffs also tend to restrict product variety in the domestic market, limit the scope for producing new products, and impact consumer welfare. Relatively high average tariffs introduce an anti-export bias into the trade regime because they make it more attractive for companies to produce for the protected domestic market rather than to sell overseas.

The tax treatment of imports in Bangladesh is complex. Average customs duties (CDs) have come down from 70.6 percent in fiscal year (FY) 1992 to 13.2 percent in FY2014 (figures 2.1 and 2.2).[1] One of the key features of tariff reform was the move toward uniformity: from about 20 tariff slabs, the tariff structure now is divided into four nonzero slabs of 2, 5, 10, and 25 percent. The system presents low tariffs of 2 percent to 5 percent for basic raw materials and capital goods, 10 percent for intermediate goods, and the top rate of 25 percent for final goods. CDs have increased by 6 percentage points since FY2009, increasing the average protection in FY2010 to FY2012 compared with the previous three years. The proliferation of other duties and taxes has added to the increase in the average protection rate. It also has become a burden for importers and the customs administration. The resultant increase in complexity and reduction in transparency raises the chances of errors and inefficiency and provides more opportunities for lobbying and rent-seeking.

Figure 2.1 Overall Protective Rate: Downward Trend but Para-Tariffs Increased in Recent Years

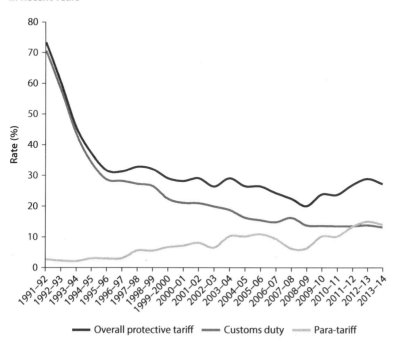

Source: Tariff data from various policy orders.
Note: Para-tariff: regulatory duty (RD) + infrastructure development surcharge (IDSC) + license fee (LF) + protective supplementary duty (SD) + protective value-added tax (VAT); overall protective tariff: customs duty + RD + IDSC + LF + SD + VAT.

Figure 2.2 Tariffs and Para-Tariffs Paid by Companies in Bangladesh, 2012

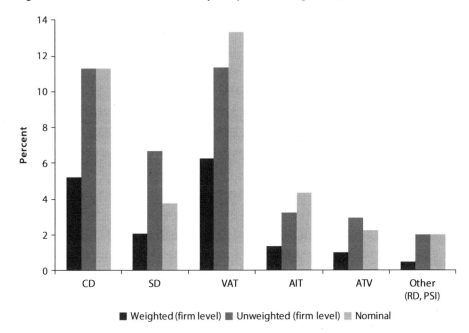

Source: Calculations based on National Board of Revenue data.
Note: For each tax, the weighted rate is the ratio of total taxes paid to total CIF import value from firm-level data; the unweighted rate is the simple average of this ratio calculated at the firm level; the nominal rate is the official rate on the books. AIT = advanced income tax; ATV = advanced trade VAT (a tax levied nominally at 3 percent of the VAT inclusive price of commercially imported goods); CD = customs duty; CIF = cost, insurance, and freight; PSI = preshipment inspection; RD = regulatory duty; SD = supplementary duty; VAT = value-added tax.

A proliferation of para-tariffs has resulted in a complex import tax regime and substantially increased the rate of border protection (see figure 2.1, above, for data up to FY2014). Para-tariffs—import taxes and levies other than customs duties—have slowly emerged as a dominant set of trade taxes since the middle of the past decade (box 2.1). Supplementary duty (SD) and regulatory duty (RD) seem to have become standard instruments for raising revenue or offering protection to domestic import-substituting industries. Such tariff changes that raise overall protection and also increase its dispersion across products potentially set back the agenda for trade diversification. The combination of the tariff rate with para-tariff rates gives an average nominal protection rate (NPR) of 26.9 percent in FY2015, up from 20.1 percent in FY2009 (albeit with a decline in FY2015, compared with the 28.1 percent rate of FY2014).

Para-tariffs are not trade neutral. The RD of 5 percent was introduced in FY2000/01 and is levied on imports only. Although an SD was introduced in 1991 under the Value-Added Tax (VAT) Act and was meant to be a trade-neutral tax, it has been increasingly applied in a non-neutral fashion; it is not applied equally on imports and domestic sales, following exemptions issued through statutory regulatory orders by the NBR. In principle, SDs are aimed at discouraging the import of luxury goods and goods considered undesirable on social or

Box 2.1 Bangladesh's Para-Tariffs

Apart from customs duties (CDs), Bangladesh's customs authorities impose a number of levies, taxes, and fees on imports, which are therefore defined as para-tariffs. CDs are the only recognized "customs tariff" for cross-country comparisons. CDs are charged under the Customs Act of 1969. The revenue authorities grant some special exemptions on the statutory rate of CDs for certain commodities through statutory regulatory orders (SROs). Duty is charged on an ad valorem basis as a percentage of the "assessable value" of imports.

The para-tariffs are:

Regulatory duty (RD). An RD is levied at a flat rate of 5 percent of assessable value. It was introduced in FY2000/01 and is levied only on imports. It is an import-specific tax, levied on an annual basis, that is, a customs tariff under a different name.

Supplementary duty (SD). An SD is levied on items listed under the Value-Added Tax Act (VAT Act), 1991. The rate depends on the product. The VAT authority issues exemptions on SDs through the SROs. In the beginning, SDs were charged according to "assessable value," but since FY1997/98, SDs have been levied on the basis of duty-paid value (assessable value plus customs duty plus regulatory duty).

Value-added tax (VAT). The VAT was introduced in 1991 in place of the Excise and Salt Tax Act of 1944. VAT is a trade-neutral tax applied at a uniform rate of 15 percent on imports and domestic production. However, the entire group of textile products, although subject to 15 percent import VAT, is exempt from VAT on domestic production, except for a levy of 2.5 percent. This non-uniform application of VAT on textiles has protective implications and serves as a para-tariff as well.

Advance income tax (AIT). The AIT is collected under the Income Tax Act and levied at a flat rate of 5 percent on the assessable value of imports, with a corresponding adjustment when the taxpayer settles his yearly income tax. Some exemptions are given via SROs. However, an AIT becomes a potential para-tariff in practice, when the AIT ends up as a final settlement, as often seems to be the case on most if not all imports.

Advance trade VAT (ATV). The ATV is applied only on commercial imports, commodities imported for retail sale. ATV is levied at a flat rate of 3 percent on "VAT paid value" (assessable value plus effective VAT).

Preshipment inspection (PSI) agent fee. The PSI agent fee is collected under the Customs Act and PSI rules, and levied at a flat rate of 1 percent on assessable value at the import stage.

Agent advance income tax. The agent advance income tax is collected under the Income Tax Act, and levied at a flat rate of 5 percent on the chargeable commission (considering the carrying and forwarding agent charges 1 percent commission on assessable value as an operating fee; from that fee the 5 percent AIT is charged at source).

moral grounds. Bangladesh applies SD rates of 350 percent on "sin goods" (alcohol and tobacco) and rates up to 156 percent on automobiles, depending on their type. However, in practice, SDs have been used as a tool to levy additional tariffs on a range of goods, as and when deemed appropriate by the authorities, including on raw materials and intermediate goods (WTO 2012). A substantial number of other products carry SD rates of 60 percent. Although punitive rates on alcohol and tobacco can easily be justified by negative externalities and high rates on luxury cars on redistribution grounds, extensive use of SDs at 60 percent, including those on a number of hygiene and consumption goods, is less justified. It does seem that a large share of the SDs has no obvious welfare justification.

The level of border protection is also high compared with other low-income economies and assessed with alternative measures of the overall stance of Bangladesh's border-tax structure. Bangladesh's tariffs, excluding para-tariffs for which we do not have comparable data across countries, remain among the highest in the region. Average most-favored-nation tariff is about 12 percent for least-developed countries (LDCs) and 9 percent for lower-middle-income countries (figure 2.3). Simple-average tariffs are known to be biased, giving too much weight to small items. Weighted-average tariffs underestimate the true rate of restrictiveness of the border-tax structure, because high tariffs reduce imports and hence the weight of items to which they apply. Two alternatives have been widely used: the Tariff Trade Restrictiveness Index (TTRI) and the Overall Trade Restrictiveness Index (OTRI).[2] Based on customs duty rates only for FY2010/11, the TTRI for Bangladesh is 13.8 percent and the OTRI is 10.4 percent. A recalculation of the TTRI and OTRI, taking into account all para-tariff charges, gives 38.9 percent for the TTRI and 28.4 percent for the OTRI. The TTRI has a higher value because of high rates of the SD in Bangladesh, which are magnified in the TTRI formula (which involves the square of the protection rate). Recalculating the TTRI after capping the import-discriminatory component of the SD at 60 percent, the TTRI goes down only marginally, to 36 percent.

Figure 2.3 Average Tariffs in Most Low-Income Countries, 2012

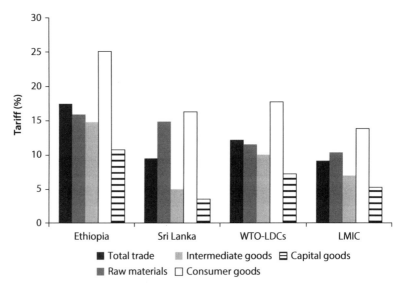

Source: TRAINS database.
Note: Data for Bangladesh are not available. LDCs = least-developed countries; LMIC = low- and middle-income countries; WTO = World Trade Organization.

Distortionary Incentives

Consumer goods are overly protected in Bangladesh, and there is a growing wedge between input and output tariffs. The government levies significant SD and RD on top of the 25 percent tariff for final goods, mostly on products that are produced domestically and are not taxed as much (table 2.1). Thus, tariff escalation is the highest at the last stage of processing—from intermediate goods to final goods. The wedge between the average NPR on inputs and final consumer goods has been rising since FY2008/09 (figure 2.4) and appears designed to offer higher protection to domestic industries primarily engaged in consumer goods production. Tariff escalation appears to be the outcome of prebudget consultations with producer groups only, without consultation with other stakeholders, such as consumers who could suffer welfare losses through higher prices or reduced choice.

There has been no critical evaluation of the impact of protection. In general, higher tariffs on a product encourage its domestic production and discourage exports, since the former is protected by the tariff and the latter is a far more competitive marketplace. The low protection for intermediate and capital goods arguably discourages domestic production of these goods; high protection for consumer goods encourages domestic production. If there is no "sunset clause" or expiration date for protection and the impact of protection on the protected sector and the rest of the economy is not evaluated, as is the case in Bangladesh, this can lead to economic inefficiencies.

Border taxation varies substantially at the sector level for tariffs and para-tariffs (table 2.2 and figure 2.5).[3] Border taxation rates vary substantially between and also *within* sectors, potentially reinforcing distortions in individual decisions, opportunities for rent-seeking, and the consequent need for enforcement. In general, tariff rates are more dispersed (less concentrated) than para-tariff rates (figure 2.6), reflecting tariff escalation.

The escalating structure of protection results in high effective rates of protection (ERPs),[4] for domestic production, which biases incentives against exports. As part of the Diagnostic Trade Integration Study, the Dhaka-based Policy

Table 2.1 Imported Consumer Goods Are Heavily Taxed Compared with Local Production, FY2013/14

percent

Type of goods	Domestic stage		Protection			
	E-SD	E-VAT	CD+RD	P-SD	P-VAT	P-Total
Basic raw materials	0.55	9.17	9.58	2.69	1.55	**13.82**
Intermediate goods	0.09	15.34	12.36	2.48	0.45	**15.29**
Capital goods	0.04	9.95	6.08	3.13	0.36	**9.56**
Final consumer goods	4.08	14.00	23.36	20.82	4.35	**48.53**
Total	1.71	13.21	15.21	10.01	2.07	**27.29**

Source: Calculations based on National Board of Revenue data.
Note: CD = customs duty; E-SD = exports supplementary duty; E-VAT = exports value-added tax; P = protection; P-SD = protection supplementary duty; P-VAT = protection value-added tax; RD = regulatory duty.

Strengthening Competitiveness in Bangladesh—Thematic Assessment
http://dx.doi.org/10.1596/978-1-4648-0898-2

Figure 2.4 Average Tariff on Import Categories, FY2000–FY2013

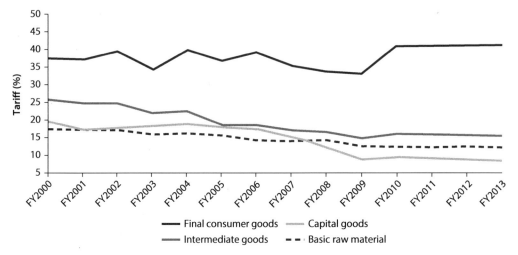

Source: Calculations based on National Board of Revenue data.

Table 2.2 Tariffs and Para-Tariffs in Bangladesh, Share of CIF Value, by Sector, FY2010/11
percent

Sector		CD	SD	VAT	AIT	ATV	Other (PSI, AIT, RD)	Total rate
01–05	Animal and animal products	7.1	1.9	14.6	4.6	0.7	2.8	33.7
06–15	Vegetable products	1.4	1.0	4.4	0.4	0.0	0.1	7.5
16–24	Foodstuffs	2.7	1.8	2.5	0.6	0.6	0.4	8.8
25–27	Mineral products	9.9	0.2	15.2	1.7	2.5	0.2	29.7
28–38	Chemicals and allied industries	3.1	0.6	5.6	2.0	0.6	0.4	12.4
39–40	Plastics and rubbers	8.2	1.3	14.6	3.5	1.5	0.9	30.1
41–43	Raw hides, skins, leather, and furs	18.7	17.6	16.8	4.8	4.0	3.1	66.1
44–49	Wood and wood products	8.8	1.4	8.3	3.1	0.8	1.1	24.2
50–59	Textiles	0.8	0.5	0.9	0.2	0.2	0.9	2.8
60–63	Garments	24.3	20.4	22.0	4.7	5.1	3.0	82.2
64–67	Footwear and headgear	24.9	27.7	23.6	5.0	5.2	3.6	92.3
68–71	Stone and glass	19.2	26.4	21.1	4.5	4.4	2.8	79.7
72–83	Metals	8.0	0.4	10.5	2.8	1.0	0.7	23.5
84–85	Machinery and electrical	5.1	1.2	2.7	0.6	1.0	0.4	11.0
86–89	Transportation	11.0	12.5	10.4	2.1	2.3	0.9	40.1
90–97	Miscellaneous	7.3	2.8	6.5	2.0	2.1	1.0	21.7

Source: Calculations based on National Board of Revenue data.
Note: Data exclude companies operating under the bonded warehouse system. AIT = advance income tax; ATV = advance trade VAT (a tax levied nominally at 3 percent of the VAT inclusive price of commercially imported goods); CD = customs duty; CIF = cost, insurance, and freight; PSI = preshipment inspection; RD = regulatory duty; SD = supplementary duty; VAT = value-added tax.

Research Institute (2012) undertook a survey of 118 manufacturing firms located in and around the cities of Dhaka and Chittagong during May–July 2012.[5] The objective was to quantify the size of the distortions for firms producing selected consumer goods with potentially high ERPs (see annex 2A for methodological issues). The analysis confirmed especially high ERPs in sectors like

Figure 2.5 Decomposition of Bangladesh's Border Taxation at the Sector Level, FY2010/11

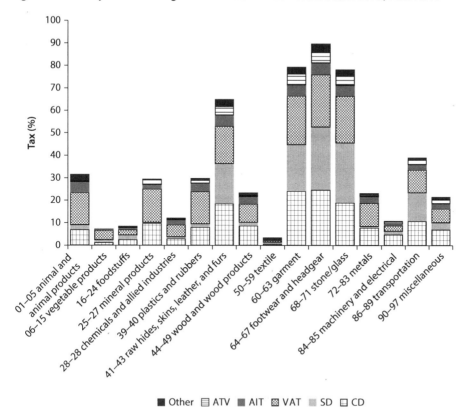

■ Other ▤ ATV ■ AIT ▨ VAT ▧ SD ▢ CD

Source: Calculations based on National Board of Revenue data.
Note: AIT = advance income tax; ATV = advance trade VAT (a tax levied nominally at 3 percent of the VAT inclusive price of commercially imported goods); CD = customs duty; PSI = preshipment inspection; RD = regulatory duty; SD = supplementary duty; VAT = value-added tax.

footwear (214–342 percent), some agri-food products (381 percent for chira/ muri), bicycles (117–386 percent), and ceramics (190–239 percent). Pharmaceuticals fall in a unique category, with ERPs only modestly positive (but this is not the full picture, since competing imports are not allowed; see Kathuria and Malouche 2016, chapter 6). Tariffs on locally produced generic equivalents of brand-name drugs are zero or 5 percent, but a highly restrictive drugs policy prohibits imports of all drugs produced domestically. Thus, local production now meets 95 percent of domestic demand, according to a World Bank study (World Bank 2008). ERPs on drugs could actually be higher than the actual tariff, but are restrained by some price controls imposed by the Drug Administration (Drug Control Act of 1982).

By contrast, output destined for exports receives no protection, and export ERPs are typically zero when imported inputs are duty exempt via mechanisms such as duty drawback. Or they are exempt from duty and other import taxes altogether through special bonded warehouse (SBW) arrangements. Often, cash

Figure 2.6 Intra-Sector Concentration of Tariffs and Para-Tariffs in Bangladesh, FY2010/11

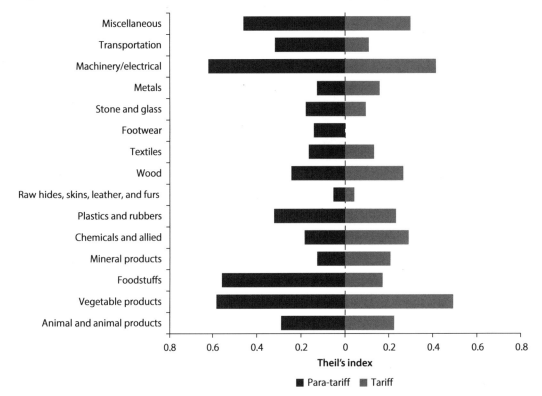

Source: Calculations based on National Board of Revenue data.
Note: The length of the bars measures the concentration of tax rates measured by Theil's concentration index. A long bar means that, within a given sector, a small number of subsectors shoulder a disproportionate share of the tax burden; a short bar means that the tax burden is spread relatively evenly within the sector.

subsidies compensate for duty drawback or SBW (box 2.2). An exporting firm may receive cash assistance (of 10–15 percent of free on board [FOB] export value) if it uses neither duty drawback nor the SBW facility. Thus, typically, ERPs for exports are expected to approach zero, be modestly positive (if receiving cash incentives), or negative if the reimbursement of duty drawback does not fully compensate for the tariff-inclusive costs of procuring imported inputs or domestic inputs that enjoy protective tariffs. Likewise, if the SBW system is effective in providing duty-free imported inputs to producers without any transaction costs, ERPs for such exports should approach zero.

With domestic market production protected at high rates, incentives to export are stifled. The bicycle industry, whose initial export drive quickly lost momentum given the asymmetry of incentives, is a case in point. Similarly, in ceramics, exports have virtually stagnated despite the industry's intrinsic strengths in terms of know-how. Given the prevailing tariffs, potential profitability in the domestic market far exceeds that in export markets, although export products are differentiated from what is sold in the domestic market. In the case of footwear,

---

Box 2.2 Three Facilities for Exporters in Bangladesh

Duty drawback system. The duty drawback facility refunds duties paid on imported inputs to exporters. It enables exporters and deemed exporters to claim, within six months of exports, the duties and taxes paid on imported inputs used in the export process. Eligible exporters can claim their drawback by filing their claim with the Duty Exemption and Drawback Office, which is an agency under the authority of the National Board of Revenue (NBR). Duties may be refunded in three ways: (a) actual drawback, (b) national drawback, and (c) flat-rate drawback. Because of the fewer complications and ease of operation, the flat-rate system remains the most preferred method of refund.

   Special bonded warehouse (SBW). Bonded warehouse facilities are licensed by NBR for the deposit and storage of imported goods, mostly intermediate inputs. SBW use is usually extended to import-dependent export industries. Industries outside export processing zones can enjoy such facilities upon assessment and approval of NBR. Under the SBW facility, companies can import required raw materials and process them for re-export without import duty and with minimum customs formalities. Ready-made goods and leather industries have been the main beneficiaries of this facility, but, in recent years, other exporters, such as leather products, light engineering (bicycles), and pharmaceuticals, have been selectively given this facility. As a policy, SBW has been excluded for new exporters or smaller exporters, or for firms whose exports are not a significant proportion of total production.

   Cash subsidy. Cash incentives, a method of offsetting input tariffs, are provided to import-dependent export industries that do not use either the duty drawback or the SBW scheme, but procure their inputs locally (imported or locally produced). Cash incentives, ranging from 10 to 15 percent, are granted on the free-on-board value of selected exports. One concern is that this facility could be abused as there is a lot of incentive to over-invoice exports.

---

anti-export incentives have been somewhat compensated by a ban on exports of raw leather, which depresses its domestic price and provides an indirect subsidy to footwear exports but also to domestic sales. Notwithstanding the fact that such indirect subsidies are actionable under the countervailing duty regulations of the WTO, they contribute to a maze of regulatory distortions, the net effect of which is unlikely to foster economic efficiency.

   Distortions also arise from variations in export facilities across sectors, including SBW and cash incentives. SBWs have been mostly provided to RMG and footwear, although they are supposedly open to all exporting sectors. The facility has been selectively offered to other sectors after much red tape, as the authorities believe it is prone to abuse if given generously; hence, SBW has not become very popular. Based on the ERP firm survey, 31 of 89 exporting firms used SBW, of which 14 were RMG accessory suppliers (deemed exporters), 11 footwear exporters, 1 leather products exporter, 2 jute textile exporters, 2 bicycle exporters, and 1 pharmaceuticals exporter. The cash incentive scheme, originally intended to offset input tariffs, has benefited jute textile exporters significantly,

Strengthening Competitiveness in Bangladesh—Thematic Assessment
http://dx.doi.org/10.1596/978-1-4648-0898-2

although their imports (less than 5 percent of output) are subject to low raw material duties. Until the end of FY2011/12, 19 export sectors were eligible to receive cash incentives (table 2.3). In FY2012/13, however, the number of export-oriented sectors eligible for incentives was reduced to 15. The sectors removed from the stimulus package were bicycles, poultry, finished leather, and crust leather. One of the primary reasons for removing bicycle exports was that the sector already enjoys duty-free access to its main market in the European Union.[6] Light engineering products other than bicycles, however, would continue to be eligible for cash incentives.

The RMG sector in particular has greatly benefited from a number of incentives that were not available to other sectors, resulting in a tilted playing field (box 2.3). The success of garments has raised questions as to why no other labor-intensive sector has emerged in Bangladesh. Has government support to garments translated into fewer incentives to other potentially competitive sectors, such as jute and leather-based products? Beyond the availability of cheap labor, four other factors have been responsible for the success in garments: (a) technology transfer through foreign direct investment (FDI); (b) the bonded warehouse system and back-to-back letters of credit, both initially extended exclusively to garment exporters; (c) a high ERP with low tariffs on inputs and high tariffs on final products; and (d) reduced tariffs in the European Union and the Multi-Fiber Arrangement, which imposed quotas on garment exports from Bangladesh's competitors. The current government program has extended the incentive schemes to new sectors, such as shipbuilding and leather footwear.

Against this policy backdrop, the incentives to engage in exports other than garments and one or two other sectors do not appear to be high. High and rising

Table 2.3 Export Promotion Cash Incentives in Bangladesh, FY2011/12–FY2013/14
percent of assessed FOB export value

Category	FY2011/12	FY2012/13	FY2013/14
Total budget, cash incentives stimulus for exporters		US$290 million	
Number of sectors receiving incentives	19	15	14
Agricultural and agro processed goods	20	20	20
Home textiles	5	5	5
All textiles (incl. home textiles) exploring new markets (excl. Canada, US and EU)	2	2	2
Jute goods	10	10	7.5
Shrimp and other fishery products	10	10	10
Ships	5	5	5
Light engineering products	10	10	10
Leather products	12.5	15	15
Finished leather	4	0	0
Crust leather	3	0	0
Poultry	15	0	0
Bicycles	15	0	0

Source: Compiled by Global Development Solutions, LLC.
Note: FOB = free on board.

Box 2.3   Bangladesh's Success Story: The Ready-Made Garments Sector

Bangladesh's ready-made garments (RMG) sector took off in the late 1970s through a transfer of technology and know-how from the Republic of Korea. In 1978, Korea's Daewoo, at that time an apparel producer, started collaborating with Desh, a Bangladeshi company, to upgrade its technology and management capabilities for joint apparel production in Bangladesh. Daewoo's plan was to relocate production to Bangladesh to escape the Multi-Fiber Arrangement's quotas, which at the time did not cover Bangladesh. By the 1980s, export growth had picked up substantially, reaching triple-digit growth in the U.S. market. In 1985, the United States slapped a quota on Bangladesh like on other Asian countries, although the quota was less constraining relative to Bangladesh's supply capabilities than it was for other Asian countries. The U.S. quota induced export redirection to the European Union, where Bangladesh benefited from reduced tariffs under the Generalized System of Preferences. From the 1990s onward, the European Union became Bangladesh's premier apparel market. It has stayed that way until now.

The RMG sector's growth was encouraged by the Government of Bangladesh through two primary incentive schemes:

- The bonded-warehouse system, under which 100 percent export-oriented firms in the RMG sector could import tariff-free instead of waiting for duty drawbacks, which to this day have been managed by an ineffective bureaucracy
- Back-to-back letters of credit, which allow RMG exporters to use export orders as collateral to obtain credit for intermediate imports.

Benefiting from wages that were, and still are, among the world's lowest, flexible labor arrangements, and very light taxation (essentially an export tax levied on the free-on-board price at a rate of 1 percent, with no corporate, profit, or payroll tax), apparel exports grew from less than 1 percent of Bangladesh's exports to more than 80 percent today. The number of apparel factories grew from 134 in 1984 to 4,825 in 2009, while employment soared from 40,000 to 3.1 million over the same period.

Knitwear (T-shirts, sweaters, tank tops, and the like) have traditionally been Bangladesh's dominant export to the EU market where, until 2010, rules of origin required a double transformation from yarn to fabric and from fabric to garment, meaning that fabric had to be sourced locally. The investment required for minimum efficient scale production of knitted fabric was only about US$3.5 million, whereas for woven products (say, trousers), it could be 10 times more. As a result, Bangladesh developed an integrated value chain in knitwear, producing 80 percent of garment exporters' needs. No such integrated value chain was developed in woven wear, which limited Bangladesh's access to the EU market for woven products until the recent reform of rules of origin.

Being targeted at the low end of the market, Bangladesh's garments sector has proved resilient in the face of the ongoing global economic crisis and, in fact, benefited from a "Wal-Mart effect" (the substitution of low-end products for more expensive ones by cash-strapped consumers). However, in the long run, raising productivity and wages will require Bangladesh to go upmarket and improve quality and positioning.

Source: World Bank.

tariffs on consumer goods and in several other areas mean that domestic market sales could be very profitable. In addition, the wide dispersion in input and output tariffs means that there are several sectors with very high rates of ERPs for domestic sales, as opposed to ERPs for exports, which are close to zero. And there are variations in export incentives across sectors, with much of the de facto support going to garments and footwear. Finally, the lack of an effective duty drawback or bonded warehouse system for most exporting sectors stifles the incentives for firms to search for new export possibilities.

Tariffs Influenced Heavily by Revenue Considerations

The good news is that Bangladesh's fiscal revenues have been increasing over the past decade, with a gradual shift from reliance on trade taxes to domestic taxes. The government's tax revenues have been rising, reaching about Tk 952 billion or 10.4 percent of gross domestic product (GDP) in FY2011/12, up from around Tk 200 billion or 9 percent a decade ago. That this has been accompanied by a decline in the share of import-based taxes is a positive development in the trade story. While import-based revenues continue to represent the largest source of tax revenue in Bangladesh, their share has declined from about 4 percent of GDP and 40 percent of revenues, to 3.5 and 29 percent, respectively (figure 2.7). At the same time, the shares of income tax and domestic VAT have risen to 23 and 18 percent of revenues, respectively. In terms of import-based revenue, NBR customs import transactions data for FY2010/11 show that one-third comes from customs and RDs, another third from VAT on imports, and the last third from para-tariffs, essentially SDs (figure 2.8). Finally, as expected, intermediate and consumer goods enjoy the highest levels of protection.

Nevertheless, Bangladesh's trade policy is heavily influenced by considerations of revenue and assistance to local industries rather than trade competitiveness. Import policy is legally set in the Import Policy Order issued by the Ministry of Commerce in consultation with customs. However, NBR, which does not have export promotion as its policy goal, seems to have the final authority on tariff setting (see also chapter 4 on institutional capacity). The FY2012/13 budget offers a case in point. Although CDs on intermediate goods and basic raw materials were reduced in a few cases (43 tariff lines), SDs were raised for a larger number of tariff lines (413) (Sattar 2012). According to local experts, these changes tend to be ad hoc in nature, implemented without any background research about how much and for how long protection is justified. And there is no obvious rationale for the variable rates of protection given to different products.

Border tax exemptions are widespread and translate into significant revenue losses. The import tax structure is marked by a large number of exemptions of all kinds, including some that benefit single companies or are under nontransparent "special order" labels. An analysis of customs transaction data at the tariff line level shows that exemptions figure in almost 30 percent of the total number of transactions and 44 percent of total trade value. These exemptions add up to significant revenue shortfalls—13 percent of collected revenue in

Figure 2.7 Decline of Import-Based Tax Revenue in Bangladesh, FY1990/91 to FY2011/12

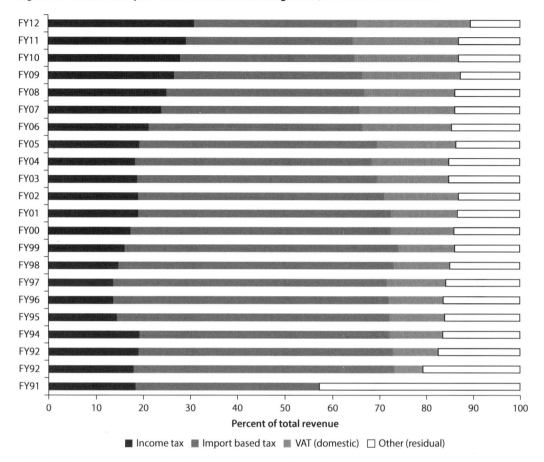

Source: Calculations based on data from the National Board of Revenue and Ministry of Finance.
Note: VAT = value-added tax.

FY2010/11—especially in the foodstuffs sector where less than 50 percent of the nominal taxes are actually collected, as shown in table 2.4. These exemptions do not seem to be associated with heavily concentrated market structures. The highest shortfalls are in foodstuffs and chemical products, where imports are relatively unconcentrated, whereas the most concentrated importer structure is mineral products, which has very low shortfalls. The machinery sector has relatively low shortfall rates and concentration, but because of its size, it accounts for almost 25 percent of the total shortfall; the transportation and mineral sectors each account for another 17–18 percent of the shortfall.

Preferential agreements do not account for much of the shortfalls. Bangladesh is a member of the South Asian Free Trade Area (SAFTA) and Asia-Pacific Trade Agreement (APTA) (also called Bangkok agreement), and as such, grants preferential treatments to other member countries. Although the SAFTA agreement covers more than 4,000 tariff lines (of a total of 5,369 tariff lines), the analysis of

Figure 2.8 Composition of Import-Based Fiscal Revenues in Bangladesh, FY2010/11

percent

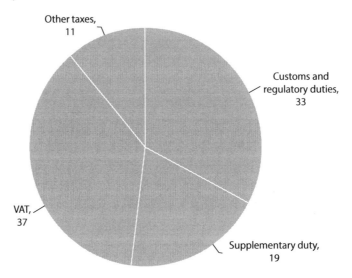

Source: Calculations based on National Board of Revenue customs data.
Note: Customs, regulatory, and supplementary duties comprise more than 50 percent of import-based fiscal revenues. VAT = value-added tax.

Table 2.4 Revenue Shortfall in Bangladesh because of Various Exemptions, FY2010/11

Sector	Actual revenue (Tk)	Revenue shortfall (Tk)[a]	Sector share in total shortfall (%)	Shortfall as share of AR (%)	Sector Herfindahl index
Animal and animal products	1,100,000,000	28,600,000	1.2	2.6	13.94
Chemicals and allied	6,630,000,000	4,440,000,000	7.1	67.0	10.78
Foodstuffs	2,000,000,000	3,010,000,000	2.1	150.5	7.29
Footwear	549,000,000	787,594	0.6	0.1	36.53
Garments	840,000,000	5,287,579	0.9	0.6	3.34
Machinery and electrical	22,700,000,000	2,480,000,000	24.3	10.9	19.24
Metals	11,000,000,000	623,000,000	11.8	5.7	3.29
Mineral products	16,500,000,000	900,000,000	17.6	5.5	110.86
Plastics and rubbers	5,500,000,000	18,400,000	5.9	0.3	0.61
Raw hides, skins, leather, and furs	129,000,000	386,266	0.1	0.3	121.84
Stone and glass	1,670,000,000	4,703,036	1.8	0.3	0.52
Textiles	1,730,000,000	5,415,670	1.8	0.3	0.52
Transportation	15,800,000,000	275,000,000	16.9	1.7	9.03
Vegetable products	4,210,000,000	206,000,000	4.5	4.9	12.42
Wood	3,190,000,000	179,000,000	3.4	5.6	1.06
Miscellaneous	1,860,000,000	42,000,000	2.0	2.3	5.23
Total	93,548,000,000	12,176,580,145	n.a.	n.a.	n.a.

Source: Calculations based on NBR data for FY2010/11.
Note: AR = actual revenue; n.a. = not applicable.
a. Revenue shortfalls are additional revenues collected in the absence of exemptions.

customs transactions data indicates that preferential treatment is virtually never claimed by importers (or granted by the customs). In the case of imports originating from India, only 156 of 185,257 transactions were recorded under SAFTA preferential treatment and 2 under the APTA agreement. For Sri Lanka, only two transactions benefited from the preferential treatment. In FY2010/11, all other potential beneficiaries (SAFTA and APTA members) had their exports entering Bangladesh under the most-favored-nation treatment. Apparently, the "Country of Origin" certificate is time-consuming and complex to obtain, and the tariff concession is very small (only 10 percent of customs duty in most cases).

In general, revenue goals are achievable with more trade-neutral border taxation. Given the magnitude of exemptions, a thorough assessment of their legitimacy would help in their rationalization and generate revenues. A goal of much greater trade neutrality in border taxation would be consistent with the NBR Modernization Plan (box 2.4).

A less distortionary tax structure could achieve the same or an even higher level of revenues. Removing exemptions would increase fiscal revenues significantly.[7] Results of a simulation that used the World Bank's Tariff Reform Impact Simulation Tool indicate that removing tariff exemptions would increase revenues by about 7–9 percent (while reducing imports by around 1 percent) and help compensate for the reduction or removal of other taxes while inducing more economic efficiency. Another simulation capping tariff peaks at 15 percent (international peak) would induce a loss in tariff revenue of 3–7 percent. Tariff revenues would actually decline by about 20–23 percent, but the induced increase in imports (between 1.7 and 3.2 percent) would increase the contribution of other taxes.[8] A third simulation that removes SDs and adopts a uniform rate of 15 percent for CD+RD would increase tax revenues by 0.9 percent, which illustrates the efficiency and revenue potential of simple and uniform taxation. These simulations do not reflect changes in the production structure and consequent changes in VAT revenues on domestic production.

Economists and policy makers might not agree on the optimal level for tariffs, but establishing a uniform tariff presents several advantages, including the following: (a) effective protection is the same for all sectors and equals the NPR; (b) it is simple, clear, and transparent and therefore reduces business costs; (c) it reduces the cost of customs administration; and (d) it reduces discretion (corruption). Moreover, the manner in which countries reduce tariffs has important implications for export incentives. Tariff-reduction schemes that exempt high tariffs or sensitive sectors could create more distortions. A strategy to reduce all tariffs—in which high tariffs are cut more than low ones—would do the most to improve export incentives and real income (Tokarick 2006).

Nontariff Measures

Overall, nontariff measures (NTMs) are moderately widespread in Bangladesh compared with other countries. Although the analysis of NTMs has long been constrained by lack of data, the World Bank, in collaboration with the Policy

Box 2.4 National Board of Revenue Modernization Plan, 2012–16

The National Board of Revenue (NBR) is responsible for end-to-end oversight and supervision of direct and indirect taxes. These include income taxes, value-added taxes, and customs. The tax base in Bangladesh is narrow with fewer than one million income tax filers.[a] Nonreporting and underreporting of taxes affect all three taxes. The present tax information gap between what the taxpayers know and what the three tax departments know about their taxpayers is wide. In effect, the taxes that get paid are what the taxpayer chooses to pay and not what he or she is obliged to pay under the law. Tax performance in Bangladesh has been registering a steady, incremental, annual improvement, with an average 20 percent growth from FY2007/08 to FY2010/11. However the gap between tax policy expectations and tax performance will widen in the future as the government expects the three taxes to more than double revenue outturns over the next five years.

As a result, NBR has recently undertaken an aggressive and comprehensive organizational renewal program that seeks to put in place an efficient, effective, fair, and responsive tax regime that is benchmarked against international best practice. The envisaged reform covers all three taxes and seeks to modernize tax policy (tax laws and statutory rules) as well as tax administration (business process, organizational design, human resource policies, taxpayer services, and so forth). One of the main goals of the reform is significant growth in revenue performance through widening and deepening of the existing tax base across the three taxes. With regard to customs tariffs restructuring and rationalization, modernization of the Customs Act will aim to rationalize tariffs to promote investments, prevent misdeclarations, and reduce distortions. NBR has also embraced information and communications technology as a key driver in its comprehensive tax administration reform effort, adopting "Digital NBR," a subset of the national program "Digital Bangladesh."

Source: National Board of Revenue.
a. NBR staff informally estimates the tax collection gap at close to 5 percent of gross domestic product.

Research Institute, has recently collected data on NTMs in Bangladesh as part of a global multi-agency effort to improve transparency in NTMs. Two indices were used to analyze the data, the frequency ratio and the coverage ratio.[9] In comparison with other countries for which NTM data are available, the analysis shows that NTMs in Bangladesh cover about 50 percent of imported products defined at the Harmonized System 6-digit level (HS-6) and around 45 percent of imports.

There is wide variation in the prevalence of NTMs across countries, as illustrated in figure 2.9. In the group of selected comparators for which NTM data are available, China, India, Pakistan, and Sri Lanka have the highest values of frequency and coverage ratios (more than 80 percent), while Indonesia, Madagascar, and South Africa have values below 50 percent for both indicators. Bangladesh shows intermediate levels of coverage and frequency ratios. However, the correlation between the frequency and coverage ratios is not perfect: some NTMs may cover few product lines but affect large import volume, while other NTMs may

Figure 2.9 Nontariff Measures Coverage in Bangladesh and Comparators, 2012

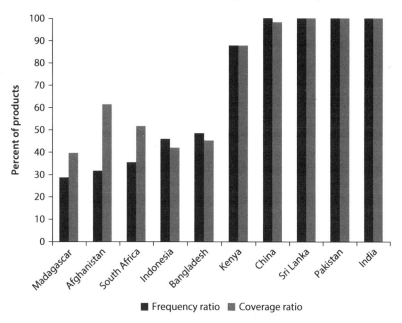

Source: Calculations based on World Integrated Trade Solution database.

cover a large number of product lines and either do not have a significant impact on the volume of trade or are more trade restrictive. Moreover, these indicators do not indicate whether NTMs are targeted to protect domestic industries or whether NTMs in Bangladesh are less trade restrictive than in other countries.

Two factors may explain a relatively higher coverage ratio. The first is import composition, especially in low-income countries that often import larger volumes of products where NTMs are more extensively used (agriculture). Second, a high coverage ratio may reflect larger use of NTM policies on most traded products (for example, for consumer protection), as is often the case in high-income countries. Overall, the trade restrictiveness of most NTMs can only be assessed case by case, depending on their justification but also their implementation procedures.

Preshipment inspection (PSI) and para-tariffs are the two largest NTM components in Bangladesh, while sanitary and phytosanitary standards (SPS) and technical barriers to trade (TBT) are increasingly the most common NTMs across countries (figure 2.10).

Multiple NTMs on the same product increase complexity and the administrative burden. One-third of Bangladeshi imports are not affected by any NTMs, half are affected by one or two NTMs, and about one-tenth of the product lines (at HS-6) are affected by three or more types of NTMs (figure 2.11). For example, a product could be subject to a sanitary standard (NTM category A) as well as a technical measure on quality (NTM category B) and finally to some licensing (NTM category E). Arguably, the greater the number of NTMs applied to the

Figure 2.10 Nontariff Measures in Bangladesh, by Category of Nontariff Measures, 2012

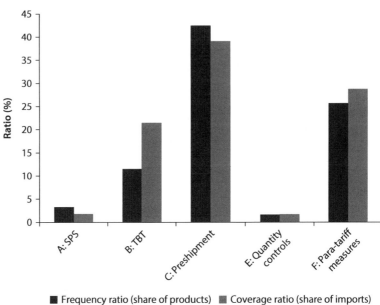

■ Frequency ratio (share of products)   ■ Coverage ratio (share of imports)

Source: Calculations based on Policy Research Institute data.
Note: SPS = sanitary and phytosanitary; TBT = technical barriers to trade.

Figure 2.11 Types of Nontariff Measures by Product, Bangladesh and Comparators, 2012

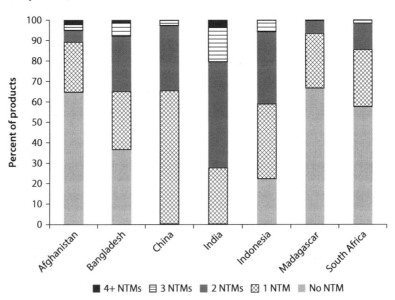

■ 4+ NTMs ▤ 3 NTMs ■ 2 NTMs ▨ 1 NTM   No NTM

Source: Calculations based on Policy Research Institute and World Integrated Trade Solution data.
Note: NTM = nontariff measures.

same product, the more regulated the commerce of that product is, especially if measures are from different chapters and ministries.[10] This suggests a source of potential inefficient domestic bureaucracy, particularly as multiple authorities are involved with the inspection and approval process. Indeed, international experience indicates that problems with NTMs often arise from lack of intragovernment coordination and burdensome bureaucratic procedures.

PSI is relatively widespread in Bangladesh, affecting all sectors, about half the product lines, and two-thirds of imports (table 2.5). These levels are high compared with the average levels found in a sample of 24 low- and middle-income countries, the European Union, and Japan, where the PSI frequency index and the coverage ratio are both about 11 percent. The relatively high incidence of PSI in low-income countries reflects the desire to fight corruption, facilitate and accelerate customs procedures, and ultimately help in the correct evaluation and taxation of imports. Although PSI is often necessary to provide some assurance on the quality and quantity of the shipment and thus may promote international trade, it adds to the cost of trading. It is also usually implemented as a temporary measure while governments improve the technical capacity of customs. However, the Bangladeshi government announced the end of PSI as of June 2013 (see chapter 6 for a broader discussion on PSI).

The relative incidence of technical measures (SPS and TBT) is currently limited in Bangladesh but likely to rise in the future. As tariffs have come down and

Table 2.5 Nontariff Measures Coverage in Bangladesh by Sector, 2012

percent

Sector	A: SPS	B: TBT	C: Preshipment	E: Quantity controls	F: Para-tariff measures
01–05 Animal	55.7	1.3	51.0	5.4	63.1
06–15 Vegetable	4.5	5.7	23.9	2.7	17.8
16–24 Foodstuffs	18.4	12.4	31.4	18.9	31.9
25–26 Minerals	..	7.4	18.5	..	11.1
27 Oil Minerals	..	41.2	41.2	..	8.8
28–38 Chemicals	1.7	35.1	36.1	0.6	4.8
39–40 Plastic/rubber	..	6.3	40.3	..	30.6
41–43 Hides/skins	..	..	31.1	1.6	23.0
44–49 Wood	0.5	1.4	38.8	2.8	22.0
50–63 Textiles, clothing	0.6	17.7	68.1	0.1	53.9
64–67 Footwear	..	..	58.3	..	58.3
68–71 Stone/glass	1.7	1.7	55.7	1.7	46.0
72–83 Metals	..	1.9	47.3	0.9	20.4
84–85 Machinery/electrical	..	3.3	33.8	0.1	10.6
86–89 Transportation	..	18.3	24.2	2.5	20.0
90–97 Miscellaneous	0.6	4.8	36.2	..	26.0
98–99 Special	..	..	..	..	..

Source: Calculations and Policy Research Institute data.

Note: Values are the percentage of product lines covered by a given nontariff measures (NTM) (category A, B, C, E, F). SPS = sanitary and phytosanitary standards; TBT = technical barriers to trade; .. = nil.

Strengthening Competitiveness in Bangladesh—Thematic Assessment
http://dx.doi.org/10.1596/978-1-4648-0898-2

the use of quantitative restrictions is more monitored, SPS and TBT have become the commonest forms of NTMs in all regions. The sector coverage of SPS and TBT measures generally reflects the technical properties of products rather than economic policy choices. Governments are increasingly called upon to respond to a variety of concerns raised by members of society in many areas, including the environment, animal welfare, and food safety, and are urged to develop technical regulations. The incidence of technical regulations rises with the level of development. In Bangladesh, most food-related products are affected by at least one form of SPS, while TBTs are applied to a much wider set of products and more uniformly across economic sectors. Their numbers peak in chemicals, vehicles, and processed food (table 2.5).

Technical regulations and standards should not unnecessarily restrict trade and hurt firms' trade competitiveness. Unlike prohibitions and quotas that are easily identifiable as nontariff barriers, technical regulations may be adopted to achieve legitimate non-trade-related domestic policy objectives. Technical regulations and product standards can increase the costs of compliance in two ways. One, they can impose additional fixed costs on exporters, who have to adapt products to the specific standards and regulations applied by the importing country. Two, conformity assessment procedures, such as testing to demonstrate compliance with these technical measures, may induce additional costs (Cadot et al. 2012). The WTO's SPS and TBT agreements contain guidance on what is regarded as international best practice in regulating quality issues, notably with respect to minimizing the trade restrictiveness of a country's quality system. The SPS and TBT agreements establish disciplines for the implementation of technical regulations and encourage and set rules for the use of trade facilitation instruments, like harmonization, equivalency, and mutual recognition. As discussed in chapter 5 on trade and standards, technical regulations should be used exclusively to regulate a narrow set of legitimate objectives.

Trade Policy and Welfare

High import tariffs may affect trade competitiveness and production structures, but they also affect consumers' welfare through prices. In Bangladesh, the average burden of border taxation on household consumption is high, but largely progressive. Analysis of data from household expenditure surveys shows that tariffs add 7.5 percent to the cost of living of the median Bangladeshi household. Adding up all border taxes can increase living costs by up to 15 percent for the median household. Moreover, the border taxes seem to tax middle-income households heavily while sparing the richest. Indeed, replacing the current array of tariff and para-tariff measures by a flat, combined border tax at a uniform 10 percent would raise real incomes by 11.3 percent on average—enough to lift 11.2 million people, or 7.4 percent of Bangladesh's population, above the poverty line.[11] The numbers indicate the large prevalence of imports in household expenditure baskets, as well as the high tariffs on many consumer goods (figure 2.12).

Figure 2.12 Consumption-Weighted Tariff and Border Taxes as a Function of Household Income in Bangladesh, by Centile

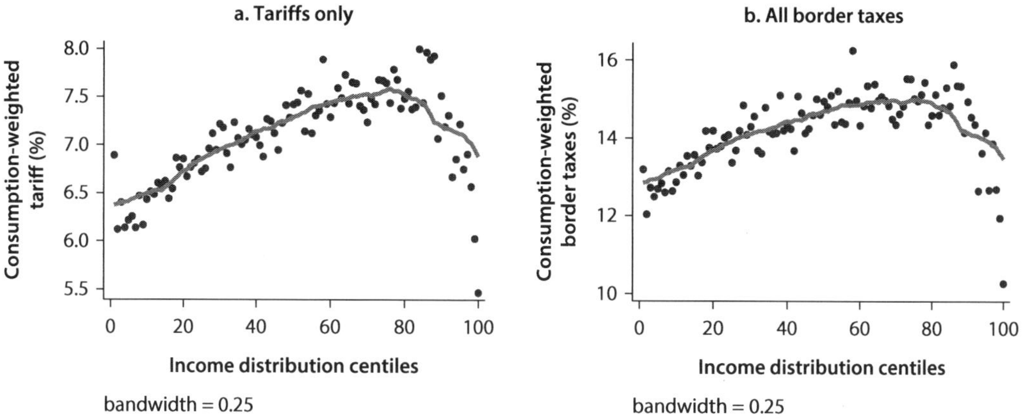

Source: Calculations based on Bangladeshi tariff data and Bangladesh's household survey.
Note: Income is approximated with total consumption. For readability, the data are aggregated by centile of the distribution of income. Thus, the point to the extreme left of the diagram is the consumption-weighted tariff affecting the lowest centile of Bangladesh's income distribution. For example, given the expenditure pattern of households in that centile, they face, on average, a tariff of 6.2 percent.

In addition to tariffs and NTMs, high prices on the domestic market seem to be attributable as much to a lack of competition and "natural" barriers to entry. For instance, interviews with the private sector suggest that in Bangladesh the market for edible oils is characterized by high prices, as imports are controlled by about eight large importers who have refining facilities. Controlling the high prices through parallel imports is difficult, because most edible oil sold in the countryside in Bangladesh is in "open" form (customers come with their own bottle to the store), which allows distributors to bypass packaging costs. Given the market's price sensitivity, the elimination of packaging costs makes a significant difference to the product's attractiveness. The government has traditionally attempted to alleviate the high prices during the Ramadan period by purchasing edible oil through the Trading Corporation of Bangladesh.[12] However the Trading Corporation of Bangladesh suffers from governance problems and is not an efficient buyer, thus limiting its ability to stabilize edible oil prices as well as sugar prices, for which the market-structure issues are similar. Competition and open trade are better price stabilizers than complex state interventions and, in addition to an easier import regime, effective operationalization of the Competition Law passed in 2012 would help to curb potential anticompetitive practices.[13]

Services Trade Policy Restrictiveness

Services trade restrictiveness is usually associated with low-quality, high-cost services, while openness has a positive impact on overall competitiveness, in particular on multifactor productivity growth.[14] According to Arnold (2010), policy reforms in the services sectors played a major role in the transformation of the manufacturing sector in India, allowing greater foreign and domestic competition with improved regulation (however, despite this, the Indian services regime remains very restrictive; see figure 2.13). Available evidence suggests that the aggregate effect of services liberalization in India was an increase in productivity of 11.7 percent for domestic firms and 13.2 percent for foreign firms for a one-standard-deviation increase in the liberalization index. An illustrative set of results from the Services Trade Restrictiveness Index (STRI) database analysis suggests that services trade policies matter for investment flows and access to services. In particular, restrictions on foreign acquisitions, discrimination in licensing, restrictions on the repatriation of earnings, and lack of legal recourse all have a significant and sizable negative effect, reducing the expected value of sector foreign investment by US$2.2 billion over a seven-year period, compared with "open" policy regimes.

Most countries exhibit fairly open services trade policies. The median STRI, which can range from 0 to 100, is about 24; that is, more than half the 103 countries in the database would on average be classified as virtually open. However, some of the fastest-growing countries in Asia and the oil-rich Gulf states have among the most restrictive policies in services trade, whereas some of the lower income countries, like Cambodia, Ghana, Mongolia, and Senegal, are remarkably open. While most Organisation for Economic Co-operation and Development (OECD) countries are generally quite open overall, they tend to exhibit greater restrictiveness in transportation services and the movement of natural persons as services suppliers. In fact, professional and transportation services are among the most protected in all countries, while retail, telecommunications, and even finance tend to be more open (Borchert, Gootiiz, and Mattoo 2012).

Figure 2.13 South Asia Services Trade Restrictiveness Index, 2010

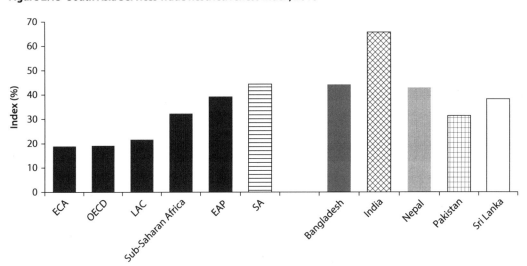

Source: Borchert, Gootiiz, and Mattoo 2012.
Note: EAP = East Asia and Pacific; ECA = Europe and Central Asia; LAC = Latin America and the Caribbean; OECD = Organisation for Economic Co-operation and Development; SA = South Asia.

In Bangladesh, services trade is more restricted than the world average, in particular in telecommunications and transportation services (figure 2.14 and figures 2A.1–2A.5). Bangladesh has the second most restrictive services trade policies in the South Asia region, with an average STRI of 44, well above the world average of 28.[15] Bangladesh's services policy restrictiveness is most acute in telecommunications and transport services, with an STRI above 60. In telecommunications, fixed-line telecommunications is completely closed in Bangladesh, as it is in only eight other countries (Belarus, Ethiopia, the Islamic Republic of Iran, Kuwait, Mozambique, Oman, Qatar, and Zambia). In mobile telecommunications, Internet group calls and voice over Internet protocol are not allowed, repatriation of earnings is subject to approval by Bangladesh Bank, and 80 percent of employees must be nationals (one foreigner for every five nationals is the governing ratio). In transportation, maritime auxiliary services and rail freight domestic services are completely closed; for domestic and international air passengers and domestic road freight services, the only requirements are that earnings repatriation needs approval by Bangladesh Bank and 80 percent of employees must be nationals.

Retail and professional services are the most open in Bangladesh, but certain regulatory inconsistencies among modes of supply also prevail for professional services. In retail services, licenses must be renewed annually upon payment of a renewal fee, repatriation of earnings is also subject to approval by Bangladesh Bank, and 80 percent of employees must be nationals. Bangladesh also maintains low levels of restrictiveness for cross-border provision of professional services, but has relatively high levels of restriction on the temporary movement of

Figure 2.14 Bangladesh Services Trade Restrictiveness by Sector

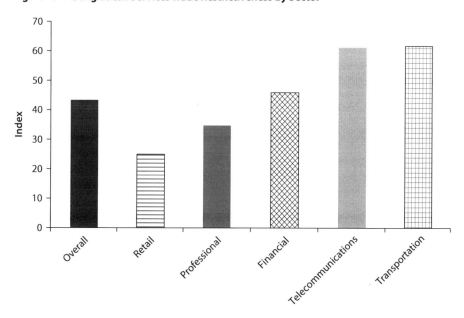

Source: Services Trade Restrictiveness Index.

Strengthening Competitiveness in Bangladesh—Thematic Assessment
http://dx.doi.org/10.1596/978-1-4648-0898-2

professionals. Therefore, if modes of supply were perfect substitutes, this would mean that although the provision of services through the latter mode is relatively restrictive, trade would take place anyway, through the cross-border provision of the service. Generally speaking, the highest barriers to trade in all countries are typically observed in professional services. One reason is that for these services, the international movement of professionals (mode 4) is critical. And such movement faces two daunting barriers: immigration-related restrictions, which make entry difficult for foreigners intending to sell services, and licensing and qualification-related restrictions, which make it difficult for foreign-trained professionals to practice their professions (Borchert, Gootiiz, and Mattoo 2012).

Lack of liberalization in some sectors is seriously constraining the quality and capacity of some services, such as air freight services. The monopoly of Civil Aviation is a major constraint. Bangladesh Biman provides ground handling services through a separate subsidiary that also operates the air cargo terminal. It rents space within the airport to United Parcel Service and other courier services. The three scanners owned and operated by Civil Aviation are only about seven years old but appear to be designed for standard ocean pallets. Since they are not large enough for airfreight pallets, all shipments must be broken down prior to scanning. Civil Aviation denied the request of Biman to introduce its own scanners. Civil Aviation has tentatively agreed to provide new storage facilities for the cargo, but would still require the use of Biman for ground handling and Civil Aviation for scanning.

Moreover, Bangladesh has not adopted an open-skies policy that allows airlines to operate freely in the country without licensing restrictions. The Association of Travel Agents of Bangladesh and the main exporters are pressing for an open-skies policy, which would reduce costs and provide more airfreight capacity for the garments sector. More generally, liberalization leads to increased air service levels and lower fares, which in turn stimulates additional traffic volumes and can bring about increased economic growth and employment. In the South Asia region, Sri Lanka has concluded a number of open-skies agreements since 2005, including with Malaysia, Singapore, Switzerland, Thailand, and the United States. Open skies has been rolling out in stages in the Association of Southeast Asian Nations since 2009, helping to make Southeast Asia home to the world's fastest-expanding low-cost airlines. The open-skies policy essentially lifts restrictions on adding flights. Between Malaysia and Thailand, for example, each country's airlines now can make as many flights as they like to the other country, assuming there is room at the airport.

Countries with open financial and telecommunications sectors have grown about 1 percentage point faster than other countries (Mattoo, Rathindran, and Subramanian 2006). The theoretical literature linking services liberalization to productivity increases in the broader economy is well developed (Francois 1990a, 1990b; Markusen 1989, 1990; Markusen, Rutherford, and Tarr 2005). A growing empirical literature that uses firm-level data and cross-country regressions also supports this relationship (Tarr 2012). The key idea is that providers of services increase the productivity of users of services in manufacturing (particularly high-tech industries and firms that use services inputs more intensively), agriculture, and the services sectors themselves. An analysis of about 4,000 firms in India finds that services reforms in the telecommunications, insurance, and transport sectors significantly increased the productivity of manufacturing firms (Arnold et al. 2012). Fernandes and Paunov (2012) find that linkages from FDI in services to downstream manufacturing industries account for almost 5 percent of the observed increase in Chilean manufacturing productivity growth.

As Bangladesh confronts the challenge of boosting productivity and exports, services policy reform should become a priority in the reform agenda. Many countries have taken action to increase competition in services markets by liberalizing FDI, opening access to foreign competition in backbone sectors such as transport and telecommunications, and privatizing state-owned or state-controlled service providers (Hoekman and Mattoo 2011). Liberalization of key services would help Bangladesh increase its share in the growing business process outsourcing and information technology (IT)–enabled services sectors. It would also help improve the productivity of key manufacturing sectors. Liberalization can lead to enhanced competition from domestic and foreign suppliers in sectors where barriers to entry are maintained—not only against foreign suppliers, but also against new domestic suppliers, such as in telecommunications.

Productivity gains from services liberalization are more pronounced for domestic and small firms. Recent empirical studies analyzing the impact of services liberalization in Eastern Europe and Central Asia indicate that small and medium enterprises are the principal beneficiaries (Tarr 2012). This is consistent with theory, as large firms can often hire service sector specialists, such as lawyers, accountants, truck drivers, and couriers, as employees. Small and medium size firms find full-time employees too costly and have to rely to a greater extent on the market for services. These results emphasize for policy makers the importance of services sector liberalization for the development of small and medium size domestic firms.

Areas of reforms include adopting a policy that encourages air freight services. Despite the importance of air courier services for the garments industry, in particular for shipping samples, Bangladesh, unlike its competitors, does not have a policy to encourage this service. Specifically, customs does not have de minimus (minimum weight below which there is no duty charged) to allow small packages to clear the airport quickly. The clearing process for packages and airfreight is the same, so that clearance times are one to two days for samples and three to five days for fabric, instead of a few hours for both as in most of the countries in the region.

Significant benefits would accrue to Bangladesh if it positioned itself as a destination for information technology enabled services–business process outsourcing (ITES-BPO). By encouraging this sector, Bangladesh can provide direct and indirect employment to the increasing number of young people entering the job market.[16] Destination ITES-BPO countries have also seen an increase in the rate of female participation in the labor force. Moreover, this sector requires low capital investment and skill levels compared with the IT sector. Finally, in addition to bringing in foreign exchange and helping build people's IT skills, the sector also helps reduce spatial inequalities as more of these activities are being located in tier 2 and 3 cities, as tier 1 cities become more expensive. The sector would benefit from government support and collaboration in a few critical areas, including more reliable Internet services, a focused and sustained promotion campaign (country and sector branding), and high-profile networking events aimed at proactively addressing the main concerns of industry players in target markets. Demonstrable and long-run commitment by the government is essential to boost investor confidence. Addressing the main hurdles to doing business in Bangladesh would also support sector growth by establishing standard legal provisions such as intellectual property rights, confidentiality, data security, and so forth. (For details, see Kathuria and Malouche 2016, chapter 7, on ITES-BPO, and World Bank 2012.)

Some reforms could also be carried out at the regional level. The regulatory heterogeneity in South Asia increases the difficulties of services integration in the region. A cross-country comparison indicates that each country maintains different regulatory measures that affect trade in services. In the case of air transport services for passengers, Bangladesh does not maintain any foreign ownership restriction; Pakistan and Sri Lanka maintain a 49 percent limit to foreign ownership, as does India, which opened its market in 2012. In India, foreign ownership limitations in telecommunications depend on the modality of entry for fixed-line and mobile telecommunications, and in Nepal, there is an 80 percent limit on foreign ownership in both services. Pakistan and Sri Lanka maintain no foreign ownership limitations. In this context, Kox and Lejour (2005) find that variations in the transparency of regulations across countries affect bilateral service exports negatively. Yet, although the policies may differ among countries, the range of restrictions applied is limited, which facilitates reaching agreements on a common regime for the region. Chapter 3 discusses areas for regional policy reforms.

Conclusions

In the pursuit of multiple objectives, Bangladesh has over the years created a complex trade regime, including tariffs and nontariff measures. As in many other countries, the consumer or exporter has not been the focus of government's policy intentions. However, much can be done to make trade policy more efficient as part of "first-generation" reforms, to be followed by more intensive reforms. Bangladesh can learn from the experience of "successful globalizers" such as Singapore; Taiwan, China; or the Republic of Korea, all of which followed consistent, long-term strategies centered on export competitiveness. In this context, balancing the interests of producers, consumers, and exporters would be useful. Extending this logic, reducing cross-sector distortions in the export incentive structure would help in Bangladesh's continued quest for export diversification.

A more harmonized and simpler import tax regime would reduce distortions and ensure a level playing field among and within sectors and firms, which would favor the development of new export sectors and small and medium enterprises.

This reform is possible without hurting the overall objective of revenue growth. There are several ways Bangladesh could deal with para-tariffs, all of which aim to phase in a more trade-neutral tariff structure: (a) eliminate para-tariffs and put everything in the import tariff to boost transparency; (b) lower para-tariff rates; and (c) ensure that para-tariffs apply to domestic production and imports, which would help reduce their distortionary impact.

Successful implementation of NBR's reform agenda will be critical to help the government shift trade policy from a focus on revenue generation to a long-term national competitiveness strategy. The objectives of the reform are (a) to continue to reduce the budget's dependence on the border tax; (b) to close tax loopholes and make the fiscal playing field less uneven across sectors and types of actors; (c) to review existing fiscal incentives and tax holidays with the objective of adopting more coherent, transparent, predictable, and time-bound (incorporating sunset clauses) policies; (d) to extend access to bonded warehouse facilities to reputable companies that use World Customs Organization Authorized Economic Operators guidelines and criteria; and (e) to generate the resources needed for the massive infrastructure investment effort that awaits national authorities if growth is to continue at the same pace.

Greater openness in some services would help boost the productivity of the manufacturing sector and expand trade in services. A priority action would require the formulation and adoption of a strategy for services trade and the establishment of a database on trade in services. Priority sectors could include air freight services and certain elements of the telecom sector.

Annex 2A: Survey Data and Computations for ERP Analysis

An industry survey of about 118 enterprises was conducted during May–July 2012, led by the Policy Research Institute of Bangladesh. However, the production, sales, and tariff data are for FY2010/11, so the analysis refers to the trade policy regime prevalent in FY2010/11. Anticipating some unusable data, the goal of the exercise was to compute effective rate of protection (ERP) estimates for at least 100 firms and this expectation was fulfilled.

Two sets of questionnaires were distributed to the surveyed firms: (a) a set of qualitative questions to elicit how enterprise management perceived and coped with the existing policy regime and how that impacted profitability and incentives for production, investment, and exports and (b) a set of quantitative questionnaires that sought data on output, employment, sales, inputs, and costs, including taxes paid or benefits received.

The objective of the exercise was to ensure that reliable data were retrieved from some 100 enterprises covering the 10 selected subsectors listed in Box 2A.1.[17] A key part of the study was to compare relative incentives between exports and domestic sales. Therefore, the survey ensured that the majority of the firms selected were engaged in domestic as well as export production.

Product ERPs were computed with NPR and tax data from the FY2010/11 Operative Tariff Schedules (OTS, available at HS-8 digit codes) and the collected

Box 2A.1 List of Subsectors for the Enterprise Survey

- Agro-based industries
- Ceramics products
- Footwear and leather products
- Plastics
- Pharmaceuticals
- Electronics and electrical products
- Bicycles
- Light engineering
- Jute textiles
- Garments and packaging

firm-level survey data. In addition, use was made of the Automated System for Customs Data (ASYCUDA) database. Disaggregated import and export transactions for FY2010/11 provided cost, insurance, and freight (CIF) and free on board (FOB) values for imported and exported commodities. In particular, the survey data included, among others, (a) the domestic price, total value, and volume of tradable outputs produced by the firm; (b) the domestic price, total value, and volume of purchased tradable inputs used in the production of outputs; and (c) the total ex ante protection, tariffs, para-tariffs (supplementary duty, SD, and regulatory duty, RD), and trade-neutral levies, such as value-added tax (VAT), on all tradable inputs and outputs. In computing ERP, to the extent that VAT and SD were trade neutral, these two taxes had to be netted out prior to computing value added at domestic and world prices. Finally, a caveat is that nontraded inputs, such as transport services, repair services, gas, electricity, water and other utilities, and so forth, are excluded to keep the survey within manageable limits. However, the main indirect tradable inputs, such as fuel oil, repair materials, and so forth used for producing the nontraded inputs, have NPRs largely around 12 percent or lower and import-substituting outputs mostly have NPRs of 50 percent or higher. As such, the current ERP estimates may, if anything, have a slight downward bias.

Methodological Issues

The ERP measures the relative difference in value added at domestic prices (protective effect on output net of protective effect on inputs) over value added measured in world prices. The formula can be simply expressed as in equation (2A.1):

$$ERP = (VADP/VAWP) - 1 \qquad\qquad (2A.1)$$

where VADP represents value added at domestic prices $[QP_q{}^*(1+NPR_q) - \sum A_i P_i{}^*(1+NPR_i)]$, and VAWP represents value added at world prices $[QP_q{}^* - \sum A_i P_i{}^*]$.

Thus, the domestic prices of output and inputs may be related by the equations:

$Pq = Pq^*(1+\text{NPR}q)$, which yields $Pq^* = Pq/(1+\text{NPR}q)$

and $Pi = Pi^* (1+\text{NPR}i)$, which yields $Pi^* = Pi/(1+\text{NPR}i)$.

It is conventional to use the results produced by the formula in equation 2A.1 and express them in percentages.

Deriving Value Added at World Prices

An industry survey typically yields data in terms of what is observable—that is, domestic prices. So the firm and product-level survey data at first yield value added at domestic prices. The challenge lies in computing VAWP, which requires data on world prices of inputs and outputs.

In the absence of observed world prices, the traditional approach (found in other studies on ERP) is to derive world prices through tariff deflation, that is, by deflating observable domestic prices of outputs (Pq) or inputs (Pi) by the nominal rates of protection (NPR). Thus VAWP (sales revenue at world prices minus input costs at world prices) could be derived through this deflation method. PRI's annual databases, titled OTS, were used as the source for NPR data. It is relevant to note that the survey responses produced data on multiple products with quantum of inputs (Ai) used in each output separately (in most cases), so that input-output coefficients were available from the data.[18] Thus, for the purpose of the present computation and analysis of firm-level product ERP, the required background data are available from OTS combined with survey data.

The second approach is to use observed world prices from import and export data. Given that the Bangladesh customs administration has adopted the ASYCUDA system for nearly two decades, the ASYCUDA database yields information on CIF or FOB prices of imports and exports, that is, world prices of traded commodities. For the present study, the ASYCUDA database was the main source of information for obtaining the world prices of the products under study. However, there is an additional challenge of picking a representative price from many import or export transactions of the same commodity with a range of prices. The approach followed here was that of picking the CIF price from the database that was the closest approximation to the tariff-deflated notional world price (used in most ERP studies).[19] The results based on this approach should be interpreted with caution.

Thus, the two approaches represent an analytical framework for effective protection analysis, whose data demands are within the scope of this study.

Addressing Tariff Redundancy

Computation of ERPs based on the estimated protective effect of nominal tariffs on outputs and inputs should take into consideration the real possibility of the existence of tariff redundancy, that is, a situation where the observed price of an import substitute product is below the price calculated by escalating the world price by the nominal rate of protection. Provided there are reliable data on CIF prices, it is possible to gauge the magnitude of tariff redundancy by comparing observed domestic and world prices. This has been done for a sample of

34 products from the survey (annex 2B), revealing that tariff redundancy is indeed widely prevalent and much higher for those products subject to very high tariffs, such as ceramic tableware, agro-based products, such as biscuits, modified rice products (chira, muri), plastic products (chairs, hangers), and so on. Pharmaceutical drugs and electronic products, such as solar home lights, which have the minimum tariffs on outputs and inputs, show no tariff redundancy.

In the context of Bangladesh, tariff redundancy can occur for several reasons:

- If the domestic product is an imperfect substitute of the comparable import, in terms of quality or any other aspect, the domestic price may be lower than the price of the comparable import that fully reflects the protective tariff.
- Under-invoicing, to evade import taxes, is widespread, particularly in cases where the tariff is high, because the incentive for evasion is higher with higher tariffs; this is reflected in a lower domestic price.
- Smuggling across the Bangladesh-India border is rampant and an option for evading import taxes.
- In the case of jute textiles (such as yarn, hessian, and sacking), the protective tariff is notional as Bangladesh is a major exporter of jute goods and little or no import takes place.
- Tariffs on locally produced, generic equivalents of brand-name drugs are zero or 5 percent, but a highly restrictive drug policy prohibits imports of all drugs produced domestically. This policy has yielded good results in that domestic production now meets practically all domestic demand for these drugs 95 percent of local demand according to World Bank (2008). The effective protective tariff in this case could be much higher than the actual tariff, although restrained by some control on prices imposed by the Drug Administration.

The implication of the existence of tariff redundancy is that when the world price of a product is derived through tariff deflation, the derived world price will be less than the actual price (since the tariff is higher than is consistent with domestic prices). Since output tariffs in Bangladesh are significantly higher than average input tariffs, derived VAWP (which uses the world price) will be lower (sometimes even negative), and estimated ERPs higher (negative if VAWP turns negative) than actual. So it is important to keep the issue of tariff redundancy in mind when computing ERPs with tariff deflation and interpreting the results. To cite some examples, the 200 percent protective tariff on biscuits is redundant by at least 100 percent (as no importer actually pays the 200 percent tariff). The 49.5 percent tariff on jute textiles is also redundant, by and large. An assumption of 0–15 percent protective tariff yields plausible ERP results for jute yarn, hessian, and jute sacks—traditional exports of Bangladesh for decades.

Protection Level in Exports
Although the preceding approach is appropriate for computing ERP for domestic sales, measuring incentives in export production arising from the tariff regime requires a slightly different approach, for the following reasons. First, there is zero

protection on the output destined for exports, where prices are actually fixed in the international markets. Second, imported inputs used in the production of exports are eligible for duty drawback, or are exempt from duty and other import taxes altogether through special bonded warehouse arrangements. Third, an exporting firm may receive cash assistance (of 10–20 percent of export volume) if it uses neither a duty drawback nor the special bonded warehouse facility.

Under the assumption of 100 percent duty drawback, ERPs are, by definition, zero, because inputs become tariff free, while outputs simultaneously receive zero protection in the international market. However, it is a known fact—also confirmed by various studies—that there are transaction costs (informal payments and delays in receipts) associated with reimbursement of duty drawback, resulting in, at best, receipt of 75 percent of the actual duties incurred on imported inputs. In the circumstances, ERPs are typically negative, since output prices are determined internationally and therefore receive no protection. Some exports are eligible for a cash subsidy of 10 percent on export volume paid in lieu of duty drawback, which might compensate for duties paid on imported inputs.

Thus, typically, ERP for exports is expected to approach zero, be modestly positive arising from cash incentives, or negative if the reimbursement of duty drawback does not fully compensate for the tariff-inclusive costs of procuring imported inputs or domestic inputs propped up by protective tariffs.

Figure 2A.1 Financial Services Restrictiveness

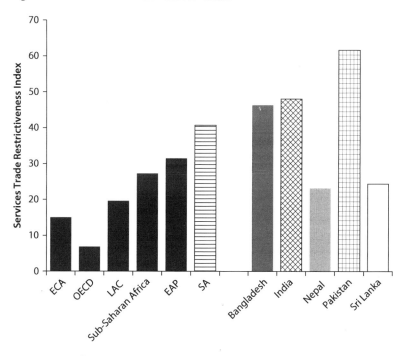

Source: Services Trade Restrictiveness Index.
Note: EAP = East Asia and Pacific; ECA = Europe and Central Asia; LAC = Latin America and the Caribbean; OECD = Organisation for Economic Co-operation and Development; SA = South Asia.

Figure 2A.2 Telecommunications Services Restrictiveness

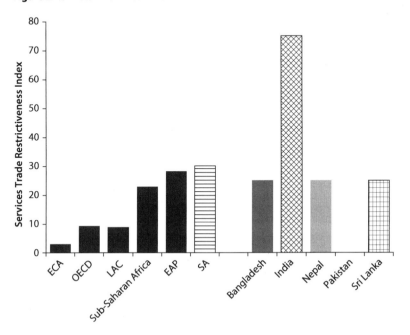

Source: Services Trade Restrictiveness Index.
Note: EAP = East Asia and Pacific; ECA = Europe and Central Asia; LAC = Latin America and the Caribbean;
OECD = Organisation for Economic Co-operation and Development; SA = South Asia.

Figure 2A.3 Retail Services Restrictiveness

Source: Services Trade Restrictiveness Index.
Note: EAP = East Asia and Pacific; ECA = Europe and Central Asia; LAC = Latin America and the Caribbean;
OECD = Organisation for Economic Co-operation and Development; SA = South Asia.

Figure 2A.4 Transport Services Restrictiveness

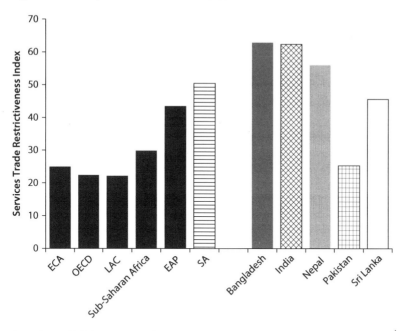

Source: Services Trade Restrictiveness Index.
Note: EAP = East Asia and Pacific; ECA = Europe and Central Asia; LAC = Latin America and the Caribbean;
OECD = Organisation for Economic Co-operation and Development; SA = South Asia.

Figure 2A.5 Professional Services Restrictiveness

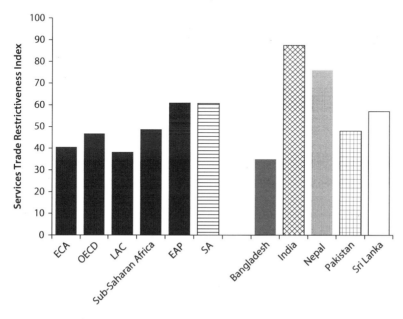

Source: Services Trade Restrictiveness Index.
Note: EAP = East Asia and Pacific; ECA = Europe and Central Asia; LAC = Latin America and the Caribbean;
OECD = Organisation for Economic Co-operation and Development; SA = South Asia.

Annex 2B: Analysis of Tariff Redundancy

Table 2B.1 Analysis of Tariff Redundancy

Enter-prise ID	Subsector	Product	Protective tariff (%)	CIF price	Survey price	Price ratio (survey/ CIF)	Tariff redun-dancy (%)
004	Agro-based industries	Chanachur	56.00	79.01	110.43	39.77	16.23
004	Agro-based industries	Mustard oil	30.00	170.14	189.57	11.42	18.58
65	Agro-based industries	Muri	56.00	43.34	47.83	10.35	45.65
065	Agro-based industries	Chira	108.00	35.50	38.26	7.78	100.22
094	Agro-based industries	Biscuit	199.00	71.01	123.00	73.22	125.78
090	Agro-based industries	Frooto mango	41.82	297.00	328.06	10.46	31.36
117	Bicycles	Mountain bicycles	56.00	3,197.00	4,521.70	41.44	14.56
119	Bicycles	Standard bikes 28"	56.00	2,984.00	4,347.80	45.70	10.30
120	Bicycles	Motor bikes 26"	56.00	2,98.00	3,913.00	31.13	24.87
086	Bicycles	Sun share (bicycles)	56.00	2,368.07	3,043.40	28.52	27.48
005	Ceramics	Dinner plates	88.50	42.65	56.52	32.52	55.98
057	Ceramics	Ceramic tableware	88.50	28.98	46.96	62.03	26.47
021	Embroidery	Three-piece embroidery	30.00	320.21	320.21	0	30.00
021	Embroidery	Child garments embroidery	30.00	1.76	2.17	23.52	6.48
033	Electronics/electrical products	Solar home lights	30.00	258.28	334.78	29.62	0.38
033	Electronics/electrical products	Solar charge controllers	3.00	507.67	507.16	−0.10046	3.10
040	Footwear	Gents leather shoes	88.50	1,210.00	1,956.50	61.70	26.80
017	Garments	Shirt	56.00	355.02	531.06	49.58	6.42
017	Garments	Panjabi	56.00	585.08	885.38	51.33	4.67
016	Jute textiles	Jute goods	49.50	81,880	101,839.40	24.38	25.12
012	Jute textiles	Yarn	49.50	79,540	92,000.00	15.67	33.83
050	Jute textiles	Hessian	49.50	87,998	101,000.00	14.78	34.72
050	Jute textiles	Sacking	49.50	63,004.20	72,000.00	14.28	35.22
111	Light engineering	Carbon rods	56.00	0.44	0.51	16.60	39.40
020	Plastics products	Plastic chairs	56.00	397.34	410.00	3.19	52.81
020	Plastics products	Plastic tables	56.00	942.95	1,260.87	33.72	22.28
020	Plastics products	Plastic wardrobes	56.00	1,026.50	1,217.39	18.60	37.40
037	Plastics products	100 ml bottles	108.00	0.60	0.88	46.67	61.33
037	Plastics products	Ponds jars	60.00	1.08	1.42	31.08	28.92
011	Pharmaceuticals	PPI-20	5.00	3.29	3.52	6.99	−1.99
011	Pharmaceuticals	Tenoloc-50	5.00	0.72	0.74	4.03	0.97
011	Pharmaceuticals	Ecosprin	5.00	0.42	0.47	11.11	−6.11
105	Pharmaceuticals	Acitrin	13.04	34.26	40.87	19.29	−6.25
105	Pharmaceuticals	Tenorin	5.00	40.45	46.00	13.72	−8.72

Sources: PRI 2012; ASYCUDA database for CIF prices. CIF = cost, insurance, and freight.

Notes

1. The import-weighted average is 10.3 percent.

2. The TTRI is the uniform tariff rate that would entail the *same deadweight losses* as the current array of border taxes at different rates. The OTRI is the uniform tariff rate that would entail the *same level of imports* (all products together) as the current array of border taxes at different rates. TTRI and OTRI formulas are as follows:

$$\text{TTRI} = \sqrt{\frac{\sum_k \varepsilon_k M_k t_k^2}{\sum_k \varepsilon_k M_k}} \quad \text{OTRI} = \frac{\sum_k \varepsilon_k M_k t_k}{\sum_k \varepsilon_k M_k} \quad \text{TTRI} = \sqrt{\frac{\sum_k \varepsilon_k M_k t_k^2}{\sum_k \varepsilon_k M_k}} \quad \text{OTRI} = \frac{\sum_k \varepsilon_k M_k t_k}{\sum_k \varepsilon_k M_k}$$

where k is imported products, ε is the price elasticity of import demand, M is the value of imports in dollars, and t is the compound rate of all border taxes.

3. Border taxation is different from protection, since VAT is levied on domestic and import transactions. The data illustrate the size of the tax relative to the transaction rather than the degree of discrimination between imports and domestic production.

4. The ERP is the proportional increase in local firms' value added (or processing margin) resulting from the combined influence of tariff rates on the final good and on intermediate inputs (a pure price effect—a higher ERP does not mean that the protected good has intrinsically higher value added). An escalating tariff structure (higher rates on final goods than on intermediates) raises local value added and protection levels compared with what would prevail under a zero or uniform tariff structure.

5. With financial support from the World Bank and in partnership with the local survey firm Data International.

6. See Kathuria and Malouche 2016, chapter 2, on bicycles for a broader discussion on the sector.

7. The analysis is based on import transaction data provided by the customs administration of Bangladesh for FY2010/11. The original database includes more than 1.2 million import transactions representing about 93–95 percent of total trade (some land customs stations are not yet connected to the customs computerized system), of which about 300,000 transactions were officially exempted imports (for example, government and diplomatic imports, re-exports) and were removed from the database (these imports are not affected by tariff reforms and would lower tariff averages artificially). Imports with specific duties (no ad valorem equivalent available) and transactions with obvious recording errors, representing close to 4,000 records, were also removed from the database. The cleanup process left 967,548 transactions for a total import value of Tk 2,135,556,832,278 (US$30,507,954,747).

8. For technical reasons, taxes had to be combined because of the large number of duties and taxes in Bangladesh. The simulation removes exemptions for CD+RD and not for other duties and taxes. The 15 percent cap is for the combination of CD and RD (considered as one single duty).

9. The frequency ratio captures the percentage of products that are subject to one or more NTMs. The coverage ratio captures the percentage of imports that are subject to one or more NTMs. In more formal terms, the frequency index of NTMs imposed by country j is calculated as:

$$F_j = \left[\frac{\sum D_i M_i}{\sum M_i} \right] * 100$$

where D_i is a dummy variable reflecting the presence of one or more NTMs and M_i indicates whether there are imports of good i (also a dummy variable).

A measure of the importance of NTMs in terms of overall imports is given by the coverage ratio. This measures the percentage of imports to country j subject to at least one NTM. In formal terms, the coverage ratio is given by:

$$C_j = \left[\frac{\sum D_i V_i}{\sum V_i} \right] * 100$$

where D_i is defined as before and V_i is the value of imports in product i.

10. The rationale is that measures in the same NTM category are similar in nature and thus often impose a relatively lower burden than measures from different NTM categories.

11. This number is a rough approximation, and should be taken as indicative. It is obtained by replacing the current total of tariff and para-tariff charges by a flat 10 percent combined border tax in each household's basket and calculating the reduction in expenditure needed to buy the same basket given the new tax rates. This reduction (an increase in real income) is then extrapolated to the population with data on household size and sampling weights. The last step consists of calculating the poverty headcount (the number of individuals below the national poverty line) before and after the simulation.

12. The Trading Corporation of Bangladesh was established in 1972—right after independence—to ensure the availability of essential commodities on the domestic market through public purchases. See http://www.tcb.gov.bd.

13. See Helal and Taslim (2010) for a detailed analysis of the edible oils market in Bangladesh.

14. Inklaar, Timmer, and van Ark (2007, 2008); Triplett and Bosworth (2004); van der Marel (2012).

15. The World Bank Services Trade Restrictions Database contains information on policies that affect international trade in services—defined to include the supply of a service through cross-border delivery, establishment of a commercial presence, or the presence of a natural person. The database collects—and makes publicly available—comparable applied services trade policy information across a large range of countries, sectors, and modes of delivery. To date, surveys for 79 low- and middle-income countries have been collected and comparable information has been obtained for 24 OECD countries. The five major services sectors covered in the database, namely financial services (banking and insurance), telecommunications, retail distribution, transportation, and professional services, are further disaggregated into subsectors. The choice of sectors was based primarily on the World Bank's assessment of their economic importance from a development perspective, the existence of meaningful restrictions on services trade, and the feasibility of collecting relevant policy data.

16. According to some estimates, every job created in the ITES-BPO sector creates three to four jobs in supporting sectors.

17. Of the 11 subsectors selected for the survey, no response was received from enterprises identified in the chemicals and batteries subsector.

18. In those few instances where inputs were not specified for multiple outputs, the method of assigning inputs on the basis of output share was applied.

19. Ideally, taking an average of the range of prices would have been the best option. However, for 165 output products and at least 500 inputs covered by the survey, this exercise would have taken time and resources that were not available to this study.

References

Arnold, J. 2010. "Bangladesh Logistics and Trade Facilitation." World Bank, Washington, DC.

Arnold, J. M., B. Javorcik, M. Lipscomb, and A. Mattoo. 2012. "Services Reform and Manufacturing Performance: Evidence from India." Policy Research Working Paper 5948, World Bank, Washington, DC.

Borchert, Ingo, Batshur Gootiiz, and Aaditya Mattoo. 2012. "Landlocked or Policy Locked? How Services Trade Protection Deepens Economic Isolation." Policy Research Working Paper 5942, World Bank, Washington, DC.

Cadot, O., A. Fernandes, J. Gourdon, and A. Mattoo. 2012. "Does Export Promotion Work? New Evidence from Tunisia." Unpublished paper, World Bank, Washington, DC.

Fernandes, Ana M., and Caroline Paunov. 2012. "Foreign Direct Investment in Services and Manufacturing Productivity: Evidence for Chile." *Journal of Development Economics* 97 (2): 305–21.

Francois, Joseph F. 1990a. "Trade in Producer Services and Returns Due to Specialization under Monopolistic Competition." *Canadian Journal of Economics* 23: 109–24.

———. 1990b. "Producer Services, Scale, and the Division of Labor." *Oxford Economic Papers* 42: 715–29.

Helal, U., and M. Taslim. 2010. "An Assessment of Competition in the Edible Oil Market of Bangladesh." Bureau of Economic Research, University of Dhaka.

Hoekman, B., and A. Mattoo. 2011. "Services Trade Liberalization and Regulatory Reform: Re-Invigorating International Cooperation." Policy Research Working Paper 5517, World Bank, Washington, DC.

Inklaar, Robert, Marcel P. Timmer, and Bart van Ark. 2007. "Mind the Gap! International Comparisons of Productivity in Services and Goods Production." *German Economic Review* (Verein für Socialpolitik) 8: 281–307.

———. 2008. "Market Services Productivity across Europe and the U.S." *Economic Policy* 53: 139–94.

Kathuria, Sanjay, and Mariem Mezghenni Malouche, eds. 2016. *Attracting Investment in Bangladesh—Sectoral Analyses: A Diagnostic Trade Integration Study*. Directions in Development. Washington, DC: World Bank.

Kox, Henk, and Arjan Lejour. 2005. "Liberalisation of the European Services Market and Its Impact on Switzerland." CPB Memorandum 130, CPB Netherlands Bureau for Economic Policy Analysis, The Hague, Netherlands.

Markusen, James R. 1989. "Trade in Producer Services and in Other Specialized Intermediate Inputs." *American Economic Review* 79: 85–95.

———. 1990. "Derationalizing Tariffs with Specialized Intermediate Inputs and Differentiated Final Goods." *Journal of International Economics* 28: 375–84.

Markusen, James R., Thomas Rutherford, and David Tarr. 2005. "Trade and Direct Investment in Producer Services and the Domestic Market for Expertise." *Canadian Journal of Economics* 38 (3): 758–77.

Mattoo, A., R. Rathindran, and A. Subramanian. 2006. "Measuring Services Trade Liberalization and Its Impact on Economic Growth: An Illustration." *Journal of Economic Integration* 21 (1): 64–98.

PRI (Policy Research Institute). 2012. "Bangladesh Assessment of Effective Rate of Protection: 2012 Survey of Selected Manufacturing Enterprises." Policy Research Institute, Dhaka.

Sattar, Z. 2012. "Is Trade Policy Losing Direction?" Policy Research Institute of Bangladesh, Dhaka.

Services Trade Restrictiveness Index (database). Organisation for Economic Co-operation and Development. http://www.oecd.org/tad/services-trade/services-trade-restrictiveness-index.htm.

Tarr, David. 2012. "Impact of Services Liberalization on Industry Productivity, Exports and Development: Six Empirical Studies in the Transition Countries." Policy Research Working Paper 6023, World Bank, Washington, DC.

Tokarick, S. 2006. "Does Import Protection Discourage Exports?" IMF Working Paper wp/06/20, International Monetary Fund, Washington, DC.

Triplett, Jack E., and Barry P. Bosworth. 2004. *Productivity in the U.S. Services Sector: New Sources of Economic Growth*. Washington, DC: Brookings Institution.

van der Marel, E. 2012. "Trade in Services and TFP: The Role of Regulation." *World Economy* 35 (11): 1530–58.

World Bank. 2008. "Public and Private Sector Approaches to Improving Pharmaceutical Quality in Bangladesh." Bangladesh Development Series Paper 23, World Bank, Washington, DC.

———. 2012. "Consolidating and Accelerating Exports in Bangladesh." Bangladesh Development Series Paper 29, World Bank, Washington, DC.

WTO (World Trade Organization). 2012. *Trade Policy Review*. Geneva: World Trade Organization.

CHAPTER 3

Market Access: From Preferences to Global Integration

Nihal Pitigala, Mariem Mezghenni Malouche, and Sanjay Kathuria

Introduction

Bangladesh's export growth has largely been driven by preferential schemes extended by the European Union and to a lesser extent by similar agreements with the United States and other high-income economies. It also benefitted from large preferential margins compared with China because of a number of anti-dumping duties and market restrictions, mostly imposed by the European Union against Chinese exports. Bangladesh is eligible for duty-free and quota-free market access for least-developed countries (LDCs) agreed to in the World Trade Organization Ministerial Conference held in Hong Kong SAR, China, in 2005, and for duty-free and quota-free access offered by India in November 2011 to all South Asian LDCs, including Bangladesh.

However, changes in the global economy will require Bangladesh to find a more sustainable path for export growth. Growth in high-income countries has been slow to recover from the dual financial and debt crisis that began in 2007, including in Bangladesh's key trading partners, the United States and the European Union. Emerging economies, led by China and India, have recovered much faster, driven by buoyant domestic demand and international trade. However, Bangladesh's share of these traditional markets will likely be challenged by countries such as Vietnam and Cambodia, which receive equal or better trade access to the United States. Any reduction in most-favored-nation (MFN) duties by the European Union and the United States under future World Trade Organization negotiations will likely reduce Bangladesh's preferences and undermine its future competitiveness in high-income country markets.

Bangladesh could better exploit regional production-sharing potential to take advantage of fundamental changes in the global economy, including global value chains and demographic shifts. Many goods and services are no longer designed,

---

This analysis was completed in 2011. While the general issues remain valid, some of the specific details, such as the revocation of US GSP privileges in June 2013, are not covered in the chapter.

produced, and sold within a single country. Rather, these functions are spread across multiple countries in regional and global supply chains. Factors that have spurred the development of these chains include falling trade costs, technological change, and institutional development in areas such as property rights. As countries have become more integrated into these chains, they have become more specialized in specific tasks based on comparative advantage. Moreover, the global financial crisis has led to large demographic shifts in East Asia and the Pacific (Ng and Yeats 2003), especially in China. This will likely create new alignments within existing global production and trade networks. For example, China is rapidly losing the advantage of low labor costs because of slow population growth and rising wage pressures. Capturing just 1 percent of China's manufacturing export markets would almost double Bangladesh's manufactured exports.

Global developments have given Bangladesh an opportunity to improve regional and South-South trade. There is growing consensus among economists about the importance of the "new markets margin," through which low- and middle-income countries (LMICs) can become more integrated in the world trading system. An extension of the welfare dimension suggests that a certain level of product and market diversification is necessary to insulate against demand shocks and obtain a minimally volatile export portfolio. India is leading the way in South Asia with its "Look East" policy to deepen trade and investment integration with East Asia. In Bangladesh, market shares of some emerging markets, such as China, India, and Turkey, have increased.

This chapter provides an overview of Bangladesh's current access conditions in its primary export markets, as well as prospects and constraints of expanding and diversifying its market access. We draw lessons from the successes and challenges of the India-Sri Lanka Free Trade Agreement (FTA) to inform Bangladesh's integration in global production chains. Finally, we discuss the role of the Export Promotion Bureau (EPB) in achieving the government's export promotion objectives.

Preferential Access for Bangladesh in High-Income Economies

EU Market Access

Bangladesh was accorded the most generous market access conditions, relative to non-LDCs, to the EU market under the Everything But Arms (EBA) initiative (box 3.1) Overall, EBA countries have significant preferences (3 percent or more) for 2 of 21 sectors (live animals and vegetable products) compared with Generalized System of Preferences (GSP) or GSP+ countries. For many products, particularly industrial products, the scheme has provided fewer benefits to LDCs than to more developed GSP or GSP+ competitors. In 2008, GSP beneficiaries accounted for 81 percent of preferential imports, GSP+ countries for 9 percent, and LDC countries for 10 percent. The top beneficiaries of EU preference regimes are five large exporters (Brazil, China, India, the Russian Federation, and Thailand); they accounted for more than 67 percent of all GSP-covered imports. The GSP imports of these beneficiaries are significantly higher than their total EU imports (non-GSP).

Box 3.1 EU Preferential Regimes

The European Union has long maintained nonreciprocal Generalized System of Preference (GSP) and reciprocal trade arrangements (principally free trade agreements) with some 176 countries and territories. GSP schemes have evolved over the past two decades into three principle regimes:

(a) A standard GSP that confers preferences to all developing countries for qualifying products, based on graduation criteria

(b) GSP+ regimes with greater preferences, which are offered to 49 vulnerable developing countries as an incentive for them to ratify and effectively implement a set of key international conventions

(c) An even more generous "Everything But Arms" (EBA) regime, which confers duty- and quota-free access to least-developed countries.

Introduced in 2001, EBA removes the uncertainties of earlier GSP schemes. Nearly 25 percent of tariff lines in the European Union have been duty free, irrespective of preferences. For GSP and GSP+ beneficiaries, 91 percent of tariff lines have been either preferential or duty free, and virtually 100 percent for EBA beneficiaries. Under such favorable market access, rules of origin and relative preference margins over other beneficiaries became key determinants of Bangladesh's exports to the European Union.

Bangladesh's export performance has thrived with strong apparel growth, despite seemingly strict rules of origin. The European Union's multiple product- and sector-specific rules of origin and options for regional cumulation are deemed too complex or too restrictive for a small and undiversified manufacturing base, as in Bangladesh (Bhattacharya, Rahman, and Raihan 2004). Nevertheless, Bangladesh's exports to the European Union increased at 13 percent per year between 2000 and 2011 (largely growth in apparel), which outpaced the European Union's average import growth of 6 percent by 200 percent. Relative to its main competitors in the ready-made garment (RMG) sector, Bangladesh's performance exceeded expectations, given the country's size. Bangladesh expanded its market share in the European Union from 3.5 percent in 2000 to 8.2 percent in 2011 (table 3.1). In comparison, China's market share in EU RMG imports in 2011 was around 30 percent, although China's gross domestic product (GDP) is 30 times larger than Bangladesh's GDP.

Bangladesh has steadily increased its share of exports to the European Union under preferential regimes since the inception of EBA, from around 51 percent in 2000 to around 83 percent in 2010 (table 3.2). Conversely, exports not meeting rules of origin declined from 90 percent in 2000 to 20 percent in 2010. The favorable trend is largely attributed to knitted garments: Bangladesh's preference utilization in knitted and crocheted garments exceeds 95 percent, about double the utilization for woven garments (tables 3.3 and 3.4). The rules of origin quite likely propagated backward linkages in knitted garments, especially in spinning of yarn.

Strengthening Competitiveness in Bangladesh—Thematic Assessment
http://dx.doi.org/10.1596/978-1-4648-0898-2

Table 3.1 Export Performance of Bangladesh and Its Competitors in the European Union, 2000–11

| | | | | | | | Market share (%) | | | |
| | | Export growth, 2000–11 (%) | | | Apparel exports (US$, billions) | | Apparel market share | | Non-apparel market share | |
Country	Regime	Total	Apparel	Non-apparel	2000	2011	2000	2011	2000	2011
Bangladesh	**EBA**	**13.4**	**14.0**	**9.5**	**2.5**	**10.6**	**3.5**	**8.2**	**0.02**	**0.03**
Cambodia	**EBA**	**17.6**	**16.6**	**20.6**	**0.3**	**1.5**	**0.4**	**1.1**	**0**	**0.01**
China	MFN	15.7	16.1	15.6	7.7	39.9	10.8	30.7	2.7	7.01
Egypt, Arab Rep.	IF	12.1	7.5	12.4	0.3	0.6	0.4	0.5	0.12	0.24
India	GSP	13.1	10.5	13.5	2.1	6.1	2.9	4.7	0.43	0.92
Indonesia	MFN	4.4	0.3	5.1	1.8	1.9	2.6	1.5	0.4	0.36
Jordan	IF	6.6	−1.1	7.6	0.0	0.02	0.0	0.0	0.00	0.01
Lao PDR	**EBA**	**2.9**	**0.2**	**11.7**	**0.1**	**0.1**	**0.2**	**0.1**	**0.00**	**0.00**
Pakistan	MFN	7.6	10.2	6.7	0.6	1.7	0.8	1.3	0.08	0.09
Sri Lanka	GSP	7.5	8.4	6.2	0.8	2.01	1.2	1.6	0.03	0.03
Vietnam	MFN	12.6	9.8	13.2	0.8	2.2	1.1	1.7	0.15	0.31

Source: Based on United Nations Commodity Trade Statistics database via World Integrated Trade Solution.
Note: Non-apparel exports represents all other exports except apparel. Countries subject to the EBA regime are in bold. EBA = Everything But Arms; GSP = Generalized System of Preferences; IF = Free Trade Agreement in force; MFN: most favored nation.

Table 3.2 Bangladesh's Total Exports under the EBA Regime, 2000, 2005, and 2010
(US$, millions)

Notation	Declarant/period	2000	2005	2010
A1	Not EBA eligible, only MFN = 0	50.9	62.7	79.1
A2	Not EBA eligible, only MFN > 0	0.0	0.0	0.0
A3	Not EBA eligible, entered unknown status	0.0	0.0	0.0
A4	EBA eligible, but entered MFN = 0	0.8	0.8	1.0
A5	EBA eligible, but entered MFN > 0; did not meet rules of origin	1,356.8	1,394.6	1,459.0
A6	EBA eligible, entered pref = 0	1,406.4	3,313.3	7,088.8
A7	EBA eligible, entered pref > 0 (specific duties)	0.0	0.0	0.0
A8	EBA eligible, entered unknown status	11.0	324.0	59.4
	EBA utilization (A6 + A7 + A4)/(A4 + A5 + A6 + A7) (%)	51	70	83
	Duty free (pref + MFN) as share of total (%)	52	66	83

Source: Calculations based on Eurostat.
Note: EBA = Everything But Arms; MFN = most favored nation.

Bangladesh's margin of preference over non-GSP countries suffered little erosion between 2000 and 2008 (table 3.5). The margin of preference erosion from 2002 to 2008 does not appear to have been significant for EBA beneficiaries, except in live animals (3.3 percent). Overall, EBA beneficiaries enjoyed at least a 4 percent margin of preferences compared with MFN countries in 10 of 21 Harmonized Commodity System (HS) sections, with a peak of 17 percent (table 3.4).[1] Bangladesh's preferential margin in apparel (HS Section 11b) is the second highest of EBA countries, and it is 11.2 percent greater than

Table 3.3 Bangladesh's Knitted and Crocheted Apparel Exports under the EBA Regime, 2000, 2005, and 2010

(US$, millions)

Notation	Declarant/period	2000	2005	2010
B1	Not EBA eligible, only MFN = 0	0.0	0.0	0.0
B2	Not EBA eligible, only MFN > 0	0.0	0.0	0.0
B3	Not EBA eligible, entered unknown status	0.0	0.0	0.0
B4	EBA eligible, but entered MFN = 0	0.0	0.0	0.0
B5	EBA eligible, but entered MFN > 0; did not meet rules of origin	367.3	252.0	206.4
B6	EBA eligible, entered pref = 0	858.0	2,326.5	5,093.7
B7	EBA eligible, entered pref > 0 (specific duties)	0.0	0.0	0.0
B8	EBA eligible, entered unknown status	6.1	157.7	37.1
	EBA utilization (B6 + B7 + B4)/(B4 + B5 + B6 + B7) (%)	70	90	96
	Duty free (pref + MFN) (%)	70	85	95

Source: Calculations based on Eurostat.
Note: EBA = Everything But Arms; MFN = most favored nation.

Table 3.4 Bangladesh's Woven Garments Exports under the EBA Regime, 2000, 2005, and 2010

(US$, millions)

Notation	Declarant/period	2000	2005	2010
C1	Not EBA eligible, only MFN = 0	0.0	0.0	0.0
C2	Not EBA eligible, only MFN > 0	0.0	0.0	0.0
C3	Not EBA eligible, entered unknown status	0.0	0.0	0.0
C4	EBA eligible, but entered MFN = 0	0.0	0.0	0.0
C5	EBA eligible, but entered MFN > 0; did not meet rules of origin	957.1	1,104.9	1,180.5
C6	EBA eligible, entered pref = 0	164.1	466.6	1,080.4
C7	EBA eligible, entered pref > 0 (specific duties)	0.0	0.0	0.0
C8	EBA eligible, entered unknown status	4.1	85.0	17.0
	EBA utilization (C6 + C7 + C4)/(C4 + C5 + C6 + C7) (%)	15	30	48
	Duty free (pref + MFN) (%)	15	28	47

Source: Calculations based on Eurostat.
Note: EBA = Everything But Arms; MFN = most favored nation.

MFN beneficiaries. Bangladesh shares the same margin of benefit with other GSP+ members, none of whom are major RMG producers or exporters.

The European Union has revised its GSP scheme to make it more equitable and in line with its external economic policy on LMICs and vulnerable economies (European Commission 2011). The new scheme was planned to be implemented in January 2014, leaving time for countries to adjust, and includes the following features. First, it aims to concentrate GSP preferences on fewer countries by withdrawing benefits to high- or upper-middle-income countries that already have GSP-level preferential access to the European Union. Preferences will be

Table 3.5 Preference Margins under the EU GSP, 2002–08

HS section	Preference margin over MFN in 2008 (%)			Change in preferences 2002–08			Margin of preferences between regimes (%)		
	GSP	GSP+	EBA	GSP	GSP+	EBA	GSP+/GSP	EBA/GSP	EBA/GSP+
Section 1	2.6	6.7	17.3	1.1	0.6	−3.3	4.2	14.8	10.6
Section 2	2	5	9.4	−0.3	0	−2.8	3	7.4	4.4
Section 3	3.3	6.5	8.6	0.4	0.7	1.4	3.2	5.3	2.1
Section 4	5.6	14.8	17	2	0.9	1.2	9.3	11.5	2.2
Section 5	0.7	0.7	0.7	0	0	0	0	0.1	0.1
Section 6	4.2	4.9	5.1	0.2	0.2	0.2	0.7	0.9	0.3
Section 7	4.4	5.5	5.5	−0.2	−0.4	−0.4	1.1	1.1	0
Section 8	2.2	2.8	3	0.1	0.1	0.1	0.7	0.9	0.2
Section 9	1.8	2.4	2.4	−0.1	−0.4	−0.4	0.6	0.6	0
Section 10	0	0	0	−1.5	−1.5	−1.5	0	0	0
Section 11a	1.3	6.2	6.2	−0.1	−0.5	−0.5	5	5	0
Section 11b	2.2	11.2	11.2	−0.1	−0.3	−0.3	9	9	0
Section 12	3.6	7.6	7.6	−0.2	−0.7	−0.7	4	4	0
Section 13	2.6	4	4	0	0	0	1.3	1.3	0
Section 14	0.7	0.7	0.7	−0.1	−0.1	−0.1	0	0	0
Section 15	1.5	1.9	2	−0.4	−0.4	−0.4	0.4	0.5	0.1
Section 16	2	2.3	2.3	−0.1	−0.1	−0.1	0.3	0.3	0
Section 17	2.9	4.6	4.6	−0.1	−0.4	−0.4	1.7	1.7	0
Section 18	2.1	2.3	2.3	−0.1	−0.2	−0.2	0.2	0.2	0
Section 19	0	0	0	0	0	0	0	0	0
Section 20	2.4	2.5	2.5	−0.1	−0.1	−0.1	0.1	0.1	0
Section 21	0	0	0	0	0	0	0	0	0

Source: European Commission 2011.
Note: EBA = Everything But Arms; EU = European Union; GSP = Generalized System of Preferences; HS = Harmonized Commodity System.

withdrawn from overseas countries and territories that have an alternative arrangement for access to high-income markets. Second, the new regime rewards respect for core human and labor rights, environmental protection, and good governance by increasing importers' access to the GSP+ scheme. Countries will have to reapply for GSP+ status after complying with about 27 requirements. Third, the new GSP scheme strengthens trade concessions for LDCs through the EBA scheme, which will reduce competitive pressure on LDCs and make their preferences more effective. Finally, revisions will increase the predictability, transparency, and stability of the GSP scheme by making it open-ended, rather than subject to review every three years as is current practice.

Bangladesh will likely be negatively impacted by the new GSP scheme. A SMART simulation of the adopted scheme indicates that the benefits will likely be concentrated on GSP+ beneficiaries, rather than on LDCs (European Commission 2011). Estimates show that Bangladesh could suffer a welfare loss of about 0.31 percent as a consequence of the potential entry of Pakistan into GSP+, which would depress the textile exports of Bangladesh. Under the current

EU GSP, specific sectors or products are graduated from the GSP or the GSP+ if they total 15 percent of EU imports over three consecutive years (the trigger is 12.5 percent for textiles and clothing). However, the sectors that will actually be graduated are not known at this stage. They will depend on the latest available import figures prior to the new regulation entering into force. Graduation of other countries' exports, such as Indian textiles, could lessen the negative impacts on Bangladesh.

Meanwhile, Bangladesh's textile and clothing industry will benefit from more favorable rules of origin. Anecdotal evidence suggests that the European Union's replacement of the "two-stage" processing requirement with "one-stage" processing, effective January 2011, has resulted in a surge in Bangladesh's apparel exports to the European Union. The new ruling allows imported fabrics in apparel exports, which makes it possible to use existing capacity in the knitted garments sector. More important, preferred exports of woven garments will likely expand.

Bangladesh should be able to use the relaxed fisheries rules to enhance exports in the fishery sector. For fish caught outside territorial waters, a prior requirement that 50 percent of the crew on the fish-catching vessel be citizens of the European Union or beneficiary countries has been removed. In addition, the value "tolerance" determination for fishery products (HS chapter 16) has been raised from 10 to 15 percent. This could enable diversification toward other fish varieties with Bangladesh's comparative advantages (including a high water-to-land ratio and an abundance of varieties, such as hilsa). In addition, a weight tolerance determination replaces value tolerance, although levels for LDCs and non-LDCs remain fixed at 15 percent. However, a number of technical requirements and rules of origin will likely continue to restrict access to the EU market. For example, some product-specific rules of origin, such as in fish and fish products, certain processed agricultural products, and a range of manufactures, remain too restrictive in accessing the EU market. In addition, restrictive cumulation may deter LMICs from fully exploiting their comparative advantage.

Beyond the EBA scheme, Bangladeshi exporters have often benefitted from EU restrictions on Chinese exports to the European Union. This is true for garment exports under the Multi-Fiber Arrangement, which governed world trade in textiles and garments from 1974 through 2004 through quotas on LMICs exports to high-income countries. However, this international agreement imposed no restrictions or duties on imports from the poorest countries, such as Bangladesh, which widened the preferential margin and contributed to textile sector expansion in these economies. Similarly, the value chain analyses conducted in the context of the Diagnostic Trade Integration Study found that the exports of a number of successful, nongarment firms benefitted from antidumping duties imposed against Chinese exports for bicycles, leather shoes, and ceramics. Although EU MFN duties on shoes were between 3 and 17 percent, the European Union imposed antidumping duties on Chinese shoes at 16.5 percent and on Vietnamese shoes at 10 percent. The EU duties were inaugurated in 2006, extended for 15 months in December 2009, and expired in 2011. European trade

Strengthening Competitiveness in Bangladesh—Thematic Assessment
http://dx.doi.org/10.1596/978-1-4648-0898-2

protection against Chinese bicycles dates to 1993, when the European Union introduced a 30.6 percent antidumping duty on imports from China. The European Union renewed that levy in 2000 before raising it to the current 48.5 percent in 2005. At the same time, the European Union introduced antidumping duties as high as 34.5 percent on imports from Vietnam.

U.S. Market Access

The United States does not provide duty-free access for some key Bangladesh exports, and only a few goods (excluding its biggest export, RMG) qualify under the U.S. GSP. The U.S. GSP program is rather straightforward. The program divides eligible countries into two groups based on their income levels: all developing countries and a subset of the LDCs. However, product coverage is far more limited than the EU program and excludes most textiles and apparel. In 2010, the GSP provided preferential duty-free entry for about 3,400 products from 129 designated beneficiaries and an additional 1,400 products from beneficiaries designated as LDCs. The program requires beneficiaries to adhere to certain criteria, among them protection of specified labor rights and intellectual property rights. In addition, the program specifies graduation of countries that exceed a per-capita income level and graduation of products that exceed "competitive-need limits," currently around US$110 million per tariff line. If the country's imports in a given category exceed 50 percent of total U.S. imports, the country may also lose GSP eligibility.[2] Although the latter is not a concern for Bangladesh, labor practices have been subject to scrutiny. Previously accepted worker rights–related petitions from Bangladesh (as well as Niger, the Philippines, Sri Lanka, and Uzbekistan) remained under review as part of the 2011 GSP Annual Review process (USTR 2011). A public hearing was held in January 2012 on Bangladesh's petition. The GSP was kept under review status.[3]

Bangladesh's performance in the U.S. market has been remarkable compared with its competitors, despite lack of substantial preferential access and distance from the market (figure 3.1). In 2005, signatories of the North American Free Trade Agreement (NAFTA) and the Dominican Republic–Central America Free Trade Agreement (CAFTA-DR) were the largest beneficiaries of U.S. trade preferences for textiles and apparel, together accounting for 30 percent of U.S. imports of these items. China, without preferences, has grown its U.S. market share of textiles and apparel more than threefold since 2004. Bangladesh's market share in these products, already a substantial 3.3 percent in 2005, increased to 7 percent in 2011, exceeding NAFTA, whose market share declined substantially over the same period.

Bangladesh's exports to the United States have gradually increased outside GSP preferences. GSP utilization has in fact sharply fallen in recent years from a high of 51 percent in 2007 to 35 percent in 2011 (table 3.6). This in part reflects a decline in U.S. preferences for all beneficiaries. Of 119 Bangladeshi products imported under preferences, the top 10 accounted for 80 percent of GSP benefits. This skewed GSP utilization and the general increase in non-preferred

Figure 3.1 U.S. Market Share of Bangladesh's Top 25 Apparel Exports, 2004–11

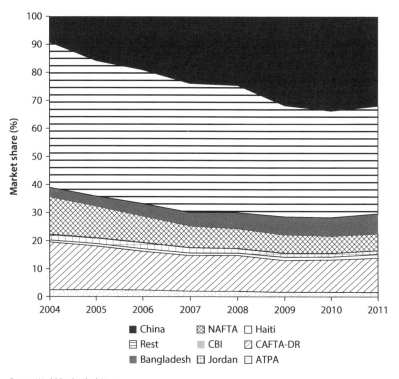

Source: World Bank calculations.
Note: ATPA = Andean Trade Preferences Act; CAFTA-DR = Dominican Republic–Central America Free Trade
Agreement; CBI = Caribbean Basin Initiative; NAFTA = North American Free Trade Agreement.

Table 3.6 Bangladesh's Utilization of U.S. GSP, 2006–11
(US$, billions)

Exports	2006	2007	2008	2009	2010	2011
GSP-eligible exports entering the United States under GSP	21	23.9	22.2	23.3	27.9	25.6
GSP-eligible exports not entering the United States under GSP	23.9	22.5	28.8	24.3	37.9	47.4
Total GSP-eligible exports entering the United States	44.9	46.4	51.1	47.6	65.8	73.1
Total exports to the United States	3,270	3,433	3,748	3,700	4,293	4,876
GSP-eligible exports entering the United States under GSP (%)	46.8	51.5	43.5	48.9	42.4	35.1
U.S. GSP exports as share of total (%)	0.6	0.8	0.7	1.1	1.2	n.a.

Source: Based on U.S. Department of Commerce and U.S. International Trade Commission statistics.
Note: GSP = Generalized System of Preferences; n.a. = not applicable.

exports indicate that the GSP has not helped Bangladeshi exports to the United
States diversify away from the RMG sector.

Bangladesh's preference margins have been limited and do not benefit
its major GSP exports to the United States, such as sleeping bags and bone china
(table 3.7). Large GSP beneficiaries, such as Brazil, China, India, and Pakistan,

Table 3.7 Margin of Preference of Bangladesh's Top 20 GSP-Eligible U.S. Exports, 2009–11

Product	HS code	GSP regime	MFN	Value (US$, millions) 2009	2010	2011
Sleeping bags	94043080	A	9%	0.2	3.3	4.0
Tobacco, partly or wholly stemmed/stripped	24012085	A+	US$0.375 per kilogram	5.4	2.1	3.4
Plastic packing of goods	39239000	A*	3%	3.9	4.2	2.8
Bone china household table and kitchenware	69111025	A	6%	0.3	1.4	2.5
Tobacco, partly or wholly stemmed/stripped	24012083	A+	US$0.375 per kilogram	2.7	4.1	1.9
Carpets and other textile floor coverings	69111037	A	8%	0.4	1.1	1.6
Porcelain or china, nonhousehold	69111010	A+	25%	1.4	1.1	1.5
Golf equipment	95063900	A	4.9%	4.0	3.6	1.3
Tobacco roots	24021030	A		0.0	0.0	0.8
Carpets and other textile floor coverings	57029920	A*	2.70%	0.7	0.7	0.5
Made-up articles of textile materials (flags)	63079098	A	7%	0.7	1.0	0.4
Plastic apparel and clothing accessories	39262090	A	5%	0.1	0.4	0.4
Prepared foods of cereals	19041000	A	1.1%	0.2	0.2	0.4
Spectacles, goggles, and the like	90049000	A	2.5%	0.1	0.0	0.4
Baskets and bags of vegetable material	46021918	A	4.5%	0.1	0.1	0.4
Juice of any other single fruit	20098060	A	0.5 cents/liter	0.0	0.0	0.3
Plastic sacks and bags	39232100	A*	3%	0.2	0.2	0.2
Other plastic goods, of polymers of ethylene	19059090	A	4.5%	0.2	0.3	0.2
Bone china household table and kitchenware	69111015	A	8.0%	0.2	0.2	0.2
Hides and skins	41044150	A*	3.3%	0.1	0.1	0.2

Sources: USITC (http://www.ustr.gov/sites/default/files/ATT%20(D)%20-%20Bangladesh%20CY08.pdf) and World Bank calculations.
Note: A+ eligibility only for LDCs. A* Articles that are GSP eligible, except for imports from specific countries that have lost GSP eligibility for that article. GSP = Generalized System of Preferences; LDCs = least-developed countries; MFN = most favored nation.

receive the same preferences as Bangladesh and other LDCs, and they benefit much more when margins are small. In addition, Bangladesh has not fully exploited products with larger preferential margins, such as nonhousehold porcelain (25 percent MFN). One explanation for the lack of penetration in the U.S. market may be the industry's principle focus on the EU market. The private sector and supporting institutions, such as the EPB, may lack the capacity to articulate strategies that align Bangladesh's competitive products with market opportunities.

Bangladesh's U.S. market prospects will likely be further reduced by preferential regimes granted to competitor countries, including free trade agreements for textiles and apparel, such as CAFTA-DR, the Andean FTA, and NAFTA. The United States has also extended unilateral preferences to a number of countries, including countries in Sub-Saharan Africa through the African Growth and Opportunity Act (AGOA), the Caribbean Basin Initiative, and Haiti. Haiti has the most advantageous access to the United States in terms of product coverage and rules of origin, where the standard "yarn forward" rule has been substantially relaxed. For example, certain apparel (chapter 61 of the United Nations Globally Harmonized System of Classification) is permitted duty-free access under tariff rate quotas subject to ad valorem de minimis rules rather than yarn forward.

Haiti and the CAFTA-DR countries are permitted to export a certain share of otherwise non-qualifying apparel on a duty-free basis.[4] Utilization rates under these preferential arrangements have been relatively high, with the exception of the Caribbean Basin (excluding Haiti) and Andean countries. NAFTA (primarily Mexico) has maintained high utilization, ranging from 89 percent in 2005 to 97 percent during the first half of 2012. The CAFTA-DR countries and Haiti have likewise attained high rates of utilization of their respective preference programs, reflecting their adaptation to strict U.S. rules of origin. NAFTA, CAFTA-DR, and Caribbean Basin Trade Promotion Act (CBTPA) countries have long benefitted from U.S. preferences. In particular, early outward processing rules encouraged the development of apparel industries specifically geared toward make-trim and cut-make-trim, which almost exclusively used U.S. fabrics.

Bangladesh will also continue to face pressure from countries that are guarding their already more favorable preferences. Bangladesh and a group of 14 countries are currently attempting to obtain GSP access in the U.S. apparel market,[5] including duty-free status like that currently enjoyed by AGOA, NAFTA, and CBTPA beneficiaries (table 3.8). This effort has resulted in U.S. legislation supporting duty-free access by Bangladesh and others. A bill presented to the U.S. Congress requesting market access equal to that of the beneficiaries faces opposition from AGOA countries and other apparel exporters, such as Pakistan, that fear erosion of their preferences. There is also domestic pressure to protect preferences to existing beneficiary countries, especially those in the Latin American and Caribbean region.

Moreover, the rapid extension of preferences to such countries as Haiti signals the geopolitical realities that are likely to impact decision making in the United States. Haiti, despite its low absolute export values, doubled its preferred exports between 2005 and 2011, and U.S. bilateral support is proactively strengthening Haiti's export capacity. Even if efforts by Bangladesh and the LDCs to obtain duty- and quota-free access under GSP are successful, such preferences would likely come with rules similar to existing yarn forward rules of origin applied to other U.S. trade regimes. The yarn forward rules give U.S. regional partners a distinct advantage, particularly in light of transportation costs that may otherwise make cut-make-trim operations with U.S. fabric in more distant locations, such as Bangladesh, less cost competitive.

Increased Role of Regional Markets for Bangladeshi Exports

Global merchandise import demand is shifting away from the European Union and the United States toward China, East Asia, and other middle-income markets. The contribution to global GDP growth of LMICs, including Brazil, China, India, and other large emerging markets, has risen—with Asia figuring as the fastest-growing region of the world. LMICs have, in turn, become increasingly important export markets in a newly multipolar global economy. Over the past three decades, the import share of emerging markets in world merchandise

Table 3.8 Comparative Benefits under U.S. Market Access Programs and Trade Agreements

Program	Description	Eligible exports and rules of origin	Beneficiaries
Caribbean Basin Trade Promotion Act (CBTPA)	A trade preference program enacted in October 2000. It provides duty-free treatment for apparel wholly assembled, knit, or knit-to-shape in beneficiary countries in the Caribbean, as long as the apparel uses U.S. fabrics and U.S. yarns, with some exceptions for knit products that are under a quota system.	Unlimited duty-free treatment for apparel manufactured in CBTPA beneficiary countries, if it is wholly assembled, knit, or knit-to-shape in CBTPA beneficiary countries, using: • U.S. yarn and fabric, cut in the United States and assembled in CBTPA beneficiary countries • U.S. yarn and fabric, cut in United States and further processed in CBTPA beneficiary countries • U.S. yarn, fabric, and thread, cut in CBTPA beneficiary countries • Brassieres cut and sewn in the United States and/or CBTPA beneficiary countries. Certain knit apparel is subject to annual quotas or TRQs. The two TRQ programs are as follows: • Knit apparel articles (excluding socks and non–underwear T-shirts) made of U.S. yarn, CBTPA knit fabric, or knit-to-shape components that are cut and sewn in CBTPA beneficiary countries • Non-underwear T-shirts of U.S. yarn and CBTPA fabric that are cut and sewn in CBTPA beneficiary countries.	Antigua and Barbuda Aruba Bahamas, The/Barbados Belize British Virgin Islands Dominica Grenada Guyana Haiti Jamaica Montserrat Netherlands Antilles Panama St. Kitts and Nevis St. Lucia St. Vincent and the Grenadines Trinidad and Tobago
Hemispheric Opportunity for Partnership (HOPE II)	Extends additional preferences above and beyond CBTPA.	Allows duty-free treatment for certain apparel wholly assembled, knit, or knit-to-shape in Haiti, using yarns and fabrics from any country. This is in contrast to CBTPA, which requires U.S. yarns and fabrics to qualify for duty-free treatment. HOPE created two preference programs: the value-added TRQ and the woven and knit apparel TRQ, each of which limits qualifying imports to certain annual quotas. The programs include: • TRQ allowing value-added rather than yarn-forward rules • An extension of duty-free access to the U.S. market for 10 years, effective October 2008 • An extension of eligible woven products from 3 to 10 years	Haiti

table continues next page

Table 3.8 Comparative Benefits under U.S. Market Access Programs and Trade Agreements *(continued)*

Program	Description	Eligible exports and rules of origin	Beneficiaries
		• An increase in the TRQ for woven and knit products from 50 million to 70 million square meter equivalents • Co-production with and direct shipment from Dominican Republic • Inclusion of luggage, headgear, and sleepwear.	
Haiti Economic Lift Program (HELP)	Enacted in May 2010, expands existing preferences for apparel under HOPE II; also establishes new preferences for certain non-apparel textile goods.	With the exception of the value-added TRQ (which expires in December 2018), HELP extends all of CBTPA's and HOPE/HOPE II/HELP's preference programs through September 2020. For programs already established by HOPE and HOPE II, HELP enacted the following modifications: • Modified the minimum percentage of value under the value-added TRQ, ranging from 50 to 60 percent • Provides a conditional increase of the woven and knit apparel TRQ quota limits from 70 million SME to 200 million SME • Modified the allowance ratio for the Haiti Earned Import Allowance Program from 1:3 to 1:2.	Haiti
Earned Import Allowance Program (EIAP), established under HOPE II, modified by HELP	Extends duty-free treatment to apparel products that do not meet the rules of origin under HOPE II and HELP—that is, products using third-party yarn or fabric.	For every two SME of qualifying fabric purchased or manufactured by the producer for apparel production in Haiti, qualifying producers can earn one SME credit. These credits can allow duty-free treatment for imports of apparel manufactured in Haiti using non-qualifying fabric. There is no quantitative limit on the Haiti EIAP.	Haiti Dominican Republic
Dominican Republic–Central America Free Trade Agreement (CAFTA-DR)	Supersedes CBTPA for member countries, extending duty-free benefits to virtually all goods; also provides provisions to open trade in services.	For textiles and apparel, most items are still subject to the yarn-forward rule, with some exceptions for specific products from selected countries. Cumulation with Mexico for purposes of rules of origin is also permitted.	Costa Rica Dominican Republic El Salvador Guatemala Honduras Nicaragua

table continues next page

Table 3.8 Comparative Benefits under U.S. Market Access Programs and Trade Agreements *(continued)*

Program	Description	Eligible exports and rules of origin	Beneficiaries
Andean Trade Preferences Act (ATPA)	Enacted in 1991 as part of U.S. efforts to reduce narcotic production and trafficking, it was modeled after the Caribbean Basin Initiative and has similar eligibility requirements and product coverage. ATPA was renewed in 2002 as the Andean Trade Promotion and Drug Eradication Act (ATPDEA) and expanded to include tuna, leather and footwear products, petroleum products, and apparel.	If apparel is assembled from U.S. fabrics, no quotas or duties apply. If local inputs are used, duty-free imports are subject to a cap of 2 percent of total U.S. imports (increasing to 5 percent in equal annual installments).	Bolivia Colombia Ecuador Peru
African Growth and Opportunity Act (AGOA)	Passed in 2000, offers beneficiary Sub-Saharan African countries duty-free and quota-free market access for essentially all products, excluding textiles.	Apparel made from U.S. yarn and fabric qualifies for duty- and quota-free treatment. If regional fabric and yarn are used, there is a cap of 1.5 percent of U.S. imports, increasing to 3.5 percent over eight years. African LDCs are exempt from all rules of origin for a limited period of time.	

Source: World Bank compilation.
Note: CBTPA = Caribbean Basin Trade Promotion Act; EIAP = Earned Import Allowance Program; HELP = Haiti Economic Lift Program; LDCs = least-developed countries; SME = small and medium enterprises; TRQ = tariff rate quota.

imports has increased rapidly and in 2010 surpassed that of the United States (figure 3.2). Most impressive has been China's emergence in global demand—a consequence of rapid growth rates and relocation of manufacturing. The secular decline in the share of world imports in high-income countries, such as in the European Union and the United States, has accelerated during the recent financial crisis and has been matched by the rise in import shares of emerging markets in Asia, such as China. This process is expected to continue as the high-income countries grapple with the long-lasting effects of the current crisis and with the recovery in capital flows to LMICs from high-income countries. Investors will seek to raise returns by investing in countries with stronger fundamentals and growth outcomes.

The rise in emerging markets provides Bangladesh with the greatest opportunity for export diversification efforts. The average factor intensity of Bangladesh's exports against each destination country's income level suggests "there is much more vertical variation at low-income levels than at high-income ones, suggesting that there is more variety in the factor content of Bangladesh's exports to low-income countries" (Cadot and Gourdon 2012). For Bangladesh, South-South trade therefore provides more opportunities for export diversification than North-South trade. The Asia region, given its growing markets and close proximity, provides the greatest opportunities for Bangladesh to diversify and expand exports. Experience suggests that geographic proximity has a powerful, positive effect on the volume of trade. Furthermore, other things being equal, the poorest countries increase their trade share with geographically closer partners when trade costs are lower than for more distant partners. A "Look East" strategy, led

Figure 3.2 World Imports, 1970–2011

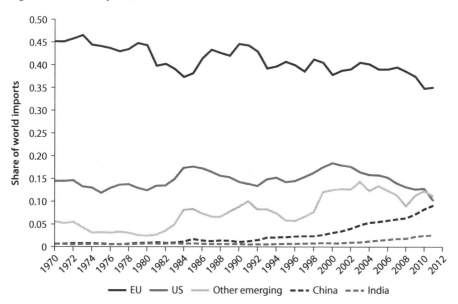

Source: World Bank, World Development Indicators.

Strengthening Competitiveness in Bangladesh—Thematic Assessment
http://dx.doi.org/10.1596/978-1-4648-0898-2

by India, is bound to have great implications for Bangladesh's long-term trade and growth prospects.

Bangladesh's imports from East Asia surpassed the level of bilateral trade with the United States in 2003; in 2011, East Asian imports were nearly at EU levels and were almost 30 percent of total imports (figure 3.3). In the absence of effective trade agreements with LMICs, the rise of trade with East Asia suggests that the region is becoming the natural trading partner for Bangladesh. As these are mostly imports, Bangladesh is discovering more competitive sources in East Asia relative to the rest of the world.

However, Bangladesh's efforts to deepen regional integration have been limited, given its focus on its preferential margins in the EU and U.S. markets. Bangladesh has signed five preferential trade agreements and 43 bilateral agreements,[6] resulting in a complex web of trading (figure 3.4). This structure seems to lack prioritization. The agreements are shallow, with selected tariff liberalization for some products, stringent rules of origin, and limited coverage of broader issues such as standards, investment, services, and labor movements (box 3.2).

An evaluation that used the trade complementarity index (TCI) suggests that Bangladesh's export capabilities have only weak complementarities with its partners' import structures (tables 3.9, 3.10, and 3.11). Complementarity has the potential to increase with a more diversified and dynamic Bangladeshi export base. Trade has potential to grow if neighboring regions start exchanging similar product lines and deepen their production relations. The smaller export shares (of total exports including the European Union and the United States) to East Asia and South Asia obscure true growth potential. Real policy barriers restrict regional trade, particularly in South Asia. Conversely, Bangladesh has significant import complementarities with key members of the

Figure 3.3 Bangladesh Imports, 1989–2011

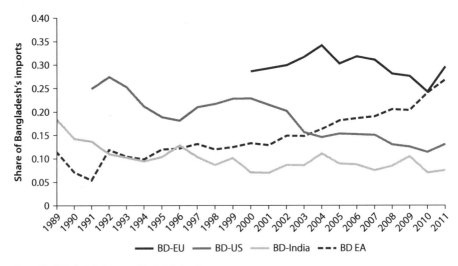

Source: World Bank World Integrated Trade Solution data.

Strengthening Competitiveness in Bangladesh—Thematic Assessment
http://dx.doi.org/10.1596/978-1-4648-0898-2

Figure 3.4 The Web of Bangladesh's Preferential Trade

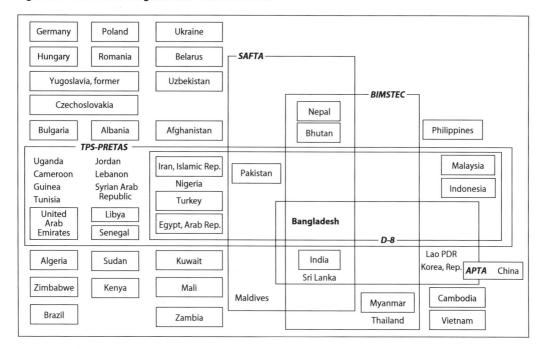

Source: Government of Bangladesh.

Note: Single-country boxes represent bilateral agreements. Multi-country boxes represent regional agreements. APTA = Asia-Pacific Trade Agreement; BIMSTEC = Bay of Bengal Initiative for Multi-Sectoral Technical and Economic Cooperation; D-8 = Developing 8; SAFTA = South Asian Free Trade Area; TPS-PRETAS =Trade Preferential System–Organization of the Islamic Conference.

Box 3.2 Bangladesh's Free Trade Agreements

First, Bangladesh is a member of the South Asian Free Trade Area (SAFTA), the free trade area (FTA) created in 2006 by members of the South Asian Association for Regional Cooperation. Other SAFTA members are Afghanistan, Bhutan, India, the Maldives, Nepal, Pakistan, and Sri Lanka. SAFTA called for the reduction of intra-bloc tariffs to below 5 percent by January 1, 2009, for non-least developed countries (non-LDCs); as an LDC, Bangladesh benefits from a phase-out period extended to 2016. Some of SAFTA's members have frontloaded their tariff reductions, including India; Bangladesh has reduced its intra-bloc tariffs by about half compared with 2006 levels. All members maintain sensitive products lists, although their size varies. For instance, Bangladesh has 987 sensitive products, Pakistan has 986, but India has only 25.

As an FTA, SAFTA maintains rules of origin. The general criterion for non-LDCs is a change of tariff heading plus 40 percent local value added, although 191 products have specific rules. That is, to qualify for preferential tariffs, a final product assembled in a member state must have an ex-factory price at least 66 percent higher than the total cost, insurance, and freight (CIF) value of its imported intermediates, and it must belong to a Harmonized Commodity

box continues next page

Box 3.2 Bangladesh's Free Trade Agreements *(continued)*

Description and Coding System (HS) tariff heading (HS-4 category) different from that of any of its imported components. This local-value content requirement is stringent. In many manufacturing activities, in particular ready-made garments (RMG), value addition rarely reaches more than 30 percent of the ex-factory price of the final good. Thus, in the RMG sector, a 40 percent local-value content amounts, de facto, to a double transformation rule; that is, assembling garments from pre-cut fabric under cut, make, and trim arrangements does not qualify as sufficient transformation. As an LDC, Bangladesh enjoys a relaxed local-value content requirement (30 percent).[a] Cumulating is allowed with 50 percent regional content.

Second, Bangladesh is a signatory to the Asia-Pacific Trade Agreement (APTA), with China, India, the Lao People's Democratic Republic, the Republic of Korea, and Sri Lanka. Tariff concessions are so far nonuniversal, with about 40 percent of the tariff lines and 20 percent of regional trade to be covered under the current round of negotiations, launched in 2007. The largest coverage is currently offered by China and Korea and includes jute products and leather goods, both of interest to Bangladesh. APTA's rules of origin are even more stringent than SAFTA, with local value contents of 35 percent for LDCs and 45 percent for non-LDCs. The current round of negotiations aims at broadening the agreement's range to trade in services.

Third, Bangladesh is part of the Bay of Bengal Initiative for Multi-Sectoral Technical and Economic Cooperation (BIMSTEC) FTA, with Bhutan, India, Myanmar, Nepal, Sri Lanka, and Thailand. Tariff reductions under the BIMSTEC FTA are planned but have not yet started. A meeting of the trade negotiating committee of the seven-nation grouping, which took place in September 2015 to revive the proposed free trade deal, failed to reach a consensus, after India's proposal to revise tariff cuts decided a decade ago was opposed by other members.[b]

Fourth, Bangladesh belongs to the Developing 8 (D-8) group, which includes the Arab Republic of Egypt, Indonesia, the Islamic Republic of Iran, Malaysia, Nigeria, Pakistan, and Turkey. A preferential tariff reduction initiative was agreed on in 2006 and entered into force in 2011, although with limited coverage (8 percent of all tariff lines). Tariff peaks (above 25 percent) are designated for reductions under the preferential scheme. As an LDC, Bangladesh enjoys longer phase-out periods.

Fifth, Bangladesh is a signatory to the Protocol on Preferential Tariff Scheme for the Trade Preferential System–Organization of the Islamic Conference (TPS-OIC) protocol of the Organization of the Islamic Conference (OIC), with Cameroon, Egypt, Guinea, Indonesia, Jordan, Lebanon, Libya, Malaysia, Nigeria, Pakistan, Senegal, the Syrian Arab Republic, Turkey, Uganda, and the United Arab Emirates.

a. Rules of origin in the garments sector are no issue for a country like Pakistan with a vertically integrated textile sector. For Bangladesh, were it not for the special LDC regime, there could be an issue in the woven wear sector, which has only weak backward linkages (because weaving machinery is expensive), although not in the knitwear sector where backward linkages are stronger.
b. http://www.livemint.com/Politics/dLv479RCsQjV2jcTwX6trO/Bimstec-meet-free-trade-talks-come-a-cropper.html.

Table 3.9 Trade Complementarity Indexes, Bangladesh versus SAFTA Partners, 2010

SAFTA countries	Complementarity with Bangladesh (TCI, 2010)	Imports (US$, thousands)
Bhutan	29.56	854
Nepal	27.17	5,127
India	19.68	341,000
Maldives	19.57	1,095
Sri Lanka	18.70	12,400
Pakistan	18.15	37,500
Simple average	22.14	—
Import-weighted average	19.62	—

Source: Calculations based on UN Comtrade data.
Note: SAFTA = South Asian Free Trade Area; TCI = trade complementarity index; — = not available.

Table 3.10 Trade Complementarity Indexes, Bangladesh versus APTA Partners, 2010

APTA countries	Complementarity with Bangladesh (TCI, 2010)	Imports (US$, thousands)
India	19.68	341,000
Korea, Rep.	22.47	425,000
Sri Lanka	18.70	12,400
Simple average	20.28	—
Import-weighted average	21.19	—

Source: Calculations based on UN Comtrade data.
Note: APTA = Asia-Pacific Trade Agreement; TCI = trade complementarity index; — = not available.

Table 3.11 Trade Complementarity Indexes, Bangladesh versus BIMSTEC Partners, 2010

BIMSTEC countries	Complementarity with Bangladesh (TCI, 2010)	Imports (US$, thousands)
Bhutan	29.56	854
Myanmar	30.99	4,164
Nepal	27.17	5,127
Thailand	21.35	180,000
Simple average	27.27	—
Import-weighted average	21.75	—

Source: Calculations based on UN Comtrade data.
Note: BIMSTEC = Bay of Bengal Initiative for Multi-Sectoral Technical and Economic Cooperation; TCI = trade complementarity index; — = not available.

Association of Southeast Asian Nations (ASEAN), China, and India. They are comparable to Eastern European countries' complementarities with high-income EU members (France, Germany, and the United Kingdom) prior to joining the European Union (a TCI in the region of 60).[7] Bangladesh maintains the highest levels of import complementarity with China, India, Indonesia, Malaysia, Singapore, and Thailand, owing to the high degree of sourcing of textiles for the RMG sector (figure 3.5). Although prospects for growing exist-ing exports to East Asia may be weak on the basis of export complementarity, dynamic, medium-term impacts may give rise to new export industries, such as the export of processed foods that are currently domestically oriented.

With less than 15 percent in services imports and exports, Bangladesh has the lowest share in trade in services among South Asian countries (Raihan 2010). Lack of regional trade is not because of the absence of complementarities. Bangladesh shares a specialization in transport services and an emerging special-ization in business services with Pakistan and Sri Lanka; it has complementarities with Maldives and Nepal in travel services; and with India in information and communications technology services (Raihan 2010). What curtails trade is the level of protection of services, which tends to be higher than the protection on goods trade. Informal trade is not uncommon among countries sharing borders with high protection in services. For example, there are suspected unofficial flows and low official trade flows between India and Bangladesh in education and health-related services. This suggests that there are prospects for gains if barriers are dismantled (De, Raihan, and Kathuria 2012).

Bangladeshi merchandise exports would be 52 percent higher, and the country could gain around US$1.8 billion from broader South Asia–East Asia integration. Export growth to East Asia has the greatest potential. A recent formal analysis that used computable general equilibrium (CGE) modeling confirms that broader South Asia–East Asia integration that includes all members of South Asia

Figure 3.5 Bangladesh's Import Complementarity with India and East Asia, Selected Years

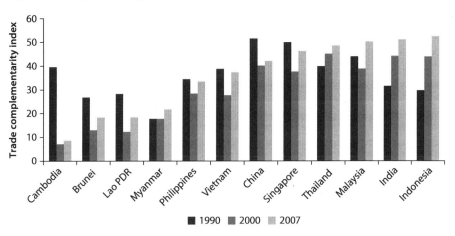

Source: Calculations based on UN Comtrade data.

would provide large gains to exports, trade, and overall welfare for Bangladesh (Francois, Rana, and Wignaraja 2009). Bangladesh's gains would have little effect, positive or negative, on outsiders. These results only illustrate the possible direction of the static gains to Bangladesh. All CGE static gain analyses considerably understate growth impacts, because the models incorporate limited dynamic effects from cross-border investment flows in support of trade. Such cross-border investment would be a much larger factor for countries like Bangladesh. Moreover, such opening to investment could raise economy-wide productivity and scale economies of domestic firms and industries (by increasing capital to an increased supply of labor, unit costs are decreased).

Bangladesh has the potential to increase trade with South Asia. Under the South Asian Free Trade Area (SAFTA), Bangladesh has secured a reduced sensitive items list and accelerated duty-free treatment for almost all items that are now subject to tariff rate quotas. Traders experience a modest level of nontariff barriers, including a 4 percent import cess on the RMG sector, rebated to domestic traders from different states. Other actions likely to yield significant dividends for Bangladeshi exporters include building product quality standards and related infrastructure; an ongoing effort by the Indian Bureau of Standards to upgrade the Bangladesh Standards and Testing Institution; and mutual recognition agreements between the two countries. The South Asian Association for Regional Cooperation provides a forum to address regional these agreements. Bangladesh's Federal Bureau of Chambers has raised a number of other policy-related issues that have hindered the movement of goods at the border with India (see box 3.3).

There is no consensus on the implications for Bangladesh of free trade in goods under SAFTA. A CGE model simulation by Francois, Rana, and Wignaraja (2009) of full free trade among South Asian countries points to a welfare gain for Bangladesh of about US$514 million over the baseline. Raihan (2010) suggests

---

Box 3.3 Policy Barriers at the Bangladesh-India Border

Selected issues identified by the India-Bangladesh Chamber of Commerce and Industry on trade flows at the border with India include the following:

• Absence of a clear transit protocol at land customs stations (LCS)
• Lack of standards and specifications at LCS
• Only certain land ports authorized for export of soap to India
• Lack of standards for commercial vehicles and lack of recognition of licensed drivers
• Six permissions required from Indian agencies to export goods to Kakarvitta in Nepal via India
• Lack of recognition of insurance policies.

Source: India-Bangladesh Chamber of Commerce and Industry.

Strengthening Competitiveness in Bangladesh—Thematic Assessment
http://dx.doi.org/10.1596/978-1-4648-0898-2

there are welfare losses to Bangladesh from potential free trade under SAFTA, largely from trade diversion outweighing the trade creation effect. However, Raihan (2010) shows a 50 percent reduction in MFN tariffs with full liberalization under SAFTA, which would mitigate the negative effects of trade diversion and improve welfare.

However, estimated gains from trade facilitation between Bangladesh and India are much larger than the gains from trade liberalization. For example, a study by De, Raihan, and Kathuria (2012) suggests that, because of the size and proximity of the countries, a Bangladesh-India FTA could increase exports to India by about 134 percent; with improved connectivity,[8] Bangladesh's exports to India could increase by about 297 percent. Improvements in connectivity provide the largest payoff in merchandise trade, and the spillovers could facilitate trade with third countries. These estimates are based on existing trade patterns, and therefore, represent a lower bound of the potential increase in Bangladesh's exports arising from an FTA. The potential gains from trade with India under SAFTA are only likely to be realized through joint efforts to reduce nontariff barriers to trade, especially with respect to standards and the transaction costs at and behind the border. Working toward mutual recognition of product standards should constitute a priority. Likewise, joint efforts to address procedural delays at the land borders can enhance trade relations. Chapters 5 and 6, on standards and trade facilitation, provide concrete recommendations on measures that can facilitate trade between the two partners. Furthermore, the experience of the India-Sri Lanka FTA shows that, beyond the exchange of preferences, the agreement has provided a "boost of confidence" in the private sector, resulting in substantial new investments by India in Sri Lanka's service sectors (box 3.4).

A bilateral FTA between Bangladesh and India should incorporate services. Steps that can reap immediate benefits include dismantling barriers to entry of service suppliers and users, which would help to formalize education and health-related areas. In India and Bangladesh, easing entry conditions and encouraging formal movement of students, for example by issuing long-term multiple-entry visas, can boost cross-border student traffic. The Bangladeshi government should help Indian universities and educational institutions set up branches in major cities in Bangladesh. Facilitating temporary movement of health, education, and information and communications technology (ICT) professionals could benefit services trade and help lay a framework for deeper integration. These steps could also attract more investment from India. Whether investment ventures were 100 percent Indian or joint ventures, they would help improve Bangladesh's export supply capability and boost exports to the region and the outside world.

Lagging border regions of Bangladesh, among the poorest in South Asia, need to be part of the new market expansion to help reduce poverty. In Bangladesh, the border districts tend to have lower than average per capita income, higher than average poverty, and poorer human development. Weak regional cooperation has hurt the poor more than other segments of the population. Regions

---

Box 3.4 India-Sri Lanka Free Trade Agreement

Sri Lanka's regional trade, particularly with India, has undergone a significant increase compared with regional neighbors. Sri Lanka's share of intraregional imports rose from 11 percent in 2000 to 23 percent in 2008, and its export share rose at a higher rate, from 2.7 percent in 2000 to 8.5 percent in 2008 (Pitigala 2010). Since the India-Sri Lanka Free Trade Agreement (ISLFTA), Sri Lanka's bilateral exports with India, traditionally small, have soared compared with the other non-landlocked countries and relative to growth levels of Indian overall imports.

There are several reasons behind the success. ISLFTA, although principally an agreement on trade in goods, boosted services trade and foreign direct investment (FDI). For example, India joined the top five providers of FDI, with cumulative investment of US$1 billion since 2003 and a lot more on the way. A liberal bilateral aviation regime between the two countries has meant that Indian tourists account for one-fifth of Sri Lanka's total foreign arrivals. And 70 percent of business at the Port of Colombo is accounted for by cargo to and from India.[a]

The scope of product coverage was enhanced by a "negative list" approach. And a faster pace of implementation was used. For example, within three years of signing, duty-free access was granted by India on 81 percent of the agreed items and similar reciprocity was pursued by Sri Lanka. Rules of origin were simplified. In practice, for India, ISLFTA is more liberal than the South Asian Free Trade Area (SAFTA), given the somewhat lower domestic value added criterion. For Sri Lanka, with the exception of the products subject to specific rules of origin under SAFTA, both agreements provide for a similar level of market access, although ISLFTA provides a more favorable framework for production sharing with India through the cumulative rules.

Source: Dasgupta, Pitigala, and Gourdon 2012.
a. See Manjula Fernando, "Bilateral Relations have Expanded Manifold - Outgoing Indian High Commissioner," *Sunday Observer,* May 13, 2013, at http://www.sundayobserver.lk/2013/05/12/fea04.asp.

---

that share a border with India are largely disconnected from the national economy and lack the market linkages and infrastructure to formalize trade. Alternative bilateral and regional mechanisms, including cross-border bazaars and related facilities, can operate in parallel with FTAs to extend local market opportunities. Cross-border trade—defined as the flow of goods and services up to 30 kilometers across international land borders—is important to the prosperity of border communities.

The *haat* program (a *haat* is a border trading area or bazaar) helps to ease the movement of goods and people across the India-Bangladesh border. The *haat* program should be expanded beyond its harvest-time trade in subsistence farming products, and the 10-mile limit of trading should be expanded. This would encourage the development of post-harvest infrastructure that would reduce harvest waste and increase returns to local communities. Participation in bazaars should be made easier (for example, through visa-free entry). Both governments should explore replicating the Korgas model for existing and new *haats* (box 3.5).

Box 3.5 Historical Role of Bazaars

Bazaars have played a vital and historical role along the India-Bangladesh border. Bazaar trading is the primary channel for cross-border trade in many regions. In 2011, the Governments of Bangladesh and India revived the border bazaar concept and opened a pilot *haat* near the Kurigram-Meghalaya border. Additional bazaars were subsequently opened, which are permitted to sell local agricultural and horticultural products, spices, minor forest products (excluding timber), fresh and dry fish, dairy and poultry products, cottage industry items, wooden furniture, and handloom and handicraft items. All sales are exempt from local taxes. By strengthening commercial ties, promoting cultural understanding, and deepening community relationships, cross-border trade nurtures amicable border relations.

Geographical and sales restrictions, however, should be relaxed. This would help create economies of scale, and encourage a post-harvest infrastructure to reduce wastage and increase returns to local communities. Although the *haat* program is a step in the right direction, it currently provides limited opportunities for local communities to expand beyond subsistence farming and toward sustainable trade development. Under existing rules, production must come from a small radius (5–10 kilometers)—within which there is little industry on the Bangladesh side of the border—and sales are limited to US$50 per person. The experience of other border bazaars suggests that relaxed entry procedures for vendors and buyers, and tariff rate quotas on small quantities, could encourage the growth of the *haat*. Such policies and facilities could provide needed services, expand the reach of local markets, create a direct stimulus for income generation and employment, and reduce poverty among households and small businesses in the border regions. This would promote the transition from subsistence-level farming to small-scale commercial farming.

The Korgas bazaar, on the Kazakhstan-China border, is an exemplary case study. It is one of the region's largest cross-border bazaars, servicing some 1,300 traders per day. The bilateral regime allows visa-free entry for traders entering for the day and limited duty-free privileges (on up to US$1,000 of cargo, with a flat rate applied thereafter). On the Kazakhstan side of the border, cross-border trading has become the most important source of employment in Jarkent, the largest border city in the district. Conservative estimates indicate that 10 percent of the local population works directly in cross-border trade activities. Estimates suggest that each trader generates employment for an additional one to two persons engaged in warehousing, local transport, or sales within the bazaar. The existence of the bazaar has generated spillover effects, creating new retail and other commercial opportunities (Kaminiski and Mitra 2010).

Integrating into Production-Sharing Networks

Bangladesh has yet to exploit regional production-sharing potential. Beyond the static comparisons of complementarity, there is much greater potential for Bangladesh to integrate with global manufacturing (and services) value chains at the labor-intensive stage. Countries are now increasingly engaged in production sharing as a means of product and market diversification (Pitigala 2010). As suggested by Sally (2010), Bangladesh has failed to insert itself into global manufacturing supply chains, processing trade supply chains, and ICT supply chains (beyond textiles and garments). The drivers of global trade go beyond relative factor endowments, to factors such as complementary use of ICT and natural geographies (clustering, agglomeration, and scale effects). The effects can be powerful enough to increase trade impacts by a factor of two or more (Hoekman and Nicita 2008). To replicate its RMG success, Bangladesh needs to address the fundamental drivers of global chains, such as lowering the trade costs and barriers to services. Regional services and cross-border investment in services can be a powerful engine for easing these constraints endogenously. Recent evidence has established a two-way relationship between regional agreements and production sharing (Orefice and Rocha 2011). The results show that, on average, "deep" trade agreements increase production-sharing–related trade between member countries by approximately 35 percent, with the highest impacts in the automotive, information, and technology product sectors.

Tariffs are an important determinant of the success of firms engaged in production sharing. For example, a 1 percent reduction in the customs duty is associated with a 0.3 percent increase in exports. Bangladeshi firm-level data for 2008–10 are used to examine how customs and supplementary duties impede exports. Total figures are calculated for each firm for export and import variables. Exports are regressed on various import impediment variables, such as customs duties, supplementary duties, and controls for the customs value of total imports. Import exemptions (such as duty drawback and export processing zones) are introduced as dummy variables.[9] The results are an attempt to measure import impediments at the border that may have an effect on exports. Figure 3.6 displays the relationship between customs duties paid (excluding other taxes) and exports.

Figure 3.6 Customs Duties versus Level of Exports in Bangladesh

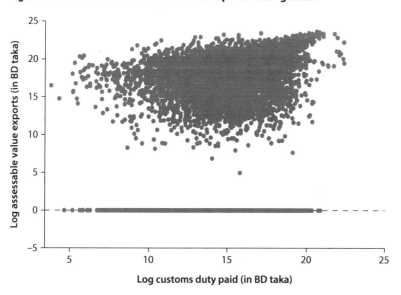

Source: Calculations based on Bangladesh Customs data.

Strengthening Competitiveness in Bangladesh—Thematic Assessment
http://dx.doi.org/10.1596/978-1-4648-0898-2

The regression results show that the level of customs duty has a strong negative effect on firms engaged in production sharing—that is, firms reporting imports and exports (annex 3A). The customs duty rate and supplementary duty rate also have a negative, but statistically insignificant, relationship to firm-level exports. As expected, exemptions from applicable duties have a strong positive relationship to exports (see tables 3A.1, 3A.2, and 3A.3 in annex 3A).

Demographic shifts and rising labor costs in China create opportunities for production sharing. While China and India are rapidly emerging as potential new markets for regional exports—including from Bangladesh—large demographic shifts in the region, especially in China, are expected to create new patterns of production and trade within existing global production networks. China emerged in the 1990s as a low-cost manufacturing powerhouse, driven by special economic zones, open coastal cities, and other incentive regimes; it had a comparative advantage in labor-intensive manufacturing, particularly basic assembly operations. However, this advantage is being rapidly eroded because of the country's slow population growth and rising wage pressures. China, like most countries in the East Asia region, is expected to experience a decline in the working age population. As population growth slows in China, the hardest hit will be the lower skilled labor market, which had already begun to shrink in 2004. In 2010, more than four million low-skilled workers entered the labor force. By 2020, new entrants in this segment will shrink to 1.5 million (figure 3.7). Hence, the comparative advantage of the economy will skew toward higher-skilled intensive manufacturing and services.

China's increasing labor costs are creating new opportunities for Bangladesh. With the shrinking labor pool, wages have increased by 15–25 percent per year since 2005 in key manufacturing and business centers, putting cost pressure on lower value–added activities in China's production chains (figure 3.8). China is expected to continue its shift toward more skill-intensive production and services. Thus, lower-wage destinations have a historic opportunity to break into the global production networks and capture a share of China's traditionally labor-intensive manufacturing industries, such as clothing, footwear, and basic electronics assembly. Moreover, while China's interior and western provinces offer an abundance of lower-cost and skilled labor, other low-wage countries in Asia, particularly those with growing labor forces (the so-called "demographic dividend"), have an opportunity to benefit from China's demographic shift.

Two factors might prevent Bangladesh from fully exploiting spillovers from China's rising wages. First, although average wages in Bangladesh are on par with other low-wage countries in Southeast Asia, Bangladesh will be at a disadvantage with the implementation of the China-ASEAN FTA, which will immediately benefit low-income countries, such as Cambodia and Vietnam (figure 3.9). Second, rising labor costs in China are offset, to some degree, by its increasing productivity and the availability of supply chains in China that may not be easily replicated by Bangladesh, except in the textiles and apparel sector. Nevertheless, there is anecdotal evidence that some opportunities will

Figure 3.7 Trends in Labor Population Growth in China, 2004–20

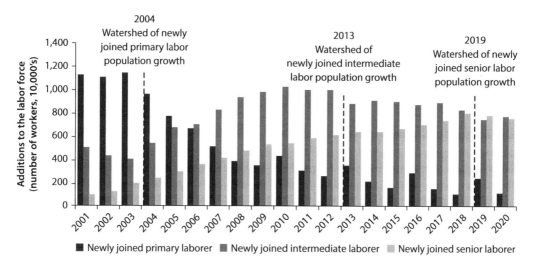

Source: NBS, Ministry of Education, World Bank Group, UN DESA Population Division, and Deloitte China Manufacturing Competitiveness Study 2011.

Note: Newly joined primary labors: 16-year-old first-time laborers at junior secondary educational levels or below; newly joined intermediate labors: 19-year-old first-time laborers at senior secondary educational or equivalent levels; but lower than tertiary or equivalent levels; newly joined senior labors: 22-year-old first-time laborers at tertiary or above educational levels.

Figure 3.8 Rising Wages in Key Geographic Nodes in China, 1985–2010

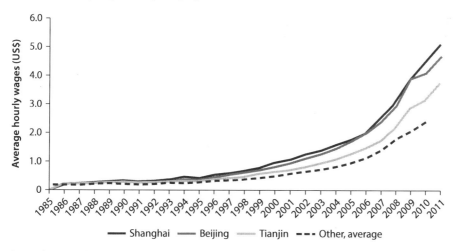

Source: China National Bureau of Statistics.

Figure 3.9 Average Hourly Labor Costs, FY2010/11

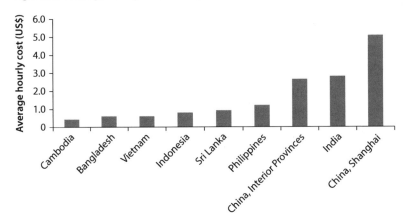

Sources: Bangladesh Export Processing Zone Authority; China National Bureau of Statistics; Economist Intelligence Unit.

arise, such as the case of a wire manufacturer that moved to Bangladesh from China. In any case, the private sector and the Government of Bangladesh need to devise a coherent strategy to exploit such opportunities.

Bangladesh has begun export diversification, albeit slowly, which could lead to new opportunities in major industrial markets. Through an initiative of the German Society for International Cooperation, the country looked at a set of nontraditional markets that could be reached by diversifying the RMG portfolio, including Brazil; Hong Kong SAR, China; Japan; the Russian Federation; South Africa; and Turkey. The markets vary in size, domestic competitiveness, climatic zone, and geographical proximity. In 2008, these countries' combined market in woven apparel was US$35 billion and accounted for 64 percent of total imports from nontraditional countries. Japan's recent relaxation of its GSP rules of origin has already provided a boost to RMG exports. Other exports, such as seafood, are at a nascent stage, constrained by fairly stringent quality and safety requirements. Bangladesh can benefit from Canada's Least Developed Country Initiative (LCDI), launched in 2003, as the quality standards are similar to those in the United States.[10] In the case of other products, like shrimp, additional measures will be needed to realize the opportunities created by the LDCI including quality that complies with Canadian product standards. There is no evidence that Canadian standards are unnecessarily high relative to those of the European Union and the United States.

Export Promotion in Bangladesh

Bangladesh's Export Promotion Bureau can play a critical role in strategically promoting exports. Countries increasingly rely on specialized agencies such as the EPB in implementing export strategies, designed principally to assist and encourage domestic firms to export goods and services and increase their foreign sales. Various methodologies have been used to study the role and effectiveness of export promotion agencies (EPAs)[11]; although country-specific studies offer valuable insights, they cannot be generalized. The World Bank's global survey of EPAs provides a rich source of information for analysis. This section briefly summarizes the key issues and performance of Bangladesh's EPB. It then compares the EPB with other EPAs through a set of key criteria, including structure, responsibilities, strategic objectives, resources and expenditures, and monitoring and evaluation systems (Lederman, Olarreaga, and Payton 2010).

The EPB could improve its effectiveness by giving the private sector more representation on its board, given empirical research that shows that such representation increases EPA efficacy (Lederman, Olarreaga, and Payton 2010). Like many EPAs, the EPB is an autonomous agency, financed by the public sector; however, the EPB has less private sector representation on its board (28 percent) compared with EPAs in countries with similar income (at least 40 percent). Moreover, the EPB's board has 14 members, higher than the world and regional average of 10 board members. The efficacy of EPAs seems to rise with public funding, but there is no evidence of increased performance with a specific legal status.

The EPB has a broad mandate with limited resources. Apart from the main functions of export and investment promotion, the EPB oversees export financing and tourism promotion. EPAs often have more than one responsibility, but promotion of tourism is usually not mentioned by other EPAs. The synergies between export promotion and investment attraction are more evident than with tourism promotion—with the exception of country image-building, an activity in which the EPB is not engaged.

The EPB's strategic objectives are much more narrowly defined than typical EPAs. Like all EPAs surveyed, the EPB is principally focused on product and market promotion. Generally, market diversification takes precedence over product diversification for most EPAs. It is not uncommon for modern EPAs to engage in strategic objectives, such as the attraction of export-oriented multinationals, the development of clusters, and inclusion in global supply chains. However, the EPB did not rank any of these strategies (value chain, clusters, or attraction of multinationals) in its response to the World Bank's survey. Given the shifting global dynamics of manufacturing, including the demographic deficit and ensuing costs in China, the EPB could be in a pivotal position to devise strategies through brand image to prop up relative country advantage and exploit production-sharing opportunities.

Image building and policy advocacy are strong functions in many EPAs, but not in Bangladesh. The EPB seems to be pursuing its objectives mainly through marketing services, which account for 50–75 percent of its budget. Less than 10 percent of its budget is allocated to technical assistance and country image-building. The effectiveness of marketing services is undetermined because the

EPB does not conduct formal follow-up with its clients or track key performance indicators. By contrast, about 80 percent of the surveyed EPAs have a formal process to follow up with clients that received assistance from them and the same share of EPAs reported having their own impact measurement mechanisms. The EPB monitors four key performance indicators: client satisfaction, number of exporters, value of exports, and number of clients. Some EPAs invest a small amount (10 percent or less of budget) on policy advocacy aimed at improving the business environment and access to foreign markets. However, the EPB is not involved in such activities. Lederman, Olarreaga, and Payton (2010) find that EPAs seem to be more effective at improving the business environment when they advocate for the removal of trade barriers abroad or when they help correct information asymmetries resulting from a large share of heterogeneous goods in the export bundle.

The EPB, with an average budget of US$3.1 million, spends slightly less than EPAs in Asian countries and LDCs in general. Survey data analysis shows a positive correlation between the budgets of EPAs and the level of exports of the country (figure 3.10), as well as the number of products the country exports (Lederman, Olarreaga, and Payton 2010). The EPB spends 50–75 percent of its budget on the garments, leather, and textiles sector (table 3.12). This pattern seems to be aligned with EPB's strategic objective (as of 2010) of diversifying exports by encouraging new destinations. However, the EPB aims to diversify exports by encouraging new products, including pharmaceutical products, ICT, ship building, and leather footwear. The relative concentration of expenditures on the garments, leather, and textiles sector seems to contradict the priority objective of promoting the exports of all sectors.

Figure 3.10 Correlation between EPA Spending and Export Volume

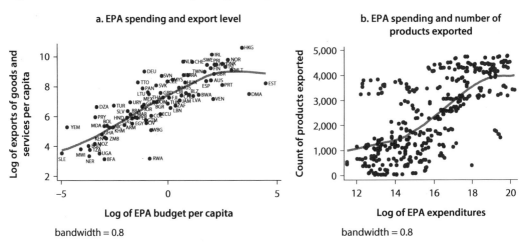

Source: Lederman, Olarreaga, and Payton 2010.
Note: Lowess smoother applied to scatterplots (bandwidth = 0.8). EPA = export promotion agency.

Table 3.12 Budget Allocations in EPAs

Sector	Share of total spending (%)		Number of respondents
	Mean	Bangladesh	
Agriculture, agro-industry, and animal products	10–25	0	67
Garments/leather/textiles	~10	50–75	65
Other manufactures	~10	0	60
Machinery	~10	10–25	64
IT services	~10	0	65
Skill-intensive IT services	~5	0	63
Tourism	~5	0	62
Other	~5	0	56

Source: World Bank survey of export promotion agencies.
Note: EPA = export promotion agency; IT = information technology.

Recommendations

Augmenting competitiveness should be the basis for greater and durable market access. Preferential market access in Bangladesh's primary export markets, such as the European Union and the United States, is determined unilaterally by their partners. This puts Bangladesh at a disadvantage in terms of influencing the level of preferential access. Coalition building to influence duty-free and quota-free access for LDCs in the U.S. market may continue as a supplementary effort rather than the norm. At the same time, Bangladesh's ambition of attaining middle-income status while maintaining higher protection is at odds with its continued reliance on LDC status as a means of securing market access. A more forward-looking, sustainable strategy would focus on robust interventions in Bangladesh to reduce logistics costs, eliminate anti-export biases in tariffs and tax policy, and improve the regulatory environment to facilitate investment. Such actions are a more sustainable means to overcome Bangladesh's preferential disadvantage in U.S. and EU markets and ensure long-term competitiveness in the RMG and non-RMG sectors.

Bangladesh should diversify export markets beyond the European Union and the United States to incorporate other Organization for Economic Co-operation and Development (OECD) countries and LMICs. Bangladesh's marketing activities are largely focused on the European Union and the United States. The new export diversification agenda should focus on OECD countries, including Canada and Japan, and LDCs, including Brazil, India, South Africa, and Turkey. Bangladesh's exports to other LDCs are more diversified than its exports to high-income countries. One of the primary barriers to new export market discovery is the lack of adequate market information (including market entry requirements, prospective buyers, and so forth), especially for small and medium enterprises. The costs of gathering information about opportunities in new export markets may be very high for a low-income country, as only a few of its firms will export to that new market at first. Any rents will be captured by new entrants. The EPB can play a critical role in this respect by collecting and disseminating market information as a public good—but it currently lacks adequate capacity.

Bangladesh should explore opportunities for production sharing beyond the RMG sector. Shifting production and trade patterns have created opportunities for new, low-cost entrants into existing global production-sharing networks that link the dominant Asian exporters. Bangladesh's potential entry into such networks depends on various factors. Recommendations include steps to improve the effectiveness of port logistics and reduce tariff barriers to improve the allocation of resources, reduce transactions costs, and increase participation in global value chains. These policy measures should be backed by a coherent image-building effort to highlight Bangladesh's comparative advantage in labor-intensive manufacturing.

The efficacy and capabilities of EPB should be improved. Increasing the number of private sector representatives on the board from four to seven will bring EPB close to the global average for private sector seats (50 percent). EPB should consider including representatives from beyond the traditional RMG sector to include the "new sectors" toward which Bangladesh aims to diversify (such as pharmaceuticals, shipbuilding, ICT, and leather footwear). EPB could address a current weakness by establishing a formal, in-house monitoring and evaluation mechanism to follow up with its clients, track key performance indicators, and monitor the export outcomes of trade missions. With the data collected, it will be possible to target the most relevant trade fairs in terms of export contracts signed.

Stronger commercial intelligence and diplomacy could help unlock opportunities in market access negotiations. There is consensus that the capacity for commercial diplomacy is weak among key officials in Bangladesh.[12] Commercial diplomacy is an area that complements the training needs addressed in chapter 4, on institutions. The targeted audience for commercial diplomacy typically constitutes senior officials (directors, secretaries, and commercial officers) of the institutions most directly engaged in negotiations, such as the Ministry of Commerce, Ministry of Foreign Affairs, Bangladesh Tariff Commission, and Bangladesh Foreign Trade Institute. A more comprehensive audience for commercial diplomacy (as conducted in India) includes chambers, key business officials, and think tanks—all stakeholders engaged in interministerial subcommittees on market access negotiations. Bangladesh can benefit, in the interim, from training programs targeted at key government agencies. A number of reputed international institutes, such as the Institute for Trade and Commercial Diplomacy and the World Trade Institute, specialize in the development of training materials in commercial diplomacy. The training generally entails a modular form and should cover, at a minimum, the following elements: (a) provide a comprehensive perspective of the global economic system and how it affects trade and investment flows; (b) explain principles and processes of commercial diplomacy and contrast with traditional diplomacy; (c) impart basic negotiation skills; (d) provide exposure to negotiation processes through conducting real case analysis and simulation of trade negotiations; and (e) explain the nuances involved in drafting an effective resolution or agreement.

Annex 3A: Regression Results

Table 3A.1 OLS Panel, Exporters and Nonexporters

Variable	Ln_exports
lnCustom_Value	1.325***
	(−0.0877)
lnCustoms_Duty	−0.304***
	(−0.0751)
CD_Rate	−0.0044
	(−0.0188)
SD_Rate	−0.000151
	(−0.0007)
Exemption	1.993***
	(−0.213)
Constant	−9.232***
	(−0.999)
Observations	7,750
R-squared	0.094

Source: World Bank calculations.
Note: Standard errors in are parentheses. CD = customs duty; SD = supplementary duty.
*** $p < .01$.

Table 3A.2 Regression Results, Exporters

Variable	Ln_Exports
lnCustom_Value	1.223***
	(−0.0876)
lnCustoms_Duty	−0.239***
	(−0.0734)
CD_Rate	0.127***
	(−0.0205)
SD_Rate	−0.0000724
	(−0.000847)
Exemption	1.753***
	(−0.213)
Constant	−10.23***
	(−1.025)
Observations	6,792
R-squared	0.098

Source: World Bank calculations.
Note: Standard errors in are parentheses. CD = customs duty; SD = supplementary duty.
*** $p < .01$.

Table 3A.3　Assessable Value of Exports, 2008–10

Variable	LnAssessableValue_ex		
	2008	2009	2010
lnCustom_Value	1.439***(−0.153)	1.289***(−0.153)	1.243***(−0.15)
lnCustoms_Duty	−0.621***(−0.13)	−0.169(−0.133)	−0.148(−0.128)
CD_Rate	0.0281(−0.0238)	−0.227*(−0.12)	0.02(−0.0376)
SD_Rate	0.000159(−0.00111)	0.00641(−0.00472)	−0.000695(−0.00114)
Exemption	1.481***(−0.371)	2.557***(−0.372)	1.991***(−0.363)
Constant	−7.132***(−1.641)	−5.27(−3.307)	−11.11***(−1.745)
Observations	2,570	2,501	2,679
R-squared	0.07	0.111	0.095

Source: World Bank calculations.
Note: Standard errors in are parentheses. CD = customs duty; SD = supplementary duty.
*** $p < .01$, * $p < .1$.

Notes

1. The 4 percent threshold can be a significant advantage, particularly in manufacturing sectors. However, the threshold may not be precise, given inter-sector variation and the impact of similar preferences can vary depending on the product concerned. It is, nevertheless, considered as sufficiently indicative. The justification is highlighted in a recent European Commission study (2011, 75–76), which finds that preferences are being used significantly although preference margins are low.

2. However, there is a de minimis waiver. The president has the discretion to waive the competitive-need limits if total imports of the United States in that category from all countries (both GSP eligible and ineligible) do not exceed US$16.5 million.

3. Bangladesh continued to enjoy GSP benefits until these were suspended in June 2013.

4. Under the Earned Import Allowance Program, Haitian producers, for every two square meter equivalents of qualifying fabric purchased or manufactured for apparel production in Haiti, can earn one square meter equivalent credit that allows duty-free treatment for imports of apparel manufactured in Haiti with non-qualifying fabric.

5. The countries include Afghanistan, Bangladesh, Bhutan, Cambodia, Kiribati, the Lao People's Democratic Republic, the Maldives, Nepal, Samoa, Sri Lanka, the Solomon Islands, Timor-Leste, Tuvalu, Vanuatu, and the Republic of Yemen.

6. Bangladesh has concluded trading agreements with Afghanistan, Albania, Algeria, the Arab Republic of Egypt, Belarus, Bhutan, Brazil, Bulgaria, Cambodia, China, the former Czechoslovakia, the Democratic People's Republic of Korea, Germany, Hungary, India, Indonesia, the Islamic Republic of Iran, Iraq, Kenya, Kuwait, Libya, Malaysia, Mali, Morocco, Myanmar, Nepal, Pakistan, the Philippines, Poland, Romania, Senegal, Sri Lanka, Sudan, Thailand, Turkey, Uganda, Ukraine, the United Arab Emirates, Uzbekistan, Vietnam, the former Yugoslavia, Zambia, and Zimbabwe.

7. The trade complementarity index (TCI) can provide useful information on prospects for intraregional trade. It shows how well the structures of a country's imports and exports match. Furthermore, countries considering the formation of a regional trade agreement can examine the TCI values of others that have formed or tried to form similar arrangements. The TCI between countries k and j is defined as:

$TCij = 100 - sum(|m_{ik} - X_{ij}|/2)$, where X_{ij} is the share of good i in global exports of country j and m_{ik} is the share of good i in all imports of country k. The index is zero when no goods are exported by one country or imported by the other, and 100 when the export and import shares exactly match.

8. To capture the improvement in connectivity, a 25 percent drop in the bilateral trade-cost margin between Bangladesh and India is simulated.

9. Exemptions conferred by preferential trade agreements were excluded from the analysis to focus specifically on domestic exemption policies.

10. Canada improved market access for LDCs by abolishing all tariffs and quotas on imports from LDCs, with the exception of dairy, poultry, and eggs. The scheme also offers generous rules of origin.

11. These include qualitative case studies (Kotabe and Czinkota 1992); econometric analysis with cross-country data (Lederman, Olarreaga, and Payton 2010); and, more recently, impact evaluation methods with firm-level data for specific countries (Cadot and Gourdon 2012; Volpe 2011; Volpe and Carballo 2010).

12. Commercial diplomacy is defined as the application of the tools of diplomacy to the removal of barriers to trade and investment, and to the resolution of policy conflicts arising from the globalization of the world economy.

References

Bhattacharya, D., M. Rahman, and A. Raihan. 2004. "The EU-EBA Initiative: Market Access Implications and Potential Benefits for Bangladesh." CPD Working Paper 43. Centre for Policy Dialogue, Dhaka.

Cadot, O., and J. Gourdon. 2012. "Bangladesh Trade Performance and Incentives." Background paper for Bangladesh Diagnostic Trade Integration Study, World Bank, Washington, DC.

Dasgupta, D., N. Pitigala, and J. Gourdon. 2012. "South Asia's Economic Prospects from Global Rebalancing and Integration." In *Economic Reform Processes in South Asia: Toward Policy Efficiency*, edited by Philippa Dee. New York: Routledge.

De, P., S. Raihan, and S. Kathuria. 2012. "Unlocking Bangladesh-India Trade, Emerging Potential and the Way Forward." Policy Research Working Paper 6155, World Bank, Washington, DC.

European Commission. 2011. "Proposal for a Regulation on the European Parliament and of the Council Applying a Scheme of Generalised Tariff Preferences. Impact Assessment Volume I." Commission Staff Working Paper SEC 536, European Commission, Brussels.

Francois., J., P. Rana, and G. Wignaraja, eds. 2009. *Pan-Asian Integration: Linking East and South Asia*. Basingstoke, United Kingdom: Palgrave MacMillan.

Hoekman, B., and A. Nicita. 2008. "Trade Policy, Trade Costs, and Developing Country Trade." Policy Research Working Paper 4797, World Bank, Washington, DC.

Kaminiski, Bartlomiej, and Saumya Mitra. 2010. *Skeins of Silk: Borderless Bazaars and Border Trade in Central Asia*. Washington, DC: World Bank.

Kotabe, Massaki, and Michael Czinkota. 1992. "State Government Promotion of Manufacturing Exports: A Gap Analysis." *Journal of International Business Studies* 23 (4): 637–58.

Lederman, D., M. Olarreaga, and L. Payton. 2010. "Export Promotion Agencies Revisited." *Journal of Development Economics* 91: 257–65.

Ng, Francis, and Alexander Yeats. 2003. "Major Trade Trends in East Asia: What Are Their Implications for Regional Cooperation and Growth?" Policy Research Working Paper 3084, World Bank, Washington, DC.

Orefice, G., and N. Rocha. 2011. "Deep Integration and Production Networks: An Empirical Analysis." Staff Working Paper ERSD-2011-11, Economic Research and Statistics Division, World Trade Organization, Geneva.

Pitigala, N. 2010. "Economic Crisis and Developing Countries: The Role of Vertical Specialization." *South Asia Economic Journal* 11 (1): 1–20.

Raihan, S. 2010. "Welfare and Poverty Impacts of Trade Liberalization: A Dynamic CGE Microsimulation Analysis." *International Journal of Microsimulation* 3 (1): 123–26.

Sally, Razeen. 2010. "Regional Economic Integration in Asia: The Track Record and Prospects." Occasional Paper 2/2010, RECIPE, London School of Economics.

USTR (Office of the United States Trade Representative). 2011. "Generalized System of Preferences (GSP): Notice of Review of Certain Pending Country Practice Petitions." *Federal Register* 76 (238).

Volpe, C. 2011. "Assessing the Impacts of Trade Promotion Interventions: Where Do We Stand?" In *Where to Spend the Next Million? Applying Impact Evaluation to Trade Assistance*, edited by O. Cadot, A. Fernandes, J. Gourdon, and A. Mattoo, 39–80. Washington, DC: World Bank and CEPR.

Volpe, C., and J. Carballo. 2010. "Beyond the Average Effects: The Distributional Impacts of Export Promotion Programs in Developing Countries." *Journal of Development Economics* 92: 201–14.

CHAPTER 4

Leveraging Institutions for Trade Development

Nihal Pitigala

Introduction

Policy makers confront an increasingly larger and more complex trade agenda. National decisions on trade policy involve a range of public institutions and agencies, all of which need to work together to address the challenges posed by the new trade agenda and ensure that policies contribute to development. Continuous consultation and consensus building among ministries and agencies involved in trade policy making and negotiations are essential for effectively responding to opportunities and challenges presented in the international trading environment. Furthermore, the consultative process needs to be broad-based as a prerequisite for good economic governance.

Although Bangladesh's Sixth Five-Year Plan and Vision 2021 recognize the critical role of trade and export diversification for economic development, actual policies are often at odds with this overall vision. This can be attributed, at least in part, to the fact that trade policy is carried out through a number of institutions in a piecemeal fashion. This fragmentation is exacerbated by the absence of a national trade strategy that could otherwise provide an overarching mandate in the formulation of each institution's individual policies. There is a lack of adequate recognition of how economy-wide costs of protective trade barriers, and other domestic policies have potentially countervailing effects on other policies designed to promote industrialization and exports. The development of an effective trade policy architecture that addresses these effects requires an efficient, capable institutional structure and coordination mechanisms.

This chapter has three main objectives. First, it assesses the process of policy making and implementation (including interagency coordination), identifies gaps and frictions that exist in the system, and assesses the capacities of existing organizations to undertake their mandated functions. Second, it suggests actionable interventions in terms of an effective institutional framework. Third, it elaborates on the associated capacity-building efforts that are required to support effective trade policy formulation and implementation.

The key messages of this chapter are the following:

- Trade policy considerations have been dominated by fiscal ones in the process of tariff setting.
- There is no uniform model of trade policy formulation. However, effective structures should allow good-quality interagency coordination, consultation among stakeholders, and research and evaluation.
- For interagency coordination, a merger of the export and import policy wings and strong coordination with the Ministry of Industries could significantly improve the consistency of trade policy. This should also help balance exporting and domestic production interests.
- Widening stakeholder consultations and making them more transparent can improve the acceptability and efficacy of trade policy. A high-level competitiveness council or similar body can help to embed trade policy in a competitiveness agenda. The existing Business Initiative Leading Development (BUILD) framework can be used to address trade-related regulatory issues. Open and transparent tools should be used to widen and legitimize stakeholder consultations.
- Strengthened research and analysis of trade policy formulation and the impact of trade policies would require the following actions: (a) involving think tanks throughout the policy-making lifecycle and (b) building up the capacity of the Ministry of Commerce (MOC) for basic research and strengthening it through the appointment of an economic advisor to help direct trade policy formulation, engage with think tanks, and so forth.
- Capacity-building efforts should focus on key institutions. Within MOC, providing trade-related training, moving staff positions from administration to trade-related wings, and providing in-house legal capability are priorities. The Bangladesh Foreign Trade Institute (BFTI) can be developed as a training institution. The Bangladesh Tariff Commission (BTC) could focus on antidumping and safeguard issues.

Trade Policy Institutions

Trade policy formulation in Bangladesh is fragmented. Policies are not linked and there is not a clearly defined focal point for implementing a unified framework (table 4.1). In terms of the official mandate, the principal responsibility of domestic and international trade in Bangladesh rests with MOC. The Imports and Exports (Control) Act of 1950 empowers MOC to regulate the import and export of goods and services. MOC regulation proceeds through a periodic Import Policy Order that encompasses a range of nontariff barriers (NTBs) (such as quotas, import controls, and licensing) and export policy that provides for incentives and other schemes. In addition, MOC is the focal point of bilateral, multilateral, and regional negotiations and for ensuring Bangladesh's compliance with World Trade Organization (WTO) agreements, including dumping, safeguards, and countervailing duties. MOC implements the policies through a

Table 4.1 Bangladesh's Institutions and Their Mandated Roles and Responsibilities, 2012

Trade policy measure	Primary policy/instrument	Primary agency responsible
Tariffs	Fiscal	MOF (NBR)
Nontariff barriers (quotas, licensing, etc.)	Import Policy Order	MOC
Subsidies	Export policy, textile policy, industrial policy	MOC/NBR/MOTJ/MOI
Standards (SPS/TBT)	Technical standards, food safety and animal health standards, Import Policy Order	MOI (BSTI)/MOC/MOHFW/MOA
Antidumping and trade remedies	Antidumping and safeguard rules under the Customs Act	MOC (BTC)
Market access (WTO, RTA, etc.)	Export policy	MOC
Trade in services	None	No focal point

Source: World Bank compilation.

Note: BSTI = Bangladesh Standards and Testing Institute; BTC = Bangladesh Tariff Commission; MOA = Ministry of Agriculture; MOC = Ministry of Commerce; MOF = Ministry of Finance; MOHFW = Ministry of Health and Family Welfare; MOI = Ministry of Industries; MOTJ = Ministry of Textile and Jute; NBR = National Board of Revenue; RTA = regional trade agreements; SPS = sanitary and phytosanitary standards; TBT = technical barriers to trade; WTO = World Trade Organization.

number of agencies under its purview: BTC, the Export Promotion Bureau (EPB), the Office of the Chief Controller of Imports and Exports, BFTI, the Trading Corporation of Bangladesh, and the Business Promotion Council.

Under the Ministry of Industries, the Bangladesh Standards and Testing Institute (BSTI) is the main body on technical standards, and the Department of Patent Designs and Trademarks deals with patents, industrial designs, and trademarks. Under the Prime Minister's Office, key agencies are the Privatization Commission, the Board of Investment, and the Bangladesh Export Processing Zones Authority. The Ministry of Industries offers a range of incentives under its industrial policy.

The following sections provide a brief overview of MOC, as the focal point of trade policy, and its two primary policy-related agencies, BTC and BFTI, including their organizational structures and staffing capacities.

MOC, as the focal point of trade policy, needs a highly professional and committed staff to make the best use of the evolving opportunities in the multilateral trading system. MOC has a number of wings and cells that are engaged in trade policy making and implementation, each headed by an additional secretary (see figure 4A.1 in annex 4A):

- The *Import & Internal Trade Wing* deals with import-related measures and domestic trade issues, including the periodic Import Policy Order, price controls, and implementation matters related to imports.
- The *Export Wing* is responsible for export policy formulation, export facilitation, engagement in bilateral trade negotiations, export promotion, compliance monitoring, and monitoring of commercial missions abroad. A *Textile Cell*, operating under the Export Wing, deals mainly with textile and apparel export-related issues.
- The *Free Trade Agreement (FTA) Wing* is responsible for bilateral and regional trade agreements and for liaison with international and multilateral trade

organizations (such as the United Nations Conference on Trade and Development [UNCTAD] and the International Trade Centre [ITC]).

- The *World Trade Organization Cell* operates at the same level as the wings and oversees WTO-related negotiations and capacity building for stakeholders on WTO rules and regulations.
- The *Directorate of Trade Organization* is responsible for relationships with trade bodies, including chambers and associations.
- The *Planning Cell* oversees the development and implementation of development projects across MOC, including trade-related programs.

In 2012, there were 38 staff cadres in the primary trade-related wings and cells (excluding the Planning Cell, where staff are not specifically assigned to trade-related programs), including five additional secretaries (heading each wing or cell) and two joint secretaries (Export and FTA Wings only), with a mix of levels in each wing or cell. Although the division and quantity of labor in MOC is logical, covering the primary mandates necessary to design and implement trade policy, several issues related to staffing and capacity impede MOC's effectiveness:

- MOC must adhere to the current civil service rules and regulations that impose mandatory rotations of staff between ministries below the deputy secretary level, leading to a lack of continuity of knowledge and accountability. Staff members, including some senior staff members, are often recruited from academic disciplines with little or no relevance, creating a weak support structure for routine operations and exerting undue pressure on directors and additional secretaries to fulfill various tasks. This necessitates a constant stream of training of officials on trade and commerce at a basic level to maintain the effectiveness of the wings.
- Although training is available, mostly through donor and multilateral programs, there are no guidelines for selecting staff for training; this leads to a mismatch of skills and jobs. In many cases, prestigious foreign training is selected regardless of whether it is aligned with training needs. The benefits of past training have, therefore, been largely unrealized.
- MOC has ongoing needs for trade-related and legal skills to review and draft legislation and regulations. But it is dependent on the Ministry of Law to provide assistance, and there is generally a lack of qualified lawyers that are familiar with trade law.
- Administrative staff numbers are disproportionately large relative to core, technical, trade-related staff. Staff of the Administration Wing has survived previous reforms where many technical departments have been abolished or downsized.

In general, MOC is constrained by lack of data and analytical resources in keeping abreast of developments in WTO and FTA negotiations, providing traders and the public with trade information, and undertaking basic research on trade issues. MOC has a weak data management system for securing and disseminating user-friendly trade data. Furthermore, there was only one statistician on its staff, under the FTA Wing, in 2012.

BTC operates as a statutory organization of the government, with the mandate to protect domestic industries from unfair trade practices and provide overall trade policy guidance. BTC is composed of a chairman and three members, each heading up a functional division (see annex 4A, figure 4A.2) :

- The *Trade Remedies Division* is responsible for adjudicating trade remedies, including antidumping, countervailing duties, and safeguard measures, as well as taking action on sanitary and phytosanitary (SPS) and technical barriers to trade (TBT) measures imposed by trade partners.
- The *Trade Policy Division* is largely designed as an analytical and advisory unit, covering industrial assistance (subsidies and other measures), sector studies, trade policy modeling, monitoring of prices of essential commodities, and other trade policies. A "Monitoring Cell" was established under the Control of Essential Commodities Act, 1956 (Act of 1956) in which BTC acts as a focal point.
- The *International Cooperation Division* advises on bilateral, regional, and multilateral trade agreements. This division conducts feasibility studies on bilateral, regional, and multilateral FTAs according to the government's FTA policy guideline 2010.

Tariff policy, one of the key mandates of BTC, has been marginalized, with the National Board of Revenue (NBR) taking the lead. On bilateral, multilateral, and regional trade negotiations, BTC plays an advisory role through the International Cooperation Division of this commission.

In terms of trade remedies, the rigorous nature of trade remedy investigations and procedures requires a high degree of analytical and legal skills. Currently, BTC has recruited some dedicated officers with an academic background in economics, international relations, computer science and engineering, and business administration, but they lack the specific skills for undertaking trade remedy investigations under WTO rules. Moreover, the Commission does not have any staff with a legal background to supplement the efforts of the Trade Remedy Division.

BFTI was established as a nonprofit research and training institution with the commerce minister as the chairman of a 15-member, public-private board of directors. BFTI is currently a shell organization with a large mandate, covering trade research, training and education, and policy advocacy (see figure 4A.3 in annex 4A). The current organizational chart calls for two fellows, one covering research and one covering training and advocacy, with four research associates shared between them. At the time of the field mission in April 2012, there was only one research fellow on staff. It is not clear whether there were any research associates currently on staff. The lack of capacity means that BFTI engagement in all three of its mandated areas has been minimal in recent years. And because of the public sector compensation levels, it is not clear that BFTI is able to recruit staff with the skills necessary to undertake the level of research that the organization is expected to undertake. BFTI competes for staff with nongovernmental organizations, such as the Bangladesh Institute of Development Studies (BIDS), Centre for Policy Dialogue (CPD), and Policy Research Institute (PRI), which are able to offer more competitive compensation and a more neutral platform for engaging in policy analysis and advice.

Interagency Coordination and Consultation

In addition to staffing and organizational weaknesses, the trade policy–making framework is weakened by a number of coordination issues. (See figure 4.1 for a schematic representation of the process.)

Tariff Policy

Following liberalization of Bangladesh's exchange rate regime and the gradual dismantling of NTBs, tariff policy has become the principal instrument of trade policy in Bangladesh. Although BTC, an autonomous agency under MOC, is mandated to advise on trade policy through its Trade Policy Wing, including tariffs and other import measures, it does not have any powers outside trade remedies. In practice, the Ministry of Finance (MOF), through NBR, takes the lead role in tariff setting in Bangladesh.

Figure 4.1 Trade Policy Formulation and Implementation Process

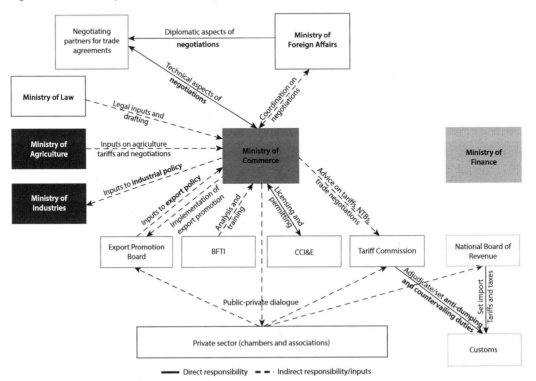

Note: BFTI = Bangladesh Foreign Trade Institute; CCI&E = Chief Controller of Imports and Exports; NTB = nontariff barrier.

The tariff-setting function led by NBR is demonstrably a distinct function in the manner it is being carried out. First, tariff policy is often treated as a subset of fiscal policy by NBR. As a consequence of low domestic revenue mobilization, the orientation of NBR is one of revenue maximization. Second, the tariff-setting process is dominated by the broader budgetary process steered by NBR. There is no forum for consulting on tariff-setting as such. However, the private sector has easy access to NBR and does manage to strongly advocate its case for protection. In the absence of a vibrant and independent counterbalancing force advocating for equity and efficiency, the process of tariff setting is prone to protectionist influences.

Moreover, in recent years, Bangladesh has demonstrated a growing tendency to set nontransparent "para-tariffs," especially supplementary duties, which are imposed on as much as 17 percent of tariff lines (in FY2010/11). Supplementary duties, such as excise duties, are expected to be neutral in their application (applied to domestic and imported goods). However, the NBR Task Force Report 2010 (NBR 2010) recognizes that such supplementary duties are de facto tariffs applied to a number of consumer goods, exacerbating effective protection rates (see chapter 2 on trade policy). The determination of supplementary and regulatory duties is spearheaded by NBR, but as in the case of tariff setting, the process lacks interagency coordination and transparency.

Ad hoc supplementary duties are often imposed as a means of circumventing MOC's role in the administration of contingency trade remedies. MOC, through BTC, is legally empowered under the Bangladesh Tariff Commission Act of 1992 to administer antidumping investigations. In practice, traders apparently opt to bypass the scrutiny of BTC, which must adhere to WTO rules, and turn to NBR to impose additional protective supplementary duties that act as proxy antidumping measures. It is difficult to observe incidences of supplementary duties attributed to circumvented antidumping measures. However, texts from the FY2011/12 MOF budget suggest that the imposition of such duties is linked to the protection of domestic industries (as well as revenue generation) (MOF 2011).

Import Policy

To regulate imports, MOC routinely formulates an Import Policy Order. The development of the Import Policy Order is time bound, and the process starts almost one year before the expiry of the existing policy, which is deemed sufficient for verification of various protective measures.

The current Import Policy Order covers the period 2012–15. It lays out the criteria and conditions for imports, including import controls and import bans; import permits, licenses, and conditions of renewal; standards and specifications set by other agencies—BSTI in the case of TBT, and the Ministry of Agriculture and the Ministry of Health and Family Welfare in the case of SPS measures (as elaborated in the next section and chapter 5 on standards); and preshipment inspection. Coordination in the formulation of the Import Policy Order is complicated by a lack of transparency; weak capacity of MOC and key agencies such as BSTI, the Ministry of Agriculture, and the Ministry of Health and Family Welfare; the lack of analytical rigor in assessing the implications of proposed measures.

First, MOC and its agencies spearhead the process of formulation and implementation of import policy through various consultative committees, and coordination is maintained through meetings at the interministerial committee and cabinet subcommittee levels (see box 4.1). Although a range of private sector stakeholders are consulted, the process is dominated by the large trade associations, including the Bangladesh Garment Manufacturers and Exporters Association and the Bangladesh Knitwear Manufacturers and Exporters Association, as well as the Chambers of Commerce and Industry, membership in which is compulsory for most industries. Other nongovernmental stakeholders (for example, representatives of consumer interests) are missing from the process.

Second, while specialized agencies, such as BSTI, the Ministry of Agriculture, and the Ministry of Health and Family Welfare (on standards) or Bangladesh Bank (on services) are expected to address any technical requirements, NBR approves bans and import restrictions on the basis of revenue concerns. MOC has the authority to reject proposals not consistent with its WTO commitments and other applicable rules. In case of disagreement, the issue is resolved through discussions and consultations. Issuing ministries or organizations have an

---

Box 4.1 Import Policy Formulation

The import policy formulation process begins with the Ministry of Commerce (MOC) and the Office of the Chief Controller of Imports and Exports inviting proposals from stakeholders, including from the private sector through the Chambers of Commerce and Industry. Issues may also be raised autonomously by stakeholders (public and private) seeking amendments to the existing policy as part of the budgetary process.

The agenda and proposals are subsequently tabled (including new measures on import bans) at a consultative committee, chaired by the Minister of Commerce and at times jointly with the president of the Federation of Bangladesh Chambers of Commerce and Industry (FBCCI). The committee generally consists of the FBCCI, Metropolitan Chamber of Commerce and Industry, Dhaka Chamber of Commerce and Industry, Bangladesh Chamber of Commerce and Industry, Malaysia-Bangladesh Chamber of Commerce and Industry, and key ministries (Industries, Agriculture, Finance, Health). Consultation with issue-specific institutions takes place at a subcommittee level, such as on coal standards. MOC consults and receives inputs from the Bangladesh Standards and Testing Institute (BSTI) (although their effectiveness remains unclear because of BSTI's capacity constraints).

The decisions reached are subsequently tabled at a Cabinet Subcommittee on Economic Affairs, which is headed by the finance minister and composed of ministers of trade-related ministries. Before being submitted to the cabinet for approval, the policy is vetted through the Law Ministry.

---

opportunity to propose alternatives and, if acceptable, particularly in terms of international rules, MOC accepts the alternate proposal. Although MOC has not provided information regarding the frequency with which it rejects measures proposed by others, there remains an overall lack of capacity to fully assess the regulatory or economic impact outside whether the measures are aligned with Bangladesh's commitments.

Finally, although the import policy is explicit about the conditions for the removal of restrictions and bans, there are no objective criteria for their imposition (for example, what qualifies as injury to domestic industries). From an institutional standpoint, BTC is mandated with recommending and monitoring protective import bans and restrictions. The legislation imposes a high burden on the commission. For example, once a restriction or ban is adjudicated in favor of an industry, BTC is required to monitor production of that industrial unit "strictly." A trader who is aggrieved by any decision regarding a ban or restriction can refer their representation to BTC, which is responsible for examining the claim and making its recommendations to MOC. Interviews point to a lack of sufficient technical capacity within BTC to analyze and monitor the impact of bans and restrictions effectively. This lack of capacity, combined with opportunities for rent-seeking, has created a framework that is potentially subject to abuse and often leads to the imposition of protective orders that are not adequately justified. A recent analysis of nontariff measures by the World Bank revealed that traditional regulatory instruments, such as quantitative restrictions (including quotas, import bans, and nonautomatic licensing), are on the decline in Bangladesh, but it has detected increasing use of import restrictions on health, environment, security, and religious grounds. This puts a spotlight on the formulation and efficacy of the import policy not only to comply with WTO norms, but to act as an instrument guiding trade development.

Other Import-Related Measures: Technical Barriers to Trade and Sanitary and Phytosanitary Standards

Although TBT and SPS measures are enforced through the Import Policy Order, they are set through regulations and other measures by the responsible line ministries and their agencies.

BSTI, an adjunct of the Ministry of Industries, is the main body mandated to formulate national technical standards for all products (except pharmaceutical products); enforce compliance with standards; and certify the quality of products for local consumption, export, or import. The BSTI Council, the highest decision-making organ of the institution, consists of representatives from various ministries, business chambers, scientific organizations, and universities. It has an internal committee on WTO affairs, is Bangladesh's WTO TBT national enquiry point (WTO 2012), and participates in the working groups on WTO agreements in the Ministry of Industries and Ministry of Agriculture. It has yet to receive a single enquiry from another WTO member.

Development of SPS consists of three areas: food safety, plant health, and animal health. Given the various technical issues, like in other countries, it is not uncommon for multiple government agencies to engage in setting, implementing, and managing SPS policy. The following are examples:

- Food safety is under the domain of the Ministry of Health. Although food safety is not highly prioritized, impacts on trade largely take place through the actions of the Department of Fisheries and BSTI.
- Plant health is under the Plant Quarantine Wing, Ministry of Agriculture. A new Plant Quarantine Act was passed in 2011. However, as this new Act greatly expands the scope of plant health, the Act is yet to be fully implemented. As the rules and regulations to implement the Act are pending approval, the Plant Quarantine Wing continues to follow the old Act.[1]
- Animal health is under the Department of Livestock, Ministry of Fisheries and Livestock. It is believed that activity and capacity in this field are low.
- Fisheries quality, including issues of food safety and animal health for fishery products, falls under the Department of Fisheries, Ministry of Fisheries and Livestock. The separation of fishery issues took place to satisfy stringent EU and U.S. demands in the shrimp sector.

For SPS and TBT, the current consultative process in developing standards is weak. Although various consultative committees are in place, they are largely dominated by BSTI (for TBT) and "private sector" representatives are often drawn from state-owned enterprises. A more open and transparent process would facilitate ongoing compliance with the government's WTO commitments and facilitate trade.

Export Policy and Industrial Policy

The government's export strategy is managed through the Export Policy (2012–15), which is formulated by MOC. The objective of the Export Policy is to enable the private sector to increase and diversify exports, stimulate higher value–added exports, and increase productivity through a series of series of incentives and other support measures (see box 4A.1 in annex 4A). Unlike the Import Policy Order, the Export Policy is an enunciation of desired programs without a legal foundation. Its implementation is an NBR prerogative, subject to revenue constraints. Nevertheless, the policy is of significance as it constitutes the government's export mandate for trade development and growth, which NBR and other institutions tend to heed.

The formulation of the Export Policy mimics the Import Policy in interministerial coordination and the stakeholder consultation process (see box 4.2). The Export Promotion Bureau spearheads the formulation and review of the Export Policy (including export incentives and facilities). The mission meeting at EPB and feedback from donors revealed weak capacity at EPB in all aspects of its core functions, including the Policy and Planning Division, which provides advocacy efforts in policy formulation, country image building, and export support services. Key decisions on Export Policy rest mainly with the additional secretary, who appears to be the principal source of institutional memory; at the deputy

---

Box 4.2 Export Policy Formulation

The consultative mechanism for the Export Policy follows the proposed initiatives of the Business Promotion Council, led by a consultative committee chaired by the Ministry of Commerce (MOC). The consultative committee consists of public and private stakeholders from the Federation of Bangladesh Chambers of Commerce and Industry, Metropolitan Chamber of Commerce and Industry, Bangladesh Garment Manufacturers and Exporters Association, Bangladesh Knitwear Manufacturers and Exporters Association, and Bangladesh Export Processing Zones Authority; other trade associations for goods such as leather, jute, and processed agricultural goods; the Bangladesh Bank (for regulations, especially foreign currency); insurance associations; raw material importers; the key ministries, including the Ministry of Finance (MOF), National Board of Revenue, Ministry of Agriculture, and Ministry of Textile and Jute, Ministry of Environment; and think tanks such as the Bangladesh Foreign Trade Institute and the Centre for Policy Dialogue. Although the Cabinet of Bangladesh approves the final draft of the Export Policy, MOF determines the rates and amounts of subsidies.

---

secretary level, there appears to be the same skills mismatch experienced by MOC. Given inadequate analytical capacity at EPB, it is highly unlikely the proposals receive adequate scrutiny, making the Export Policy susceptible to an even higher degree of industry lobbying efforts than the Import Policy. The vetting process relies heavily on NBR's (unknown) internal evaluation criteria and therefore is not transparent.

Further incentives are provided through the Industrial Policy formulated by the Ministry of Industries to support private sector industrial growth. Despite a common orientation toward export growth, there is no coherent vision guiding the implementation of an export strategy in Bangladesh. The recent European Union–funded Comprehensive Trade Strategy asserts that the selection criteria for identification of priority sectors under the Export Policy and Industrial Policy are vague. Moreover, performance of the priority sectors that receive incentives is not adequately monitored, partly owing to a lack of capacity and resources.

Equally important, there is little coherence between the Import Policy (which promotes the protection of import-substituting, domestic market-oriented, and labor-intensive industries) and export incentives as propagated through the Export Policy and Industrial Policy. This has created a highly distorted incentive environment in which selected domestic and export sectors are subsidized through high effective rates of protection. The disconnected policy-making processes and policies that result fail to take into account the countervailing effect that import restrictions have on exports (see chapter 2 on trade policy).

Multilateral, Regional, and Bilateral Trade Agreements
In Bangladesh, MOC is the focal point for evaluation and negotiation of, and compliance with, multilateral, regional, and bilateral trade agreements, including WTO agreements. MOC's FTA Wing suffers from the same civil service appointment

and rotation policy that prevents "institutional memory" and efficient functioning (box 4.3). At the individual level, the joint chief of BTC appears to be a key official contributing to negotiations. His long tenure (an exception to the civil service rotation policy) and acquired knowledge on market access and NTBs have made him an indispensable source for preparations and negotiations on bilateral trade and FTAs.

Preparations for negotiations on the South Asian Free Trade Area (SAFTA), the Asia-Pacific Trade Agreement (APTA), and other agreements are made through an interministerial committee established for each agreement. The committees are chaired by MOC leadership, through the additional secretary and joint secretary, both of whom are seasoned negotiators with a long history of experience. The committees consist of public and private institutions, with a mechanism for receiving inputs from stakeholders in preparations for negotiations (see box 4A.2 in annex 4A).

Preparations for regional trade negotiations follow a standard norm of coordination between government bodies and the private sector. However, there is a lack of continuity in the consultative process. According to senior officials, stakeholder configuration (public and private sectors) is not "permanent" and is subject to change during the course of the interagency coordination process, partly owing to prolonged regional trade negotiations. Furthermore, MOC and the committees seem to have little ability to generate interest in the private sector.

Box 4.3 Ministry of Commerce's FTA Wing

The Free Trade Area (FTA) Wing comprises five deputy secretaries and three senior assistant secretaries or assistant secretaries who report to the additional secretary. Administrative functions are assigned to deputy secretaries based on multilateral, regional, or bilateral FTAs. For example:

- The South Asian Free Trade Area, Asia-Pacific Trade Agreement, and Agreement on South Asian Association for Regional Cooperation preferential trading arrangement issues are under the Deputy Secretary (FTA-1 Branch).
- The United Nations Conference on Trade and Development, D-8, and the Framework Agreement on Trade Preferential System among the Organization of the Islamic Conference Member States are dealt with by the Deputy Secretary (FTA-2 Branch).
- The Bay of Bengal Initiative for Multi-Sectoral Technical and Economic Cooperation, Indian Ocean Rim Association for Regional Cooperation, the European Union, and Pakistan are dealt with by the Deputy Secretary (FTA-3 Branch).
- Bhutan, Myanmar, Sri Lanka, and rules of origin are dealt with by the Trade Consultant (Deputy Secretary).
- India is dealt with by the Deputy Secretary (FTA-1 Branch).

All these deputy secretaries report to the additional-joint secretary (FTA); the additional secretary reports to the Ministry of Commerce secretary, who ultimately reports to the Minister of Commerce.

Leading commercial enterprises interviewed were not aware of the existence of the consultative process; nor have they made any inquiries on the "offer list" or "market access" in recent negotiations under SAFTA or APTA. In contrast, in countries such as India, Pakistan, and Sri Lanka, industry organizations collectively and individually play a key role in shaping the government agenda through their chambers or associations on issues related to market access (or on protection through negative lists). Moreover, despite the large number of sectors affected by negotiations, there is no mechanism in place for broader public consultation with affected parties, which include service industries, labor, consumers, and households.

The agenda for regional and bilateral trade negotiations is set through intergovernmental negotiations (see box 4.4). MOC routinely consults private think tanks, especially CPD, which has a leading role in policy-oriented regional trade. MOC also draws on its affiliations with the South Asian research network, its relatively active engagement in regional workshops and seminars, and research and articles on regional trade.

The head of the FTA Wing of MOC (additional secretary or joint secretary of FTA) is typically considered the highest-ranking authority in trade negotiations and is the head of the Trade Negotiations Committees. Deputy Secretaries from the FTA Wing have also served as the negotiating authority. Preparations for negotiations are supported by the International Cooperation Wing of BTC and BFTI. They provide MOC with independent analysis, research, information, and recommendations on FTAs. Their capacity to do so, in practice, remains limited.

Stakeholder Consultation

Stakeholder consultation on trade policy is largely dominated by the large chambers and associations: the Federation of Bangladesh Chambers of Commerce and Industry (FBCCI), Dhaka Chamber of Commerce and Industry, Metropolitan

---

Box 4.4 Interagency Coordination on Trade Agreements

Initiated by the Ministry of Commerce (MOC), interministerial committees on trade negotiations are usually agreement-specific. The Ministry of Foreign Affairs spearheads the diplomatic affairs in close collaboration with MOC. Other key government members of the committee include the Ministry of Industries, National Board of Revenue, Ministry of Law and Parliamentary Affairs, Ministry of Agriculture, Ministry of Home Affairs, Bangladesh Tariff Commission, Export Promotion Bureau, Office of the Chief Controller of Imports and Exports, and Bangladesh Foreign Trade Institute. The private sector is represented by the Federation of Bangladesh Chambers of Commerce and Industry, Metropolitan Chamber of Commerce and Industry, and Dhaka Chamber of Commerce and Industry. Policy research institutes such as the Centre for Policy Dialogue and the Policy Research Institute are also invited to sit on interministerial committees.

Chamber of Commerce and Industry, and key trade associations, such as the Bangladesh Garment Manufacturers and Exporters Association (BGMEA), Bangladesh Knitwear Manufacturers and Exporters Association (BKMEA), the Jute and Textile Association, and the Leather Producers Association. These chambers and associations are engaged as standing committee members at the preliminary stages of the policy-making process. Chambers and associations routinely engage MOC, Ministry of Industries, EPB, and NBR on regulatory or other business-related issues. FBCCI, the apex body of all the chambers, plays a pivotal role from the policy initiation stage until the draft policy is submitted to the Cabinet for approval. At the final vetting stages, FBCCI is the only private sector representative consulted.

The lack of transparent and inclusive structures for consultation can be broadly highlighted from two perspectives. First, the FBCCI secretariat, with its small research staff (for example, comprising two staff with MBAs, two with bachelor's degrees, and the support of a relatively senior associate in economics in 2013) and limited budget, is expected to make an effective contribution to the 50 or so public sector forums in which it is engaged every year. Given FBCCI's prominence in consultative committees and standing committees on key sectors of trade, the lack of research capacity needed to support private sector interests has undermined the effectiveness of its inputs.

Second, often the interests of only a handful of selected sectors are represented. The BGMEA, BKMEA, Jute and Textile Association, and Leather Producers Association together exert undue influence on trade policy. This enables them to benefit from the most favorable incentive regime, which creates sizable bias across sectors. Small traders and producers are often marginalized because they have few resources to analyze and respond to such issues in a timely manner. Moreover, few, if any, representatives from other sectors of the economy that will be affected by trade policy are consulted, including consumers, labor, and service industries. This contributes to a policy-making environment that is heavily skewed toward the large, established industries, which can lead to policies that are not in the best interests of Bangladesh. This is partly a historical legacy of the import-substitution model that characterizes many low- and middle-income countries, whereby businesses in only a few sectors hold sway and the interests of the broader constituency of consumers, labor, and civil society are marginalized.

Toward a New Trade Policy Framework

The preceding discussion highlighted several weaknesses in the existing institutional framework for trade policy in Bangladesh. The weaknesses have contributed to the fragmented trade policy framework and conflicting roles and responsibilities. The main issues are summarized as follows:

- Policy making is carried out through several government institutions in a piecemeal fashion, blurring the lines of responsibility.

- Stakeholder consultation is weak in transparency and accountability, as the policy-making process is largely captured by special interests.
- An active dialogue with representatives of civil society such as labor, households, and consumers is either nascent or absent in Bangladesh.
- Public and private institutions that are intimately engaged in trade policy formulation and implementation lack the capacity to analyze and respond to such issues in a timely manner.

A more cohesive trade policy framework would recognize that trade policies encompass a much broader agenda, including the direct and indirect ways in which trade and trade-related policies affect welfare. This requires recognition of the need for consensus on national interests and the role of trade in meeting the broad economic objectives of growth, exports, and poverty reduction.

Trade policy formulation is not a one-off event but an iterative process that requires effective interagency coordination and stakeholder consultation, backed by data and analysis throughout the policy-making lifecycle. No single correct structure for a trade policy *initiation, formulation, implementation,* and *evaluation* framework exists; they vary according to the existing governance structures, legal frameworks, and institutional proficiencies. Improving the quality of trade policy formulation in Bangladesh requires an individualized and more systematized approach that encompasses complementary elements that work together throughout the policy-making lifecycle (see figure 4.2).

Figure 4.2 Trade Policy Lifecycle

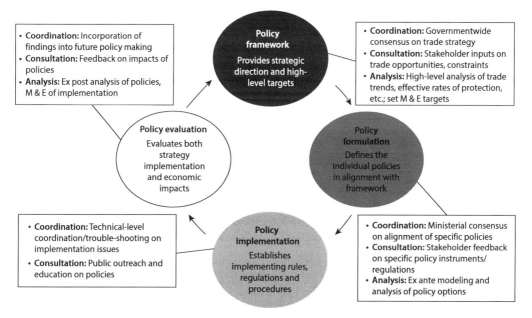

Note: M&E = monitoring and evaluation.

Strengthening Competitiveness in Bangladesh—Thematic Assessment
http://dx.doi.org/10.1596/978-1-4648-0898-2

The starting point for creating a more cohesive policy-making process starts with consensus on a national vision and the strategic direction of trade policy reform that is aligned with Bangladesh's broader economic development objectives, as laid out in Vision 2021 and the Sixth Five-Year Plan. The objective of such an agenda is to create a unified framework for developing trade-related policies that balances the interests of all key stakeholders (including the often-forgotten consumer). The agenda is linked with Bangladesh's international commitments and helps guide future positions on international negotiations, and has a clear monitoring and implementation plan that clarifies roles and responsibilities. This Diagnostic Trade Integration Study (DTIS), together with the European Union–supported Comprehensive Trade Policy, can provide the analytical foundation and the core links that need to be kept in mind for such a reform plan.

Addressing the lack of synergies and inefficiencies in Bangladesh's trade policy formulation system would entail the following actions:

- *More effective interagency coordination.* Coordination among the numerous public sector actors engaged in trade policy is critical for realizing the benefits of Bangladesh's participation in global trade. Effective coordination mechanisms need to be adaptable to the evolving demands of the global trading environment. These demands include the ongoing fiscal and financial crisis, rebalancing after the crisis, and the expected shifts of global growth toward a more multipolar world. The shifting global environment will make necessary the regular reassessment of the scope and priorities of Bangladesh's trade policies. It is recommended that all trade policies, including tariffs, import taxes, and standards, should be vetted through a uniform, standardized process.
- *Inclusive and transparent stakeholder consultation.* Without broader policy consultation with economic and social partners, interagency coordination alone cannot achieve national consensus on trade policy objectives. Interagency coordination and stakeholder consultation processes are complementary and need to be conducted systematically across all stages of the policy-making process.
- *Evidence-based research and analysis.* Coordination and consultation can only be effective if they are built on a sound foundation of economic research and analysis. This foundation will help stakeholders understand the potential ex ante economic impacts of trade policy reforms and the ex post impacts on the economy.

These principles are well illustrated in the case of trade negotiations, which increasingly encompass a broad spectrum of regulatory issues beyond tariff concessions. Interagency coordination and stakeholder consultations are critical in the early stages to identify interests and options and the development of a negotiating position. Ex ante partial and general equilibrium analyses can provide the basis for quantifying the potential impact of policies on revenues, trade flows, and sector output and employment. Stakeholder consultations in the early stages can build support at home for identifying priority demands for increased market access.

Although one or two agencies take the lead during negotiations, open channels to other ministries and agencies are critical to reach consensus rapidly on non-tariff-related provisions. Post-negotiations, implementation often requires ongoing interagency coordination to ensure compliance with the provisions of the agreement; continued awareness building among stakeholders, especially in the private sector, to promote diversification into the new market; as well as ex ante monitoring and evaluation of economic outcomes to inform future rounds of negotiations.

Although there is no one-size-fits-all approach to organizing trade institutions, international experience provides examples of good practices that could be incorporated into Bangladesh's existing framework to improve the quality of trade policy making through a systematic approach to make interagency coordination more effective, increase the transparency and scope of stakeholder consultation, and strengthen the quality of research and analysis required to support the policy-making process. Figure 4.3 provides an illustrative approach to organizing Bangladesh's trade-related institutions and stakeholders to initiate, formulate, implement, and monitor trade policy reforms.

Any redesign of Bangladesh's institutional structure for trade should be designed to build on existing capacities and institutions, with a focus on strengthening linkages within government and among the public sector, private sector, research and academic community, and other stakeholders, such as labor, consumers, and others.

Figure 4.3 Toward a New Institutional Framework in Bangladesh

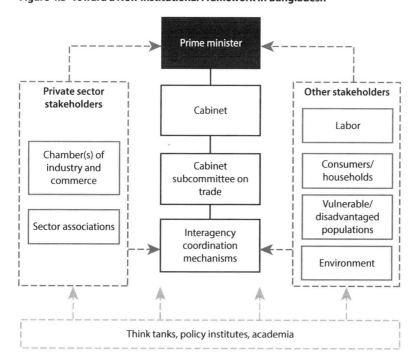

Strengthening Competitiveness in Bangladesh—Thematic Assessment
http://dx.doi.org/10.1596/978-1-4648-0898-2

The following sections provide a detailed assessment of options, including a discussion of international practices, for the main components of a more systematic trade policy framework. The options include improved mechanisms for interagency coordination and more effective and transparent stakeholder consultation. In addition, better access to robust research and analysis will support policy making and help build the capacity of public and private institutions to improve the coherence of trade policy.

Improving Interagency Coordination

Although a number of mechanisms are in place to support interagency coordination in Bangladesh, their fragmented nature has contributed to fragmented trade policies. Effective trade policy coordination is based on achieving three important targets: (a) integrating Bangladesh's domestic trade policies with its many existing and future international trade agreements into a coherent trade and development strategy; (b) eliminating contradictions in trade policies, such as the Import Policy and Export Policy; and (c) streamlining the approaches of various government institutions engaged in trade policy formulation and implementation. The Ministries of Commerce, Finance, Agriculture, Health, and Industries and their respective agencies must work together to ensure efficient policy making.

Although there is no one-size-fits-all approach to interagency coordination, two broad typologies of coordination are observed. They are not necessarily mutually exclusive, and elements of each may be present in a single country:

- *A strong, centralized, executive-level agency, often outside the ministerial structure.* Given that trade policy has broad impacts beyond the traded sectors of the economy—including, for example, labor, households, and the environment—some countries have established agencies that are not bound to the narrow interests of a single ministry. An executive-level agency offers several advantages for strengthening the trade policy framework. But the most valuable feature is the autonomy given to the lead agency, providing an arm's length relationship from the vested interests of a single ministry. In the United States, for example, the U.S. Trade Representative is a cabinet-level agency reporting directly to the U.S. president. The agency is responsible for setting the policy agenda, although it coordinates with line agencies through a series of committees.

- *A high-level, interministerial committee with a formal mandate.* Where no centralized institution exists, many countries rely on interagency committees to formulate, rationalize, and monitor the implementation of trade policies. Unlike Bangladesh, many countries have a multi-tiered network of committees that ensures that interactions take place at the right level, as some but not all decisions require minister-level engagement. This tiered approach also imposes a greater level of discipline and accountability in the policy-making process and reduces the potential for rent-seeking behavior, since certain policy changes can be mandated for approval at a higher level. In Indonesia, for example, a National Team for Increasing Exports and Investment was established in 2003, with the president as chair, to formulate trade and investment policies.

In 2005, an interagency Indonesian National Trade Negotiation Team was established to improve Indonesian participation in international trade negotiations. In the United States, the U.S. Trade Representative relies on a multi-tier, multi-channel approach to interagency coordination. An interagency Trade Policy Review Group is chaired by the Deputy Trade Representative and brings together undersecretary-level officials from more than 20 agencies to consult on the trade agenda and coordinate implementation. The latter role is largely delegated to a Trade Policy Staff Committee comprised of senior officials from the same set of agencies to coordinate implementation, which is supported by some 80 subcommittees that work on various policy issues.

Establishing a new trade agency in Bangladesh, while potentially advantageous, would be a long and complex process of parliamentary approvals. More expedient would be a reworking of the existing structure of trade-related committees under MOC as the focal point, drawing on and adapting the experiences of other countries. Reconstituting and embedding the existing technical committees in a multi-tiered system, with clearly defined mandates for decision authorities at each tier and defined roles and responsibilities for each agency, can instill greater discipline and accountability for policy decisions.

Although not significantly different from the current setup, such a structure would provide a more systematic approach that, in combination with a more formal vetting process, backed by consultation and analysis, would lead to greater discipline and accountability. A more structured system of coordination would also help reduce the incentives for rent-seeking behavior that are present in the current system. It is recommended that a new, streamlined framework be applied across the full spectrum of trade policy issues, including tariffs and taxes, which are largely outside the existing coordination and consultation process where no formal committee currently exists to balance the interests between MOC, NBR, and others. Similarly, in the case of standards, a more structured vetting process through the committee framework, tied to transparent consultation and research and analysis, can better ensure that TBTs and SPS measures meet the needs of the market and are in compliance with the spirit of Bangladesh's WTO and other international commitments.

Creating a Transparent and Inclusive Consultative Process

Even if the trade policy is guided by a clear agenda for trade development, poor consultative mechanisms can dampen the outcomes of policies. Often there are fixed costs related to trade and they disproportionately affect small and medium enterprises (SMEs), the poor, and rural and urban farmers, prohibiting their participation in trade and limiting inclusiveness. Furthermore, it can be argued that structures that allow broader participation by public and private sector stakeholders are more likely to be considered legitimate and will therefore be more sustainable and effective. Although the existing coordinating committees have engaged the private sector to some degree at the technical level, the diagnostic study points to the absence of engagement at a higher level of decision making to define the vision and direction of trade policy, as well as the exclusion of other

Strengthening Competitiveness in Bangladesh—Thematic Assessment
http://dx.doi.org/10.1596/978-1-4648-0898-2

stakeholders from the policy-making process. The following discussion offers options that use existing institutions that could be augmented and other mechanisms that could be evolved over time.

Potential Role of BUILD in the Consultative Process

Business Initiative Leading Development is a joint initiative of the Dhaka Chamber of Commerce and Industry, the Metropolitan Chamber of Commerce and Industry, and the SME Foundation as a platform for the government and the private sector through which the two sides can work together and address the key constraints that are impeding the growth of the private sector. BUILD works through four thematic working committees: Financial Sector Development, SME Development, Trade and Investment, and Taxation. BUILD can potentially be expanded to improve stakeholder consultation on trade policy, particularly in areas that are related to the regulatory and procedural aspects, such as those covered by the Import Policy Order. By bringing in SME representation and creating an effective partnership with think tanks, academia, and chambers of commerce and maintaining coordination and continuity between public and private sector understanding for better reforms, the engagement of BUILD can tilt the "playing field" that is skewed toward established and large-scale enterprises that have captured the trade policy-making process. The more open process will improve transparency, reducing the incidence of rent-seeking behavior. BUILD will be able to address, on a priority basis, the most punitive of the regulatory issues that disproportionately impact SMEs, such as licensing, customs, and other trade-related transactions costs.

Mechanisms for Broader Consultation

BUILD and the existing committees can be effective mechanisms for engaging broader private sector consultation. However, their focus is currently limited to the *tactical* rather than *strategic* level of policy making, and their participation, outside government, is limited to the private sector. The following provides options and recommendations for creating a broader framework for stakeholder consultation that is more strategic in nature and has broader participation.

Role of Competitiveness Councils in Trade Policy Strategy. Many countries have instituted competitiveness councils or similar advisory bodies to provide the government with strategic inputs into developing policies to support a competitive private sector. Competitiveness councils and advisory boards encompass "behind the border" issues with a mandate for greater regulatory scrutiny. They act as a "sounding board" for major trade policy initiatives (import, export, and industrial) that elude the existing institutional framework in Bangladesh. The merit of competitiveness councils is not just broader scope—such councils are typically comprised of prominent members of the business and research communities and have access to the highest levels of decision-making apparatus in a country, typically the prime minister's or president's office. For example, in the Philippines, the National Competitiveness Council was formed by executive decree in 2006 as a public-private task force to address the improvement of the country's competitiveness. The council is co-chaired by the Trade and Industry Secretary (a minister-level post) and a prominent private sector representative. Its working groups cover a broad range of private sector competitiveness issues, including trade and customs, business licensing, and anticorruption, among others. The National Competitiveness Council maintains strong links to academia, which plays an important role in providing policy research and analysis to back the policy agenda. Similarly, in Indonesia, Export Expansion and Investment Promotion was established to formulate policies and evaluate strategic issues related to export and investment promotion with a mandate to engage government in regulatory issues at the policy formulation stage. Export Expansion and Investment Promotion has been credited with remarkable recent successes in preventing some of the punitive regulations that are in violation of WTO obligations.

The modes of operation of such councils include sector and functional working groups, some permanent and others ad hoc, as may be deemed necessary. One option in Bangladesh may be to develop working groups to discuss draft decisions and regulations under a council structure—to collect more detailed and precise information on specific policies and regulations not covered by BUILD. Working groups can also ensure deeper participation from a wider private sector.

There does not appear to be single "best" approach to the formation of councils of this type. However, successful competitiveness councils appear to share several characteristics that should be considered in Bangladesh:

- Councils are of relatively small size (15–20 individuals at most) and include representatives from the public sector, the private sector, academia, and labor to guarantee multiple perspectives.
- Councils should have a bipartisan, multipartisan, or nonpartisan composition. This helps build consensus in the country around the goal of competitiveness and allows it to survive a change of government.
- Councils should be recognized by the government, enabling the council to exert real influence over government policy. This does not always necessitate that government officials formally sit on the council. In Ireland, for example, links between the council and the government come via direct meetings between the council chair and the prime minister, while senior civil servants attend council meetings and participate in deliberations.

Transparency through Broader Stakeholder Consultation. Establishing an active dialogue with the private sector and representatives of civil society, such as labor unions, consumer associations, vulnerable and disadvantaged populations (gender, youth, rural), and academia and research institutes, is essential to generate the support needed for reform. Active dialogue can be an expedient mechanism for exposing excessive economic rent-seeking behavior of businesses and aligning it with other stakeholder interests.

Strengthening Competitiveness in Bangladesh—Thematic Assessment
http://dx.doi.org/10.1596/978-1-4648-0898-2

In Bangladesh, the existing consultative committees are not designed for a broader stakeholder regime, let alone broad private sector representation. There is, therefore, a need to develop new mechanisms that can create a more transparent and participatory process, and that are focused largely on engaging the private sector. An effort should be made to include academia and think tanks to inject an analytical dimension into debates and discussions, providing a balanced outcome to proceedings. The participation of academia and think tanks in common forums would help in identifying "beneficiaries" and the impact of "consumers." It would also help in avoiding common misunderstandings among broader groups with competing interests that would otherwise find no common ground.

Although MOC has a key role to play, effective consultation should be the responsibility of all trade-related agencies. Effective consultation requires the development of systematic and structured mechanisms to engage stakeholders throughout the policy-making lifecycle. This should include more structured and standardized methods of work, such as channels of consultation through open hearings on key policy matters, the Gazette, roundtables and forums, as well as public access to deliberations of the interministerial committees.[2] Consultation should be based on the following principles:

- *Timely information and agenda-setting.* Meeting dates and agendas should be available to participants well in advance. Short reports on meetings should be produced and distributed as soon as possible.
- *Broad representation.* The widest possible range of interest groups from the private sector and civil society should be encouraged to participate. Participation by groups that lack financial resources can be funded if doing so ensures broad representation.
- *Transparency of participation.* Organizations intending to participate in national trade dialogue meetings should register to do so, and a database of all participating organizations should be maintained with standardized practices for consultation. Such a policy will require investment in new procedures and staff training in how to consult and how to use information from consultations. Some developed countries have invested in web-based platforms for dialogue and dissemination, and low- and middle-income countries are beginning to do the same. For example, the business sector in Jamaica has developed a website called "The Briefing Room," which provides information to private sector stakeholders on external trade negotiations. Operationalizing this process requires a public outreach plan and staff training in how to consult and how to use information from consultations.

If needed, the Government of Bangladesh should consider the development and implementation of a mandatory consultation policy, based on international practice and e-government tools, which lays out goals, standard methods, and an implementation plan.

Enhancing Analytical Capability to Support Trade Policy

Measuring and exposing the economy-wide costs of trade barriers has been crucial and unique to successful reformers of less developed countries (in Latin America, East Asia, and Eastern Europe) that have made great strides in improving the quality of trade policy decision making, largely on the back of unilateral reforms. Bangladesh has, for the most part, enjoyed preferential status in key markets but has largely ignored the potential costs of protecting the domestic market—costs that have significant welfare implications that potentially thwart the emergence of new and more dynamic products and services.

The current structure of economic and regulatory impact analysis supporting government trade policy formation is weak. A major challenge confronting Bangladesh is the need for an objective, independent, rigorous, and authoritative policy evaluation mechanism that would provide analysis of the impact of proposed reforms. A policy impact mechanism can otherwise persuade policy makers of the merits of trade liberalization. The following offers two complementary paths to strengthening the capacity for trade-related research and analysis—the first relies on existing institutions, while the second is a more robust platform, modeled on a tried and tested mechanism adopted by Australia.

Building on Existing Institutions

Strengthening Links with Think Tanks and Academia. In Bangladesh, the knowledge pool and expertise capable of comprehending the demands of the emerging trade agenda and the competing paradigms for trade development are sparse and difficult to attract to the public sector, because of low compensation and the poor image of public institutes. Eminent economists with competence in Bangladesh are attached to academic institutes, international organizations, or leading think tanks, such as CPD, PRI, or BIDS. They have often obliged the government with research and advocacy, either formally, such as through BIDS' statutory role under the Ministry of Planning and the CPD's role in the European Union–funded work to develop a "comprehensive trade policy" or through various consultative committees.

Mobilizing key economists from Bangladesh's existing think tanks and policy institutes more formally to support policy making throughout the lifecycle would be beneficial. It would bring to bear the analytical and research capacity of these institutes to support policy making and to undertake ex ante studies of options, for example, for trade negotiations, regulatory impact assessments such as for licensing and standards, and ex post measurement of impacts of trade policy reforms. The Policy Coordination Committee already has established linkages with the various think tanks and institutes—creating a funding mechanism would allow trade-related ministries and agencies to commission studies on an as-needed basis.

Building In-House Capacity in MOC. These mechanisms need to be complemented by greater capacity within the government to commission and absorb the results of the research and analysis. As the lead trade policy institution, there is an urgent need to ensure that MOC has the capacity, at a minimum, to undertake this role, as well as some basic research and analysis (such as trade trends and tracking various trade indicators with World Integrated Trade Solution and other tools). A dedicated economic advisor to the ministry should be considered to provide ongoing advice to the minister on trade policy matters, although donor support may be required to attract eminent economists and overcome salary constraints. The advisor could play a key role in supporting the development of an in-house unit that would undertake basic research and manage and digest external research on behalf of MOC.

Leveraging the PFF Framework. Following the model of India's National Institute of Public Finance and Policy (NIPFP), the Public Finance Foundation (PFF) was set up in Bangladesh with a mandate to promote research and policy guidance on public finance, including fiscal policy. PFF is expected to act as an advisory body for providing effective public finance management and consultative services and liaison with academic institutes and development partners, contributing to and shaping the public economics agenda in Bangladesh. Thus far, progress has been limited to helping design courses and guidelines for public financial management and providing a training course.

Evidence suggests that many countries are facing the need for specialized capacity for providing an analytical basis for influential fiscal policy and public economics through institutions like NIPFP. These institutions have permanent structures led by professional economists and are typically outside the civil service—to improve the recruitment and retention of trained economists and to provide for greater autonomy from the government and private sector. Although PFF has the potential to play an important role, as it is currently structured, as an extended arm of the Finance Division of MOF, it lacks the degree of desired independence from NBR. A more desirable structure would provide PFF with a degree of autonomy, similar to that of India's NIPFP (see box 4A.3 in annex 4A). With appropriate resources and autonomy, PFF could fulfill a large void in public finance–related research and advocacy as well as provide the analytical rigor that is missing in current policy deliberations.

The PFF framework, if successfully developed, has the potential to play a critical role in supporting trade policy formulation in areas directly linked to PFF. These include ex ante and ex post analyses of the economic, sector, and financial impacts of policy changes. Such policies might include changes in trade-related taxes, including tariffs, supplementary duties, and other trade taxes, as well as other tax policies with direct or indirect impacts on government revenues or expenditures, including incentives, subsidies, grants, and other concessions to the private sector.

Establishing a Productivity Commission

A well-defined, funded, and staffed PFF could be effective in resolving key frictions in trade and tax policy tariffs, import taxes (supplementary duties), and multiple incentives. Existing think tanks are well geared toward providing modeling work on tariff-related policy analysis related to unilateral trade liberalization as well as trade agreements. A clear understanding of the impacts of the remaining trade agenda—NTBs, standards (SPS and TBT), licensing requirements, nonrecognition of foreign qualifications or accreditation, local presence or ownership requirements, intellectual property rights, and so forth—will be critical for developing a coherent trade policy agenda in Bangladesh.

New models addressing the broader incentive and regulatory environment linking national development strategies to trade have proliferated in recent years. For example, the role played by the Productivity Commission of Australia provides a profound lesson for an independent source of analysis for development-oriented trade policy for Bangladesh and low- and middle-income countries elsewhere (see box 4A.4 in annex 4A). The Productivity Commission is set up as an independent principal evaluation and advisory body on microeconomic policy and regulation. Its rigorous and authoritative quantitative estimates of the costs of trade barriers and other forms of government assistance to industries, consumers, and the economy as a whole have helped persuade policy makers of the merits of trade liberalization. Transparency, independence, and the evaluation of economy-wide effects of policies have become three fundamental principles of the Productivity Commission—all essential attributes that are currently missing from the policy-making apparatus in Bangladesh.

The platform for a Productivity Commission–type institution may be germinated in Bangladesh by starting a dialogue with the key stakeholders willing to champion the cause. In the early stages, it can take the form of an advisory board, commissioning independent studies through eminent local economists in academia or think tanks, to provide strategic advice on trade policy. This would be a complement to a competitive council type of body and, with the support of an enhanced consultation framework, the advisory board would offer insights on trade and investment issues of relevance to regulatory reform or trade negotiations.

Building Institutional Capacity

Improved mechanisms for policy coordination and consultation must be complemented by improved skills and capacities in the key government institutions. The resource needs to implement a reasonably comprehensive and coherent approach to trade policy may seem daunting, but most of the interventions are for improving institutional effectiveness in its present form. The European Union's proposed capacity building under its trade policy support program addresses much of the training needs. The EU trade policy support program targets three institutions: MOC, EPB, and BFTI. In addition to the Comprehensive Trade Policy, designed to provide a road map for institutions for production and exports, training programs targeted at these entities at functional levels fulfill a significant void highlighted in the diagnostics. In particular, training of key MOC officials (including on trade policy, WTO agreements and trade-related data sources, and trade negotiations including regional trade agreements) are in line with the recommendations of the DTIS. The additional interventions need to be viewed as necessary complements to operationalize the new trade policy–making architecture.

Ministry of Commerce

To mitigate the impact of the civil service rotation policy and facilitate the effective administration of key areas of trade policy, a consistent stream of training, targeting deputy secretaries, assistant secretaries, and the support staff at MOC should be considered. The training should focus on the basics of trade policy, as well as on multilateral, bilateral, and regional trade, including the WTO agreements. Additional training should focus on identification of interests and options in multilateral agreements, the prioritization of negotiating positions on bilateral and regional agreements, and trade diplomacy (the latter targeting the higher officials). In addition, joint secretaries and directors should be exposed to the new trade agenda defined by trade competitiveness; traditional trade policy, especially the impact of tariffs and NTBs on trade; the behind-the-border and regulatory dimensions of trade reform; and the importance of the international supply chain.

Data and Analytical Competence

MOC is constrained by the lack of data and analytical resources it needs to keep abreast of the developments within WTO and FTA negotiations, provide traders and the public with trade information, and undertake basic research on trade issues for the benefit of trade policy making, negotiation, and advocacy. First, MOC has a weak data network for securing and disseminating user-friendly trade data. At present, MOC's Export Wing receives data from EPB, which are only in aggregated form (Harmonized Classification 2-digit level). Data are presented by EPB to the Export Wing in monthly or annual format and then distributed to other wings. A framework for receiving up-to-date, product-level (6-digit, at a minimum), country-wise, and sector-wise data for dissemination among the wings and for traders and the public is a core function of a typical ministry, but is absent in Bangladesh. MOC should coordinate with the Bangladesh Bureau of Statistics to develop such a trade database.

MOC maintains a rudimentary website that is inadequately designed to deliver basic trade-related data and information to the public at home and traders abroad. For example, the existing website provides an introduction to the various bilateral trade agreements and FTAs, but offers no information on concessions available or application of existing FTAs (such as the share of exports benefitting from preferential duties and rules of origin). A fully integrated website with access to all legislation pertaining to trade policies and a portal dedicated to interacting with various stakeholders are prerequisites for a new trade policy consultation. In addition, the website should provide information on WTO notification and General Agreement on Trade in Services inquiry points and access to trade statistics (or links to available sources, such as the Bangladesh Bureau of Statistics). To operationalize the broader stakeholder consultation agenda, the Planning Cell (Wing) needs adequate information technology equipment and systems, including help-desk support, e-mail, and electronic file sharing through secure web-based platforms.

Legal Competence

Currently, there is no internal capacity to assimilate and interpret the legal implications of trade agreements, including those of the WTO. This void is fulfilled routinely through the Law Ministry's "Drafting Wing" or other entities. For example, in the recent case of antidumping sanctions imposed by Turkey, MOC sought counseling from a private sector WTO expert (PhD from Oxford) on a pro bono basis. A more expedient option, as an interim measure, would be the secondment of a legal expert trained in trade issues from the Ministry of Law to provide legal advice to MOC. There is sufficient demand within MOC for a permanent legal advisor. The duties would include interpreting treaties and other international agreements in relation to MOC functions. The advisor would also draft, vet, and approve agreements, memoranda of understanding, and any other legal documents required by MOC, including interpretation of domestic law related to MOC or agencies under MOC in accordance with the Federal Constitution.

Supporting Bangladesh Tariff Commission's Core Mandates

In its present form, BTC does not demonstrate the requisite capacity to reestablish the leadership role in tariff setting that is currently held by NBR. The status of its role in tariff setting must be further examined along with reestablishing its leadership on antidumping, safeguard, and countervailing measures, since the tools are already in place and BTC has the legal mandate to adjudicate antidumping and countervailing duty measures. This would reduce the incentive to misuse tariffs in the protection of domestic industries and would require a robust process to determine injury. To build BTC's role in trade policy and negotiations, capacity building should focus on issues related to WTO and regional trade agreements, research and analytical skills to support trade policy analysis, and data management.

Strengthening the Training Role of the Bangladesh Foreign Trade Institute

BFTI was established as a nonprofit research and training institution with the Minister of Commerce as the chairperson. BFTI was tasked to enhance the trade and business knowledge of the government (especially MOC) and private sector through research, policy advice, and education and training on issues such as the WTO and FTAs.

The trade policy support program of the European Union is focused largely on building BFTI's capacity as the research arm of MOC. The sustainability of this effort needs to be clearly established, given the difficulties associated with attracting and maintaining staff with the requisite skill sets. At the same time, the program overlooks BFTI's role as a training institute, including the mandate to provide specialized and general training on trade and business issues for officials of the government and the private sector. Given the deficit in basic training of trade officials within MOC and in light of the rotation of civil servants, BFTI's role should be to help address the training needs of MOC and other trade-related agencies.

Capacity Building for Policy Makers

Policy makers, especially secretaries and additional secretaries of the Ministries of Commerce, Industries, and Agriculture, would benefit from programs such as the Practitioner Knowledge Exchange on Economic Reform of the World Bank Institute (WBI). This WBI program could facilitate the exchange of knowledge and experience among policy makers with a combination of face-to-face activities, video conferencing, and interactive online discussions. These exchanges often draw on the expertise of top experts, academics, ministers from low- and middle-income country governments, and central bank governors, who share their views on existing and new approaches to development and associated policies. WBI designs and delivers learning programs on Leadership and Coalition Building to support "change agents" in their efforts to effect reforms in various sectors of the economy.

In addition, study tours for policy makers could expose them to systems and practices of successful reformers such as India, Malaysia, and even the United States. The tours could focus on building capacity for the key institutional reform areas identified here, including the process and institutional arrangements for formulating tariff policies, standards, and other nontariff measures, among others.

Outreach Activities for Civil Society

More inclusive and transparent trade policy making requires a broader outreach strategy. This includes continued efforts to encourage dialogue and exchanges of views and ideas between MOC and civil society representatives (such as nongovernmental organizations, rural farmers, and social service organizations, local and international) on trade-related and development-related issues. In addition to the introduction of trade issues in laymen's terms, MOC and civil society representatives are encouraged to consider their respective roles in multilateral processes and ways to increase public awareness of the international trade agenda. These may take the form of workshops in Dhaka and other major economic centers (perhaps Chittagong and border areas such as Benapole and Agratala).

Conclusion and Recommendations

The foregoing analysis points to a number of weaknesses in Bangladesh's current institutional framework for trade policy making, including the following:

- Lack of a cohesive and uniform trade policy–making strategy to guide the direction of trade policies and the dominance of narrowly vested interests (such as the protection of selected large industry players and revenue considerations of NBR) in designing trade policies

- Frictions in coordinating the various government agencies engaged in policy making
- Narrowly based consultation with the private sector
- Lack of rigorous research and analysis to support policy formulation and evaluation
- Deficits in skills and capacities in individual institutions for effective implementation of policy reform.

The following summarizes some broad recommendations for improving the trade policy–making framework in each of these areas:

- *Adopt a Strategic Trade Policy Agenda.* It is recommended that the Government of Bangladesh adopt the recommendations of this DTIS, which provides the analytical foundations for the elements of strategic trade policy, and support ongoing EU efforts on trade policy, to form the foundation of a strategic and cohesive trade policy strategy to govern import and export policies, tariff reform, trade-related aspects of industrial policies, and other policies affecting nontariff barriers, such as standards formulation. The trade policy agenda should be adopted at the highest levels of government, for example, through the Council of Ministers, to promote consensus between the ministries and agencies engaged in formulating or implementing policies affecting trade. The goal is to create an overarching set of objectives for trade policy, aligned with the Sixth Five-Year Plan and Vision 2021, to form a coherent strategy that the other policy mechanisms will support, eliminating conflicts and counterproductive policies.
- *Strengthen mechanisms for interagency coordination.* To reinforce the Strategic Trade Policy Agenda, serious consideration should be given to rationalizing the current institutional framework to clarify roles and responsibilities and create a more formal process for mandated coordination that creates greater accountability and transparency. Specific aspects of such a rationalization should include the following:
  - *Integration or merger of MOC's Import Policy and Export Policy Wings.* As the first component of the rationalization, it is recommended that the two Wings be merged into a single Import-Export Policy Wing, backed by a process that aligns the two policy documents toward a single set of objectives to provide better harmonization between the Import and Export Policies that reinforces the government's stated objectives to promote trade-led development.
  - *Improved coordination between the Ministries of Industry, Commerce, and Finance on import, export, and industrial policies.* It is recommended that interagency coordination on import, export, and industrial policies be strengthened through the establishment of a standing interagency committee, comprised of the merged Import-Export Policy Wing and the relevant wing of the Ministry of Industries. The goal of this committee will be to harmonize trade policy measures, including a consistent approach to

balancing the interests between exporting and domestic-oriented industries. This would include the selection of "thrust industries" that are granted incentives to promote export growth. On the implementation side, greater coordination between EPB, MOF, and Bangladesh Bank will be required to ensure that incentives are aligned, with increased monitoring by the standing interagency committee.

- *A formal mechanism for tariff setting.* A clear delineation of roles and responsibilities with respect to tariffs and other import duties that limits rent-seeking behavior is urgently required to improve transparency, reduce rent-seeking behavior, and ensure that a balance of interests are considered, beyond revenues and individual special interests. This includes the establishment of a joint committee comprising MOC, through the merged Import-Export Policy Wing, and NBR that will bring a greater balance between the interests of export industries, domestic industries, and revenue collection. This must be accompanied by a transparent consultation process with strict criteria for changes to the schedule outside a standardized tariff-setting cycle.

- *A structured vetting process for standards and other NTBs.* A more structured vetting process should be implemented for standards. This could be done through a formal committee framework that is tied to transparent consultation and research and analysis, including use of the tools of regulatory impact analysis, to ensure that TBT and SPS measures are not unnecessarily restrictive. Similarly, in the case of other NTBs, they should conduct more rigorous and transparent vetting and impact analysis, with broader stakeholder consultation, to guard against protective measures that impose undue costs on the broader economy (the BUILD framework may be leveraged)—and increase reliance on contingency trade remedies to address unfair competition from imports or import surges that threaten domestic industries in place of protective bans and restrictions.

- *Promotion of greater consultation with Bangladesh Bank.* Several other policies, while not directly under the purview of "trade policy," have a potential impact on competitiveness. These include such policies as the letter of credit, margin, and exchange rate, which are undertaken directly by Bangladesh Bank. Although the importance of maintaining Bangladesh Bank's autonomy in setting such policies is recognized, to promote a culture of greater transparency and accountability, it is recommended that some form of consultation would be appropriate, perhaps through an advisory council based on the U.S. Federal Reserve's Advisory Councils, with representatives from the Ministries of Commerce and Industries, as well as from private sector associations, to discuss the impact of monetary policies on competitiveness.

• *Broaden stakeholder consultation and improve transparency.* The reach of consultation should be broadened to engage SMEs, labor, consumers, and others in civil society as well as the trade-related implementing agencies (for example,

EPB, Bangladesh Export Processing Zones Authority [BEPZA], and Bangladesh Board of Investment [BOI]):

- *Establish a competitiveness council.* Consider establishment of a competitiveness council or similar body that can provide strategic direction to government on trade policy and its integration into a broader competitiveness agenda. Membership would be 50:50 public-private, with representation from MOC, EPB, BEPZA, BOI, and key private sector chambers, sector associations, and SMEs.

- *Expand BUILD to address trade-related regulations.* The BUILD framework, which includes SME representation, should be leveraged to address trade-related regulatory issues (including, again, vetting processes that prevent bad polices from being introduced, such as regulatory impact analysis).

- *Implement inclusive and transparent stakeholder consultation.* Inclusive consultation and transparency should be enabled through new, standardized mechanisms, including open tools to promote dialogue and feedback on policy (making the draft policy recommendations available online and, once established, making them available through Gazette notifications and so forth) and established standards of consultation. It is recommended that a single unit, such as MOC's Planning Cell, take responsibility for putting in place and monitoring these mechanisms and their standard operating procedures for the functioning of standing or ad hoc committees, as well as procedures for conducting broader stakeholder outreach. The individual policy wings and cells in MOC and its agencies would then be responsible for implementation or utilization of the established mechanisms. This will require that all units have adequate information technology equipment and systems for managing file sharing and communications.

- *Strengthen research and analysis.* Several intermediate steps can strengthen the rigor of research and analysis to support policy formulation and monitoring and evaluation. This includes several types of research and analysis, including providing periodic reports on trade developments, including Bangladesh's own performance and other regional or international trends; the ex ante analysis necessary to formulate the periodic Import and Export Policies and analyze the impacts of trade agreements under negotiation, including tariff and nontariff concessions, rules of origin, and other aspects of agreements; tracking, assessing, and recommending policy options in response to national, regional, and international economic trends and shocks; responding to the policies and strategies of related ministries as they impact the trade environment; and monitoring and assessing the impact of trade policies, including the Import and Export Policies.

  - *Build analytical capacity within relevant government bodies through a central trade analysis unit.* MOC and its agencies (BFTI and BTC) should have at their disposal a minimum in-house capacity to support trade policy decisions, including the tracking and analysis of industry trends impacting trade or resulting from trade policy (for example, calculating effective rates of protection), analysis of trade policy and FTAs with simple partial equilibrium modeling and scenario analysis, and analysis of the impacts of domestic regulations on trade. A comprehensive program should be developed, in coordination with the donor community, to develop such capacity through a single unit, perhaps BTC's Trade Policy Unit. This would include training on the use of standardized tools from the World Bank, ITC, and others. This should be complemented by high-level training for officials in the various wings and cells of MOC, BTC, and BFTI to develop basic knowledge and understanding of the research and analytical results used in policy making. BFTI, as the primary training mechanism for trade issues, should be the recipient of a train-the-trainers program to ensure that such training can be sustained through the development of its own curricula and materials for research and non-research staff.

- *Develop a data management center.* To support the government's ongoing research needs and address gaps in data, it is recommended that a data management center be incorporated into the proposed research unit in BTC's Trade Policy Unit, as a central resource for access to domestic and international trade databases, domestic production data, and other research and information sources. A simple, web-based system could be developed to provide government researchers with access to domestic (for example, detailed customs data) and subscribed data sources, many of which are available for free to the government, through the World Bank, UNCTAD, ITC, and others. The system could be configured to generate automatic reports, with data derived from selected sources and generated on a regular basis (such as monthly trade data).

- *Strengthen links with external research institutes.* Although basic analytical skills would be developed in MOC, BTC, and BFTI, the government will require more complex trade policy analysis, such as advanced statistical modeling or general equilibrium modeling, from time to time to support policy making and trade negotiations, as well as independent analysis. It is recommended that links with existing research and policy institutes, such as BIDS, CPD, PRI, and academic institutions, be strengthened to engage researchers throughout the policy-making lifecycle. Should PFF be launched, the new institution could be leveraged, as well, to provide analytical support on tariff- and tax-related analysis. In parallel, the central trade policy unit would need capacity building to coordinate and manage the research carried out by external researchers, including the ability to define its research requirements.

- *Appoint an economic advisor.* It is recommended that the government seek donor assistance to recruit an economic advisor, to be embedded in MOC, to provide high-level advice to MOC, and to support capacity building in

MOC and other trade-related bodies. The role of the economic advisor would be to provide overall strategic advice to MOC and its implementing agencies on the development and implementation of a cohesive Strategic Trade Policy Agenda, help direct trade policy formulation, engage with think tanks, and support the development of analytical capacity in BTC, with the aim of enabling BTC to play a more prominent role, in this respect, over the longer term.

- *Build institutional capacities.* The following outlines key capacity-building areas:
  - *At MOC:* The following key capacities need to be built:
    + Train staff (through BFTI and available World Bank, ITC, UNCTAD, and other international programs) on trade policy; multilateral, bilateral, and regional trade; identification of interests and options in multilateral agreements; prioritizing negotiating positions on bilateral and regional agreements; and trade diplomacy and negotiations. The latter area will be targeted specifically at senior officials at MOC and BTC that are actively engaged in negotiations, either at the WTO or through regional agreements, and provided by BFTI.
    + Consider options for providing legal expertise in MOC on a permanent basis, as there is sufficient demand within MOC, either through direct hire or on retainer through a local law firm or, if neither of those options is feasible, through the secondment of a legal expert from the Law Ministry. Depending on available capacities, further training on trade law may be required.
  - *At BTC:* Build capacity as shared in-house resource for trade research, analysis, and data management to enable BTC to develop fully its role as the primary source of trade policy advice to MOC and the rest of the government.
  - *At BFTI:* Given the constraints imposed by the civil service rotation practices, there is a need to build a sustainable framework to address the many gaps in human resource skills and capacities at MOC and its agencies. There is an opportunity to strengthen BFTI, through a train-the-trainer program, to provide ongoing training and professional development to the other trade-related agencies with ongoing external training reserved for more advanced skills development, to supplement BFTI programming. Two separate sets of curricula are recommended to build the basic analytical capacity of trade officials in MOC and other trade-related institutions designed to provide a consistent, broad level of knowledge of basic principles of trade policy, the role of the WTO and its agreements, trade negotiation skills, and the role of regional trade integration. Several sources of existing training modules are available through the WTO, WBI, UNCTAD, ITC, and others that can be leveraged to design a train-the-trainers program and curriculum. An illustrative BFTI Train-the-Trainers program is outlined in box 4.5.

Box 4.5 Outline for a BFTI Train-the-Trainers Program

Basic Principles of Trade Policy
- Process within the Ministry of Commerce
- International Trade Policy
- Principles of Trade Theory
- Basics of Empirical Analysis
- Overview of Bangladesh's Trade Agreements
- Bangladesh Trade Policy Regime
- Industrial Policy
- Principles of Industrial Policy Theory
- Overview of Bangladesh's Industrial Policy Regime

Analytical Tools for Trade Policy Research
Quantitative Policy Analysis Tools
- Trade Indicators and Use of WITS and Other Indicator Databases
- Partial Equilibrium Analysis
- Introduction to Forecasting Techniques
- Interpretation of CGE Models
- Cost/Benefit Analysis and Impact Assessment Methodologies

Economic Data
- Survey of National Data Sources
- International Data Sources
- International Reports
- Assessing the Consistency and Reliability of Data

Trade Negotiations
- Role and Development of Negotiations in Commercial Diplomacy
- Overview of Trade Negotiations
- Elements of Interest-Based Negotiations
- Identification of Problems and Opportunities
- Establishing Negotiating Goals and Objectives
- Research, Planning, and Pre-Negotiation Negotiations
- Skills to Employ at the Negotiating Table
- Drafting Agreements
- Dispute Resolution Mechanisms
- Modules on Specific Trade Agreement Topics (Agriculture, Services, Rules of Origin, TRIPS and Intellectual Property Rights, Trade Facilitation, SPS, TBTs).

Note: BFTI = Bangladesh Foreign Trade Institute; CGE = computable general equilibrium; SPS = sanitary and phytosanitary; TBTs = technical barriers to trade; TRIPS = the Agreement on Trade-Related Aspects of Intellectual Property Rights; WITS = World Integrated Trade Solution.

Annex 4A: Details of Organizations in Bangladesh and Overseas

Figure 4A.1 Ministry of Commerce: Organizational Structure

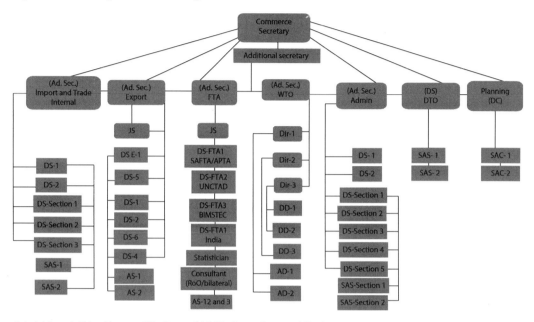

Note: Ad. Sec. = Additional Secretary; DC = Deputy Chief; DS = Deputy Secretary; SAS = Senior Assistant Secretary; AS = Assistant Secretary; Dir = Deputy Director; AD = Assistant Director; SAC = Senior Assistant Chief.

Figure 4A.2 Bangladesh Tariff Commission: Organizational Structure

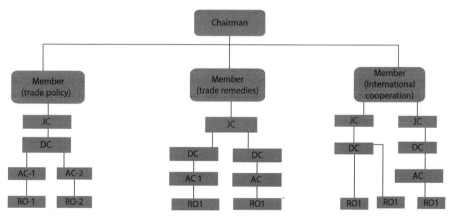

Note: JC = Joint Commissioner; DC = Deputy Chief; AC = Assistant Commissioner; RO = Research Officer.

Strengthening Competitiveness in Bangladesh—Thematic Assessment
http://dx.doi.org/10.1596/978-1-4648-0898-2

Figure 4A.3 Bangladesh Foreign Trade Institute: Organizational Structure

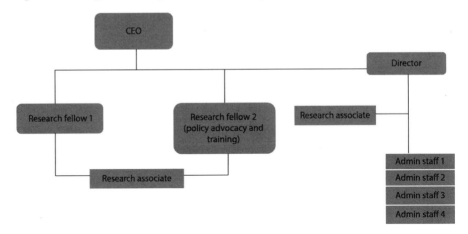

Box 4A.1 Export Policy and Priority Sector Incentives

The Export Policy stipulates General Provisions for Export, Steps toward Export Diversification, General Export Facilities, and Product-Specific Export Facilities. Under General Export Facilities, the Export Policy enunciates an Export Promotion Fund (providing venture capital at lower interest rates and with soft terms for production of goods, exhibitions, and so forth) and other financial facilities (incentives such as tax exemptions and cash incentives, export credit, and exemptions from insurance premiums, bond facilities, airfreight, and other subsidies). The Export Policy also contains provisions for prohibited products and products subject to "conditional exports."

As a step toward augmenting and diversifying exports, the Export Policy stipulates (a) "highest priority sectors," referred to as "products and sectors which have special export potentials, but such potentials could not be utilized properly due to certain constraints, and more success is attainable if adequate support is rendered to them" and (b) "special development sectors," referred to as products or sectors "which have export potentials but whose production, supply and export base are not consolidated." The Export Policy further states that "government will regularly modify this list, and provide special privileges to encourage the export of these products."

Box 4A.2 Standards of Consultation

Standard of consultation. Create a standardized format for consultation documents, such as a summary of policy goals, main issues, and options, to permit easier access by stakeholders.

Scope of consultation (policy decisions). Make consultation accessible to all businesses and stakeholders.

box continues next page

Box 4A.2 Standards of Consultation *(continued)*

Method of consultation. Build a unique Internet website for publication of and consultation on draft regulations and decisions. This would significantly improve the visibility and accessibility of ministerial documents and place the Ministry of Commerce in the mainstream of international practice. Plan, for example, to publish open public consultations that are announced at a "single access point" or central webpage. Timely information, meeting dates, and agendas should be available to participants well in advance. Short reports on meetings should also be produced and distributed as soon as possible.

Timing of consultation.

1. Revise procedures inside the Ministry to require consultation early in policy development, before drafting is done, to improve the quality of documents submitted to the minister.
2. Allow sufficient time for response to information. Ministry staff should allow at least eight weeks for responses to be written for public consultations and 20 working days for meetings.
3. Receipt of contributions should be acknowledged.
4. Results of open public consultation should be displayed on a website linked to a single access point on the Internet.
5. Ministerial reactions to stakeholder comments should be summarized in the final policy decision.

Source: OECD 2010.

Box 4A.3 National Institute of Public Finance and Policy of India

Objectives. The National Institute of Public Finance and Policy (NIPFP) was founded in 1976. It is an independent center for excellence in applied research in sustainable public finance policy for development, including strong advocacy and capacity development of public and private institutions.

Governance. NIPFP's governing body comprises three eminent economists, taxation experts, and 12 other members representing state governments, research institutions, scientific societies, chambers, and senior officials from the Ministry of Finance (MOF). NIPFP works closely with the Department of Economic Affairs (DEA) of the MOF, and the chief executive director of NIPFP is a member of the Economic Advisory Council to the Prime Minister of India. The Advisory Board of the DEA of the MOF provides overall policy guidance to NIPFP, while a steering committee headed by the Secretary of DEA reviews various policy notes and outlines future areas of research.

Funding. NIPFP receives an annual grant-in-aid from the MOF (Government of India) and from various state governments. This grant is supplemented by funds from its sponsoring, corporate, permanent, and ordinary members.

Key activities. NIPFP's three major activities encompass research, training, and advocacy work.

• **Research.** Major research includes work on contemporary fiscal issues; several studies on central, state, and local finances; and studies on neighboring countries. NIPFP has also

box continues next page

Box 4A.3 National Institute of Public Finance and Policy of India *(continued)*

conducted more than 230 sponsored studies on tax systems of central, state, and local governments; the indirect taxes enquiry committee; reform of domestic trade taxes in India; goods and service tax reform; other state and local taxes; and public expenditures. NIPFP provides fee-for-service consultancies within and outside India.

- **Training**. Training programs in the form of day and residential courses, lectures, workshops, and so forth are organized for government and nongovernment officials as well as international participants.
- **Advocacy**. NIPFP identifies various public interest–related issues and conducts advocacy through dissemination events. These advocacies have had significant influence on the policy making of the Government of India.

Source: Knowledge Sharing Workshop: Visit to National Institute of Public Finance and Policy (NIPFP); India Finance Division, Ministry of Finance and World Bank, Bangladesh, November 8–9, 2010.

Box 4A.4 Australia's Productivity Commission

The Productivity Commission of Australia is set up as principal evaluation and advisory body on microeconomic policy and regulation. It conducts rigorous and authoritative quantitative estimates of the costs of trade barriers and other forms of government assistance to industries, consumers, and the economy as a whole. These have helped persuade policy makers of the merits of trade liberalization, transparency, and independence. Evaluation of the economy-wide effects of policies has become one of the three fundamental principles of the Productivity Commission and its predecessor—all essential attributes that are currently missing from current policy-making apparatus in Bangladesh. Before discussing the shape and form of how the Productivity Commission may be relevant, it is incumbent to understand the commission's evolution. It operates independently, under the authority of an Act of Parliament, *as an advisory body*. The commission has a chairman and commissioners who are statutory appointees, and they cannot be removed except by Parliament. Transparency is ensured through the commission's public hearing process and its public release of inquiry and annual reports.

The Productivity Commission has the following personnel:

- Associate commissioners, who enhance the work of the commission and the community's understanding of the commission's approach. Although usually appointed for their expertise on a particular inquiry, some have been appointed on a permanent basis.
- Recruited staff with economics and quantitative skills, especially key staff with the highest quantitative acumen.

The Productivity Commission Act specifies that the commission's formal functions are as follows:

- Hold inquiries and report on matters relating to industry development and productivity
- Provide secretariat and research services to government bodies such as the Council of Australian Governments

box continues next page

Box 4A.4 Australia's Productivity Commission *(continued)*

- Investigate competitive neutrality complaints
- Initiate its own research on industry development and productivity
- Promote public understanding of industry development and productivity matters
- Undertake other functions, including providing advice to the treasurer, on request, on industry development and productivity matters.

    These functions translate into a wide range of activities:

- Government-commissioned projects
    - Major inquiries with public hearings
    - Inquiries without formal hearings
    - Public inquiries on safeguard action against imports
    - Evaluations of departmental programs
    - Advice to the Treasurer.
- Standing research and advisory responsibilities:
    - Commonwealth and state service provision for the Council of Australian Governments
    - Performance monitoring of government trading enterprises
    - International benchmarking, especially of economic infrastructure
    - Case studies on workplace arrangements
    - Regulation review, including advice to the Cabinet, vetting, and compliance monitoring
    - Competitive neutrality complaints mechanism
    - Annual reporting on productivity, assistance, and regulation.
- Supporting research.

Source: Australian Productivity Commission 2000.

Notes

1. As of 2012, phytosanitary certification is required for all imported plants and plant products. There are 26 quarantine stations at the border: 20 at land borders, 3 in airports, 2 in sea ports, and 1 in a river port. Each quarantine station has a staff of six to eight people; Chittagong has 14 staff members. About 190 people in total work in quarantine.

2. The main formal consultative committees on trade-related issues are the National Committee on Exports; Consultative Committees, one each on imports and exports; and the High-Powered Committee on WTO issues. Among those committees, some are permanent and some are issue-specific (and exist only up to resolution of the issue).

References

Australian Productivity Commission. 2000. *Australian Productivity Commission Annual Report (1999–2000).* Melbourne: Government of Australia.

MOF (Ministry of Finance). 2011. "Towards Building a Happy, Prosperous and Caring Bangladesh." Budget Speech 2011–12, paragraphs 38 and 331. Government of Bangladesh, Dhaka.

NBR (National Board of Revenue). 2010. *Structure of Customs Tariffs Imperative of Rationalization.* An Interim Report of the NBR Task Force on Tariff Rationalization, Presentation, NBR, February 11. http://xa.yimg.com/kq/groups/19207362/710104351 /name/Tariffs_Rationalization.pdf.

OECD (Organisation for Economic Co-operation and Development). 2010. *Jordan Trade Capacity Building Program.* Paris: OECD Guidelines, OECD.

WTO (World Trade Organization). 2012. *Trade Policy Review: Bangladesh 2012.* Geneva, Switzerland: WTO Secretariat.

CHAPTER 5

Meeting the Quality Challenge: Technical Regulation, Sanitary and Phytosanitary Measures, and Quality Infrastructure

Michael Friss Jensen

Introduction

In the future, Bangladesh's ability to harness economic opportunities from global trade will depend on its management of the quality of the products it exports and imports. Bangladesh faces a quality challenge for its exports and imports. For exports, buyers and importing countries will set more stringent standards and technical regulations in the future. The success of Bangladesh's attempts to develop and diversify its exports will depend on how the country meets this quality challenge. Simultaneously, in the future, the population of Bangladesh will demand better regulation of imports to address an expanding array of issues, like public safety, food safety, and plant and animal health. Meeting the quality challenge in export and import markets will help maximize trade, accelerate growth, and eradicate poverty.

This chapter assesses the quality challenge. It argues that in export markets quality management is essentially a private undertaking, but the government and the donors that support it play a key role in setting the rules right and providing support infrastructure and technical assistance. It is the private sector that picks markets and has to comply with the quality requirements. The role of the government is to help producers, notably small and medium enterprises (SMEs), meet quality standards and with an appropriate supply of national infrastructure. This supply usually consists of a combination of private and government services for quality, supplemented by imported services.

The chapter focuses on the key concerns of meeting quality demands in Bangladesh. Because of the complex and dynamic nature of the quality challenge, the chapter is necessarily nonexhaustive. Careful choices were made to ensure that the chapter was not too long or too detailed to be of use to the practitioner. The chapter does not discuss all—or even a majority—of the specific standards and quality requirements that Bangladeshi exporters face. These specifications change so rapidly that detailed information would soon be outdated. Timely specifics should be sought elsewhere. The chapter focuses on general issues and includes specifics only to illustrate generic points.

The chapter supplements existing material on how low- and middle-income countries (LMICs) may meet the quality challenge. Many international agencies have produced guides and handbooks on quality policy and export development.[1] Most such publications draw heavily on the experiences of high- and middle-income economies and less on economies like Bangladesh. Therefore, this chapter occasionally deviates from some common recommendations. Notably, the chapter urges prioritization and exploitation of the capacities of private market suppliers of services for quality where these exist. To develop an appropriate quality system, the scarce resources and capacities of government institutions must complement existing private efforts rather than replace them. The garment industry, for example, uses services for quality testing and certification extensively, and this demand is met satisfactorily by private suppliers.

The chapter is based on stakeholder interviews and existing research on the challenges Bangladesh faces with respect to technical regulation, sanitary and phytosanitary (SPS) measures, and quality infrastructure. The authors visited Bangladesh from March 18 to March 29, 2012, and again from November 24 to December 13, 2012. Officials in the Bangladeshi government were interviewed (at the Ministry of Commerce, the Bangladesh Standards and Testing Institute, Plant Protection Wing, and Department of Fisheries). Private sector and nongovernmental stakeholders were also consulted, including industry associations (Dhaka Chamber of Commerce and Industry), individual firms (in garments, footwear, ceramics, food, and quality service providers), donors, and academics. The chapter was finally revised following a validation workshop in Dhaka on October 22–23, 2013.

The chapter is structured as follows. The next section presents background information on international best practice. The following section identifies Bangladeshi export quality requirements and discusses how Bangladesh meets them. Then the chapter presents Bangladeshi import regulations and analyzes the operation of two major import regulation agencies, the Bangladesh Standards and Testing Institute (BSTI) and the Plant Protection Wing. The following section reviews quality-related barriers to trade between Bangladesh and India. The last section concludes and makes policy recommendations on how to improve Bangladesh's technical regulation, SPS measures, and quality infrastructure.

Background

When judging the way a country meets the quality challenge, two approaches dominate. The first approach, which we call the benchmark approach, uses international best practices as a benchmark. Reform is directed toward incorporating international best practice into the country's quality system. The second approach, which we call the demand assessment approach, analyzes and identifies the country's needs in terms of export market requirements, domestic demand for consumer protection, demand for technical interoperability of components, and so forth. Demand assessment seeks to tailor reform to the challenges the country faces. Although these two approaches appear conceptually distinct, in practice, the practitioner will often use them in combination.

This chapter elaborates on these two approaches, but first there is a discussion about terminology. The key concept of "quality" is in one way in the legal literature much inspired by the Agreement on Technical Barriers to Trade (TBT Agreement) of the World Trade Organization (WTO) and in another by the vast literature on quality management. The legal literature distinguishes sharply between "quality" and "safety." Thus, a fruit, for example, has quality characteristics like taste and color and safety characteristics like pesticide residues. The reason for this distinction is that the TBT Agreement allows government to regulate what it understands as safety issues but not quality. In the quality management literature, the concept of quality is broader and includes whatever characteristics may cause two variants of a product to differ. Thus, in this tradition, safety characteristics are just another form of quality characteristics. This chapter uses the quality management terminology because the key areas it discusses, like quality infrastructure and conformity assessment, are used to control all sorts of quality characteristics, including what a WTO lawyer would call safety.

The benchmark approach has been used to evaluate the needs of many LMICs and to inform capacity building for standardization and quality. The approach addresses two basic problems. First, although many practitioners refer to international best practice, there is no consensus on what it contains. Best practice likely varies with the country context. Second, technical regulation and the quality infrastructure are basic in many LMICs. Thus, benchmarking with any given definition of best practice yields so many deficiencies that prioritization becomes difficult without further analysis.

The demand assessment approach suffers from severe methodological difficulties. Cost-benefit analysis and similar economic valuation methods are conceptually simple and often recommended. Yet in practice, these methods depend on the availability of data, as well as human and financial resources that are in limited supply in LMICs. The practitioner therefore often combines the two approaches, for example, the benchmark approach may be used to focus the demand assessment on a few alternative policy choices. The benchmark approach may also be used as a quality control of the outcome of a demand assessment. If the demand assessment leads to recommendations of a policy course contradicted by best-practice lessons, great care should be taken to argue for the deviation. In essence, deviations from international best practice in a country's quality system should always be substantiated in objective circumstances, like institutional weakness.

Best Practice in Drafting Technical Regulations and Standards

The concept of international best practice plays a central role in the discussions of a country's quality system. This section seeks to discuss what international

Strengthening Competitiveness in Bangladesh—Thematic Assessment
http://dx.doi.org/10.1596/978-1-4648-0898-2

practice is and how good practice may vary with country contexts. Although many observers and practitioners refer to the concept of best practice, no commonly accepted definition exists on what it is. This chapter discusses best practice using three sources of information.

First, recent joint work by the Organisation for Economic Co-operation and Development (OECD) and the Asia-Pacific Economic Cooperation (APEC) has searched for common ground on the understanding of best practice. The memberships of the OECD and APEC cover the major part of the world economy and this initiative subsequently constitutes the initiative with the broadest anchor currently available. In addition, the OECD and APEC have developed a joint work program on regulatory reform (APEC and OECD n.d.). Among the program's outcomes is a checklist on regulatory reform and a note entitled "Information Notes on Good Practice for Technical Regulation" (APEC 2000). The checklist is meant to be used by economies desiring to move closer to good international practice by establishing a framework of key concepts for decision makers. The note discusses elements of best practice more specifically for technical regulations and conformity assessment.

Second, the WTO SPS and TBT agreements contain guidance on international best practice in regulating quality issues, notably with respect to minimizing the trade restrictiveness of a country's quality system. The SPS and TBT agreements establish regimes for the implementation of technical regulations. They also encourage and set out rules for the use of trade facilitation instruments, like harmonization, equivalency, and mutual recognition.

Third, analytical work and capacity-building efforts in LMICs are beginning to influence the understanding of what constitutes best practice. In many LMICs, recent capacity-building efforts by multilateral organizations like the United Nations Industrial Development Organization (UNIDO) and bilateral agencies like the German Metrological Institute have generated new thinking on how best to address the quality challenge in LMICs (see, for example, Kellermann 2011; UNIDO 2007). In many least-developed and low-income countries, capacity will have to be built almost from scratch. To establish a quality system that serves the needs of a low- or middle-income developing country, careful prioritization of interventions will be crucial and policy measures will need to match a country's human, institutional, technological, and financial resources. The remainder of this section identifies and discusses lessons of best practice as witnessed in the APEC-OECD work program; the WTO SPS and TBT agreements; and in LMIC work on quality issues.

Technical regulations should be used exclusively to regulate a narrow set of legitimate objectives. In many LMICs, the institutions working on quality issues—such as national standardization bodies (NSBs) and various government agencies—traditionally see themselves as regulatory agencies rather than service providers to industry and consumers. The international best practice is to reserve technical regulation for a short list of legitimate objectives, such as consumer safety and safeguarding the environment, while leaving other quality-management issues to market forces and private initiatives, often in the form of voluntary standards. Furthermore, a division of labor is established in many successful economies between NSBs and government agencies like ministries. NSBs set voluntary standards while regulatory functions are reserved for the government agencies. Sometimes governments will use the voluntary standards as the basis for the technical regulations they issue, thereby making the regulations voluntary. NSBs are not directly involved in regulatory decision making, but are service providers to industry, consumers, and government.

Performance-based and prescriptive technical regulations are the two main types of technical regulation. Performance-based regulations focus on defining the objective of the regulation while prescriptive regulations define the objectives and the means through which these must be met. Prescriptive means reduce the flexibility of industry to choose the most efficient means to comply with regulatory objectives and generate great demand on the regulatory authority's ability to deal with complex technical issues. Performance-based regulation is seen as a proper way to decentralize decision making on technical issues to the level where the best knowledge exists, the industry. However, a limited role remains for prescriptive technical regulations in situations where a high degree of control of the compliance process is desirable. Typically, these are situations where there are limited ways of achieving a desired objective or when the problem addressed by regulation is static. Performance-based regulations may introduce uncertainty regarding what constitutes compliance and may pose difficulties for regulators that monitor and enforce compliance. Furthermore, in high-income countries, performance-based regulations are often used in combination with additional controls, such as post-market surveillance. The WTO TBT Agreement Article 2.8 encourages WTO members to apply performance-based regulations:

> Wherever appropriate Members shall specify technical regulations based on product requirements in terms of performance rather than design or descriptive characteristics.[2]

The major advantage of performance-based regulations is that they can accommodate a range of technical compliance solutions, thus encouraging innovation and technological change.

The referencing of voluntary standards may reduce the uncertainty of how to comply with performance-based standards if used properly. Regulatory authorities may stipulate that the compliance with certain voluntary standards developed by national or international standard-setting bodies is an optional way of ensuring compliance. This approach provides guidance on how to comply while ensuring flexibility. However, many voluntary standards are not developed to assess compliance and may include many features irrelevant to the question of compliance. Regulatory authorities should exercise care that only aspects of voluntary standards relevant to compliance are referenced by a technical regulation.

Alignment with international standards reduces the trade restrictiveness of technical regulations. Harmonization may lead to cost savings through economies of scale and may lead to the transfer of technology to LMICs. However, the positive effects of harmonization depend on the appropriateness of the international standards with which harmonization takes place. Some international standards address problems for which the optimal configuration of the standards depends on local conditions, such as weather or institutional capacity. The WTO SPS and TBT Agreements encourage the use of international harmonization as a trade facilitation tool, but stop short of making harmonization mandatory (Jensen and Vergano 2009). APEC (2000) emphasizes that to be valuable for harmonization, international standards must have been drafted through a process that is transparent, open, and nondiscriminatory, and that properly reflects the conditions in all countries expected to use the standard. Many international standards are developed without inputs from LMICs.

Equivalency and mutual recognition are alternative trade facilitation instruments to harmonization (APEC 2000; Jensen and Vergano 2009). Acceptance of the technical regulations of other economies, even when standards are not identical, may still result in efficiency gains for industry and regulators through the means of equivalency and mutual recognition as recognized in the WTO SPS and TBT Agreements. The usefulness of these alternative trade facilitation instruments depends on the ability of different economies to achieve the same levels of protection of health and safety. For trade between countries with highly varying income levels, this may be difficult. Yet, successful cases do exist where LMICs have established equivalent regulatory frameworks for compliance with highly demanding OECD country regulations. These successes are typified by Vietnam's ability to gain recognition for its regulatory framework in seafood by the European Union, an achievement that has allowed Vietnam to gain EU market access and make the European Union its most important seafood destination.

In summary, a country may take a number of steps to minimize the restrictions that technical regulations impose on domestic industry and trade. These steps include the following:

- Limit the use of technical regulations (in some countries, also called mandatory standards) to issues of product safety, environmental protection, and similar issues requiring tight government control. Make standards voluntary when legitimate objectives are not in play.
- When regulating legitimate objectives, adopt performance-based rather than prescriptive technical regulations.
- Ensure that when referencing voluntary standards only the parts of the voluntary standards necessary to achieve the legitimate objective are referenced.
- Use the appropriate trade facilitation instruments (such as harmonization, equivalency, or mutual recognition) to reduce the difference in regulatory requirements across borders.

Best Practice in Conformity Assessment

A country should seek to choose the appropriate conformity assessment regime. The appropriate system meets the needs of industry and consumers at the lowest costs, exploits available sources of conformity assessment services (that is, private, public, and imported services) efficiently, and ensures the greatest degree of compliance with technical regulations with the lowest degree of government interference (APEC 2000; Kellermann 2011).

Inspection is a highly stringent form of conformity assessment and places a significant burden on industry and consumers. Furthermore, inspection regimes often put severe strain on government resources because they demand many personnel and financial resources. APEC (2000) recommends that inspection should only be used in high-risk situations or in cases where the product is constructed on-site and does not reach final form until ready to be put in use (as with buildings, for example). Border management procedures often include testing and inspection activities. Efficiency concerns dictate that the often severely limited public resources available for border management should be directed toward their most effective use. Risk profiling may generate considerable gains in cost-effective inspection and meeting the objectives of regulation. In risk profiling, available product and trader information is used to identify trade most likely not to comply with technical regulations. Border management resources are subsequently directed toward these segments.

Batch testing samples each batch or shipment of a mass-produced product and reduces the burden associated with testing. According to APEC (2000), batch testing is declining in popularity because increasingly effective quality management systems in firms ensure that each product made has the same quality. Batch testing remains useful when the regulator or buying company lacks confidence that the quality of the product is consistent.

Licensing assesses the competence of an individual or firm to undertake a specific task. Licensing is applicable in situations where the quality characteristics of the resulting product are difficult to observe. The need for certainty that technical regulations will be met necessitates that competent individuals or firms should make the product. Such individuals or firms should be licensed, and the license may be subject to periodic renewal to ensure that competencies are maintained.

Approvals are currently the most common form of pre-market conformity assessment in OECD countries. Approvals involve the assessment of a product sample. The assessment may be done either by a government body or by an accredited test facility. In either case, the regulatory body retains the final decision based on the test to approve or disallow the sale of the product. Approval systems are normally complemented by systems of post-market surveillance. Post-market surveillance involves the monitoring of products put on the market, including batch testing if necessary, to ensure that the goods on sale correspond to the originally approved product.

Most certification activities are undertaken effectively and efficiently by private certification companies. Certification is a third-party attestation related to products, processes, systems, or persons. Certification is based on the results of tests, inspections, and audits, and gives confidence to the customer or buying company on account of the systematic intervention of a competent third body. In some countries, mainly LMICs, the government is active in certification, but for the most part, private companies specialize in the provision of such conformity assessment services. Globally, a range of multinational conformity service providers has developed to serve business and government needs in LMICs and high-income countries.

Listing or registration is a less intrusive alternative to approval. Listing or registration accomplishes the same outcome as approval without the direct activity of the regulatory body prior to putting a product on the market. Producers or traders simply submit appropriate documentation such as testing reports. On the basis of this documentation, the regulatory body makes a decision. Listing or registration of products allows the regulatory body to identify the manufacturer or trader should a problem of nonconformity arise. Best practice in the use of approval, listing, and registration is to reserve these instruments for products with relevant critical characteristics, for example, for objectives like consumer safety. Pre-market approval may be avoided for products with less critical characteristics.

Supplier declarations provide significant advantages to industry. Supplier declarations require the producer or trader to demonstrate due diligence in the form of, for instance, testing by a conformity assessment body or the supplier's own testing facility. Supplier declarations allow industry to choose the facility used to demonstrate conformity with technical regulation. Industry is not required to seek approval from the regulatory body prior to placing its product on the market. Such a system leads to time and cost savings for industry and lessens the administrative burden of the regulatory body. Naturally, a minimum level of trust is an essential requirement for the efficient functioning of supplier declarations.

An efficient conformity assessment regime exploits the potential of the private market. In all countries, quality regulation is only a small part of quality management. Technical regulations address mandatory quality standards, but quality management also deals with nonmandatory requirements such as size, shape, design, and so forth. Nonmandatory requirements are nevertheless crucial for achieving international competitiveness. Quality management, including regulation, is constantly evolving. This is particularly so in LMICs, which are under pressure to meet international requirements exceeding domestic ones and simultaneously meeting the expectations of the local populations to upgrade domestic quality management and regulation. As discussed, complying with technical regulations often involves working with private sector bodies. Similarly, complying with private market requirements in the form of voluntary standards or company quality specifications is often exclusively a private market issue. In this case, the government's role is to allow the private market for quality services to operate efficiently.

Furthermore, the conformity assessment regime should harness the resources of the global economy. Many conformity assessment services are highly tradable. Simultaneously, many LMICs are small and lack the capacity to supply necessary quality services. Even among high-income countries, such as EU member states, quality services are often provided across the border.

In summary, a country may take several steps to increase the effectiveness and efficiency of its conformity assessment regime. These steps include the following:

- Use all available sources of conformity assessment services to establish a conformity assessment regime that economizes on scarce public resources and meets regulatory demands as well as other quality management demands.
- Allow private and imported conformity assessment services to complement the national conformity assessment regime.
- Consider carefully the choice of conformity assessment instruments and pick the one that meets the objective of regulation while creating minimal government interference.
- Consider the range of alternative instruments used in more developed economies and evaluate their usefulness in the context of the relevant economy.

Meeting the Quality Challenge Abroad: How Bangladesh Manages Export Quality

Access to export markets is influenced by many quality requirements that vary greatly across markets. Garments and ceramics are examples of markets where such requirements are predominantly set by private firms. However, some quality characteristics are regulated by importing countries that enforce technical regulations. Garments, for instance, have to comply with, among other things, consumer expectations about design and washing resistance; buyer requirements about pilling, durability, and labor conditions; and regulatory demands from the end-markets about dyes, other chemicals, and heavy metals. These value chains are very much buyer-driven; that is, large foreign buyers set the rules, including quality requirements. In contrast, seafood is an example of a market in which stringent technical regulations are most important: these are set by importing countries, most notably the European Union and the United States. Horticulture is yet another story. The main exports of fresh fruits and vegetables from Bangladesh go to the Middle East, where quality requirements are easy to meet. Some processed and manufactured products are exported to India and are burdened by cumbersome Indian import procedures and the lack of mutual recognition of certification between India and Bangladesh. Table 5.1 illustrates the range of quality requirements that apply to exports.

Producers need to tailor-make products for buyers. As an example, the Plant Protection Wing of the Ministry of Agriculture, the national Bangladeshi plant health authority, reports that it has received numerous notifications from

Table 5.1 Illustrative Quality Issues for Bangladeshi Export Products

		Standards, private protocols, and technical regulations relating to			
Product group	Quality attributes	Consumer safety standards	Food safety	Plant and animal health	Environmental and social issues
Garments and footwear	Design durability	Azo dyes, heavy metals, EU REACH[a]	n.a.	n.a.	Private labor standards and codes of practice Private environmental codes of practice Waste water treatment
Ceramics	Shapes Glaze Decor	Lead and cadmium content	n.a.	n.a.	Private labor standards and codes of practice
Fresh produce	Demand for traditional Bangladeshi varieties by expat Bangladeshi communities Packaging standards	n.a.	Pesticide residue limits Hygiene requirements	Phytosanitary certification Fumigation Pest risk analysis Traceability	n.a.
Seafood	Size Species Taste Color	n.a.	Hygiene requirements Antibiotics residue limits HACCP[b]	n.a.	n.a.

Note: n.a. = not applicable.
a. European Union's REACH (Registration, Evaluation, Authorization and Restriction of Chemicals) chemical control program.
b. Hazard Analysis and Critical Control Points.

the European Union on the detection of harmful pests on citrus exports bound for the United Kingdom. In collaboration, the citrus producers and the Plant Protection Wing have developed the Bangladeshi plant health system with the aim of meeting the phytosanitary requirements of the European Union. Such problems are typical for the extremely stringent EU market. By contrast, the Plant Protection Wing has not received any complaints on sanitary or phytosanitary problems from markets in the Middle East, Bangladesh's largest market for airfreighted fresh produce. Even when receiving apparently similar products, like vegetables for Bangladeshi expatriate communities, the European Union and the Middle East have different requirements for food safety and plant health. Successful Bangladeshi exporters carefully target export markets that demand quality characteristics with which they can comply. They upgrade their products to target more demanding and higher paying markets in tandem with improving quality management capabilities.

Export Quality Management in Bangladesh

Quality management is a necessary condition for successful export performance. Meeting quality requirements in international markets is a multidimensional process, ranging from working in the value chain to ensure that the right quality is produced, to demonstrating that the product meets the relevant quality requirements. The International Trade Centre (ITC) in Geneva has identified four dimensions of quality management:[3]

- Obtaining information about the mandatory technical regulations and voluntary standards applicable in the export market
- Adapting the product to meet these quality requirements efficiently
- Demonstrating that the product meets the relevant quality requirements
- Obtaining the necessary support at each step from the national quality infrastructure.

The sections below discuss quality management in four export sectors in Bangladesh: garments and footwear, ceramics, fresh produce, and seafood. The discussion uses the four dimensions of quality management identified by the ITC.

Garments and Footwear

Garments and footwear comprise the bulk of Bangladeshi exports. Most of Bangladesh's exports are positioned in the lower quality segments of EU and U.S. markets. The buyers are a mix of branded companies and unbranded importers selling through discount outlets. Some Bangladeshi exporters are targeting higher value markets, like more fashion-oriented brands with season-oriented shifts of designs. The quality requirements in this trade are primarily private market standards and company codes, although there are some importing-country regulations on issues like chemicals (such as dyes) and heavy metals. Bangladeshi producers source market information on quality requirements exclusively through market channels, in particular their buyers. As one exporter put it in an interview, "exporting is about meeting the buyer's requirements." Bangladeshi technical regulations and standards do not play much of a role for the export trade, except for labor standards. Compliance with labor standards is a growing issue. These standards are formulated as private buyer standards and codes of conduct and as Bangladeshi regulations.

In the main garment markets, such as the European Union and the United States, nongovernmental organizations (NGOs) and labor unions have campaigned for better working conditions in the producing countries. NGOs and labor unions argue that such improved conditions should include, for example, a safe work environment, regulation of child labor, and higher wages. The campaigns have successfully influenced global garment markets and today, the large international brands that purchase most of Bangladesh's garments view compliance with labor standards as a key factor of competitiveness. Initially, each brand created its own corporate code of conduct. But influencing working conditions through private means is difficult because of the structure of the global garment industry. Most Bangladeshi garment producers supply numerous brands and cannot operate with equally numerous and differently formulated codes of conduct. For example, paying workers different wages depending on which brand will buy their output is impractical. Therefore, in 2006, the Bangladeshi government adopted a "uniform code of conduct" and updated and consolidated the old labor laws into a single one. The new labor law includes adjustments of the minimum wage every five years (World Bank 2012).

Naturally, complying with buyer requirements necessitates producing the right kind of product. Various interventions in the value chain support the adaption of the product to quality requirements. These interventions include garment and footwear manufacturers' own interventions and quality upgrading efforts, assistance from buyers, and interventions from the Bangladeshi government and the donors that support it. The manufacturers' own interventions include investment in technology and training of workers to meet quality requirements. Buyers constantly interact with manufacturers, particularly in the more quality-oriented parts of the value chain. For example, one garment manufacturer with its own design department worked closely with the designers of major international brands to develop styles for the export market. The close interaction allowed the brands to enjoy the benefits of relatively cheap design services in Bangladesh. It also helped the Bangladeshi manufacturer learn about export market requirements and adapt the company's production technology to market demands. Government and donors generally are not very involved in garment and footwear supply chains; however, work to upgrade Bangladeshi garments to higher value segments is supported by industry association–run training centers, like the University of Fashion and Technology in Dhaka.

Garments and footwear exporters use a combination of first-, second-, and third-party services to ensure and demonstrate that their products meet the relevant quality requirements. First-party services include the services that exporters provide themselves. Larger manufacturers have testing laboratories and other facilities that enable them to manage quality as the product moves through the value chain. For example, a large garment manufacturer that was visited tested its own produced textiles for various quality characteristics, including color, washing, and dry cleaning color fastness; pilling; wrinkle recovery; and similar physical characteristics for which the buyer sets exacting quality standards. This garment manufacturer primarily used testing equipment from the leading U.K. manufacturer James Heal.[4] James Heal has a global network of agents, including an agent in Bangladesh, which supplies calibration services to its customers to maintain the accuracy of the testing equipment. The calibration procedures conform to the International Organization for Standardization's (ISO) 17025, and the calibration tools are traceable to the National Physical Laboratory in the United Kingdom.

The quality of Bangladeshi garments and footwear is continuously monitored by the international buyers who do their own testing and inspection, known as second-party services. Samples of goods are tested on arrival, and large buyers even have agents in Bangladesh that may inspect facilities, with or without notice, and test the products at the end stage of production or in the production process.

Many buyers and markets require third-party quality services, which are independent from the manufacturer, exporter, and buyer. A global industry has developed to provide such services, and the size of the Bangladeshi garment industry has attracted a large number of these providers. Present providers include Intertek,[5] SGS,[6] Bureau Veritas,[7] TÜV Rheinland,[8] TÜV SÜD,[9] MTS,[10] and others. They service such areas as standardization, testing, certification, accreditation, and calibration. These providers can use their global networks to create economies of scale and thus supply services to Bangladesh that were previously unprofitable. One service provider interviewed, for example, explained that to provide certification in Good Agricultural Practices in Bangladesh, it used its Sri Lanka office, and to provide inspection services in the oil industry, it relied on its India office. When governments set import market regulations, typically to address consumer safety issues, they require third-party certification. In Bangladesh, private services for the quality industry supply such certification.

The national quality infrastructure supporting quality management in garments and footwear consists almost exclusively of private sector services supplied by a combination of domestic and foreign sources. This situation is typical for industries consisting of buyer-driven supply chains. The large international buyers dominating these supply chains manage quality by establishing a large number of private standards and codes of conduct, which in turn necessitates access to services for quality. There is particularly strong demand for private quality services in countries with large industries like Bangladesh (see lessons from Sri Lanka in box 5.2). The Bangladeshi government supplies a limited set of services for quality, including standards and testing, inspection, certification, accreditation, and calibration services (as explained in box 5.1). Remarkably, international buyers and the governments setting import regulations are fully satisfied with private services for quality.

Box 5.1 Quality Infrastructure Components

Quality requirements. Quality requirements specify the nature of a product, including its production methods as demanded by buyers or regulated by regulatory agencies, both of which may be either domestic or foreign, depending on the end market of the product. Quality requirements may be expressed as purely private requirements determined by a single buyer or a group of buyers, as formal standards, or as technical regulations. Some private quality requirements may operate like standards in the marketplace because of their market dominance.

Standards. Standards are codified quality requirements providing the basis for the evaluation of compliance with the demands of buyers and regulatory agencies. Standards may be set by a variety of actors, including national, regional, and international bodies. National standardization bodies (NSBs) bring together public and private stakeholders to

box continues next page

Box 5.1 Quality Infrastructure Components *(continued)*

develop formal consensus on national standards. Such standards may become international standards if adopted by national NSBs following certain procedural rules about the development of standards. Following the Technical Barriers to Trade (TBT) Agreement by the World Trade Organization, compliance with standards is voluntary.

Technical regulations. Technical regulations are mandatory quality requirements providing the basis of the regulation of legitimate issues such as product safety or environmental protection. Technical regulations are highly variable, ranging from very prescriptive to those that mostly set general objectives, thereby allowing the private sector the choice of how to comply. Often, technical regulations refer to standards as the technical basis of regulation. This approach ensures that a consensus exists between public and private sector actors on the most efficient ways to comply with regulation. In some countries (for example, Bangladesh), technical regulations are often called "mandatory standards," a contradiction in terms according to the TBT Agreement.

Conformity assessment. This is the process of ensuring those quality requirements are met, for example testing, inspection, and certification.

Testing and inspection. Testing and inspection demonstrate compliance with quality requirements, standards, and technical regulations. Testing and inspection may be done by first parties (in-house), second parties (buyers or regulatory agencies), or third parties (bodies independent from both transaction parties). For many needs, testing and inspection services are tradable. Small and large service providers supply testing and inspection services across borders and in low- and middle-income countries, typically to exporters.

Certification. Certification is the assurance by an independent body that a product, service, system, or process conforms to quality requirements, standards, or technical regulations. The certification bodies are often private, but may be public, especially in markets for which conformity assessment services are little developed. As with testing and inspection, certification services are tradable, and many global firms provide such services across borders.

Accreditation. Accreditation is the assurance by an authoritative body (the accreditation body) that an organization or person is competent to conduct specific tasks. Conformity assessment bodies undertaking testing, inspection, and certification can seek accreditation on a voluntary basis as proof of competence in a given area. The accreditation body may be a domestic or a foreign entity. More-developed countries often have a single national accreditation body responsible for all areas.

Calibration. Calibration is the comparison of measuring equipment against a standard instrument of higher accuracy. Firms often use calibration laboratories to calibrate their measurement equipment, although some firms calibrate their own equipment. Private or public service actors may provide calibration services that may be produced domestically or imported.

Metrology. Metrology is the science of measurement. More developed countries have established a national measurement system designed to maintain, develop, and diffuse measurement standards. This system provides calibration services to independent calibration laboratories and other institutions involved in measurement. Calibration laboratories in turn provide services to firms and public sector agencies that use measurement equipment. Measurements are traceable through a chain of comparisons back to the national system and eventually to global measurement standards, thereby guaranteeing the accuracy of the primary users of measurement equipment.

Box 5.2 Lessons from Sri Lanka on Developing Garment Testing Services

The Sri Lankan garment industry procures testing services from a variety of sources. Facilities have their own testing laboratories, and when independent testing is needed, the garment exporters use global service providers present in Sri Lanka, like Bureau Veritas and Société Générale de Surveillance. In the case of certain highly technical tests, exporters seek laboratory facilities available in India and Singapore.

In a project funded by the Norwegian Agency for Development Cooperation, the United Nations Industrial Development Organization (UNIDO) has supported the establishment of garment testing capacity at the Textile Training and Support Centre (TTSC). TTSC is a government body established in 1984 that provides training, consultancy, and testing services to the garment industry, with training as the main activity. From 1999 to 2003, UNIDO assisted TTSC with the upgrading of its textile testing laboratory. Nevertheless, an independent evaluation published in 2010 found that, contrary to expectations, the testing laboratory lost clients after the capacity building took place.

The evaluation report analyzed the Sri Lankan demand for testing services and concluded that the lack of demand for TTSC services was caused by garment exporters' preference for private laboratories. TTSC lacked accreditation by the major international garment buyers. It also suffered from a poor service culture, exemplified by weaknesses in diligence; speed of service; and lack of ancillary services like packaging, house-to-house delivery, and mailing. The rationale for developing government-supplied testing services in a market already supplied by private service suppliers is unclear.

Source: UNIDO 2010.

Ceramics

The export of ceramics is a small but growing activity in Bangladesh. Bangladeshi exports target lower quality segments in neighboring countries and the high-end market in high-income countries. Buyer-driven value chains dominate the high-end ceramics market, and quality management in such chains bears a resemblance to that in garments and footwear. Bangladeshi manufacturers work with leading ceramics brands to learn about and satisfy a mixture of buyer requirements and government-mandated import regulations; they use a variety of mostly private services for quality.

Meeting high-end quality requirements necessitates the use of modern technology, the efficient operation of the technology, and the ongoing adaption and optimization of the technology. One ceramics producer interviewed had imported cutting-edge technology from Japan, allowing the manufacture of high-quality products. The Japanese supplier provided training and technical assistance as an integrated part of the technology purchase. Details like shaping and decals are other important quality aspects in high-end ceramics and will eventually help determine market success. The producer interviewed had regular, week-long visits from buyers providing advice on how to adjust the production process to meet the buyers' quality requirements.

As with garments and footwear, Bangladeshi ceramics producers use a combination of first-, second-, and third-party services to ensure and demonstrate compliance with quality requirements. Leading ceramics producers have their own testing laboratories to test, for example, for color, dishwasher safety, and resistance to acids and detergents. Buyers test samples and inspect production facilities themselves. Buyers and importing country regulations may require independent third-party testing and certification. The use of private quality services is demonstrated by compliance with California State Proposition 65. Proposition 65 requires companies producing for the U.S. state of California to notify consumers about the presence of any harmful substances in their products. A high-end Bangladeshi ceramics manufacturer explained that to meet this regulation and similar ones in the EU market, no heavy metals like lead or cadmium were used in the glaze of the manufacturer's ceramics. To demonstrate that the ceramics were free of heavy metals, the manufacturer tested its own products and procured testing services from private services providers like Ceram UK[11] and SGS Thailand. Ceram is a materials testing, analysis, and consultancy company based in the United Kingdom but operating testing laboratories around the world. Furthermore, the manufacturer was certified ISO 9001:2008 by the Netherlands department of the service provider Det Norske Veritas.[12] The same leading Bangladeshi ceramics manufacturer reported that it purchased weight calibration services from BSTI.

The national infrastructure supporting quality management in ceramics consists almost exclusively of private sector services supplied by a combination of domestic and foreign providers. Recently, a European Union–funded and UNIDO-implemented project has updated the metrology department of BSTI, allowing ceramics manufacturers to procure weight calibration services from BSTI. Nevertheless, the ceramics industry's interaction with government quality infrastructure is limited. However, the absence of government services does not prevent Bangladeshi companies from successfully targeting high-end export markets. One ceramics manufacturer felt interaction with the government quality infrastructure could be an irritant. This manufacturer had initially assisted BSTI in the development of a mandatory Bangladeshi standard for ceramics, including rules for lead- and cadmium-free glaze. The manufacturer was inspected by BSTI every three years to achieve mandatory certification, a service for which the manufacturer paid US$25,000 and which has no commercial value.

Fresh Produce

Airfreighted fresh produce exports constitute a new but so far marginal source of export diversification. Although other LMICs have successfully developed fresh produce markets in the European Union (including asparagus from Peru, fresh vegetables from Kenya, and mangoes from Mali), Bangladesh faces a range of problems, including logistics, competitiveness, quality issues, and problems of compliance with plant health measures. Bangladesh targets such exports to communities of ethnic Bangladeshis in the United Kingdom as well as the Middle East. The requirements for quality and plant health in these markets are considerably lower than for the rapidly growing EU supermarket trade. Although the supermarket trade puts forward exacting and demanding requirements on food safety management and intrinsic product quality, ethnic markets are more price-sensitive and demand traditional Bangladeshi products. The ethnic spot market is unable to transfer complex quality signals to the producer; consumers procuring vegetables through the market are unwilling to pay for supermarket quality characteristics. Exports bound for the European Union must nevertheless satisfy EU regulations on food safety and plant health.

EU plant health rules have challenged Bangladesh. The Plant Protection Wing of the Ministry of Agriculture, the national Bangladeshi plant health authority, reports that it has received many notifications from the European Union concerning harmful pests detected on citrus exports bound for the United Kingdom. In collaboration, the citrus producers and the Plant Protection Wing have developed the Bangladeshi plant health system with the aim of meeting the plant health requirements of the European Union. Such problems are typical for the extremely stringent EU market. By contrast, the Plant Protection Wing has not received any complaints on food safety or plant health problems from markets in the Middle East, Bangladesh's largest market for airfreighted fresh produce.

Even when receiving apparently similar products, like vegetables for Bangladeshi ethnic communities, the European Union and Middle East have different standards for food safety and plant health. Successful Bangladeshi exporters carefully target export markets demanding quality characteristics with which they can comply. This strategy is one way of coping with the quality challenge: rather than adapting the product to the market, the exporter selects the right market for the product. In the longer term, breaking into larger volume trading segments in the European Union, like the supermarket trade, would require considerable upgrading of the Bangladeshi supply chain. Bangladesh faces a host of challenges in this regard, only some of which are related to quality. Given the country's geographical location and the intense competition in the world market, it remains to be seen whether Bangladeshi fresh produce will be competitive in the European Union outside ethnic markets, even if quality is raised significantly and EU private and public food safety and plant health requirements can be met.

Contrary to garments, footwear, and ceramics, the challenge for airfreighted Bangladeshi produce is primarily related to government regulations. Private quality requirements for the market segment currently targeted by Bangladeshi exporters are relatively lax. However, the European Union has intercepted banned pests, like the citrus canker and exotic fruit flies, in plant consignments from Bangladesh (FVO 2010). An EU inspection of the Bangladeshi plant health system in 2010 concluded that:

> The organisms of concern to the EU, in particular citrus canker and citrus blackspot, are known to occur in Bangladesh and no pest free areas have been established for these.

> Action has been taken in response to the continued EU interceptions of harmful organisms on fruit and vegetables exported from Bangladesh, however, the lack of

traceability and use of exporter declarations, combined with the limited awareness of EU import requirements and harmful organisms of concern, and very limited laboratory and technical support for the NPPO and records of activities, means that the current system of official export checks does not ensure compliance with EU import requirements, and until the shortcomings identified are corrected, there will be a continued risk of introduction of harmful organisms to the EU. This is particularly so for *Xanthamonas axonopodis* and *Guignardia citricarpa*, on citrus fruits (FVO 2010, p. I).

The national infrastructure supporting quality management for airfreighted fresh produce exports is weak. The private service industry that serves garments, footwear, and ceramics exports well has found no clients able to pay for services in fresh produce. This is primarily because of the small size of the sector with many small farmers and SMEs in the supply chain. The European Union's Food and Veterinary Office (FVO) report demanded significant changes in the government's quality infrastructure. The demands included upgrading the system of issuing plant health certificates; investment in government equipment and facilities necessary to carry out inspection, testing, consignment verification, plant health certification, and heat treatment of wood packaging materials; and training of officials responsible for export checks. In the future, such upgrading of the government quality infrastructure is inevitable, but it is debatable whether the demands of the tiny fresh produce industry would by themselves justify new investments at this point. The fresh produce industry already suffers from many hurdles to becoming competitive in the EU market. Prematurely upgrading quality infrastructure will not increase exports, as other problems are likely more constraining. Such problems include long, uncoordinated supply chains and higher airfreight rates along with longer flights for Bangladesh than for competitor regions like Northern and Eastern Africa and the Middle East. Therefore, if the Bangladeshi government wishes to upgrade the phytosanitary management component of the quality infrastructure, it should target the domestic and regional markets before looking at the demands of faraway markets.

Seafood

Seafood exports, in particular frozen shrimp, are a growing source of export diversification, but success has been hampered by inconsistent quality. Bangladeshi seafood is primarily exported to the European Union and the United States, where food safety regulation is tight. EU regulations are generally seen as the most stringent ones. To be allowed to export seafood to the European Union, a country needs a seafood safety regime deemed equivalent to the EU system. Additional requirements like the establishment of a national residue control system apply too. The European Union has approved the Bangladeshi Department of Fisheries as a national Competent Authority to monitor the Bangladeshi industry and approve individual processing facilities for export to the European Union. The European Union regularly inspects the regulatory system and the industry. In addition, the

European Union monitors seafood safety at points of import. If violations are detected either during country inspections or at the point of import, the European Union demands corrective actions and may impose additional requirements in case of grave violations of its food safety policy (European Commission n.d.).

The European Union has frequently imposed additional requirements for Bangladeshi seafood. In 1997, the European Union banned imports of Bangladeshi seafood following EU inspections of Bangladeshi processing plants. Inspections found deficiencies in the infrastructure and hygiene of the plants and insufficient government quality controls (Cato and Subasinge 2003). The ban sparked more investment in processing plants and government regulatory capacity by industry, government, and donors. Subsequent EU inspections determined that six processing plants met EU requirements and lifted the ban for the six plants by the end of 1997. In the following years, the upgrading of the Bangladeshi industry continued and by 2002, 65 plants held Bangladeshi government licenses for exports, of which 48 plants had EU approval. However, frequent inspections by the European Union since 2002 have pointed out additional problems. The EU Rapid Alert System for Food and Feed has regularly reported interception of Bangladeshi consignments with food safety problems, such as banned antibiotics and microbiological contamination. As late as November 2011, the European Union lifted a requirement for 20 percent mandatory testing of Bangladeshi seafood after progress had been made in the Bangladeshi residue monitoring system.

Contrary to garments, footwear, and ceramics, compliance with quality requirements in seafood is essentially about meeting government-set regulations. The organization of the industry is radically different from light manufacturing industries. The value chain of the most important product, frozen shrimp, is long and dominated by small farms linked to exports by middlemen. Respect of food safety regulation requires action from a large number of small operators, including shrimp fry hatcheries, small farmers, processors, and input providers like the suppliers of feed and animal medicine. The uncoordinated nature of shrimp value chains coupled with import market regulations has created a strong demand for government involvement and private industry coordination. In Bangladesh, the Department of Fisheries regulates the seafood value chains. Import market food safety rules are complex and continuously evolving and seafood operators from primary producers to processors as well as Bangladeshi government officials have struggled to understand the regulations and keep up with the changes. Information about the applicable regulations flows from the European Union and donor technical assistance projects as well as the Department of Fisheries to value chain participants.

Adapting Bangladeshi seafood to high-paying import market requirements necessitates completely new production and processing methods. Bangladesh traditionally produces and consumes seafood in large quantities, but past experiences in the Bangladesh market provide poor guidance for export market success. Seafood is highly perishable and prone to food safety hazards. Import markets are far away and require quality characteristics that traditionally have been of no value in the domestic market. Successful domestic producers trying to base export production on their domestic experiences will eventually fail.

To adapt Bangladeshi seafood to the new quality requirements, industry, government, and donors are undertaking several supply chain interventions. Individual processors have updated their plants and developed links with downstream suppliers. The Bangladesh Frozen Food Exporters Association organizes processors and advises government and its members on quality management. The Department of Fisheries has overall responsibility for regulatory oversight and inspection. Donors, acting through Bangladeshi government departments, notably the Department of Fisheries, have provided strong support to the seafood sector.

For example a project funded by the U.S. Agency for International Development (USAID) called Poverty Reduction by Increasing Competitiveness of Enterprises has contracted the World Fish Centre to implement the Greater Harvest and Economic Returns from Shrimp (GHERS) initiative. GHERS is focused on piloting greater integration in the value chain to increase productivity and quality. Under GHERS, shrimp depot owners work with hatcheries to ensure the supply of disease-free shrimp fry to farmers, thereby reducing future demand for antibiotics and subsequently reducing the risk of exported shrimp being rejected in the European Union and elsewhere because of antibiotic residues. The GHERS initiative builds on the experiences of two previous USAID projects, namely the Shrimp Seal of Quality Project and the Shrimp Quality Support Project (World Fish Centre 2011). The Better Work and Standards—Better Fisheries Quality (BEST-BFQ) program is funded by the European Union, the Norwegian Agency for Development Cooperation, and the government of Bangladesh and implemented by UNIDO. The program is a follow-up to the Bangladesh Quality Support Program implemented during 2006–10. BEST-BFQ applies a "farm to fork" approach that focuses on strengthening the national fisheries quality infrastructure of Bangladesh. BEST-BFQ supports the value chain by upgrading through training farmers in good aquacultural practice and by training processors and other value chain participants on traceability and the hazard analysis and critical control points (HACCP) approach. Several other donor projects support the upgrading of the Bangladeshi seafood industry.

Seafood exporters primarily use Bangladeshi government services to demonstrate compliance with the stringent regulatory requirements of the export market. Compliance necessitates regulatory oversight and intense monitoring and testing, which, according to Bangladeshi law and in compliance with EU rules, must be provided by the Department of Fisheries. EU regulations are extensive and stringent. Imports of seafood into the European Union are subject to official certification. The certification is supplied by the Department of Fisheries, recognized as the Competent Authority by the European Union. As the Competent Authority, the Department of Fisheries ensures inspection and control throughout the value chain. It monitors all relevant aspects of hygiene, public health, and, in the case of aquaculture products like frozen shrimp, animal health. Live aquatic animals, their eggs, and fry must fulfill animal health standards, which require veterinary services to enforce health controls and monitoring programs.

The Department of Fisheries must also guarantee compliance with hygiene and public health requirements, including rules on the structure of vessels, landing sites, and processing plants, as well as rules on processing, freezing, and storage. A control plan on heavy metals, contaminants, residues of pesticides, and veterinary drugs must be in place for aquacultural products like frozen shrimp. Only approved vessels and establishments, inspected by the Department of Fisheries and found to meet EU requirements, may export to the European Union. As the Competent Authority, the Department of Fisheries regularly inspects approved vessels and establishments and guarantees the respect of EU rules. Inspections by the European Union's FVO confirm Bangladesh's compliance with EU requirements. Finally, Bangladeshi seafood consignments are subject to border inspections where each consignment is subject to a documentary check, identity check, and, as appropriate, a physical check. The frequency of physical checks depends on the risk profile of the product and the results of previous checks.

The Bangladeshi government and supporting donors have invested many resources in the establishment of a seafood quality infrastructure that meets the demand of the major export markets. This development has been entirely focused on government services. The capabilities of private quality services that work for other export industries, such as garments, footwear, and ceramics, have not been developed. Other countries in the region use a different approach. In Indonesia, the Competent Authority allows private laboratories to conduct testing for monitoring programs, while it uses its own laboratory for the testing needed to issue health certificates. In Thailand, testing for monitoring and for the issue of health certificates may both be undertaken by private laboratories.

The Department of Fisheries should consider allowing a private market for seafood quality assessment. International best practice demonstrates that quality assessment services can be efficiently provided by the private sector. For example, current Bangladeshi law dictates that testing for nitrofurans, chloramphenicol, and similar substances must be done at a government laboratory. A leading private quality services provider interviewed stated that although the company currently had no capacity to test for such substances, a change in the law would, in its view, create a sufficiently large market to warrant investing in laboratory facilities to service the seafood export industry. This company has already undertaken physical inspection for shrimp exporters and certified seafood processing plants against HACCP, another mandatory EU requirement.

Summing Up: Sources of Supply of Services for Quality

The private provision of services is an integral part of Bangladesh's quality infrastructure. Private providers supply services relating to standardization, testing, certification, accreditation, and calibration. Bangladesh has a thriving private market for quality services. In light manufacturing exports, international service providers with an office in Bangladesh, like Intertek, SGS, Bureau Veritas,

TUV Rheinland, TUV SUD, MTS, and others, supply conformity assessment services. A conformity assessment need that cannot be satisfied by suppliers based in Bangladesh is often supplied through trade. Bangladesh benefits from its proximity to service providers serving larger and more mature markets, like India and Thailand, but also Malaysia, Singapore, and Sri Lanka. The presence of a large variety of service providers in the region is an advantage that Bangladesh can exploit while gradually building the national quality system. Initially, Bangladesh may wish to focus on a few high-priority areas while supplementing its own limited range of services with imports. Eventually, the amount and diversity of services offered in Bangladesh will be much increased; however, even advanced economies like those in the European Union trade intensively in services for quality. An efficient national quality system would continue to exploit the gains from imports as it matured.

At present, India's National Accreditation Board for Testing and Calibration Laboratories (NABL) exemplifies the gains from trade in services for quality. From its base in New Delhi, NABL has served both BSTI and SGS with services. Although attempts to establish a national accreditation board in Bangladesh have proven difficult, the sourcing of Indian services has allowed BSTI to acquire accreditation for a part of its laboratory capabilities and to continue working toward achieving accreditation for the rest. Meanwhile, SGS has imported metrology services from NABL. In this way, Bangladesh has saved resources otherwise needed for the development of national accreditation and metrology supplies—resources that may be used to develop other and higher prioritized parts of a national quality system.

Whether the private service providers cover the needs of SMEs is questionable. The services of international service providers tend to be costly. SMEs, especially those operating in small sectors poorly covered by private providers, may be constrained to operate in market segments in which the demand for services for quality is low or where this demand may be met by their international buyers. Knowledge of the demand for services for quality by SMEs is limited. Potentially, the needs of SMEs are covered by working with larger operators, which are in a better position to provide quality management.

Government provision of services for quality is minimal. Although a range of government institutions is theoretically in position to provide services, few services are indeed provided. In light manufacturing industries, none of the private sector operators interviewed expressed any desire to use government services for vital tasks, but preferred to rely on private services for quality. BSTI and a range of laboratories in various parts of the government and in universities could in theory provide conformity assessment services, like testing and certification. However, the poor quality of most of the laboratories and the lack of a business-oriented service mentality severely limit the provision (Raj Sud 2010).

The situation is different in the seafood industry because the governments of high-income import markets require the Bangladeshi government—represented by the Department of Fisheries—to safeguard quality. In the case of seafood exported to the European Union, the European Union requires that the

Department of Fisheries act as a Competent Authority, with legal powers and resources to ensure credible inspection and controls throughout the value chain. Therefore, the Department of Fisheries must be competent in matters of hygiene, public health, and, for farmed shrimp, animal health it must be able to provide services for quality like testing and certification. Given the importing market requirements, both the efforts of the Department of Fisheries and of the private sector operators have been crucial to the seafood industry's export success.

BSTI acts like a regulatory agency rather than a service provider. BSTI primarily provides testing and certification against its own mandatory standards, most of which cover domestic and imported products. These mandatory standards have no value to export industries (Raj Sud 2010). BSTI has attempted to set up some services in areas of interest to export industries. However, the rationale behind these attempts is unclear. Exemplified by investments in a textile laboratory, these attempts risk unnecessarily duplicating already successful provision of such services by the private sector. The only part of BSTI that does provide some level of services is the metrology department, supported by the European Union–funded and UNIDO-implemented project Better Work and Standards—Better Quality Infrastructure (BEST-BQI). BSTI mainly impacts Bangladeshi trade by mandating standards and associated inspection and testing. Thus, BSTI is further discussed in the next section, which focuses on import regulation.

Meeting the Quality Challenge at Home: How Bangladesh Manages Import Procedures

Quality Requirements for Imports into Bangladesh

Many Bangladeshi quality-related laws and regulations and SPS measures influence trade and disturb the free flow of imports unnecessarily. Imports need to flow smoothly to support the import needs of the export sectors and the needs of the domestic population. The problematic laws and regulations may be divided into three broad groups. The first group consists of technical regulations, in Bangladesh known as mandatory standards, on a range of products including food and agricultural products, chemical products, textiles, electrical and electronic products, and engineering products. The second group consists of SPS measures, notably food safety laws and regulations and plant health laws and regulations. The third group includes a number of "special rules" stated in the Import Policy Order (Ministry of Commerce 2010).

Mandatory standards require inspection and testing at the border. BSTI under the Ministry of Industries coordinates and heads a system of technical committees that draft Bangladeshi standards. The committees have some private sector participation, although not to the same degree as observed in countries with a strong history of standards development. Although the standards are voluntary in principle, around 150 products have currently been brought under the Mandatory Certification Marks Scheme and are therefore mandatory. The Ministry of Industries has the power to make standards mandatory, often acting on the recommendation of BSTI. Currently, 64 food and agricultural products, 39 chemical products, 11 textile products, 25 electrical and electronic products, and 14 engineering products are under the Mandatory Certification Marks Scheme.[13] Products subject to mandatory certification are inspected at the border, and testing is undertaken if the present BSTI inspector deems it necessary. According to BSTI, a total of 65 inspectors are available for ensuring compliance with the mandatory standards for imported and domestically produced products and for voluntary certification. BSTI reports that all consignments are inspected, and no risk profiling is used to prioritize the burden of conformity assessment.

Exporters to Bangladesh meet a range of quality-related demands at the border. Bangladesh is a net food importer. In FY2008/09, about 5.63 metric tons of food, including rice, wheat, pulses, sugar, edible oil, and onions, were imported, representing a value of US$1.9 billion. About 80 percent of all imported food enters the country through the Chittagong seaport and Benapole land port (FAO 2010a). Bangladeshi food safety standards are set by BSTI, which generally seeks to base them on the international Codex Alimentarius[14] standards. BSTI focuses on the implementation of the mandatory food standards for which it is responsible. In general, food inspection in Bangladesh is rather complicated and involves multiple ministries and agencies. Fifteen ministries are involved in food safety and quality control, and 10 ministries are directly involved in food inspection and enforcement services. The roles and responsibilities of the concerned ministries and agencies are unclear. The overall coordination body for food safety and food control at the national level is the National Food Safety Advisory Council (FAO 2010a).

The Department of Customs, working in close collaboration with port authorities, is responsible for border food inspection. Inspection is carried out as prescribed by the Import Policy Order as well as a number of subsidiary acts and standards. All food imports are inspected without adherence to any clear procedures, protocols, or guidelines (FAO 2010a). Preshipment inspection was mandatory for products imported to Bangladesh until June 2013. Shipping documents must include radioactivity test reports and certificates declaring "fit for human consumption," "not mixed with harmful substances," and country of origin. Meat imported from EU countries must be certified as free from Mad Cow disease. As part of the document verification process, customs authorities carry out physical tests, including organoleptic tests, at the port. According to a report from the Food and Agriculture Organization of the United Nations (FAO), imported food samples may be analyzed by laboratories at BSTI, the Bangladesh Atomic Energy Commission, the Plant Protection Wing, the Department of Agricultural Extension, the Fish Inspection and Quality Control Wing of the Department of Fisheries, the Bangladesh Council of Scientific and Industrial Research, and the Customs Department laboratory in Chittagong (FAO 2010a). The requirement for radioactivity tests is reported not to be strictly implemented on food products originating from countries from the South Asian Association for Regional Cooperation (SAARC) and the Association of Southeast Asian Nations (ASEAN). The BSTI laboratory only analyzes products for which mandatory BSTI standards exist. Products not complying with Bangladesh's rules may be labeled correctly, downgraded to purposes other than human consumption, destroyed, or returned to the country of origin, depending on the nature of the problem. Customs does not keep information on the compliance history of importers, effectively making risk profiling impossible.

Domestically, the food safety regime is weak. A 2010 FAO report reviewing Bangladesh's food safety and quality policies argues that "[w]hile a range of national policies and other documents make some reference to aspects of food safety and quality in Bangladesh, there is only limited focus on food safety and important issues are dealt with only superficially" (FAO 2010b). Historically, Bangladesh's food policy has focused on food security because of the country's tragic past experiences with famine catastrophes.

Potential exporters to Bangladesh encounter uncertainty about the prevailing plant health regime. All exporters need a phytosanitary certification to export plants and plant products to Bangladesh. According to the Bangladeshi authority for plant health, the Plant Protection Wing of the Ministry of Agriculture, there are 26 quarantine stations at the border: 20 at land borders, 3 in airports, 2 in sea ports, and 1 in a river port. Each quarantine station has a staff of 68 people, except Chittagong, which has a staff of 14. In total, 190 people work in quarantine. The import procedure is the following:

- The exporter gets a phytosanitary certificate from the authorities of the exporting country.
- The Plant Protection Wing issues an import permit, either centrally in Dhaka or at the border.
- When the product arrives at a border post, Plant Protection Wing personnel check the documentation and inspect the product for plant health problems.
- If the Plant Protection Wing observes a problem, they take samples and test in a laboratory. They have 10 plant quarantine labs at border posts. If they observe insects, they send samples to a laboratory in Dhaka.

According to the Plant Protection Wing, transaction times are typically low, one to two hours if documents are satisfactory and inspection does not find any problems. If testing is needed, up to three days may be needed to finalize the transaction. In the case of seeds, the transaction time may exceed three days.

The Import Policy Order includes a number of special import regulations that address quality issues. The Order stipulates that imports must be accompanied by certificates for absence of melamine for the import of milk and milk products; by certificates for radioactivity (presence of CS-137), required for many products and origins, issued by the exporting country and by the Bangladesh Atomic Energy Commission; and certificates for the "purity" of oil palm products (including palm oil, palm olein, and RBD palm stearin). The scientific basis for such requirements is not obvious. In general, for many Bangladeshi import requirements, neither the process through which they are adopted nor the form in which they are published meets international best practice. While the import requirements often, at least in principle, target legitimate needs, like food safety, they are formulated in a way that offers little protection but inflicts costs unnecessarily on the private sector and the consumer.

Import Regulation Agencies in Bangladesh
Bangladesh Standards and Testing Institute

BSTI is simultaneously the Bangladesh national standardization body (a regulatory agency) and a supplier of conformity assessment services. BSTI coordinates and heads a system of technical committees that draft voluntary Bangladeshi standards. The system consists of a mixture of government, academia, and private sector representatives. At the same time, BSTI is involved in the process of setting mandatory standards (that is, technical regulations) by advising the Ministry of Industries, which ultimately adopts mandatory standards. In most cases, the Ministry of Industries follows the advice of BSTI. Finally, BSTI provides testing, inspection, and certification against "Quality Marks" for products under mandatory certification.

Two European Union–funded and UNIDO-implemented projects have recently provided assistance to BSTI. The Bangladesh Quality Support Program (BQSP) provided support in 2006–10, while the BEST-BQI program continued support right after termination of BQSP and was to end in 2014. BSTI is implementing or planning a number of other projects that are supported by a mix of government and donor funding; these are presented in annex 5A. As evidenced in project documentation from BQSP and BEST-BQI projects, strong disagreements exist between quality infrastructure actors in Bangladesh about the functioning of BSTI (Raj Sud 2010). The disagreements focus on conflicts of interest inherent in BSTI as a result of its many responsibilities. A baseline study report concludes that:

> The conflict between regulatory functions and government's role in providing a national standards, conformity assessment, measurements infrastructure to support trade and industry was noted to be a central concern within BSTI as reported by several BWSP consultants. BSTI, the main national agency that provides conformity assessment, standards and calibration services is ineffective in providing services to exporters or industry due to its focus on regulatory functions such as mandatory standards enforcement and weights and measures enforcement. It remains ill equipped to serve industry due to non-availability of human resources for functions that service industry, poor management practices and a certain lack of credibility and recognition of the reports issued. (Raj Sud 2010, p. 2)

A survey of BSTI clients in various sectors conducted in September 2010 revealed a high degree of dissatisfaction with BSTI services. The survey covered the four major services delivered by BSTI—product certification, testing, calibration, and standards development. The survey collected 217 responses from randomly selected respondents among BSTI's clients and standards committee members. Fifty-eight percent of the respondents were large firms (more than 500 employees) and the rest were small firms (less than 500 employees). Table 5.2 presents the survey results. Overall, 41 percent of the respondents were dissatisfied with the services of BSTI. Respondents indicated a number of reasons for their dissatisfaction, including slow service, unreasonable requirements, no benefits provided (from mandatory certification), and lack of credibility (from testing services). Respondents were especially dissatisfied with mandatory certification (Raj Sud 2010).

To increase its effectiveness and efficiency, BSTI could draw on lessons from international best practice in technical regulation and standardization in three areas: use of mandatory standards, avoidance of conflicts of interest, and standards development. Mandatory standards, which are known internationally as technical regulations, should only be used when core regulatory objectives are at stake. Such objectives vary by country, yet typically include issues like consumer safety, environmental protection, and compatibility issues. The list of mandatory standards applied in Bangladesh gives the impression that no clear guidelines are followed when determining whether a particular standard should be voluntary or not.

The products and issues regulated by mandatory standards appear to be chosen somewhat randomly. A small, randomly chosen sample of BSTI mandatory standards reveals the lack of adherence to international best practice. While interviewing BSTI officials, the consultant was given copies of the BSTI mandatory standard for yogurt entitled "BDS CAC-A-11 (a): 2002 for yoghurt and sweetened yoghurt." The yogurt standard regulates fat content, milk solids, which bacteria cultures to add, and similar issues with no direct implications for food safety or other regulatory objectives normally considered legitimate. Hygiene issues like bacterial counts are curiously absent. The yogurt standard appears to be a trade standard—that is, a standard defining the nature of the products. Such standards are typically voluntary. Surprisingly, common food safety issues regulated in technical regulations for yogurt in many countries are not addressed by the Bangladeshi standard.

By restricting the use of mandatory standards to issues seen as legitimate in other countries, the Bangladeshi government would achieve more efficient regulation. This would allow the private sector to set quality characteristics according to market needs for issues considered suitable for market determination. At the

Table 5.2 BSTI Client Satisfaction
percent

Service	Satisfied	Dissatisfied	Neither satisfied or dissatisfied
Certification marking	29	71	0
Calibration	50	47	3
Testing	31	26	52
Standards purchasers	81	19	0
Average	**48**	**41**	**11**

Source: Raj Sud 2010.

Strengthening Competitiveness in Bangladesh—Thematic Assessment
http://dx.doi.org/10.1596/978-1-4648-0898-2

same time, more efficient regulation would economize on the government's enforcement resources and provide more effective regulation of legitimate issues like consumer protection.

It is international best practice to separate regulatory powers (such as setting mandatory standards) and conformity assessment (such as testing, inspection, and certification). In contrast, BSTI strongly influences the adoption and formulation of mandatory standards while simultaneously benefitting from the incomes derived from testing, inspection, and certification against these mandatory standards. In OECD countries, it is highly unusual to give NSBs regulatory functions. In some countries, NSB is merely a standards developer, while in others, it has departments involved in the provision of conformity assessment services. Regulation is the domain of other agencies, typically government ministries. In Bangladesh, the Ministry of Industries has delegated the functions of standardization, quality, certification, technical regulation, and metrology to BSTI.

Accreditation is the responsibility of the Bangladesh Accreditation Board, which functions as a department under the Ministry. BSTI is the regulatory agency responsible for the implementation of mandatory standards, the Pure Food Rules, and import consignment approval for 39 items. The BSTI Certification Wing undertakes these functions. In 2010, 15 officers were responsible for implementing product certification for approximately 14,500 licenses. These officers processed 10–15 new applications per day, participated in mobile courts for prosecuting offenders, approved imported consignments, and implemented the Pure Food Rules (Raj Sud 2010). Mandatory standards are approved by the Ministry of Industries, usually following BSTI recommendations. The combined provision of standards development responsibilities, regulatory functions, and conformity assessment services damages the credibility of BSTI. The current structures do not meet international best practice to ensure independence and impartiality.

Standards development in BSTI suffers from poor quality and nonpublication of a large portion of the approved standards and noncompliance with the WTO/TBT Code for Standards, according to UNIDO's baseline study report (Raj Sud 2010). Of 3,300 adopted standards, 1,000 have remained unpublished for years. The Standards Law focuses on mandatory standards but not on the economic and social benefits of a well-functioning system of voluntary standardization. The two UNIDO projects, BQSP and BEST-BQI, have worked to increase the quality of BSTI standards development:

A quality manual and procedures were developed during the BQSP interventions. A small portion of these has been implemented. These require review and formal implementation. The current process and practices for standards development do not fully comply with ISO Guide 59 and the WTO/TBT Code for Standards. BSTI has established a functioning committee structure for standards development. The membership of the committees and rules for operation require review to assure consensus process is followed and wider stakeholder participation. There is a corresponding concern with the quality and relevance of many existing BDS standards due to obsolete content and errors.

BSTI does not provide information services or undertake any promotional activities on standards for trade and industry. The awareness of the utility and benefits of standards is low with many officials equating standards with technical regulation. It has developed some capacity to participate in international standards during BQSP, but participation mostly remains on observation basis for limited sectors. (Raj Sud 2010, p. 13)

The Bangladesh Accreditation Board is being upgraded with assistance from an UNIDO-led technical assistance project. The Bangladesh Accreditation Board was established by an Act of the Parliament in 2006 (Act No. 29, July 16, 2006) as the national accreditation authority. The Board currently functions as a department of the Ministry of Industries (Raj Sud 2010). The vision of the Bangladesh Accreditation Board is to improve national capacity in testing and measurement, thereby assisting the overall development of Bangladesh by strengthening production capability, competition, consumer protection, and trade facilitation. BEST-BQI is a program funded by the European Union, Norwegian Agency for Development Cooperation, and the Government of Bangladesh and implemented by UNIDO; it is a follow-up to BQSP, implemented during 2006–10. BEST-BQI seeks to make the Bangladesh Accreditation Board an internationally recognized accreditation body. International recognition necessitates that the Board becomes a full member of the International Laboratory Accreditation Cooperation (ILAC) and the International Accreditation Forum (IAF). Today, the Board is only an affiliate member of ILAC and plans to seek membership from IAF.

UNIDO activities aim at building capacity in laboratory accreditation. UNIDO's opinion is that the demand for an inspection body and certification body accreditation is too small to justify developing capacity in these areas (Raj Sud 2010). BEST-BQI currently works to accredit a number of Bangladeshi public and private laboratories. This accreditation will be granted by a foreign entity, which will work with the Bangladesh Accreditation Board to build its capacity in laboratory accreditation. This current UNIDO activity builds on assistance provided under BQSP, where 15 laboratories—many of them seafood laboratories—received assistance for accreditation.

International accreditation bodies already operate in Bangladesh and will in the future compete with the Bangladesh Accreditation Board. For example, NABL (India), U.K. Accreditation Service, and Dutch Accreditation Council (RvA, the Netherlands) have accredited private test laboratories of SGS, Bureau Veritas, and Intertek (Raj Sud 2010). These international bodies primarily service the garment industry and similar export-oriented light manufacturing industries. Competing with these international bodies will be a severe challenge for the Bangladesh Accreditation Body. Foreign buyers only appoint laboratories, inspection services, and management system certifiers accredited by known and trustworthy accreditation bodies. The Bangladesh Accreditation Board is yet far from achieving the level of credibility of its international competitors.

Strengthening Competitiveness in Bangladesh—Thematic Assessment
http://dx.doi.org/10.1596/978-1-4648-0898-2

The Plant Protection Wing

In 2011, the new Plant Protection Act was enacted, which largely expands the regulatory scope of the Plant Protection Wing. However, it lacks the capacity to implement the additional responsibilities. Therefore, the Plant Protection Wing still instructs its personnel to act according to the old rules. The current procedures are based on the 1940 rules as amended in 1985. The Plant Protection Wing has not developed a plan for transitioning from the old to the new regulatory framework. It is to be expected that a gradual transition will take place over many years. Exporters will face difficulties in understanding which requirements to follow, as the regulations implemented will deviate substantially and likely unpredictably from the ones in the 2011 Plant Protection Act.

Meeting the Quality Challenge Next Door: Regional Trade and Quality

The bilateral trade balance between India and Bangladesh reveals that India exports much more to Bangladesh than vice versa. Although this may be the result of Bangladesh's specialization in light manufacturing exports for more distant markets, suspicions run deep that nontariff barriers (NTBs) on the Indian side severely hamper Bangladeshi export opportunities. Bangladeshi media frequently report on such NTBs, and one area suspected to give rise to barriers is technical regulations and standards. In particular, one company interviewed expressed deep concerns over the complicated SPS measures met when exporting processed food to India. The story is that the Indian authorities demand excessive testing on the Indian side. The company's processed food is subject to mandatory Bangladeshi standards and, thus, is already tested and approved by BSTI. Indian authorities merely repeat these tests. The company interviewed states that India requires laboratory testing from its Central Food Laboratory prior to issuing sales permissions. Central Food Laboratory testing is required for each product of every consignment. In northeast India, the Central Food Laboratory is located in Guwahati in the state of Assam. It takes 45 days to get the health report from the Public Health Analyst office of Guwahati, which is located 300–600 kilometers from border crossings. In the meantime, products are kept in a bonded warehouse at the port area. Ultimately, the products reach the Indian market with nearly two months delay.

This trade dispute might be addressed by the conclusion of a mutual recognition agreement (MRA). An MRA states that technical regulations, standards, and conformity assessment procedures undertaken on one side of the border are essentially equal to the ones undertaken on the other side. Thus, goods produced in one country can be freely marketed in the other. MRAs facilitate trade by enabling manufacturers to have their products tested and certified in the country of origin, for compliance with the regulatory requirements of the importing country. By eliminating the time delays and costs associated with obtaining regulatory approval in the importing country, MRAs benefit the parties' businesses by delivering significant savings in time and money. Under MRAs, one government agrees to recognize the results of another's testing, inspection, SPS certification, or other procedures. Therefore, the manufacturer can meet both parties' standards by undergoing one inspection, testing, or certification procedure by approved bodies in whichever country is most convenient. For example, mutual recognition may apply to all foods traded between countries that are parties to an agreement or only to specified foods. Similarly, recognition may apply to all requirements applicable to specified foods (including food standards) or only some (such as conformity assessment procedures). Countries may elect to enter into an umbrella agreement consisting of general provisions and specific sector arrangements made under the umbrella agreement.

The feasibility of establishing mutual recognition will be greatest between countries that have broadly similar attitudes to the appropriate level of protection against health risks and deception of consumers and between countries that have broadly similar capabilities for monitoring and enforcement of requirements. Often, such countries will be neighbors with a long tradition of trading food and other SPS-regulated products. For example, MRA initiatives in ASEAN and APEC are a clear testimony to the validity and commercial attractiveness of the approach.

The negotiation and conclusion of equivalency agreements and MRAs is often costly and time-consuming. An MRA requires a thorough evaluation of a number of factors. Economic considerations are one factor (for example, the level of trade in the product concerned, prioritization, availability of relevant statistics, tangible benefits accruing from the conclusion of such agreements, and so forth). Other considerations include the compatibility between regulatory systems, the impact on domestic regulatory systems, the regulatory challenges imposed by the negotiation, the cost assessment and time forecast of the negotiating process, the availability of resources, and domestic support. Negotiations are lengthy as they involve a number of steps, including the process of documentary review and comparison. Problems may arise as a consequence of different legal structures, from difficulties in identifying a single authority for overall control of the system (especially where more than one regulatory body is involved), and from a counterpart's relative lack of willingness and readiness to negotiate. In addition, such negotiations often require the commitment of technical and trade specialists to review materials.

Recent media reports have claimed that India will accept the certification of BSTI, thus expediting exports by avoiding testing on the Indian side of the border (*Daily Star* 2012b). This development should be the result of Indian institutions accrediting BSTI product certification (*Daily Star* 2012a). But a major Bangladeshi exporter of processed foods to India states that although accreditation has been granted to some but not all BSTI tests, no formal agreement has been signed to accept BSTI's certification. Therefore, India continues to test Bangladeshi products on the Indian side of the border.

Solving frequent complaints about Indian NTBs may require deep institutional reforms of the Bangladeshi system of standardization and inspection. Ideally, Bangladesh should negotiate an MRA or pursue equivalence of the relevant SPS measures with India. However, in reality, the successful completion of an agreement with India may require much more work than commonly believed in Bangladesh. The current Bangladeshi system is subject to criticism because of its very large agenda, limited resources for enforcement, and strong conflicts of interests within BSTI (the main regulatory agency). The Indian authorities may argue convincingly that the guarantees of product safety offered by the Bangladeshi system are not convincing. The Bangladeshi authorities could greatly improve the odds of an MRA with India if they aligned the present certification system more closely with international best practice.

To start negotiation of mutual recognition, donors could fund a road map of mutual recognition of food-related border procedures. The elements of this road map are:

- Examine the concurrent Indian and Bangladeshi legislation.
- Assess the standards and conformity assessment procedures applied.
- Promote mutual trust and bilateral cooperation in food production and trade.
- Work toward mutually recognizing the critical elements of each other's regulations.
- Hold technical discussions about the necessary steps for achieving mutual recognition.
- Identify and support necessary reforms.
- Establish regular contacts and communication concerning standards, technical regulations (mandatory standards), and conformity assessments in the Indian-Bangladesh border trade.

Conclusions and Recommendations

The government and the donors need to be pragmatic when assessing Bangladesh's efforts in quality management and realistic about the opportunities for the rapid upgrading of government capacities. In most least-developed countries, the general picture of the public and private sectors is one of limited quality management capacity. This emphasizes the need for prioritization. Although most high-income countries possess extensive national quality infrastructure, resource constraints and genuine economic needs dictate that LMICs develop their quality infrastructure step by step. In that regard, government and donors should recognize that the private sector and the government play complementary roles in quality management. In the buyer-driven value chains to which Bangladesh caters, standard setting, testing, certification, and even the provision of metrology services are dominated by private service providers. This characteristic should not be seen as a threat to the existing government quality infrastructure, but as an opportunity allowing the government to build capacity in the most crucial areas first, while ensuring that exporter demand for quality management is met.

Bangladeshi quality management may be improved through a variety of means. These include value chain interventions, ensuring the supply of services for quality, and promoting the smooth flow of imports while respecting legitimate needs for import regulation like food safety. Potentially fruitful areas for reform of the existing quality infrastructure in Bangladesh include the following:

- Consider opportunities to open fishery testing markets for private sector service providers.
- Review the new Plant Protection Act and develop an implementation plan that provides clarity to importers about the prevailing rules. At the same time, meet the regulatory needs of Bangladesh.
- Introduce international best practice among border management agencies. These practices include developing the use of risk profiling and similar modern techniques to increase regulatory effectiveness while facilitating trade.
- Review the list of mandatory standards to determine whether they meet legitimate regulatory objectives and can be effectively enforced.
- Continue ongoing work by UNIDO to reform BSTI, with the aim of bringing the BSTI structure into closer alignment with international best practice and avoiding conflicts of interest.
- Develop a mutual recognition agreement or pursue equivalence with India.

Annex 5A: Current and Upcoming BSTI Projects

Table 5A.1 Current and Upcoming BSTI Projects

Project	Objective	Source of funding	Time frame	Estimated costs
Establishment, modernization, and development of BSTI regional offices at Sylhet and Barisal	Establish BSTI Regional Office cum laboratories in Sylhet and Barisal division to strengthen the Metrology and Certification Marks activities. Enhance the capabilities of BSTI Regional Offices at Sylhet and Barishal with procurement of modern and sophisticated equipment for testing and metrology laboratories; procurement of vehicles for market verification, inspection, and mobile courts.	Government of Bangladesh	July 2005– December 2011	Tk. 1,873,131,873 (US$2.2 million)
Modernization of BSTI through procurement of sophisticated equipment and infrastructure development of laboratories for accreditation	Construct and refurbish laboratories for accreditation. Procure sophisticated equipment for different laboratories. Upgrade laboratories at Headquarters and Chittagong Regional Office for creating accredited facilities of calibration, testing, and certification. Ensure accredited quality of exports from Bangladesh. Ensure accredited quality of products to the customer.	Japan Debt Cancellation Fund; Government of Bangladesh	January 2009– December 2011	Tk. 2,295.00 lakh (US$2.7 million)

table continues next page

Table 5A.1 Current and Upcoming BSTI Projects (continued)

Project	Objective	Source of funding	Time frame	Estimated costs
Barrier removal to the cost-effective development and implementation of energy standards and labeling	Remove barriers to the development and effective implementation of energy efficiency standards and labeling programs in the region. Facilitate the transformation of regional product markets of targeted energy consuming appliances, equipment, and lighting products.	GEF; Government of Bangladesh	June 2010– June 2014	Tk. 1,863.00 lakh (US$2.2 million)
Modernization and strengthening of BSTI	Component 1: Develop food testing facilities in BSTI; establish food testing lab with modern and sophisticated equipment. Component 2: Establish gold testing facilities in BSTI; establish gold testing lab with modern and sophisticated equipment. Component 3: Establish cement and brick testing facilities in BSTI; establish cement and brick testing lab with modern and sophisticated equipment. Component 4: Build capacity in accreditation in BSTI and establish traceability of BSTI Metrology Laboratory to S.I. units with the help of NPL India. Furthermore, achieve recognition of licenses issued on the basis of BSTI product certificates.	Exim Bank of India; Government of Bangladesh	October 2010–June 2012	Tk. 7,291.51 lakh (US$8.7 million)
Establishment of the office of the South Asian Regional Standards Organization in Bangladesh	Promote and undertake harmonization of national standards of the South Asian Association for Regional Cooperation member states with a view to removing technical barriers to trade and enhancing the flow of goods and services in the region. Encourage exchange of information and expertise among the NSBs of SAARC member states in the field of standardization and conformity assessment. Explore the possibility of having a common mark of conformity among member states. Establish the South Asian Regional Standards Organization in Dhaka, Bangladesh, to achieve these objectives.	Government of Bangladesh	July 2011– June 2013	Tk. 2,211.92 lakh (US$2.6 million)

table continues next page

Table 5A.1 Current and Upcoming BSTI Projects *(continued)*

Project	Objective	Source of funding	Time frame	Estimated costs
Establishment of calibration and verification facilities for the CNG mass flow meter at the CNG filing station at the regional level	Establish infrastructure development of CNG mass calibration/verification laboratories at Dhaka and Chittagong regional offices and a tanker truck calibration center at the Chittagong regional office. Procure modern, sophisticated equipment for Dhaka. Ensure correct measurement of flow at CNG filling stations and protect meters from tampering.	Government of Bangladesh	July 2011–June 2013	Tk. 520.00 lakh (US$0.6 million)
Better quality infrastructure for the BEST program	Improve the system of quality management, standards, and conformity assessment of commodities, products, and equipment to international standards. Build awareness and capacity of the government and private sector to cope with international quality standards and TBT/SPS enhancement. Strengthen legal framework for standards, metrology, and testing in line with the accepted international practice. Accredit five labs (mass, temperature, dimension, force and pressure, volume, viscosity and density, electrical, time and frequency) of the National Metrology Laboratory and other existing labs of BSTI. Establish national certification bodies for HACCP, ISO 9000, ISO 14000, etc. Strengthen the recently established Bangladesh Accreditation Board with technical and financial support from UNIDO. Get Bangladesh Accreditation Board full membership from APLAC and ILAC through the BEST project and increase promotional activities of lead assessors/ auditors.	EU/UNIDO; Government of Bangladesh	July 2011– December 2014	Tk. 4,826.00 lakh (US$5.7 million)
Expansion and strengthening of BSTI (five districts)	Expand and strengthen BSTI in five districts.	Government of Bangladesh	March 2011–June 2014	Tk. 4,747.45 lakh (US$5.6 million)

table continues next page

Strengthening Competitiveness in Bangladesh—Thematic Assessment
http://dx.doi.org/10.1596/978-1-4648-0898-2

Table 5A.1 Current and Upcoming BSTI Projects *(continued)*

Project	Objective	Source of funding	Time frame	Estimated costs
Establishment of Chemical Metrology Laboratory at NMI in BSTI	Contribute to the growth of industrialization and reduction of poverty by assisting trade with calibration; help build conformity assessment infrastructure support services at the backward linkage for the development, strengthening, and diversification of the production and export base of Bangladesh. Develop, improve, and apply primary methods and reference materials for chemical measurements. Provide a pragmatic approach to measurement, traceability, and measurement uncertainty; establish links to S.I. units where appropriate. Disseminate expertise and knowledge on chemical metrology through seminars, guides, conferences, comparisons, etc. Establish infrastructure for chemical metrology; build and procure sophisticated laboratory equipment and furniture. Procure vehicle. Procure Certified Reference Materials.	Government of Bangladesh	July 2011– June 2014	Tk. 2,085.00 lakh (US$2.5 million)

Sources: BSTI websites, http://www.bsti.gov.bd/bstiOnGoingDevProject.html; http://www.bsti.gov.bd/bstiUpComingDevProject.html.
Note: APLAC = Administrative Panel on Laboratory Animal Care; BEST = Better Work and Standards; BSTI = Bangladesh Standards and Testing Institute; CNG = compressed natural gas; GEF = Global Environment Facility; HACCP = hazard analysis and critical control points; ILAC = International Laboratory Accreditation Corporation; ISO = International Organization for Standardization; NMI = National Metrology Institute; NPL = National Physical Laboratory; NSBs = national standardization bodies; SAARC = South Asian Association for Regional Cooperation; S.I. = International System; SPS = sanitary and phytosanitary; TBT = technical barriers to trade; UNIDO = United Nations Industrial Development Organization.

Notes

1. Such agencies include the International Trade Centre, the International Organization for Standardization, the United Nations Industrial Development Organization, and the World Bank; and bilateral agencies like the German Metrology Institute and the Swedish International Development Cooperation Agency. For examples of specific publications, see Foss (2004), Guasch et al. (2007), ISO and ITC (2010), ITC (2011), and Kellermann (2011).

2. http://www.wto.org/english/res_e/booksp_e/analytic_index_e/tbt_01_e.htm#article2.

3. See www.intracen.org/exporters/quality-management.

4. See http://www.james-heal.co.uk for the company website containing additional information on textile testing.

5. http://www.intertek.com/.

6. http://www.sgs.com/.

7. http://www.bureauveritas.com/.

8. http://www.tuv.com/.

9. http://www.tuvamerica.com/.

10. http://www.mts.com/.

11. See www.ceram.com for the company website.

12. See www.dnv.com for the company website.

13. See http://www.bsti.gov.bd/list.html for a full list of the products under the Mandatory Certification Marks Scheme.

14. http://www.codexalimentarius.org/.

References

APEC (Asia-Pacific Economic Cooperation). 2000. "Information Notes on Good Practice for Technical Regulation." APEC Sub-Committee on Standards and Conformance (SCSC). APEC. http://www.jisc.go.jp/eng/apec-asem/pdf/grp_info.pdf.

APEC and OECD (Asia-Pacific Economic Cooperation and the Organisation for Economic Co-operation and Development). n.d. "APEC-OECD Integrated Checklist on Regulatory Reform—A Policy Instrument for Regulatory Quality, Competition Policy and Market Openness." The APEC-OECD Co-operative Initiative on Regulatory Reform. APEC and OECD. http://www.oecd.org/dataoecd/41/9/34989455.pdf.

Cato, J. C., and S. Subasinge. 2003. "Food Safety in Food Security and Food Trade—Case Study: The Shrimp Export Industry in Bangladesh." International Food Policy Research Institute. http://www.ifpri.org/sites/default/files/publications/focus10_09.pdf.

Daily Star. 2012a. "BSTI Gets Indian Accreditation." January 28, 2012 (accessed February 21, 2013). http://www.thedailystar.net/newDesign/news-details.php?nid=220184.

———. 2012b. "India to Accept BSTI Certification." December 5, 2012 (accessed February 21, 2013), http://www.thedailystar.net/newDesign/news-details.php?nid=260014.

European Commission. n.d. "EU Import Conditions for Seafood and Other Fishery Products." Directorate-General for Health and Consumers, European Commission. http://ec.europa.eu/food/international/trade/im_cond_fish_en.pdf.

FAO (Food and Agricultural Organization of the United Nations). 2010a. "Food Inspection and Enforcement in Bangladesh: Current Arrangement and Challenges." FAO, Rome.

———. 2010b. "Review of Food Safety and Quality Related Policies in Bangladesh." FAO, Rome.

Foss, I. 2004. Development of Trade in Africa: Promoting Exports through Quality and Safety. Oslo and Stockholm: Norwegian Agency for Development Cooperation (NORAD) and Swedish International Development Cooperation Agency.

FVO (Food and Veterinary Office). 2010. "Final Report of a Mission Carried Out in Bangladesh from 02 June to 10 June 2010 in Order to Evaluate the System of Official Controls and the Certification of Plants for Export to the European Union." DG(SANCO) 2010-8616—MR FINAL. FVO, Health and Consumers Directorate-General, European Commission. http://ec.europa.eu/food/fvo/act_getPDF.cfm?PDF_ID=8458.

Guasch, L., J.-L. Racine, I. Sánchez, and M. Diop. 2007. *Quality Systems and Standards for a Competitive Edge*. Washington, DC: World Bank.

ISO and ITC (International Standardization Organization and International Trade Centre). 2010. *Building Linkages for Export Success: Trade Promotion Organizations and National Standards Bodies Working Together*. Geneva: ISO and ITC.

ITC (International Trade Centre). 2011. *A Guide for Small and Medium-Sized Exporters*. Geneva: ITC.

Jensen, M., and P. Vergano. 2009. *Does One Size Really Fit All? Guidelines for Understanding Harmonization in the SPS and TBT Agreements*. Report submitted to the World Bank, Washington, DC.

Kellermann, M. 2011. "Thought on a National Quality Policy." Discussion Paper 4/2011, Physikalisch Technische Bundesanstalt (PTB), Berlin. http://www.ptb.de/de/org/q/q5/docs/broschueren/broschuere_discussion4_2011_02.pdf.

Ministry of Commerce. 2010. "Import Policy Order 2009–2012." Published in *Bangladesh Gazette Extra-ordinary*. January 26, 2010. Ministry of Commerce, Government of the People's Republic of Bangladesh.

Raj Sud, R. 2010. *Better Work and Standards Programme (BEST)—Better Quality Infrastructure (BQI) Component—Baseline Report*. Vienna: United Nations Industrial Development Organization (UNIDO).

UNIDO (United Nations Industrial Development Organization). 2007. *A Roadmap to Quality: An e-Learning Manual for Implementing Total Quality Management*. Vienna: United Nations Industrial Development Organization. http://www.unido.org/index.php?id=o72358.

———. 2010. *Independent Evaluation—Sri Lanka: Impact of UNIDO SMTQ Projects in Sri Lanka*." Vienna: United Nations Industrial Development Organization.

World Bank. 2012. "Consolidating and Accelerating Exports in Bangladesh." Bangladesh Development Series Paper 29, World Bank, Washington, DC.

World Fish Centre. 2011. "Untitled Brochure of the Greater Harvest and Economic Returns from Shrimp (GHERS) Initiative." The World Fish Centre, Bangladesh and South Asia Office. http://www.worldfishcentre.org/ressource_centre/WF_2768.pdf.

CHAPTER 6

Trade Facilitation and Logistics

Charles Kunaka and Nadeem Rizwan

Introduction

Efficient logistics are important for enhancing Bangladesh's competitive edge in exports. They reduce costs and delays for exports, and they expedite imports for consumption and as inputs for domestic production. High logistics costs can be seen as an implicit tax that biases the economy away from exports. Generally, superior logistics performance offers a competitive advantage in an era of increasing globalization, more production sharing across countries, and shortened product lifecycles. To date, low wages have benefitted Bangladesh's ready-made garments (RMG) exports and have partially compensated for poor logistics performance. But to ensure general growth of exports, logistics performance in Bangladesh will need to improve considerably.

The objective of this chapter is to identify options for tackling four interrelated issues that are critical to Bangladesh's logistics efficiency: (a) the limited use of containers on the Dhaka-Chittagong Corridor (DCC) and options for reform, (b) customs and border management modernization, (c) air transport capacity and connectivity, and (d) regional transit and connectivity. The assessment is based on extensive consultations with a broad range of stakeholders. These included government ministries (railways, commerce, communications), transport and logistics regulatory authorities (road transport, inland waterways), port authorities, private sector associations (freight forwarders, cargo agents), exporting firms, the research community, customs, chambers of commerce, shipping lines, export processing zones authorities and investors, and site visits to the Port of Chittagong and the Benapole border post (shared with India).

Logistics Performance

In parallel with the rapid growth in exports of garments in recent years, Bangladesh has already made some progress in improving its logistics performance. There are ongoing reforms in customs, and there has been considerable expansion of the road network and performance improvements at the main trade gateway port of Chittagong. However, the 2010 Logistics Performance Index published by the World Bank (2010) suggests that although Bangladesh performs above the regional average for South Asia in logistics, it generally ranks below India, which leads the region in performance, as well as other countries at similar income levels. In general, Bangladeshi logistics performance lags in customs, infrastructure, competence of logistics service providers, and tracking and tracing (figure 6.1).

Growth in Bangladesh's export performance is best illustrated by the rapid increase in cargo traffic through its main international trade gateway of Chittagong. Chittagong handles more than 90 percent of Bangladesh's foreign trade and is the main fulcrum of the Bangladesh logistics system. The port is the fifth largest in South Asia after Jawaharlal Nehru (Mumbai) and Chennai in India, Colombo in Sri Lanka, and Karachi in Pakistan (figure 6.2). In 2010, Chittagong handled just less than 1.4 million 20-foot equivalent units (TEUs) of containerized traffic.

Traffic volumes have been increasing strongly in recent years, especially of containerized cargo (figure 6.3). Containerization of cargo through Chittagong started growing in the late 1980s, and in 2010, it was just less than half of total cargo volumes. As more and more cargo is containerized, it presents a good opportunity to provide door-to-door containerized service. In 2009/10, containers accounted for almost 39 percent of railway freight traffic revenues, three times larger than petroleum products, which were the second highest source of revenue.

Figure 6.1 Bangladesh's Logistics Performance, 2010

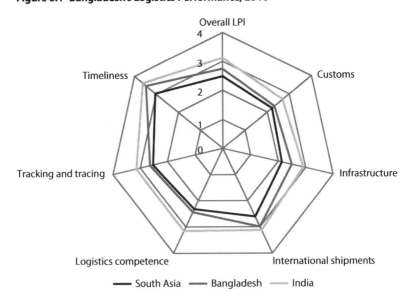

Source: World Bank 2010.
Note: The following countries had to be excluded from the 2012 international LPI sample because there were an insufficient number of responses or other data reliability concerns: Bangladesh, Israel, Mali, Mozambique, Nicaragua, Somalia, Turkmenistan, Uganda, and Zambia. LPI = Logistics Performance Index.

Figure 6.2 South Asia Port Size as Measured by Volume of Containerized Traffic, 2010

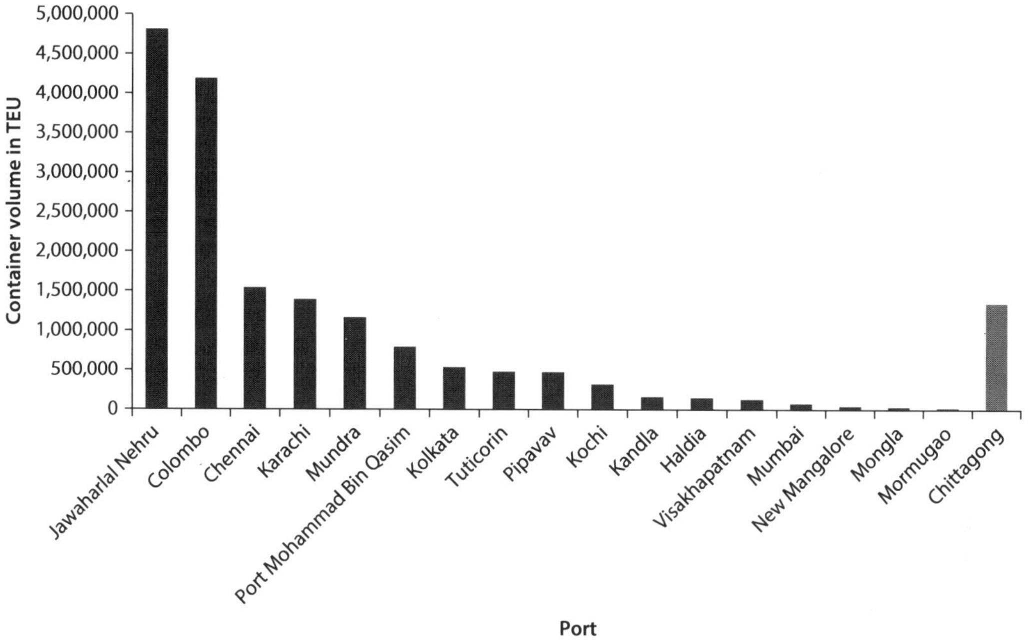

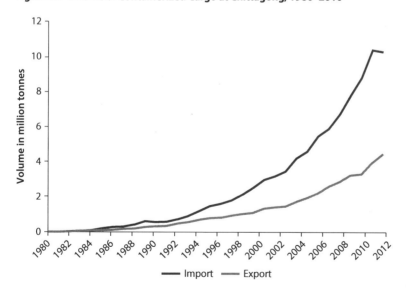

Source: Data from Containerization International (http://www.lloydslist.com/ll/sector/containers/).
Note: TEU = 20-foot equivalent unit.

Figure 6.3 Volume of Containerized Cargo at Chittagong, 1980–2010

Source: World Bank estimates, data from Chittagong Port Authority.

Strengthening Competitiveness in Bangladesh—Thematic Assessment
http://dx.doi.org/10.1596/978-1-4648-0898-2

Containerization over the past six decades has fundamentally transformed logistics. Containers offer several advantages, including the following:

- They are standardized and can therefore be deployed anywhere in the world. Most vehicles, vessels, and railway wagons are designed to accommodate containers.
- They are versatile in that they can be adapted to carry dry cargo, bulk commodities such as coal and grain, cars, and frozen products.
- They can be reused, although ownership largely remains with the shipping lines or specialized leasing firms.
- They can be used to simplify transport management, because charges are often in number of units moved rather than the number of loads or consignments.
- They can be used to secure cargo in transit so that clearances can be done inland rather than at seaports.
- They have lower costs compared with bulk handling of cargo.

Despite the rapid growth of containerization in Bangladesh, they are not used much in the domestic movement of cargo. There is still limited movement of containers inland, with such movement, especially by rail, lagging the growth in containerized traffic handled at the port. Although Bangladesh joined the containerization revolution in 1981, it has largely not fully exploited the benefits of containerization, although the authorities are keen to improve the systems for inland container movement. Presently, although approximately 50 percent the cargo passing through the port of Chittagong is containerized, less than 15 percent of containers are moved inland. The rest are stuffed and unloaded either in the port or in privately operated inland container depots (ICDs) outside the port but within its vicinity. The containers that move inland are transported mostly by rail (figures 6.4 and 6.5), with only a few transported by road. In 2009, rail moved around 3 and 5 percent of loaded import and export containers, respectively. Inland waterways in Bangladesh are generally not used to ship containers, although the authorities see great potential in utilizing waterways. In fact, the government recently commissioned a new inland port, and others are planned by the government and the private sector.

Growing container volumes moved by rail and inland waterways are keys to better integration in the domestic logistics system. This would require arresting a two-decade decline in railway capacity (figure 6.5) and improving inland waterway infrastructure. The latter would help in two respects: (a) it would avoid congestion at Chittagong port and (b) it would move containers by a cheaper mode than road and railways. Improvements in infrastructure at the Pangaon Inland Container Terminal and the introduction of customs facilities will help reduce cargo dwell time, as cargo would be cleared inland; this is already the case with railway-borne cargo. The government has reportedly authorized the construction of privately owned inland container terminals that will operate the same way. A few such facilities are already being developed near Dhaka

Figure 6.4 Dhaka-Chittagong Corridor: Number of Containers Carried by Rail, FY1995/96–FY2009/10

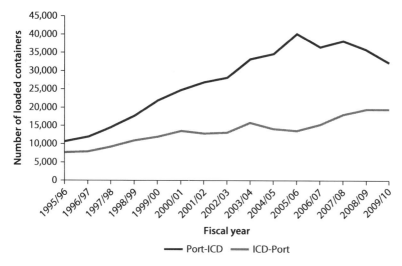

Source: Estimates based on data from Bangladesh Railway.
Note: ICD = inland container depot.

Figure 6.5 Proportion of Chittagong Containers Moved In and Out by Rail, FY1995/96–FY2009/10

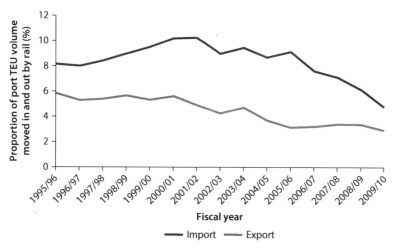

Source: Estimates based on data from Bangladesh Railway.
Note: TEU = 20-foot equivalent unit.

and Narayanganj. However, a major constraint with the inland waterway system is the slow speed of movement.

A complex picture of several intertwined practices reinforces the established patterns of port clearance of cargo, the loading and unloading of containers in port, and port congestion. To illustrate, unloading increases demand for trucks on the corridor between Dhaka and Chittagong, which in turn increases

Strengthening Competitiveness in Bangladesh—Thematic Assessment
http://dx.doi.org/10.1596/978-1-4648-0898-2

congestion on the roads. Furthermore, unloading takes place in the port, which leads to congestion in the port area and uptake of space; this can then lead to higher infrastructure improvement costs. The main patterns of operation of goods along the DCC are described in the following.

A large proportion of import containers in particular are stripped in the port itself (around 60 percent).[1] Customs allows only 17 types of goods that can be cleared in off-dock yards in the Chittagong area (annex 6A). These are mostly bulk commodities that are not containerized. By customs regulation, containerized cargo may only be removed from the port by rail (to the ICD in Dhaka) or to bonded facilities in the export processing zones. As the volumes of containers that are removed by rail are small, current practice is that containers are stripped within the port and then the goods are loaded into covered trucks for removal.

One consequence of these practices is that trucks are overloaded, often with the contents of more than one container. Current practice increases the demand for storage space in the port and the average dwell time for cargo in the port area. Although the port has room to grow, further expansion is taking an infrastructure solution to a problem that probably could be addressed by changing customs clearance procedures.

The stripping of containers adds to handling costs as the goods are then loaded into trucks instead of the more efficient route of transporting containers. As a result, many road trucks move cargo between Dhaka and Chittagong. The Dhaka-Chittagong highway is congested from the high volume of traffic, as well as from bottlenecks at specific locations such as bridges and intermediate centers. Congestion increases transit times and decreases reliability on the corridor. Transit times can be as high as 12 hours when they should be less than 4 hours with free-flowing traffic. Transit times by rail, the only other mode of transport, are even longer (close to 20 hours). The long transit times by road and rail discourage shipping lines from shipping containers to the ICD in Dhaka. In general, shipping lines want empty boxes to be returned to the port and repositioned to other ports globally where they will be needed.

To summarize, the inadequate use of containers is caused by a combination of factors. These include inadequate application of risk management procedures in customs clearance and a preference for clearing different types of goods in the port of Chittagong, the limited and unreliable capacity of rail and inland water transport services, and road infrastructure constraints along the corridor. These factors lead to minimal containerization of trade on the DCC, which in itself then becomes the most pragmatic and cost-efficient mode of transport.

Dhaka-Chittagong Corridor

A large proportion of the trade traffic handled at Chittagong Port moves on the DCC. The corridor is the most important trade link in the country; estimates are that it directly serves regions accounting for more than 50 percent the national population, 57 percent of gross domestic product, and more than

66 percent of the country's import and export flows. The DCC has multimodal transport possibilities as it is comprised of road, rail, and inland waterway links. In the corridor, road transport handles just over 50 percent the traffic, followed by inland waters with 43 percent and rail with just over 6 percent. Nationally, road transport is the most important mode of transport, moving more than 80 percent of traffic. Inland waterways handle 16 percent and rail 4 percent. The share of traffic moved by road transport has been growing while that by the other modes has been in decline.

The poor performance of the DCC has been identified as one of the constraints to further expansion of the garments sector. Berg et al. (2011) identify low railway capacity, poor direct connectivity of the port to international markets, and congestion along the corridor as the major sources of inefficiency. However, railways are presently the most important mode for container movement inland.

Although Bangladesh Railway has achieved substantial growth in market share in recent years, its potential is much greater than its current share would imply. In 2012, Bangladesh Railway operated unit trains of 76–80 TEU twice a day between Chittagong and the Dhaka ICD in Kamalapur.[2] When properly run, the service has the potential to reduce costs significantly for importers and exporters in the Dhaka area in particular. The published freight rate for this inbound movement is Tk 6,000 per TEU, while that for backhaul is Tk 3,000 per TEU for loaded boxes and Tk 1,500 for empties. These rates are much lower than those for road freight transport. In addition, when operating efficiently, rail can offer other advantages, including the following:

- There is less risk of damage to the cargo by keeping it in the container.
- Service is faster, with delivery in about eight hours, although waiting time in the port can be high. The high level of demand for inbound movements has created a wait of three to five days for wagon space. Importers have been willing to incur this delay, although the cost for port-to-factory multimodal rail-truck movement is higher, at about Tk 10,000, than for pure road movement.
- There are better customs service and lower informal charges for unloading and clearing containers at the Dhaka ICD relative to Chittagong Port (although both are operated by Chittagong Port Authority).

Inbound movements are loaded containers while most outbound containers are empty. Because there are capacity constraints, loaded boxes are given priority. Capacity is limited by short train length caused by track configuration and loop lengths. Long headways are needed because of the signaling and loop configuration. For freight train operations, there is the additional constraint of the wagon braking systems that limit maximum speed to 29 kilometers per hour. The large number of train operations has meant high levels of utilization on the major rail links, especially on the route between Dhaka and Chittagong.

Despite the high level of demand and the potential for future growth, Bangladesh Railway has not increased the frequency of unit train operation.

Yet, unit train operation is Bangladesh Railway's only profitable service and has helped to offset some of the losses from passenger services. The reasons for not increasing the container service include the following:

- There is heavy demand on those sections that serve the passenger traffic from the northeast, for example, between Tongi and Bhairab Bazaar and between Laksam and Chakisasma. This is compounded by the limitations of a single track between Tongi and Chinki Astana. The government is building another track with financing from the Asian Development Bank. This should remove a major operational bottleneck on the railways, although a shortage of wagons and locomotives will still constrain improvements in capacity.
- Government policy favors passenger services over freight services. Most of Bangladesh Railway's capacity is dedicated to interurban passenger train movements.[3]
- There is a lack of commercial incentives for management, which is satisfied with rationing capacity to collect a premium (formal and informal) for the service.
- Rail ICD capacity has difficulty handling three trains a day in each direction.

Several initiatives would increase the capacity of the existing network with relatively modest investments and changes in procedures. The measures would include increasing port capacity. The Chittagong Port Authority is planning a new terminal, the Karnaphuli Container Terminal. A feasibility study has already been commissioned. In addition, the authorities are looking at a deep-sea port at Sonadia, south of Chittagong.

A major constraint that is faced at Chittagong is that as a river port it cannot accommodate large vessels, because of limited width and water depth. This is a key reason why Bangladesh's cargo is transshipped in Singapore or Colombo. The government has therefore proposed to build a deepwater port on Sonadia Island, some 150 kilometers south of Chittagong. Feasibility studies for the port were completed in 2009, and the authorities are currently assessing options for the financing and construction of the port. The port project, which is considered as high priority, has attracted interest from some of the largest port operators, shipping lines, and port developers. However, given that construction of the new port as well as efficient hinterland connections will take time to materialize, focus in the short term should be on improving operations of the current port and inland connections.

One way to increase capacity is to reduce container dwell time in the port. Cargo dwell time in the port of Chittagong is much higher than the most efficient ports even in middle-income countries (figure 6.6). The dwell time has been reduced from approximately 25 days in 2005 to 16 days in 2012, which is higher than the dwell time in the larger ports in the South Asia region. Dwell times in efficient ports would be around three to four days. Long dwell times impose costs on importers and exporters, as they have to maintain higher inventories while the port also suffers from poor capacity utilization.

Figure 6.6 Container Dwell Time in the Port of Chittagong, 2005–2012

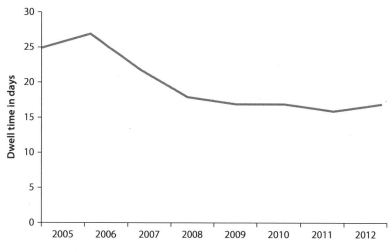

Source: Chittagong Port Authority.

Dwell time of cargo in the port can be reduced by procedural reforms as well as by improving the efficiency of the hinterland logistics connectivity system. SwedeRail proposed to increase average train speed through better track maintenance and improvements in rolling stock as one way of increasing system capacity.[4] In lieu of operational improvements, Bangladesh Railway would have to reduce the frequency of underutilized passenger services. Since the container trains can be run at any time during the day or night, the effect on passenger services should be minimal. Furthermore, SwedeRail proposed dual gauges for the line connecting Dhaka and Chittagong as a method to reduce congestion (the link connecting Tongi and Dhaka already has dual gauges), but this idea was rejected in favor of incremental introduction of dual track or construction of a new link connecting Dhaka and Laksam. If Bangladesh Railway changes its policy or increases track capacity, then limited space and road congestion around the rail ICD in Dhaka would create some new problems. As a solution, it has been proposed to establish a new ICD in Tongi, which would be closer to most of the garment factories. It is clear that to increase the proportion of traffic moved by rail, various measures will have to be taken to increase efficiency and capacity.

The rail service provides a cost-effective means for repositioning of empties through lower backhaul tariffs. There are no serious delays for the southbound movement from Dhaka to Chittagong, and the ICD provides sufficient storage for empties. However, the benefits to exporters are limited since the ICD does not currently operate as a dry port with a through bill of lading. The shipping lines continue to charge exporters for the round-trip movement of the boxes, even if they are loaded in both directions. Further, the shipping lines require a bank guarantee for movement of empties from the ICD to the factory for loading cargo. Given their interest in controlling how the boxes are used and coordinating their repositioning, the shipping lines have little incentive for offering attractive rates for a backhaul-loaded movement. It is left to the freight forwarders to encourage the loading of the empties stored at the ICD with export cargo. They are able to move the boxes to the factory under a company guarantee rather than a bank guarantee, and they can negotiate lower rates with the shipping lines for a loaded southbound movement. The relocation of the ICD to Tongi should encourage this business.

With expanded services, the railroad would have to reduce its price to attract container traffic currently moving by road—and thus ensure a high level of utilization of its service as well as commercially oriented management. Rail tariffs are supposed to be based on train operating costs, but container tariffs are comparable to truck operating costs. This is surprising, especially given the age of the rolling stock. As experience with India's Concor service clearly demonstrates, efficient rail transport of containers requires commercial management—if not by the private sector, then by a corporatized body operating along commercial lines.[5] Concor is part of Indian Railways and operated as a for-profit corporation along commercial lines. Most of its rolling stock was financed through the World Bank. It provides unit train service with rail ICDs stretching across the country, and in 2011 it handled about 1.4 million TEUs per year. Concor operates a number of unit trains daily to and from various ports, most notably Nhava Sheva and Kolkata. It has demonstrated a willingness to open new markets, such as Nepal's rail ICD and various joint ventures with private transport companies. It has also expanded service where there was sufficient growth in demand. At the same time, it has stopped service where traffic has not materialized.

The plan to establish a rail ICD at Tongi should be implemented as soon as possible. The existing Dhaka rail ICD in Kamalapur operates more efficiently than the container yard in Chittagong Port, but its location in the congested city center restricts access. A better location for this facility would be a site nearer to the garment factories with good road access. Since a significant number of the garment factories are located northwest of Dhaka, Tongi seems to be a good choice. A similar facility in the Narayaganj area would not be needed: the knitwear manufacturers use less imported fabric and yarn and are more likely to use road transport, which is faster and cheaper. Although the Dhaka rail ICD serves traders supplying imports to the consumers in Dhaka, it is unclear whether this facility should remain open, given the increasing congestion and the potential value of the site if used for commercial purposes.

Logistics Services

The government has invested heavily in improving roads in recent years, but several problems remain. The road network comprises more than 270,000 kilometers, most of which was constructed over the past 40 years. A new bridge across the Jamuna River improved east-west connectivity in the country; another that is planned across the Padma River will do the same for the southwest part of the country. The bridges, which carry railway lines as well, are important not just for Bangladesh, but also for connectivity with India.

There are two trucking markets in Bangladesh, one modern and the other largely informal and underdeveloped. The relatively modern market is based on the RMG industry, which has played a major role in the development of the sector, especially on the DCC. The RMG industry accounts for as much as two-thirds of the volume carried on the DCC (Raihan, Eusuf, and Ifthekhar 2010). The sector has encouraged the emergence of modern trucking services based on contracts for services at an agreed price. Although these services tend to be expensive, they offer a predetermined quality of service, for which they charge a premium. The non-RMG trucking services suffer from poor quality and low reliability. The services are highly competitive, perhaps because they are highly fragmented. Many operators use old fleets. In addition, there is a high level of vehicle overloading. In an effort to mitigate competition, the operators typically have to go through transport brokers to obtain loads, especially on the Benapole-Dhaka route. The market is therefore distorted, because the brokerage industry or clearing and forwarding agents control access to and competition for services. Going through agents is often the only way to obtain loads. One of the major constraints faced in this secondary market is the lack access to financing that could be used to modernize fleets and improve access to new business. To expand, operators either use their own savings or borrow from relatives. Reform of trucking services in Bangladesh should therefore target the non-RMG market, which accounts for approximately half the trucking services in the country (Raihan, Eusuf, and Ifthekhar 2010).

Bangladesh has a well-established logistics industry, although it concentrates mostly on clearing and forwarding services. There are more than 500 registered clearing and forwarding agents in the country, including major global players. Since 2008, the industry has been regulated through a statutory regulatory order (SRO) issued by government. The SRO clarifies the ownership of freight forwarding firms and the requirements for licensing. Reportedly, the SRO has contributed to improved quality of forwarding services. However, most forwarders only handle the domestic components of import and export logistics, except to a few markets such as Africa. Most exports are free on board to Chittagong. The main constraints to the operation and efficiency of logistics services providers are as follows:

- *Restrictions on establishing bonded warehouses.* Although the government allows the private sector to operate ICDs and container freight stations, there are still restrictions on clearing and forwarding firms, particularly for establishing bonded facilities. The ability of such firms to have bonded facilities is a characteristic of modern logistics in other countries. It is particularly helpful to small and medium enterprises that ship less than container loads and can then benefit from consolidation possibilities in bonded facilities. Forwarders and major trading firms in Bangladesh are interested in investing in such facilities, as this would allow them to pack cargo into containers and receive imports on their premises. Customs could take immediate steps to allow the opening of bonded warehouse facilities around the country, but especially along the core DCC.

This may increase costs for customs, but it will likely lead to significant cost reductions for exporting firms. The facility to establish bonded facilities could be extended to reputable firms, consistent with the proposed move to have authorized economic operators.

- *Restrictive foreign exchange controls, especially for foreign direct investment.* Clearing and forwarding firms face onerous requirements to access foreign exchange approvals to invest in other countries as part of their networks to offer door-to-door services, especially to the main trade markets. These make it impossible for Bangladeshi operators to establish a presence in key overseas markets. As a result, they are limited to playing mostly a domestic role.

Inland Waterways

Water transport in Bangladesh has a large but unutilized potential. More than 10 percent of the population of Bangladesh has direct access to the inland waterways transport system (IWT). There are three main types of services offered:

- *Trunk haulage of passengers and freight along major waterways, between economic centers and port gateways, and between India and Bangladesh.* Volumes are highest on these services, which have tended to have some of the most modern vessels in the system. Types of cargo have been dominated by bulk and petroleum products, fertilizers, construction materials, and grains.
- *Feeder services.* These are usually short trips with modest traffic volumes for small enterprises and farmers.
- *Ferry services.* These provide continuity of road transport services. They are essentially part of the road networks rather than the IWT.

Although inland waterways are cheaper than other modes of transport, they suffer from poor performance. Generally, the volumes of cargo moved by the IWT have stagnated over the past decade. This mode is slow (16–20 hours between Chittagong and the ICD to the south of Dhaka). Although this is somewhat faster than the current rail service for inbound containers, it is slower than road transport, especially when door-to-door movement is considered.

The IWT has been promoted as an alternative mode for transporting containers between Dhaka and Chittagong, but not many containers are moved by water. Earlier efforts were motivated by the limited capacity of road infrastructure. More recent efforts have focused on reducing congestion and delays. Still, interest in exploiting the IWT remains high. For instance, the government recently built the Pangaon Inland Container Terminal, although full operations are being limited in part by a shortage of vessels. There is a proposal to establish barge facilities for containers moving between Chittagong and Narayanganj, involving private barge terminal operations at either end. The barge service would be privately operated under a separate contract. The operating costs for barging would be less than for other modes, but the door-to-door costs are likely to be comparable when the terminal handling and road transport from Narayanganj to the destination are included. In the end, the market share for the proposed barge service will depend on the behavior of the other two modes, specifically the level of congestion on the roads and the pricing and frequency of the unit train service. An IWT service could capture a significant share of the movement of empties, but it would have difficulty capturing a significant share of the movement of loaded containers.

Development of the IWT sector would require strengthening the regulatory oversight of transport services. There are two bodies with regulatory responsibilities for IWT in Bangladesh. These are the Department of Shipping, which is responsible for the safety and overall regulation of the sector, and the Bangladesh Inland Water Transport Authority (BIWTA), which is responsible for dredging services, navigational aids, management of inland ports, and regulation of transport operations, among other functions. Often the separation and allocation of responsibilities between the two is not clear. For the development of water transport, it is important that the functions of the two regulators are streamlined and the allocation of roles clarified.

Priorities for improving use of the IWT should include the following (see also Kathuria and Malouche 2016, chapter 1, on shipbuilding):

- *Improving service performance.* The IWT has great potential to move higher volumes of cargo, especially between Dhaka and Chittagong and between India and Bangladesh. It can help relieve some of the pressure from low railway capacity and congested roads. However, making this happen would require dredging channels, improving IWT port capacity near Dhaka, and acquisition of more efficient vessels. Some of the improvements can be made by the private sector.
- *Streamlining regulation of the IWT.* Presently, there is overlap of regulatory functions between the Department of Shipping and the BIWTA. Developing the sector to its full potential requires streamlining sector management. With proper regulation, inland water transport can help Bangladesh reduce the environmental impacts of transport operations, as it is more efficient and generates lower carbon emissions than other modes.

Air Shipments

Airfreight in Bangladesh has been growing steadily over the past few years (figure 6.7). The principal gateway for airfreight is Dhaka's Shahjalal International Airport. There are several scheduled airfreight services by most of the airlines from East Asia, the Middle East, and other regions (including Biman Bangladesh Airlines, Cathay Pacific Emirates, and China, Qatar, Saudi, and Singapore airlines). Services are typically twice per week. Through hubs in the Middle East and the East Asia region, Bangladesh is connected to the rest of the world. Air charters are also used, especially during the period of high demand, July to October. Airfreight is used mostly by the garment industry, usually at the buyer's request, and sometimes in the case of a missed ocean shipping date. For normal shipments, one of the practices is to use a sea-air combination: ship by sea to Dubai and air freight from Dubai to Europe and the United States.

Figure 6.7 Airfreight from Dhaka Airport, 1998–2010

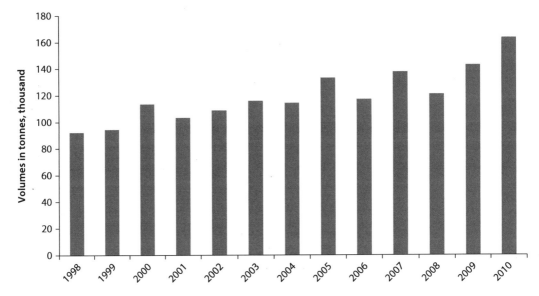

Source: Bangladesh Bureau of Statistics, various years.

The forwarding community and exporters do not experience many problems with air transport except during the peak period.

Most of the problems with air freight are experienced on the ground, in particular with respect to the management of the air cargo terminal in Bangladesh:

- *Performance of the terminal and ground handling monopoly.* Ground handling and management of the air cargo terminal at the airport in Dhaka is performed by a subsidiary of the national carrier, Biman Airlines. Cargo is brought in by the cargo agents, typically 30 hours before departure. Clearing and forwarding agents report two problems with the current arrangements, the first of which the mission was able to confirm. First, the terminal area is often congested, partly because of increasing cargo volumes, but also because of poor performance in the handling and clearance processes. Second, although agents pay Biman for all services, they often have to hire their own labor for the same purpose. Current management and practices therefore increase costs for airfreight logistics. Biman maintains that its role is not driven solely by commercial interests, but its operation should nevertheless be scrutinized for practices that could be detrimental to efficiency in logistics services. Infrastructure improvements are necessary at the terminal to increase capacity and space, including the acquisition of scanners able to handle airfreight pallets and other unit loads.
- *The clearance process for small consignments.* A contributory factor to congestion at the cargo terminal is the clearance process, even for small shipments. Although Bangladesh has a simplified procedure for small shipments and

Section 18 of the Customs Act provides for the non-levy of duties and taxes on such shipments, the limit in value of Tk 1,000 per consignment is low. As a result, most shipments of samples for the garment industry exceed this value and are caught. As a result, the packages are treated the same as all other shipments, resulting in clearance times that take one to five days even for garment samples. The adoption and introduction of procedures for expedited clearance of small shipments, consistent with World Trade Organization (WTO) guidelines, could be one possible solution to this problem.

Customs and Border Management

Risk Management

The National Board of Revenue (NBR), which manages customs, has implemented various reforms that have led to some improvement in customs performance in Bangladesh. It is possible for customs brokers to submit data electronically to the customs system[6] and for ship agents to electronically file vessel manifests (although the two systems are not integrated). In 2008, Chittagong Customs House, in cooperation with Chittagong Chamber of Commerce and the private sector, was involved in an automation project to interface their systems and enable online access to the customs system. Under that initiative, the Bill of Entry Module for online submission of customs declarations (Direct Traders Input) by importers or carrying and forwarding agents was implemented at Chittagong Customs House and Dhaka Customs House. It is now possible for importers or their agents to submit declarations online from their own premises, unlike in the past when they could only do so at a customs station.

NBR is taking steps to automate customs processes further. It was working on introducing Automated System for Customs Data (ASYCUDA) World[7] in 2013, starting at the Port of Chittagong. The plan is to interconnect all the customs stations so that declarations can be lodged from anywhere. In addition, NBR is working to introduce a "single window system" starting at Chittagong Customs House. Already, ship agents can file vessel manifests electronically, although hard copies still have to be submitted.

However, despite the improvements, informal payments are still common to facilitate clearance of goods. A major accomplishment in July 2013 was the phasing out of preshipment inspection. Until then, Bangladesh customs relied on the preshipment inspection (PSI) services provided by four firms: Bureau Veritas, Intertek Testing, SGS (formerly Société Générale de Surveillance), and Overseas Merchandise Inspection Company. Although it was claimed that PSI improved revenue collection, reporting on the declarations,[8] and cargo clearance time by one to two days on average, the program has not been without controversy (Arnold 2010). Globally, PSI firms provide customs with important risk-related functions and can enhance integrity in the clearance process. The PSI program requires pre-arrival processing of documents. It is used to verify the description, quantity, classification, and valuation of the goods being exported to Bangladesh and to issue a Clear Report of Findings. In Bangladesh, the PSI system was not working as efficiently as could be expected. On paper, 10 percent of PSI and 100 percent of non-PSI shipments were supposed to be subject to physical examination. However, the actual physical examination rate for PSI shipments was much higher (close to 50 percent). There are around 8,000 disputes pending in the courts relating to the certifications by the PSI agencies—a small proportion of the total declarations. The disputes were usually about classification and valuation of imports and what was regarded as poor performance by the PSI companies (Mahmud and Rossette 2007; Uzzaman and Abu Yusuf 2011).

With the phase-out of PSI, the services previously offered by the private firms have become part of the normal functions of customs administration. In any case, risk management is a core component of a modern customs administration. Customs should therefore provide the resources and training of their staff to target their interventions better on areas that pose the most risk. The International Finance Corporation, the private sector arm of the World Bank Group, reviewed the government strategy and identified some priority actions that could be undertaken as part of capacity building upon phasing out PSI in Bangladesh (see box 6.1).

Box 6.1 Priority Actions to Phase Out Preshipment Inspection

- *Risk management.* Establish a risk management unit with officers able to analyze, prioritize, and design responses to risks associated with particular kinds of cargo shipments. The program should include a risk management policy, a standard risk profile, extensive coordination and communication with all entities (companies and other government agencies) involved in the trade process, a post-clearance audit program and unit, trained analysts, and a formalized compliance program.
- *Customs valuation.* Follow World Trade Organization Valuation Agreement standards, where the preferred basis of appraisement is "transaction value," defined as the "price actually paid or payable" by the buyer for the imported goods.[a] This expanded role for customs may require a significant change in current work processes for customs officers and will require specialized training.
- *The World Customs Organization (WCO) Harmonized System.* Develop classification capacity for customs based on the Harmonized System, the WCO's system of code numbers for identifying products, since the classification and explanatory notes can be quite complex. Refresher training for customs officers may be required.
- *Trade compliance and enforcement.* Provide support to staff and management to balance the actions taken when reviewing import or export documentation or physically inspecting commercial goods.
- *Customs automation.* Enhance current processes and procedures through automation, in preparation for transition from the existing preshipment inspection regime.

Source: World Bank 2012.
a. http://www.wto.org/english/tratop_e/cusval_e/cusval_info_e.htm.

The government has taken measures consistent with the priority actions in preparation for the phasing-out of PSI. Chief among the actions taken was a significant increase in and training of customs staff, to accompany the July 2013 phase-out of PSI.

A complementary action that authorities could also take would be to implement an Authorized Economic Operators (AEO) program.[9] An AEO is a party involved in the international movement of goods in whatever function that has been approved by or on behalf of a national customs administration as complying with World Customs Organization (WCO) or equivalent supply chain security standards. The operator satisfies certain criteria and is considered to be reliable in customs-related operations. The operator is therefore entitled to certain benefits and greater trade facilitation, such as simplified and rapid release procedures on the provision of minimum information. The criteria include having an appropriate record of compliance with customs requirements, a demonstrated commitment to supply chain security, and a satisfactory system for managing commercial records. Typically, an AEO program is developed and implemented in phases, reflecting the capacity of the authorities and private sector readiness to participate in such a program. The Revised Kyoto Convention already provides some of the steps that customs could implement to facilitate authorized operators, forming the basis for an AEO program.

An AEO program for Bangladesh would help address several objectives, including faster clearance of some goods and, as a corollary, freeing customs and other border management resources to target those consignments that pose the most risk.

To summarize, specific actions to improve risk management in Bangladesh include the following:

- Focus on specific tariff lines or products that pose the highest risks. A national risk profile, based in part on the experience of customs and PSI firms, could be created to identify activities that have the most impact on revenue protection and collection and regulatory compliance. The profiles can be tuned to the flows handled at different customs houses; for example, traffic at Chittagong is different from that handled at Benapole.
- The management of risk should be automated as much as possible, based on international best practices. The ASYCUDA World system that is being developed has a capability to enhance risk management in a flexible manner. To improve the system, customs should record examination results in a systematic and consistent manner. For a start, customs should obtain data from the PSI firms so that it can develop a risk management database.
- Define a clear risk management policy that identifies roles and responsibilities for different levels of customs staff. In addition, it is important to strengthen the post-clearance audit system. Presently the post-clearance audit function is performed by the same commissionerate that deals with customs valuation. It would be important to have a dedicated post-clearance audit unit that is fully staffed, especially at the offer level, and equipped to offer

Strengthening Competitiveness in Bangladesh—Thematic Assessment
http://dx.doi.org/10.1596/978-1-4648-0898-2

services at all major ports. This should be considered as part of a comprehensive risk management regime.

- Introduce an AEO regime for selected supply chain participants. This could start with the established garment manufacturers. Such a program would free customs resources to target those consignments that pose the most risk, especially following the phasing out of PSI.

Land Customs Station Management

Presently, most of the land customs stations are not automated and use manual systems. Bangladesh has an extensive network of land customs stations. The most dominant one is Benapole, which is on the main land trade route with India. A project is underway whereby NBR is working with the United Nations Conference on Trade and Development and customs to introduce ASYCUDA World software, which would enable the connecting of the five major customs houses and the 10 largest land customs ports. This was expected to be in place in late 2013. Customs intends to build on this system to introduce a single-window system to integrate all border agencies at the various customs houses around the country.

Clearance times are typically two to three days at the smaller stations and within five to six days at Benapole (figure 6.8). At Benapole, 80 percent of declarations are assessed within a day of being lodged, whereas it takes up to five days to clear 80 percent of goods for release after declaration. The clearance times at the land customs stations are affected by several practices that increase time and cost. The main one is the current practice of transloading cargo between

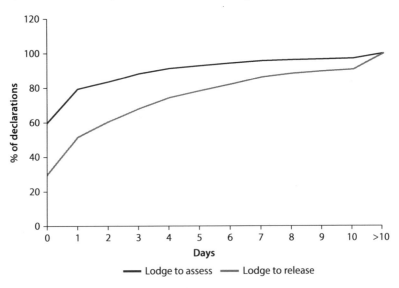

Figure 6.8 Cumulative Distribution of Customs Clearance Times at Benapole Land Customs Station, November 2011 to February 2012

Source: World Bank estimates, data from Bangladesh Customs.

trucks registered in Bangladesh and those registered in India. This practice has several consequences, including the need to provide warehousing space and equipment to handle and store goods, and labor to handle the goods. A solution to these inefficient practices lies in the two countries agreeing on modalities for the penetration of trucking services into each other's territory.

The problems and possible solutions to problems often found at Bangladesh's land border crossing points are summarized in table 6.1. The problems are most commonly found at the major land customs stations, such as Petrapole-Benapole and Akhaura-Argatala, the largest ports between mainland India and Bangladesh and Bangladesh and northeastern India, respectively.

Generally, there are common issues that could be addressed to improve overall efficiency at the land border posts. Some of the measures can be short-term measures including the following:

- *Increase and harmonize border working hours.* The land ports do not operate fully on Friday in Bangladesh and on Sunday in India. Two days of clearance are therefore lost each week.
- *Allow pre-arrival clearance of goods.* Some countries have realized significant gains from allowing the processing of documents to start before goods get to the border. The goods can therefore be cleared as soon as they arrive and customs and other agencies are able to carry out any physical verification they may desire.

Table 6.1 Common Problems and Possible Solutions at Land Customs Stations

Problem	Possible solutions
Access roads to land border crossing points are often narrow with not enough space for vehicles to be parked on the roadside. This creates congestion and delays, which result in high truck demurrage charges to Bangladeshi exporters.	India has built or is planning integrated check posts at several borders with Bangladesh. However, while the facilities should help address the space constraints that are faced, the access roads between the two sides are not always properly aligned. There should be active engagement between the two sides on development plans.
There is often not enough space or sheds for transloading.	Space for transloading should be larger on the side that is importing more volume than the other. There is need to match capacity to need.
Differences in border opening hours on the Bangladesh and India sides as the early closure at 5 pm reduces the average work day to 6–7 hours.	There is need to synchronize border opening hours between the two sides.
In addition, there are differences in holidays each week, further reducing the commercial work week by two days.	A system of pre-arrival processing of documents could be introduced to expedite clearance.
There are labor syndicates on both sides of the borders that increase transloading costs.	Measures should be taken to abolish syndicate practices at the border posts.
	Transloading could also be mechanized to improve efficiency.
Customs only clears goods if the complete consignment has arrived.	Processing could be allowed for split consignments.

• *Increase capacity for handling transloaded goods.* In the interim before phasing out transloading of goods, the capacity for handling such cargo should be increased. Current practices are designed around significant use of manual labor and the involvement of hundreds of people at each border post in the transloading business. Some of the processes can be automated to expedite the movement of goods.

Regional Integration and Trade Facilitation

A review of trade facilitation and logistics performance in South Asia illustrates continued weakness in several areas. This is reflected in the low intraregional trade volume compared with trade with other regions, although South Asia has great potential as one of the main sources of global growth. Recent political developments have opened the possibility that the objectives of the South Asian Free Trade Agreement of 2006 can move further ahead. As the countries look toward deeper integration, it becomes increasingly obvious that there is a need to address some of the constraints that increase transport and logistics costs.

Infrastructure interconnectivity is a fundamental building block for a regionally integrated transport system. Although South Asia has a basic, interconnected road network, road transport operations are hampered by differences in market access policies, axle load limits, quality requirements, and so forth. Cargo that is compliant in one country may exceed limits in the next country. Similarly, railways in the region have a combination of meter and broad gauge lines. This impedes cross-border movements, where these are allowed. Bangladesh has had to construct both gauges in some parts of the network to interface with the Indian system. Infrastructure differences take time and are costly to accommodate. However, some of the major constraints lie in the policy choices of the countries.

For example, there are differences in axle load limits between Bangladesh and India, with which it shares the longest border (table 6.2). Axle load limits in Bangladesh are consistently lower than those in India, for the same class of trucks. This could be a reflection of weaker pavements in Bangladesh; or it could reflect a regulatory legacy where the limits have not kept pace with

Table 6.2 Gross Vehicle Weight Limits in Bangladesh and India
tonnes

Vehicle type	Bangladesh	India
3 axle (1 front, 2 back)	22	25
4 axle (steering + 3 axles)	25	31
5 axle (3 prime mover, 3 trailer)	38	44
6 axle (3 prime mover, 3 trailer)	41	44[a]
7 axle (3 prime mover, 4 axle)	44	—

Source: World Bank estimates, data from various sources.
Note: — = not available.
a. Nominal weights are 45.4 and 54.2 tonnes, but 6-axle vehicles are restricted to 44 tonnes.

recent trends in trucking technology. In fact, the differences in axle load limits are cited as one reason for denying India transit rights across Bangladeshi territory. This is only one reason and possibly not the main reason for denying such transit rights. Various other political, social, and economic considerations are also pertinent. There are whole industries and a large number of people already engaged in transloading cargo at the borders. These stakeholders would be affected by a change in policy, regardless of the economic inefficiencies involved in the status quo.

For efficient cross-border movement of cargo, it is essential that road, rail, and inland waterway vehicles are allowed to cross borders and deliver goods from origin to destination seamlessly. Because of the shape of the borders in the region, Bangladesh could serve as a transit country for trade between mainland India and India's northeastern states and for Nepal and Bhutan. As discussed earlier, movement of vehicles is not possible across Bangladesh's borders, whether for transit or for goods bound for Bangladesh. Goods therefore have to be offloaded at the border and transferred to vehicles from the other country. This practice is inefficient. The same applies to railways where locomotives have to be changed. Recently, however, the Governments of India and Bangladesh have been discussing how Indian traffic can cross from the mainland to the northeast states across Bangladesh. The intention is primarily to allow traffic between western Bengal and the landlocked Indian states in the northeast. Such transit would halve travel distance to about 500 kilometers.

Dealing with transit rights between two coastal countries is possible but much more complex than between coastal and landlocked countries, where there are clear international rules and traditions. The complexity is apparent in the ongoing discussions and negotiations between India and Bangladesh. Each side has undertaken studies on what the impacts could be. It would appear Bangladesh's preference is for a regional approach so that transit is dealt with from a broader perspective that includes landlocked Bhutan and Nepal. The countries have some mechanisms in place to exchange traffic, including standard operating procedures for movement of vehicles from and to India, Nepal, and Bhutan up to customs-controlled areas on each side of a border. However, the existing arrangements still require the transloading of cargo from the vehicles of one country into those of the other, a practice that is inefficient.

Meanwhile, the discussions on a broader framework are ongoing, and India is already developing alternative routes to reduce costs between the northeast states and the mainland. It is financing the development of a port (Sittwe), road, and mode interchange facility in Myanmar that will be part of a multimodal system between Kolkata and Sittwe to the state of Mizoram and the rest of the northeast region.

A comprehensive transit framework has the potential to transform the trade facilitation environment in South Asia, particularly if it is extended to accommodate traffic to and from Nepal and Bhutan. The latter may then be able to access Bangladeshi ports much more efficiently, especially Mongla. The problem here is a specific one that requires a practical transit solution on a few identified road corridors with significant traffic potential. Two of the main considerations are as follows:

- A functional transit procedure through Bangladesh that would allow seamless movement of goods between western Bengal and the northeast states of India, with no significant waiting time at the border or en route for inspections or transloading.
- Adequate cost recovery mechanisms for Bangladesh, to recoup the costs associated with required infrastructure and services, according to universal principles on freedom of transit.

A formal agreement between the countries would be required for any new initiative to work. The alternative to the transit procedure would be through the Siliguri Corridor or "chicken neck" in India,[10] which would essentially set an upper bound for the performance of the transit route across Bangladesh. For example, in the case of a tractor-trailer rig that travels at least 500 kilometers a day, delays probably should not exceed three hours at each border. This is a demanding target, given current levels of performance where delays of several days are not uncommon. A formal agreement may open the way for a multilateral approach that includes and benefits the landlocked countries of Bhutan and Nepal.

Ratification of international instruments can help with regional harmonization of trade facilitation practices. A possible solution to all these problems could be the ratification of a set of seven international conventions by all South Asian countries. This could become the foundation for integrated trade and transport systems as recommended by the United Nations Economic and Social Commission for Asia Pacific in 1992 (see table 6.3) (UNESCAP 2007).

The seven international instruments cover infrastructure and service and transit needs for a regionally integrated system. Among the instruments is the Customs Convention on the International Transport of Goods under Cover of TIR Carnets (Transports Internationaux Routiers, TIR, Customs Transit Procedure). TIR is a system of bonds, operated in nearly 70 countries, that

Table 6.3 The Seven UNESCAP Conventions

Title	Date
1. Convention on Road Traffic	Vienna, November 8, 1968
2. Convention on Road Signs and Signals	Vienna, November 8, 1968
3. Customs Convention on the International Transport of Goods under Cover of TIR Carnets	Geneva, November 14, 1975
4. Customs Convention on the Temporary Importation of Commercial Road Vehicles	Geneva, May 18, 1956
5. Customs Convention on Containers	Geneva, December 2, 1972
6. International Convention on the Harmonization of Frontier Controls of Goods	Geneva, October 21, 1982
7. Convention on the Contract for the International Carriage of Goods by Road	Geneva, May 19, 1956

Source: UNESCAP (http://www.unescap.org).
Note: TIR = Transports Internationaux Routiers; UNESCAP = United Nations Economic and Social Commission for Asia Pacific.

guarantees that any customs and other duties will be paid on goods transported in transit trucks. Its objective is the improvement of transport conditions and the simplification and harmonization of administrative formalities in international transport, particularly at frontiers. TIR has three important principles:

- Goods carried under TIR procedures in sealed road vehicles are not as a general rule submitted to examination in customs offices en route. But they may be inspected when an irregularity is suspected. Customs authorities do not require vehicles to be escorted at the carrier's expense on the territory of their country.
- The contracting parties authorize agreed upon professional associations to issue TIR carnets. These associations guarantee that they will pay the import or export duties (of course, if the goods are moving from India to India via Bangladesh, there should be no duties) and taxes, including penalty interest in case of irregularities. For the purpose of identification of the goods on which duties have to be paid, details of these goods are entered in the TIR carnet. Customs authorities discharge TIR carnets after conclusion of the transport operation. Discharge is equivalent to clearance, and customs authorities cannot claim taxes and duties after discharge.
- Irregularities render the offender liable to the penalties of the country where the offense was committed. In case of doubt, the offense is deemed to have been committed in the country where it was detected. Any person guilty of irregularities may be in future excluded from the operation of the TIR.

In South Asia, only Afghanistan has ratified the TIR Convention. One of the likely benefits of India and Bangladesh, in particular, acceding to the TIR is the potential spillover effects beyond South Asia. Nepal and Bhutan are landlocked and need access to seaports and harmonized agreements to reduce time and costs.[11] They could therefore more easily access the ports of Bangladesh, which are the closest. A functional regional transit system is therefore an imperative for South Asia. The TIR would also greatly benefit transit trade with Afghanistan, as it can be an instrument to address concerns over likely diversion of goods in transit into the Pakistani domestic market. However, Pakistan and India have only made tentative moves to accede to the TIR Convention. In the case of Pakistan, progress stalled over attempts to have reservations on some provisions of the TIR Convention, which is not allowed. Acceding to the convention seems contentious in Pakistan, and an official decision has been made to suspend the efforts until there is consensus.

Bangladesh does not presently have an effective institutional mechanism to promote trade facilitation and logistics upgrading. The existing mechanism, through the National Trade Facilitation Committee, does not have the powers necessary for a proactive and robust definition of a trade logistics strategy. It certainly does meet the trade facilitation obligations under the WTO framework, but some of the constraints now faced are much more about the interface between the physical infrastructure and meeting regulatory requirements

Strengthening Competitiveness in Bangladesh—Thematic Assessment
http://dx.doi.org/10.1596/978-1-4648-0898-2

for the movement of goods. Like other countries, Bangladesh has several agencies that play a role in trade facilitation and logistics. These include customs, chambers of commerce, the land port authority, port operators, railways, roads, inland waterways, clearing and forwarding agents, security services, and so forth. However, the country does not presently have an effective institutional mechanism for these players to coordinate their actions to improve overall performance. The lack of proper coordination is evident in the manner in which transit issues have been pursued, where a holistic assessment of the costs and benefits of transit has not gained enough traction. In other countries, such as Pakistan, coordination of trade facilitation reforms is pursued through a national trade facilitation committee. Bangladesh should broaden the coverage and strengthen the capacity of the national trade facilitation committee to play a more proactive role in guiding trade facilitation and logistics reforms in the country.

Options for Improving Trade Facilitation and Logistics Performance in Bangladesh

The main findings of the analysis presented in this chapter that could frame the action matrix are as follows:

- The current practice of stripping containers in the port or in the Chittagong area increases cargo clearance time, costs, and port development costs. The practice denies Bangladeshi exporters the benefits of containerization, which is fundamental to modern logistics.
- The railways are fundamental to increased utilization of containers on the domestic corridor. Presently, the railways suffer from low capacity and poor reliability, which contribute to limited movement of containerized cargo. Proposed plans to dual track the main line between Dhaka and Chittagong should address capacity constraints, but would require improved procedures at the port to expedite movement.
- Development of an inland waterway transport and logistics system will increase its viability as an option for moving containers inland. However, the overriding issue is the comparatively slow speed of water transport. This makes it less attractive to shippers, especially in the garment industry. A more comprehensive approach is needed that will include modernization of the vessel fleet.
- There is poor coordination among agencies at the border, which increases costs and clearance time and reduces reliability.
- There are high costs and disputes associated with using PSI. Some PSI shipments are subject to price and quality disputes. The intention of government to phase out PSI is validated by the evidence, but customs needs to build adequate internal capacity to take over proper valuation of goods.
- Air shipments can be expedited through the adoption of WCO's Immediate Release Guidelines. Presently, even samples are subjected to the same clearance formalities as all other cargo.

- The trucking industry needs a reform strategy for modernization and improved performance. Most trucks deployed on the DCC are not designed to carry containers. Long transit times and congestion limit movement of containers by road. This is partly caused by infrastructure constraints, especially two narrow bridges that act as choke points.
- Whole industries and communities have grown up around the land customs stations, largely to facilitate transloading—moving goods from vehicles of one country into another. Thus, significant political economy issues will have to be addressed if the South Asia region is to facilitate seamless trucking across international borders. Countries would first have to negotiate either regional or bilateral instruments allowing the cross-border movement of trucks.
- Air transport is inefficient because of congestion and lack of capacity at the air terminal. The terminal is run as a monopoly. Options to increase competition should be explored.
- Exchange control rules force clearing and forwarding agents to play only a local role. The main constraints to the operation and efficiency of logistics services providers are (a) restrictions on establishing bonded warehouses and (b) restrictive foreign exchange controls, especially for foreign direct investment. As product value chains become more sophisticated, Bangladeshi operators will want to manage outbound chains as well. However, this issue goes beyond just logistics services providers and is relevant to several other aspects of the Diagnostic Trade Integration Study.

Good logistics are important for enhancing Bangladesh's competitive edge in exports. To date, low wages have benefitted Bangladesh's RMG exports and have partially compensated for poor logistics performance. But to ensure continued rapid growth of exports, logistics performance in Bangladesh will need to improve considerably. This chapter has identified options for tackling interrelated issues that are critical for enhancing Bangladesh's logistics efficiency.

Annex 6A: List of Goods That Can Be Cleared in Off-Dock Yards

Headings are from the Harmonized System, the World Customs Organization's system of code numbers for identifying products.

1. Rice (Heading 1006)
2. Scrap (includes meltable and rollable scrap under Heading 72.04)
3. Wheat (Heading 1001)
4. Mustard (Heading 21033000)
5. Waste Paper (under Heading 48.07)
6. Chick Peas (under Heading 07.13)
7. Pulses (under Heading 07.13)
8. Raw Cotton (Heading 52)
9. Hard Coke (Heading 27040000)
10. Carbon Black (Heading 27030000)
11. Marble Chips (Heading 251741000)

12. Ball Clay (bulk good, Heading 25083000)
13. Onions (Heading 07021019)
14. Ginger (Heading 09101090)
15. Garlic (Heading 07032090)
16. Fertilizer (Heading 31010000–310590000)
17. Animal Feed (Heading 23.09)

Notes

1. Export containers are loaded outside the Port of Chittagong at various private inland container depots or container freight stations. Once loaded and customs approval has been obtained, they are then transferred to the port for loading.

2. Dhaka ICD has a storage capacity for only 1,000 TEU at any one time. It was established in 1987 under the joint ownership of Bangladesh Railways and Chittagong Port Authority. Container handling operations are under the control of Chittagong Port Authority. Since August 1991, dedicated container block trains have operated between Dhaka and Chittagong.

3. About 90 percent of train kilometers are passenger services, nearly all of which are customers traveling second class.

4. Bangladesh Regional Rail Traffic Enhancement Project, TA 3490 Ban, November 2003, SwedeRail, RITES, CPCS Transcom, BETS. See http://www.adb.org/projects/32234-012/main.

5. There are some examples of public railroads successfully operating high-volume container train services, such as the Republic of Korea's Pusan-Seoul service, but these are generally correlated with strong government policies promoting the service.

6. Bangladeshi customs uses a version of the United Nations' Automated System for Customs Data (ASYCUDA++). See http://www.asycuda.org/.

7. See http://www.asycuda.org/.

8. Review of preshipment inspection in Bangladesh, Manzur Ahmed, http://www.thefinancialexpress-bd.com/more.php?news_id=17515.

9. The World Customs Organization (WCO) SAFE Framework of Standards defines the SAFE Authorized Economic Operator (AEO) as an entity complying with WCO or equivalent supply chain security standards and with legal obligations in relation to tariff and nontariff requirements on the import, export, and transit of goods.

10. See http://en.wikipedia.org/wiki/Siliguri_Corridor.

11. Although countries may negotiate regional agreements on transit, TIR remains the only proven functional system for international transit.

References

Arnold, J. 2010. *Bangladesh Logistics and Trade Facilitation.* Washington, DC: World Bank.

Bangladesh Bureau of Statistics. Various years. *Statistical Yearbook of Bangladesh.* http://www.bbs.gov.bd.

Berg, A., S. Hedrich, S. Kempf, and T. Tochtermann. 2011. *Bangladesh's Readymade Garments Landscape: The Challenge of Growth.* Dusseldorf: McKinsey and Company.

Kathuria, Sanjay, and Mariem Mezghenni Malouche, eds. 2016. *Attracting Investment in Bangladesh—Sectoral Analyses: A Diagnostic Trade Integration Study.* Directions in Development. Washington, DC: World Bank.

Mahmud, T., and J. Rossette. 2007. "Problems and Potentials of Chittagong Port: A Follow-up Diagnostic Study," (accessed June 28, 2013), www.ti-bangladesh.org/research/ES_CTG_Port2007%28eng%29.pdf.

Raihan, S., A. Eusuf, and S. Ifthekhar. 2010. "Competition Issues in the Trucking Sector in Bangladesh." *Bangladesh Economic Outlook* 2 (4): 7–14.

UNESCAP (United Nations Economic and Social Commission for Asia Pacific). 2007. *Towards a Harmonized Legal Regime on Transport Facilitation in the ESCAP Region: Guidelines.* ST/ESCAP/2489. Bangkok: UNESCAP.

Uzzaman, A., and M. Abu Yusuf. 2011. "The Role of Customs and Other Agencies in Trade Facilitation in Bangladesh: Hindrances and Ways Forward." *World Customs Journal* 5 (1): 29–42.

World Bank. 2010. *Connecting to Compete 2010: Trade Logistics in the Global Economy.* Washington, DC: World Bank.

———. 2012. *Connecting to Compete: Trade Logistics in the Global Economy.* Washington, DC: World Bank.

CHAPTER 7

Constraints to Trade Finance

Hugh Baylis

Introduction

Lack of access to finance and to competitive trade financing instruments has often been identified as a hindrance to trade. The shortage of medium-term finance for the purchase of capital equipment is of crucial importance to new exporters and companies wishing to diversify their exports. Despite significant efforts by the government and nongovernmental organizations, only 33 percent of all small and medium enterprises (SMEs) in Bangladesh have received at least one loan from a formal financing institution. This means a large majority of existing SMEs do not have access to bank finance, and this acts as a constraint to export growth and the entry of potential new exporters into the market.

Moreover, at a time of general liquidity shortages, access to finance can get further squeezed, as happened in FY2011/12, when a surge in government borrowing crowded out affordable access by the private sector. This squeeze severely inhibited the banking sector's ability to finance the growing export industry. Tight monetary conditions resulted in reduced availability of trade finance and working capital loans. The banks were also requested by Bangladesh Bank (BB) at that time to decline requests to open import letters of credit (L/Cs) for "luxury" products.

The provision of trade finance support is important for lowering risks for exporters and helps mitigate the local currency shortage. Trade finance is particularly important during the initial stages of exporting (for example, for new firms and at the extensive margin where new products and new markets are being established) as well as during periods of macroeconomic uncertainty. Lower risk reduces barriers to entering and sustaining exports (increasing export survival) as well as lowering trade cost (through financing costs). Moreover, while foreign currency financing at usually low interest rates has recently become easier to obtain in Bangladesh, unsecured working capital loans from abroad are notoriously difficult to attract. The perceived credit and political risks are high, and new Basel II capital adequacy requirements make the finance unattractive to foreign lenders. Therefore, the best alternative solution is trade finance, especially export finance, which traditionally has a lower risk profile than regular, unsecured, working-capital finance. The transactions are backed by shipping documents and the underlying goods; tenors are short, and the credit risk lies with a (usually) better credit-rated buyer in a stronger economy. Bangladesh's finance risk becomes performance risk, which is manageable where the exporter has an established track record.

This chapter brings international experience to bear on trade finance and identifies instruments that could benefit small companies and new exporters. In particular, the chapter focuses on companies that are not part of supply chains, including the garment industry, and discusses issues relating to general access to credit.

Role of Trade Finance

Much of international trade is conducted directly between firms without direct intermediation of the banking sector (figure 7.1).[1] Some 80–90 percent of total world merchandise trade, valued at US$18 trillion in 2011, is reportedly financed between firms in a supply chain or between different units of individual firms. Transactions conducted directly between firms can involve cash in advance from the buyer to the seller, or be done on an "open account" basis, with the buyer paying the seller at a later point. According to messaging data from the Society for Worldwide Interbank Financial Telecommunication, approximately 90 percent of trade finance occurs through interfirm transactions, including "open account" exchange.[2] Direct cash-in-advance payments are most prevalent among micro businesses and SMEs in low- and middle-income countries (LMICs), while open-account transactions tend to be used in more developed, competitive markets (Chauffour and Farole 2009; IMF-BAFT 2009). In addition to making payment arrangements directly between themselves, importers and exporters have the option to use the banking sector to intermediate transactions. Intermediation of the banking sector can provide risk mitigation, improve the liquidity and cash flow of the trading parties, and provide locally oriented firms with access to the hard currency needed to finance imports (Chauffour and Farole 2009). Some 20–40 percent of world trade is estimated at being intermediated in this manner.

Figure 7.1 Trade Finance Agreements Worldwide

Market share of financing arrangements			
Cash in advance	**Bank trade finance**	**Open account** (38%–45%, US$6.0 trillion to US$7.2 trillion)		
19%–22% US$3 trillion to US$3.5 trillion	35%–40% US$5.5 trillion to US$6.4 trillion	**ECA guaranteed** US$1.25 trillion to US$1.5 trillion	**Arm's-length non-guaranteed**	**Intra-firm**
$15.9 trillion in global merchandise trade (2008 IMF estimate)			

Source: Chauffour and Malouche 2011, global trade data.
Note: ECA = Export Credit Agency; IMF = International Monetary Fund.

The choice of direct or banking sector–intermediated trade transactions will depend on the familiarity and degree of trust between the buyer and the seller, as well as broader country, sector, and institutional factors that increase or decrease the risk of nonpayment for the goods and services being traded (Chauffour and Malouche 2011).

Trade finance generally consists of two main components, payment risk mitigation and provision of the working capital necessary for exporters and importers to manufacture or sell their goods. Working capital finance for exports is generally short term, up to 180 days, depending on the merchandise, increasing to 360 days, for example, in the case of shipbuilding. Relative to a standard credit line or working capital loan, trade finance—whether offered through banks or within the supply chain—is relatively illiquid, which means that it cannot easily be diverted for another purpose. It is also highly collateralized—credit and insurance are provided directly against the sale of specific products or services whose value can, by and large, be calculated and secured.[3] This suggests that the risk of strategic default on trade finance should be relatively low, as should be the scale of loss in the event of default.

Exporters must offer their customers attractive sales terms supported by appropriate payment methods to win markets and be competitive (box 7.1). Because getting paid in full and on time is the ultimate goal for each export sale, an appropriate payment method must be chosen carefully to minimize the payment risk while accommodating the needs of the buyer. As shown in figure 7.2, there are four primary methods of payment for international transactions that companies should consider during or before contract negotiations and that would be mutually desirable for the exporter and the buyer. Exporters want to receive payment as soon as possible, preferably as soon as an order is placed or before the goods are sent to the importer. For importers, any payment is like a donation until the goods are received. Therefore, importers want to receive the goods as soon as possible but to delay payment as long as possible, preferably until after the goods are resold to generate enough income to pay the exporter.

A "confirmed" letter of credit transaction is the most prevalent instrument in trade between high-income countries and LMICs. In a confirmed L/C transaction, a second bank (the *confirming bank*), usually in the exporter's country or region, is involved. If an exporter is unwilling to take the payment risk of the local issuing bank, then it can request that a second bank add its commitment (or confirmation) that payment will be made to the exporter. A confirmed L/C is generally used when there is a perception that there is a risk that the local bank issuing the L/C may not fulfill its obligation to pay for any reason, including bank failure, country instability, or country regulations. In this case, the confirming bank takes the payment risk of the local issuing bank in the country of the importer. The confirmed L/C is the most prevalent instrument among trade between high-income countries and LMICs. For a confirming bank to take the payment risk of the local issuing bank, it has to establish a relationship with this bank, conduct its due diligence on the bank, and establish a prudential credit limit up to which it is willing to be exposed to this bank. The majority of Global Trade Finance

Box 7.1 Payment Methods for International Trade Transactions

Cash-in-advance. With cash-in-advance payment terms, the exporter can avoid credit risk because payment is received before the ownership of the goods is transferred. Wire transfers and credit cards are the most commonly used cash-in-advance options available to exporters. However, requiring payment in advance is the least attractive option for the buyer because it creates cash-flow problems. Foreign buyers are also concerned that the goods may not be sent if payment is made in advance. Thus, exporters who insist on this payment method as their sole manner of doing business may lose to competitors who offer more attractive payment terms.

Letters of credit. Letters of credit (L/Cs) are one of the most secure instruments available to international traders. An L/C is a commitment by a bank on behalf of the buyer that payment will be made to the exporter provided that the terms and conditions stated in the L/C have been met, as verified through the presentation of all required documents. The buyer pays his or her bank to render this service. An L/C is useful when reliable credit information about a foreign buyer is difficult to obtain, but the exporter is satisfied with the creditworthiness of the buyer's foreign bank. An L/C protects the buyer because no payment obligation arises until the goods have been shipped or delivered as promised. An L/C can be either "unconfirmed" or "confirmed." In an unconfirmed L/C transaction, an importer requests a local bank (that is, in the importer's country) to issue an L/C in favor of the exporter. The local bank (the *issuing bank*) then issues an L/C through which it irrevocably agrees to pay the exporter on agreed terms (such as presentation of relevant documents). In this transaction, there is only one bank that is financially involved—the bank that issues the L/C. The exporter takes the risk that the local issuing bank will not honor its obligations (for example, because of credit or country events). Such unconfirmed L/Cs are more common when the local issuing bank has a strong balance sheet and is in an economically and politically stable country.

Documentary collections. A documentary collection (D/C) is a transaction whereby the exporter entrusts the collection of a payment to the remitting bank (exporter's bank), which sends documents to a collecting bank (importer's bank), along with instructions for payment. Funds are received from the importer and remitted to the exporter through the banks involved in the collection in exchange for those documents. With D/Cs, a draft is used that requires the importer to pay the face amount either at sight (document against payment) or on a specified date (document against acceptance). The draft gives instructions that specify the documents required for the transfer of title to the goods. Although banks do act as facilitators for their clients, D/Cs offer no verification process and limited recourse in the event of nonpayment. Drafts are generally less expensive than L/Cs.

Open account. An open account transaction is a sale where the goods are shipped and delivered before payment is due, which is usually in 30–90 days. Obviously, this option is the most advantageous option to the importer in terms of cash flow and cost, but it is consequently the highest-risk option for an exporter. Because of intense competition in export markets, foreign buyers often press exporters for open-account terms since the extension of credit by the seller to the buyer is more common abroad. Therefore, exporters who are reluctant to extend credit may lose a sale to their competitors. However, the exporter can offer competitive open account terms while substantially mitigating the risk of nonpayment through the use of one or more of the appropriate trade finance techniques, such as export credit insurance.

Figure 7.2 Payment Risk Diagram for Exporters and Importers

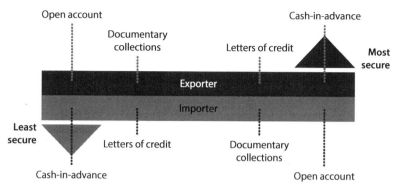

Source: U.S. Department of Commerce 2008.

Program transactions (70 percent) involve confirmed letters of credit (with the balance supporting other instruments such as pre-export and pre-import finance).

Recognizing the fundamental role of trade finance as an engine for global trade and the movement of goods at all stages of the supply chain, especially in emerging markets, international institutions such as the World Bank Group and regional development banks, including the Asian Development Bank (ADB), have programs to support trade finance in LMICs (box 7.2). The International Finance Corporation (IFC), the World Bank Group's private-sector lending arm, has a number of programs that support trade finance, including the following:

- The Global Trade Finance Program, which offers confirming banks guarantees covering payment risk on banks in emerging markets for trade-related transactions
- The Global Trade Supplier Finance (GTSF) Program, which provides short-term finance to emerging-market suppliers and exporting SMEs
- The Critical Commodities Finance Program, which supports global agricultural commodities trade and imports of energy-related goods in the world's poorest countries
- The Global Trade Liquidity Program, conceived to channel liquidity quickly to targeted markets by providing trade credit lines and refinancing portfolios of trade assets held by selected banks.

All of these programs were scaled up during the 2008–09 financial crisis (Chauffour and Malouche 2011).

However, the analysis of the flow and availability of trade finance continues to be constrained by the lack of trade finance data worldwide. This limitation became evident during the 2008–09 global financial crisis as trade volumes plummeted and trade credit froze in most LMICs. As a consequence, the G20 has undertaken some initiatives to improve information on trade finance, mostly through the International Chamber of Commerce (ICC) annual and

Box 7.2 Asian Development Bank Trade Finance Program during the 2008–09 Financial Crisis

The Asian Development Bank's (ADB's) Trade Finance Program (TFP) provides guarantees and loans to banks in support of trade and does so within 24–48 hours from the time it receives guarantee and loan applications from partner banks. TFP currently works with more than 180 banks. TFP has made a point of not assuming risk in China and India, preferring to focus resources on more challenging Asian markets where the private sector is not very active. TFP had the bulk of its exposure in Bangladesh, Pakistan, and Vietnam, but was active in Azerbaijan, Indonesia, Mongolia, Nepal, Sri Lanka, and Uzbekistan as well as other markets. In March 2009, ADB ramped up the activities of its TFP. TFP supported US$2 billion in trade, an increase of over 300 percent compared with 2008.

The program delivers tangible and measurable development impact. For example, in 2009, TFP provided trade support for 263 small and medium-sized enterprises (SMEs). Supporting the growth of SMEs is a priority for ADB since smaller firms employ the largest number of people in most Asian countries. Increased trading activities and cross-border relationships enabled by TFP are helping boost economic integration and cooperation in challenging Asian markets, which should, in turn, spur faster economic growth and help reduce poverty. In 2009, 56 percent of TFP's portfolio supported intraregional trade. Furthermore, 47 percent of TFP's 2009 US$2 billion portfolio supported trade between ADB's low- and middle-income member countries (South-South trade).

Source: Chauffour and Malouche 2011.

snapshot bank surveys. The Trade Finance Registry was also established by the ICC and the ADB to capture the default and recovery rate of short-term documentary export and import loans, and guarantees of about 19 international banks for 2005–10. It helped show that the default and loss percentages on these trade finance instruments, even in severe economic times, were minimal. Nonetheless, comprehensive data on bank-intermediated trade finance remain unavailable. More data would help in monitoring the trade finance market, especially for low-income countries, small banks, and SMEs. It would also help make the case for the relative safety of trade finance to the Basel Committee.

Trade Finance in Bangladesh

Most exports from Bangladesh are based on L/Cs. BB feels more comfortable with the stronger control mechanisms provided in L/C regulations. In Bangladesh, trade finance is governed by the Foreign Exchange Regulations Act, 1947 and the Foreign Exchange Guidelines of BB. These are updated on a regular basis through the issuance of BB circulars and other instructions. The regulations are relatively complex, especially for imports, with the aim of controlling the country's balance of payments and limiting outflows of foreign currency. As a result, all official trade passes through the local banking sector and trade financing from abroad (except through foreign bank branches) is difficult to acquire. Also, the government has amended the Foreign Exchange Regulation Act which appears to have tightened some of the controls and expanded the authority of Bangladesh Bank to cover a wider range of transactions, ask for information, and cover foreign nationals living in Bangladesh.

Other guidelines constrain export industries, despite some relaxation over the years. BB Export Guidelines require that title documents to export transactions be assigned in favor of a local Bangladeshi bank. This effectively prohibits the ability of offshore lenders to enter the market and provide diversified trade finance from abroad. The title documents cannot be released to the overseas buyers without the local bank first receiving payment. The restriction means that trade finance lending is almost always in taka (in short supply during the liquidity shortage) and at current high interest rates (up to 18 percent per year). Foreign exchange regulations have been relaxed to some extent over the years owing to lobbying by the strong garment industry, which has forced change and some simplification. Nevertheless, there remain areas where more can be done to eliminate constraints and create a more open environment.

In contrast to this scenario, bank-intermediated trade finance accounts for only about 20 percent of total world trade. The remaining 80 percent is conducted on an open-account basis or cash in advance. Of the large exporting countries in Asia, only Pakistan and Bangladesh maintain these controls. In most countries, the title documents to an export transaction are issued to order (left open) or are assigned to a specific party or foreign bank as determined in the contract between the exporter and importer. India, coming from a regulatory environment similar to Bangladesh's, successfully boosted exports through introducing open-account trading while continuing to maintain strong exchange controls. Sri Lanka also provides a good example of how the procedures have successfully been introduced.

Several private banks do provide high-quality trade finance services and the state banks, too, have improved their trade capabilities. Interviews with select banks evidenced strong management and an open approach to developing modern trade finance services. However, in FY2011/12, the liquidity shortage restricted the banks' ability to support their clients; moreover, local banks are severely constrained by a lack of access to offshore funding. Some local banks have recently initiated cash-flow lending and take collateral only as a secondary fallback. However, in most cases, collateral is taken for the majority of bank risk, including short-term working capital and trade finance. Sometimes security up to 150 percent of the loan is taken, together with the personal guarantees of the company's owners and directors. This places a strain on the borrower's resources, especially smaller companies. SMEs often do not have sufficient collateral available, or have assigned it to other risk. The result is they are unable to raise the finance necessary to enter the export market or increase their export business.

Strengthening Competitiveness in Bangladesh—Thematic Assessment
http://dx.doi.org/10.1596/978-1-4648-0898-2

There is a need to enhance cash-flow lending among local banks, especially for trade finance, which provides lower risk lending opportunities.

The foreign banks in Bangladesh have a number of advantages over local banks.[4] They are able to run offshore (U.S. dollar) and local currency balance sheets. They have easy access to U.S. dollars from their offshore offices. Nevertheless, the foreign banks are constrained in their overall U.S. dollar exposure by their internal country limit restrictions (table 7.1). In addition, the requirement to assign export title documents to a local bank does not impact the foreign banks to such an extent because they can finance a transaction from overseas, knowing the title documents are fully assigned to the local branch. Bangladeshi banks do not have this advantage.

The government has two main schemes to support SME exporters. First, the Export Refinancing Scheme finances working capital at 10 percent per year. Under the Export Refinancing Scheme, BB no longer refinances the loans, and the banks have to bear the negative interest differential themselves (10 percent versus 12 percent cost of funds). Consequently, the facility is not popular with the banks, and they find other ways of financing exporters at higher rates of interest. Second, the Export Development Fund finances capital investment at 7 percent per year. Under the Export Development Fund, the local banks lend to the SMEs and retain the credit risk. They refinance themselves from BB at 7 percent per year. The scheme is popular. Bangladesh's Eastern Bank commits 8 percent of its US$1 billion export finance under the scheme (for the import of capital equipment). However, the national average is believed to be lower, perhaps around 1.5 percent. There is also a Women's SME facility, which has not been well utilized so far. Nevertheless, SME exporters express a need for easier access to working capital and, where imports are required, the facility to open import L/Cs.

The lack of finance and high interest rates impact smaller companies more than their larger counterparts. SME lending is a specialized area. The risks are high, and SMEs must prove themselves before a bank can entertain lending to them. Less than half the banks in Bangladesh have SME lending as a strategic goal, although those that do have well-organized SME operations. Standard Chartered Bank has a significant SME division with 30 percent of its assets lent to SMEs. Eastern Bank and Janata Bank, among those interviewed, also have a strong SME focus. Bangladesh is a world leader in microfinance and the skills and motivation for cash-flow and SME financing are improving. The average loan size

Table 7.1 Bangladesh's Export Finance Exposure by Bank Sector
2011 estimated

Bank sector	Exposure (US$, billions)	Percent
State-owned banks	6.9	30
Privately owned banks	8.1	35
International banks (U.S. dollar)	4.4	19
International banks (local currency)	3.6	16
Total	23.0	100

Source: World Bank calculations.

for BRAC Bank (formerly the Bangladesh Rural Advancement Committee) is US$8,000, spread across nearly a million borrowers; some of this lending supports the export industry.

The Export Credit Guarantee Scheme (ECGS) operates as Bangladesh's Export Credit Agency (ECA). ECGS was started in 1978, based on the initiative of the Export Promotion Bureau to provide insurance against export risk. The scheme is administered by the Sadharan Bima Corporation (SBC), a state-owned general insurance company. The scheme encourages exporters to initiate exports of new products and enter new markets by covering the risk of buyer insolvency as well as political risks. The also guarantees bank loans taken by exporters to meet their working capital needs prior to receiving payment from their foreign buyers. The facility provides credit up to 180 days, including preshipment and post-shipment finance. Coverage is 75–80 percent in case of commercial credit and 95 percent in case of political risks. The following trade guarantees are issued by ECGS: (a) export preshipment guarantees, (b) export post-shipment guarantees, and (c) export payment risk policies. For preshipment and post-shipment guarantees, the exporters must first be accepted for credit risk by their local bank. The bank then makes the application for the guarantee to SBC. The cost of the guarantee is a low 0.10 percent, subsidized by the government for "promotional" reasons. At present, ECGS is a minor department within SBC, does little business, and has a modest reputation among banks and exporters.

Although expansion of ECA operations can mitigate credit risk and keep trade finance markets from drying up, the potential impact of these agencies on the financial and real sectors of the economy should be carefully evaluated. The choice of a sustainable business model is crucial, involving a strong governance structure as well as an adequate capital base that would allow the institution to be independent and have a strong enough operational footprint to achieve its objectives. These are two preconditions that are seldom met in low-income economies, which often suffer from weak institutional capacity, poor governance practices, and difficulties in applying the rule of law (Chauffour, Saborowski, and Soylemezoglu 2011). Examples of countries that have successfully strengthened their export credit agencies to good effect are Sri Lanka and Indonesia. Sri Lanka's Sri Lanka Export Credit Insurance Corporation is strongly market oriented and supports small as well as large companies. It has been especially successful in supporting the garment industry, including small suppliers to the sector. More than 70 percent of Sri Lankan exporters are SMEs, and the Sri Lanka Export Credit Insurance Corporation has developed a number of schemes to facilitate their export operations.

A Modern Approach to Trade Finance

The local bank assignment requirement should be changed. This would open up Bangladesh to new trade financing structures from abroad, improve liquidity, and significantly lower financing costs. BB should allow title documents to be endorsed directly in favor of the overseas buyer in select cases. An example would be buyers that are highly rated companies or exporters that have a long-standing and good export performance record of, say, a minimum of three years. This would be highly beneficial to the exporter, since buyers could trade with the Bangladeshi exporter on the same terms as exporters in other countries and acceptance of documents by the buyer would be faster and more efficient.

The risk of fraud is generally limited. One of the main concerns of BB and Bangladeshi authorities is how to ensure the correct repatriation of foreign currencies and the risk of fraud under the proposed new procedure. The risk of fraud essentially revolves around under-invoicing to pay reduced charges, or over-invoicing to obtain higher amounts of foreign currency from a country than are due. Alternatively, it is conceivable that goods other than those invoiced could be shipped. In all cases, fraud is extremely difficult to perpetrate. First, there are two parties to the contract, buyer and seller, and both must be willing to enter into the subversion. As most buyers of Bangladeshi ready-made garments exports are well-established companies with strong reputations, such activity would not be easy to accomplish. The buyer is always required to "accept" the invoices before a bank will purchase them. Second, in most cases, documents such as quality and standards certificates are issued, which require third parties to sign off on the goods against the invoice. Third, the goods must be processed through customs, which checks the value and quantity of goods against invoices and other documents. And finally, the shipping documents are issued by authorized agents upon loading the goods, which are again checked for quantity and content. The possibility of shipping goods other than those stipulated in the invoice is deemed near impossible.

The risk of fraud can be managed by establishing a centralized risk registry (CRR). Mortgages and charges on real estate and fixed assets can be registered at the land registry in Bangladesh. However, there does not appear to be an efficient register of pledges of movable assets. Some institutions register the charge at the Registrar of Joint Stock Companies.[5] Other banks say this procedure is inefficient and not always complied with. Much time and effort is spent on agreeing on pari passu terms between creditors. Even if a bank does not take collateral, it will fear being subordinated to other lenders through the pledges. A CRR will include complete and accurate registration of all pledges or liens on movable assets, including receivables. This would eliminate the risk of companies financing the same export receivable more than once (through secured loans or through the sale of receivables), since financiers would be able to check existing pledges or liens on receivables. A CRR would enable potential lenders to see immediately which assets have been pledged and eliminate the possibility of fraud and double pledging. The issue will become more acute as offshore trade finance becomes commonplace following the proposed change in assignment of title documents. The World Bank in Dhaka has initiated discussions on the implementation of such a register in the export processing zones (also referred to as EPZs). This should be expanded to include the entire country.

IFC's new GTSF Program could be introduced to create a controlled environment under which to implement this proposal, at least in the initial stages.[6] This would provide for a high level of comfort for BB and local authorities, because the offshore lending bank would be IFC, a triple A–rated financial institution within the World Bank Group. Under GTSF, IFC would purchase up to 100 percent of the export receivables from agreed foreign buyers of ready-made garments and other exports, after their acceptance of the documents, paying the net discounted amounts to the Bangladeshi exporters (through their local banks) without recourse. Since the financing is based on the (better) credit risk of the overseas buyer, discount rates would be highly competitive and represent significant cost benefits to the exporter. Implementation would typically be through an electronic platform (provided by IFC) between the buyer, the exporter, and IFC (financier). This would allow for efficient, streamlined processing since the exporter could view invoices accepted by the buyer and request financing through the platform. GTSF could be introduced quickly, within two months.

If even 20 percent of garments sector exports could be financed through GTSF, reducing export receivables credit delays by 45 days, this could release up to US$350 million annually in cash flow for exporters. The program would significantly enhance liquidity in Bangladesh's financial system and substantially reduce financing costs. The change would primarily support the garment industry because it is the largest sector, but would also assist the increasing number of other exporters in Bangladesh. Garment exporters require pre- and post-shipment finance, as most garment sales are at 60–90 days post-shipment credit terms (some even extending to 120 days). GTSF would provide a preshipment solution by discounting the receivables, improving cash flow, and reducing working capital requirements for Bangladeshi exporters.

Exporters would greatly benefit if modern trade finance instruments such as export receivables (post-shipment finance) were widely adopted (box 7.3). In trade finance, export finance in particular has an especially low risk profile.[7] This is because in most cases, goods exported from LMICs are sold to stronger buyers in more-developed economies where the risk is lower. The credit risk is of the buyer, and the country risk is that of the country of the buyer. In many cases, the buyers are creditworthy companies located in the United States or Europe. There is no foreign exchange risk as payment is made by the buyer in the currency of the loan. Therefore, Bangladesh's risk is reduced to performance risk—that the exporter will manufacture and ship the correct quality and quantity of goods on time. Provided the exporter has a good track record and the shipment is properly insured, the risk is manageable. Trade finance loss rates for LMICs are not significantly higher than those of high-income nations. If 20 percent of Bangladesh's total exports were financed through receivables purchases, it would release up to US$575 million annually in cash flow for manufacturers. In addition, assuming international financing costs of around 5 percent per year compared with Bangladeshi local interest rates of nearer 18 percent per year, the overall interest rate savings would be in the region of US$75 million per year. If this is extrapolated through 2015 (assuming a conservative 10 percent per year export growth rate), working capital savings could reach US$900 million and interest savings US$72 million (assuming a reduced interest rate differential of 8 percent per year).

Box 7.3 Main Export Finance Instruments

Pre-export finance. Working capital loans made to the exporting firm, enabling it to manufacture the goods for export. The risk is structured on the strength of the export letter of credit or export contract. In most cases, the bank is repaid from the export proceeds in the buyer's country.

Post-shipment finance. Finance provided to the exporter to finance the post-shipment terms demanded by the buyer. Often structured in the form of purchase of export receivables, funds are paid to the exporting firm upon shipment, thereby reducing its working capital requirements. The loan is repaid by the buyer upon final payment.

Supply chain finance. Supply chain finance can include both pre- and post-shipment finance. Usually the financing would commence early in the production cycle and continue until final payment, including the post-shipment period. Finance could be provided to an exporter's supplier or the exporter, with repayment made from the final export proceeds.

Contract finance. Contract finance can include pre- and post-shipment finance. Finance would start upon contract signing and continue until final payment. It is usually provided only to the exporter.

Factoring. The purchase of invoices (receivables), but for smaller companies, factoring can be international or local.

Forfaiting. Purchase of larger, medium-term trade receivables.

A more open trade finance market should also initiate access to supply chain finance and export contract finance. Supply chain finance can include financing the exporter (the anchor company), enabling it to finance its suppliers, or lending to the suppliers directly, based on the strength of their orders from the anchor company. Repayment would be made from the export proceeds. In either case, the performance record of the supplier in relation to the anchor company is crucial to the supplier's ability to raise finance. A prerequisite for the success of such an instrument is the existence of organized and creditworthy companies supplying the main exporters. In Bangladesh, the delivery record of some suppliers can be uncertain, and even the well-established garment industry consists of a hub of many less creditworthy companies supplying the main exporters. However, Bangladeshi export supply chains are relatively straightforward, and it should not be long before international banks start financing the better suppliers as well as the main exporters. This would be a major step forward in providing finance to the suppliers that have proved difficult to finance in the past.[8] A simpler and more realistic means of financing exporters, at least to start with, is lending against export *contracts*. Contract finance creates liquidity for the exporter from the outset of the production cycle (as opposed to receivables purchases, which are post shipment). This creates longer periods of finance, enabling the exporters to provide better terms to their suppliers. The mechanism would be quick to establish itself following the assignment change and would rapidly reduce working capital requirements and interest rate costs.

Small firms could benefit from local factoring.[9] Factoring could provide a good means of financing the suppliers to the export industry, "the deemed exporters," as well as creating liquidity in the local economy. In other words, it could help finance the supply chain. Factoring is a method of financing small businesses that do not have easy access to regular bank finance. The factor purchases the company's invoices (receivables) at a discount, crediting the company with the net proceeds. Upon payment by the buyer, the factor pays the remaining balance to the company. In some economies, such as Portugal, Sri Lanka, and Taiwan, China, local factoring has proved to be highly successful in financing the SME sector. Factoring is more costly than bank finance, especially on a nonrecourse basis, but it can help small, less creditworthy companies obtain finance outside the banking sector. Factoring can sometimes benefit from legislation being passed to clarify the transfer of ownership of assigned receivables and the rights and obligations of the parties involved. India, for example, passed factoring legislation in 2011 that has significantly boosted the factoring business. Sri Lanka, by contrast, does not have a factoring law.

Taking these new mechanisms into consideration, the scenario suggests half of Bangladesh's exports could be financed from offshore, generating US$3.6 billion in additional working capital by 2015. By way of comparison, consider Sri Lanka, which had total exports of US$8.4 billion in 2011, of which approximately 52 percent comprised garment exports. It is estimated that 40 percent of total exports were financed from offshore, generating approximately US$800 million of working capital—that is, 9.5 percent of total exports or slightly lower than the 10.3 percent estimated for Bangladesh in 2015 (table 7.2). However, Sri Lanka has a more liquid banking system with greater access to local currency finance and lower interest rates.

Back-to-back (BTB) L/Cs and bonded warehouses (BWH) could largely benefit non-garment exporters. BWHs enable exporters or "deemed exporters" to import inputs without paying import duties and value-added tax on the materials (manufacturers must export 80 percent of their production to be able to obtain a BWH license and BHWs may be located within or outside an export processing zone). Because BWHs were initially designed solely for use by the garment industry and a few specially approved exporters, subsequent licensing seems to have been authorized on a piecemeal basis. As a result, there is uncertainty over who can obtain a license. The complexities of applying for a BWH license constrain many small companies. The BTB L/C scheme has been a great success in enabling SME garment suppliers to open L/Cs to import inputs without posting collateral.[10] The BTB scheme can only be used together with a BWH and there appears to be uncertainty about who can use BWH and BTBs and who cannot. Some major exporters stated they were unable to use BTB L/Cs because they did not export 100 percent of their production; the requirement has been reduced to 80 percent. In the Sixth Five-Year Plan, the government has extended the benefits to the shipbuilding and leather industries. The uncertainty is constraining smaller companies from expanding their operations and potentially building export businesses. BTB L/Cs could also be issued without the support

Table 7.2 Estimated Scenario for Bangladesh's Offshore Trade Finance, 2015
US$, billions

Product	Total exports (US$, billions)	Financing percentage	Finance provided (US$, billions)	Days financed	Working capital generated (US$, billions)
Pre-export finance	—	20	—	—	—
Contract finance	—	12	4.2	120	1.4
Supply chain finance	—	8	2.8	120	0.9
Post-shipment finance	—	30	—	—	—
Receivables finance	—	20	7.0	45	0.9
Other	—	10	3.5	45	0.4
Total exports	35.0	50	17.5	—	3.6

Source: World Bank calculations.
Note: — = not available.

of a BWH. The deemed exporter would not benefit from nonpayment of import duties, but the important collateral benefits would remain.

Policy Options

Given the constraints of the local marketplace, there is a clear need to open the door to easier access to foreign financing. This could be achieved through a change in the local assignment requirement for export title documents. The change would enhance competition, increase liquidity, and reduce interest costs. It would be most helpful to the garment industry, because it is the largest, but would benefit Bangladesh's other exporting sectors as well as potential new exporters. In addition, it would help support the SME suppliers to the export industry, which have traditionally been difficult to finance.

To help achieve these aims, the following concrete policy options are proposed:

- Review the Foreign Exchange Regulation Act to allow more flexible and competitive international payment mechanisms.
- Change the assignment rule for export title documents.
- Phase in the new procedure by implementing IFC's GTSF program. GTSF would help introduce the "assignment" change, at least in the initial stages, as IFC would be the "foreign financing bank."
- Implement an automated CRR. Use it to log pledges of movable assets, thus providing clear information on all charges or pledges made by lenders. Alternatively, automate the Registrar of Joint Stock Companies, where charges on movable assets are often registered.
- Make access to BTB L/Cs and BWH more transparent and broader in terms of sectors and firms (for example, deemed exporters).
- Consider introducing factoring in Bangladesh, which would be especially relevant for small firms.

These recommendations should help Bangladesh modernize its trade finance business and expedite access to trade finance and working capital at more affordable and competitive rates. They would help the export sector to compete better and support its quest for expansion and diversification.

Notes

1. Society for Worldwide Interbank Financial Telecommunication data from http://www.swift.com/. There are substantial variations in the estimates. This estimate is assumed to exclude financing by the banking sector further up or down the supply chain.

2. Estimates from IMF-BAFT (2009) suggest that 10–20 percent of trade finance is composed of cash-in-advance payments (these mainly involve SMEs, especially in LMICs); 45–80 percent is on open account (of which 30–40 percent is intra-firm); and 10–35 percent is bank intermediated. See http://www.fimetrix.com/.

3. This is, of course, not true in all cases. Specific problems occur with products that are perishable (and whose value erodes quickly or immediately), that are extremely differentiated (where there is little or no market value outside the intended buyer), and for services (which are not generally able to be collateralized).

4. An example of a creative new import finance product was designed by a foreign bank branch in Dhaka. The bank provides post-shipment finance to importers in U.S. dollars against usance L/Cs, payable 180 days after shipment. The importer issues the usance L/C but pays the supplier at sight with the proceeds of the loan. He repays the loan after 180 days. This enables the provision of a foreign currency loan at international interest rates for the usance period. BB has authorized the foreign currency borrowing under generic approval because it is trade-related. The foreign banks are already looking for more creative ways of working within the regulations.

5. It is recommended that analysis be conducted on the need either to upgrade and automate the Registrar of Joint Stock Companies or to establish a separate CRR.

6. The GTSF Program has been approved for an overall worldwide limit of US$500 million, and it would be beneficial if Bangladesh were able to benefit from this availability.

7. Trade finance has historically had a lower default record than most unsecured bank risk.

8. IFC could provide training in supply chain management if Bangladesh decides to take GTSF.

9. International factoring requires a steady flow of sales and invoicing. If only a couple of export sales are achieved a year, it is doubtful international factoring could add much value. In addition, a Bangladeshi company exporting to a stronger buyer overseas should be able to raise more cost-effective finance, as the risk in this case is that of the buyer. Therefore, international factoring is not considered to be suitable for Bangladesh.

10. The "master L/C" is opened by the foreign buyer in favor of the Bangladeshi exporter. The L/C then provides the collateral on which smaller import L/Cs can be opened by the suppliers without posting collateral. This helps increase liquidity and facilitates the production process. The master L/C can also be used as collateral for working capital loans required by non-importing local suppliers.

References

Chauffour, Jean-Pierre, and Thomas Farole. 2009. "Trade Finance in Crisis: Market Adjustment or Market Failure?" Policy Research Working Paper 5003, World Bank, Washington, DC.

Chauffour, J.-P., and M. Malouche. 2011. *Trade Finance during the Great Trade Collapse.* Washington, DC: World Bank. http://siteresources.worldbank.org/INTRANETTRADE /Resources/TradeFinanceEntire.pdf.

Chauffour, J.-P., C. Saborowski, and A. Soylemezoglu. 2011. "Should Developing Countries Establish Export Credit Agencies?" In *Trade Finance during the Great Trade Collapse,* edited by J.-P. Chauffour and M. Malouche. Washington, DC: World Bank.

IMF-BAFT (International Monetary Fund–Bankers Association for Finance and Trade). 2009. *IMF-BAFT Trade Finance Survey: A Survey among Banks Assessing the Current Trade Finance Environment.* Market Research & Intelligence for Financial Institutions, FImetrix.

U.S. Department of Commerce. 2008. *Trade Finance Guide: A Quick Reference for U.S. Exporters.* Washington, DC: International Trade Administration, U.S. Department of Commerce.

CHAPTER 8

Attracting Foreign Direct Investment

Sanjay Kathuria, Mariem Mezghenni Malouche, Peter Kusek, and
Nadeem Rizwan

Introduction

To reach East Asian growth rates of 7–8 percent, private investment levels in
Bangladesh need to rise to at least 33 percent of gross domestic product (GDP)
(World Bank 2012). Foreign direct investment (FDI) could help to augment the
quality and quantity of investment. Foreign-owned firms are a source of innovation spillovers and perform significantly better than domestic firms in terms of
labor productivity and profit margins. Foreign-owned firms can help to increase
the overall amount of private investment by accessing their own savings as well
as international financial markets, thereby easing at least a part of Bangladesh's
financial sector limitations.

The rapid rise of China and forecasts of it outsourcing 80 million jobs over the
next four to five years because of rising wages present an opportunity for countries like Bangladesh to attract FDI, but this will not happen automatically. Japan,
for example, is actively following a so-called "China Plus One" policy, where it is
searching for alternative countries from which to source. But there are several
countries that could provide viable options for Japan, including, for example,
Indonesia, Vietnam, and others. So far, despite being considered relatively open
to FDI, capital inflows have remained small in Bangladesh. The share of FDI in
GDP and private investment is low, even when compared with levels in other
low-income economies. Several studies have identified the main constraints to
economic growth, productivity gains, and FDI as follows: bureaucracy, corruption, electricity shortages, inadequate access to land and finance, skill shortages,
ineffective implementation of measures to attract FDI inflows, and lack of confidence in sustained sociopolitical stability (Hossain 2008; Kafi, Uddin, and Islam
2007; Nasrin, Baskaran, and Muchie 2010).

The benefits of FDI for economic development and export diversification are
well established. A global network of multinational corporations and foreign

affiliates has helped create millions of jobs, transfer technology, upgrade skills, open export markets, and foster domestic competition. In the long run, FDI's most important benefits are spillovers of technology and knowledge (such as management and organizational practices) to local firms and workers, rather than easily observable things like capital inflows, jobs, and taxes. Spillovers can diffuse from foreign firms to local producers within the same industry (intra-industry or horizontal spillovers) or to another industry (inter-industry or vertical spillovers). However, the impact of FDI on the host country is stronger when its linkages with the economy are high, which in turn depends on skill availability, the type of foreign ownership, the characteristics of local firms, and the host country's institutions.

This chapter reviews the main bottlenecks to overall private investment in Bangladesh and then focuses on FDI performance and the openness of Bangladesh to FDI, relying extensively on 2012 indicators from the World Bank's Investing Across Borders (IAB) Initiative.[1] Although Bangladesh is one of the most open countries to foreign equity ownership, the IAB data point to the following hindrances to FDI: (a) a gap between policies and practice, (b) lengthy and discretionary administrative procedures, (c) weak dispute arbitration systems, and (d) poor access to land-related information in Bangladesh. The chapter also relies on the United Nations Conference on Trade and Development's (UNCTAD's) 2013 Bangladesh Investment Policy Review, which examines the regulatory and legal framework needed to support a larger role for FDI in Bangladesh's economic development. In particular, the report highlights the need to examine FDI entry procedures, weaknesses in the general regime of regulations and operating conditions for business, and poor promotion of foreign investment in Bangladesh (UNCTAD 2013).

Constraints to Private Investment in Bangladesh

Investment in Bangladesh has stagnated at a relatively low level in recent years, at around 26–27 percent of GDP. This reflects feeble growth in private investment and declining public investment, to the extent that national savings could not be fully absorbed domestically. Weak incentives for investment appear to be the more binding constraints. Bangladesh has failed to improve its business environment and investment climate. The repetitive political uncertainty during election times, together with frequent general strikes and associated violence, has added to the long-standing energy and infrastructure deficits in dampening the investment climate. Deficiency of infrastructure has been a binding constraint to domestic investment, of which inadequate supply of power and gas is at the top of the list. In 2012, the demand-supply gap of electricity was around 5,000 gigawatt hours (Ministry of Finance 2013). Bangladesh ranks nearly last among its Asian competitors (only above Nepal) in the prevalence of power outages. It was ranked 109th in the Global Competitiveness Index 2014–15 of 144 countries, and 173 of 189 countries in the Ease of Doing Business 2015 ranking (World Bank 2015).

The consequences of deficiency of infrastructure and chronic power shortages are lower manufacturing productivity in Bangladesh than in Vietnam and China, and the use of costly captive generation to compensate for outages (World Bank 2012). Bangladesh ranks last among 189 countries surveyed in World Bank's *Doing Business 2014* report in terms of getting an electricity connection, which takes 404 days (World Bank 2014). Transport infrastructure is also inadequate. Roads predominate as railways are inefficient, and waterways and barge container transport are underutilized. Bangladesh is at a competitive disadvantage in terms of port infrastructure, paved roads, airport density, quality of air transport, and railroads. The share of paved roads in total roads in Bangladesh is some 20 percentage points below the norm after controlling for the country's stage of development. This is a large drawback for a country with one of the highest population densities in the world. In terms of infrastructure and institutions, Bangladesh continued to rank poorly (131st and 132nd, respectively, of 148) in the Global Competitiveness Index 2012–13.

Access to land is another major impediment to new investments, particularly in manufacturing. Land availability is severely limited, as large, unused tracts are not available. What does exist is either owned by state-owned enterprises or the government or used for agriculture, housing, and roads. Smaller firms are cut off more severely from access to land and that access has worsened over time. In 2002, 29.2 percent of firms considered it a major problem, which had risen to 41.7 percent by 2007. Unavailability of serviced land is a prominent investment hurdle (World Bank 2012). Moreover, the property registration process is inordinately slow. According to the World Bank's *Doing Business Report 2015*, Bangladesh ranks 184 of 189 economies, with property registration typically taking 244 days, compared with 47 days in India, 25 days in Indonesia, 57 days in Vietnam, and only 2 days in Thailand (World Bank 2014).

Corruption, access to finance, and an inefficient government bureaucracy are extremely problematic obstacles to doing business in Bangladesh. These impose costs on doing business and hurt the country's chances to attract private investment and compete in global markets. Poor property rights protection magnifies risk perceptions; limits on user rights discourage private initiative and slow the process of economic diversification. Although many countries have improved their respective processes of contract enforcement, Bangladesh has not made any significant globally benchmarked reforms in this regard. With contract enforcement taking on average more than 1,442 days, Bangladesh is slowest among its comparator countries and ranked at 185th of 189 countries surveyed (World Bank 2014). Long-term lending and lending to small firms in the rural nonfarm sector is inadequate. Financial depth (measured as M2-to-GDP) is low and the range of financial services is quite rudimentary. Many of the important contractual savings institutions are absent and capital markets are extremely shallow.

Investors do not find sufficiently high return on investment because of low human capital productivity or shortage of skills. Bangladesh lags behind competing countries in terms of educational attainment. The country is unable to take full advantage of globalization with a poorly educated and relatively unskilled workforce. Firms are less able to adopt technologies from more advanced economies. Investors are less likely to try ventures that require specialist skills. Although the shortage of skills and low labor productivity did not constrain investment and growth in the past, they are becoming increasingly important.

Poor Performance of FDI Inflows in Bangladesh: A Snapshot

In the context of an unfriendly business environment, FDI has persistently been low (figure 8.1 shows the small increase, relative to other countries, in FDI inflows over 1990–2012, despite the low base) and represented a tiny fraction of GDP and private investment in Bangladesh.[2] Bangladeshi FDI inflows reached around US$1.6 billion in 2013, but overall FDI stocks remain below 6 percent of GDP (as of 2012, see figure 8.2). Average FDI as a percentage of GDP was about 23 percent in the 2000s in least-developed countries (LDCs). FDI stock as a share of GDP was also higher in comparator countries, such as Vietnam (an average of 45 percent of GDP), Pakistan (over 10 percent despite difficult conditions there), South Asia as a whole (almost 10 percent), and Sub-Saharan Africa (30 percent) (figure 8.2).

Figure 8.1 FDI Inflows, 1990–2012

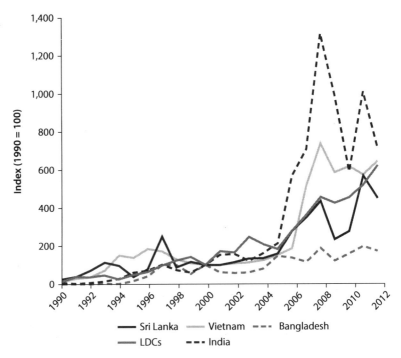

Source: UNCTAD World Investment Report 2012 online database, http://unctad.org/en/Pages/DIAE /World%20Investment%20Report/Annex-Tables.aspx.
Note: FDI = foreign direct investment; LDCs = least-developed countries.

Figure 8.2 Foreign Direct Investment Stock as a Share of GDP in Bangladesh and Selected Low- and Middle-Income Countries, 2012

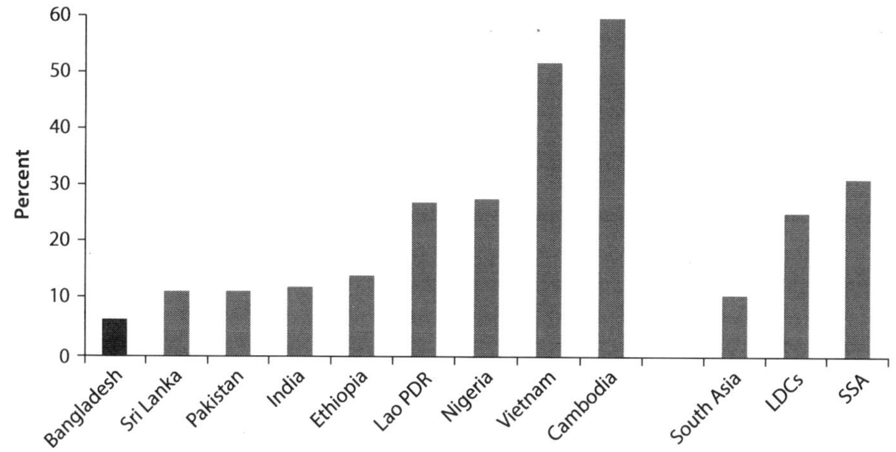

Source: UNCTAD World Investment Report 2012 online database, http://unctad.org/en/Pages/DIAE/World%20 Investment%20Report/Annex-Tables.aspx.
Note: South Asia includes Iran. GDP = gross domestic product; LDCs = least-developed countries; SSA = Sub-Saharan Africa.

FDI in Bangladesh has mostly flowed into the services sector. The telecommunications industries and the banking sector have attracted the most FDI, followed by the garment, gas, and petroleum sectors. Bangladesh has attracted three totally foreign-owned mobile telephone providers, as well as a majority foreign investor in the firm with the largest market share. The banking sector includes a number of globally renowned banks. The textile and clothing industry has received less FDI, which is partially because of obstacles in this sector (UNCTAD 2013).[3] Moreover, Bangladesh has attracted investment from a diverse set of countries. The Arab Republic of Egypt was the largest foreign investor during 2005–11, with investment concentrated in telecommunications. The next largest foreign investors are the United Kingdom, the United States, and Singapore.

An important share of FDI in Bangladesh takes place in export processing zones (EPZs). EPZs are export-oriented industrial enclaves that provide the infrastructure, facilities, and administrative and support services for a wide variety of enterprises. Bangladesh's successful EPZs in Dhaka and Chittagong are complemented by new EPZ developments around the country. As of December 2014, 405,166 jobs were created in EPZs, mostly in Chittagong and Dhaka (see table 8.1 for complete data), although these cannot be attributed to foreign firms alone, since some domestic firms also locate in EPZs.

Sector studies conducted for the Diagnostic Trade Integration Study point to the important role FDI can play in terms of export diversification and technology transfer in Bangladesh. The Republic of Korea has led investment in the garment industry. FDI was critical in the emergence of bicycle exports in Bangladesh. Malaysian investors seized an opportunity in the EU market by establishing the first bicycle exporting firm in Bangladesh in 1995. They invested US$2 million

Table 8.1 Overview of EPZs in Bangladesh, December 2012

| | No. of industries | | | | |
Name of EPZ	Manufacturing	Under implementation	Investment (US$, millions)	Export (US$, millions)	No. of employees
Adamjee	36	27	179.41	683.47	25,470
Chittagong	170	10	1,033.62	16,053.77	178,889
Comilla	32	31	163.02	799.0	13,428
Dhaka	102	11	888.46	13,395.99	86,873
Ishwardi	9	20	70.15	112.43	5,342
Karnaphuli	38	19	236.28	647.68	30,793
Mongla	16	14	6.26	159.76	1,551
Uttara	9	9	30.13	34.46	7,917
Total	412	141	2,607.33	31,886.56	350,263

Source: Ministry of Finance 2013.
Note: EPZ = export processing zone.

in a new plant named Alita in Chittagong. FDI in the shipbuilding sector is close to zero for the moment; however, FDI and joint ventures could help gradually improve Bangladesh's capacity and reputation in shipbuilding. FDI could especially help the linkage industries through technological advancement and improvement of processes as well as worker skills. Korean and Chinese investors in particular seek to capture some of the growth in Bangladesh's textile and services sectors.

However, the most defining characteristic of the recent period of globalization has been the proliferation of global capital flows, including FDI. Between 1990 and 2011, global FDI flows expanded more than eightfold, two and half times faster than world GDP and more than 60 percent faster than world trade growth over this period. Foreign affiliates of multinational corporations employ 69 million workers and contribute US$7 million in value added (UNCTAD 2012), equivalent to more than 10 percent of all global output. FDI inflows to low-income and middle-income countries expanded by 30 times in just 20 years, almost 6 times faster than they did in high-income countries. As a result, the average annual share of inward global FDI flows in non-OECD countries rose from 16 percent during the 1970s and 1980s to reach 45 percent in 2010.[4] This trend has been supported by liberalization in global trade and investment regimes that, along with advances in transport and communications, have allowed multinational firms to expand their market reach and exploit resource opportunities and offshore activities across global production networks. Moreover, FDI is becoming an increasingly significant component of output and trade in low- and middle-income countries (LMICs), in part because of the major expansion in the scope of global value chains (box 8.1).

Lessons learned from FDI policies oriented toward protected LMIC markets indicate that the policies have typically resulted in plants that were too small to capture economies of scale in the industry, leading to inefficient

---

Box 8.1 Why Do Global Value Chains Matter in the Discussion of FDI Spillovers?

Reduced policy barriers to cross-border trade and investment combined with substantial improvements in transport and communications technology have allowed for significant fragmented and geographical dispersion of production. This "second unbundling" (Baldwin 2012) has contributed to a major shift in global trade and investment patterns in recent decades, with production in individual countries increasingly forming just one stage in a product's value chain. The networks that have emerged from this process are typically led by large firms (normally in industrialized countries) and involve networks of suppliers across many countries in various stages (Milberg and Winkler 2013) from value addition of raw materials through component stages and to final production, assembly, and delivery. The networks are often referred to as "global value chains" (GVCs). It is estimated that more than half the value of world trade is made up of products traded in the context of GVCs. And in low-income countries, particularly small ones, the vast majority of non-resource-seeking investment takes place in the context of GVCs.

But aside from their sheer scale, the context of GVCs potentially has important implications when considering the prospects for achieving spillovers:

- Joining GVCs creates significant opportunities for spillovers through rapid insertion of host countries into global networks, but actually realizing and sustaining these spillover benefits may be mediated by the governance structures of value chains (Gereffi and Fernandez-Stark 2011) as well as the specific value chain strategies of lead firms.
- While GVC structures allow the potential for low- and middle-income countries to participate in global trade without building up full sector-specific supply chains (Baldwin 2012), it also means they may have little to no domestic expertise in the value chains that are investing in their country, limiting the potential for spillovers.
- In addition, GVC-oriented investments have in many cases become enclaves, relatively disconnected from their host country economies. This has perhaps been aggravated by the tendency of GVC-oriented investment to be located within export processing zones.

Thus, while many of the issues regarding spillovers are relevant for considering any type of foreign direct investment (FDI), investment under the context of GVCs raises an additional set of concerns. Understanding how these impact spillover potential and how they differ across sector and locational contexts is critical to considering how to maximize the potential benefits from FDI for low-income countries.

Source: Farole and Winkler 2014.

---

operations and expensive output. For example, in the automotive industry, the import substitution strategy led to a proliferation of small assembly facilities whose output did not typically exceed 20,000 units a year, whereas economies of scale demanded output on the order of 150,000–225,000 a year. These boutique plants depended on ongoing trade protection to keep them profitable, forcing host country consumers to pay a premium of 20–60 percent above the international market price (Moran 2006). A car assembled in 2003 at one of the mandatory joint venture plants in the protected Vietnamese market, with 10–30 percent locally produced auto parts, cost US$34,340 compared with US$16,500 for a vehicle of the same size produced under free trade and investment conditions in neighboring Association of Southeast Asian Nations countries.

Import-substituting FDI may generate local employment, but it is at a high cost and generally at the expense of local consumers. General Motors' Hungarian affiliate, by assembling 15,000 Opels behind a 22.5 percent tariff wall (before accession to the European Union in 2004 forced an end to Hungary's trade protection), created 213 jobs at a cost of more than US$250,000 each, paid for by domestic car buyers. Even learning among workers and managers and the potential to turn protected infant industries into full-scale competitive operations are limited. The parent firms delivered semi-knocked-down and completely-knocked-down "kits" to the small-scale assembly plants in the host country's protected local market. The procedures for screwing together an automobile from these car-in-a-box kits are different from assembly procedures in world-scale plants and cannot be used as building blocks for the larger operations (Moran 2006). Cost-benefit analysis of 83 foreign-owned assembly and processing projects in some 30 LMICs over more than a decade, valuing all inputs and outputs at world market prices, shows that those projects oriented toward protected local markets actually subtracted from host country welfare. These industries include industrial equipment, agribusiness, textiles, pharmaceuticals, chemicals, and petrochemicals, as well as automotive equipment and electrical equipment.

To sum up, gains from FDI can be substantial at the macro and micro levels, provided that FDI occurs in a competitive environment. At the macro level, gains materialize through increases in investment, employment, foreign exchange, and tax revenues (Paus and Gallagher 2008). Moreover, FDI often contributes to integrate host countries into the world economy (as foreign firms are engaged in exporting and use their global sales and supply networks) and, thus, stimulates trade in the long run. FDI might have an indirect impact on skills, infrastructure, and the business environment, as countries seeking to attract foreign investment tend to put policies in place to improve these factors. Finally, foreign entry may result in higher competition in the host country, leading to lower prices, more efficient resource allocation, and higher aggregate productivity (OECD 2002). At the micro level, FDI can benefit local suppliers directly through increased demand for quality intermediates, thus raising their output, profits, and possibly investments and labor demand. FDI can impact directly on domestic firms that use the output of foreign firms as inputs, possibly providing access to cheaper, higher quality, and more reliable inputs (Farole and Winkler 2014). The arrival of Suzuki in India in the late 1970s, for example, stimulated the growth of a highly competitive automotive components industry that is now a major exporter.

Constraints to FDI

UNCTAD indices of FDI attraction and potential show Bangladesh to be among the underperformers.[5] The UNCTAD FDI Potential Index has shown two groups of economies that have attracted significantly more (or significantly less) FDI than expected on the basis of their economic determinants alone (figure 8.3). The "below-potential" group includes economies that have not traditionally relied on foreign investment for capital formation, as well as a group of LMICs with emerging market status and with growing investment potential. Underperformers include the Philippines and South Africa and, to a lesser extent, countries such as India, Indonesia, and Mexico (UNCTAD 2012).

Bangladesh should be able to triple its FDI, given its advantages and the average FDI inflows to LDCs (figure 8.2). Compared with other LDCs, Bangladesh benefits from its large domestic market, competitively priced labor, and the powerful garment industry. These conditions should allow for increased domestic and foreign investment. Bangladesh underperforms compared with large,

Figure 8.3 Matrix of FDI Attraction versus FDI Potential, 2011

	4th quartile	3rd quartile	2nd quartile	1st quartile
1st quartile	Chad; Liberia; Madagascar; Niger	Albania; Bahamas; Congo, Rep.; Congo, Dem. Rep.; Equatorial Guinea; Jordan; Lebanon; Luxembourg; Mongolia; Mozambique; Zambia	Bulgaria; Ghana; Ireland; Israel; Nigeria; Norway; Panama; Turkmenistan; Uruguay	Australia; Belarus; Belgium; Brazil; Chile; China; Colombia; Hong Kong SAR, China; Kazakhstan; Malaysia; Peru; Poland; Russian Federation; Saudi Arabia; Singapore; Switzerland; Ukraine; United Kingdom; Vietnam
2nd quartile	Armenia; Cambodia; Guinea; Nicaragua; Saint Vincent and the Grenadines; Solomon Islands	Costa Rica; Georgia; Honduras; Kyrgyz Republic; Libya; Maldives; Malta; Namibia; Seychelles; Sudan; Tanzania	Brunei Darussalam; Croatia; Dominican Republic; Egypt, Arab Rep.; Estonia; Iraq; Portugal; Qatar; Serbia; Tunisia; Uzbekistan	Austria; Canada; Czech Republic; France; Germany; Hungary; India; Indonesia; Spain; Thailand; Turkey; United Arab Emirates; United States
3rd quartile	Antigua and Barbuda; Belize; Cape Verde; Central African Republic; Djibouti; Dominica; Fiji; Grenada; Guyana; Mali; São Tomé and Principe; Vanuatu	Barbados; Botswana; Cameroon; Lao PDR; Macedonia, FYR; Myanmar; Uganda; Zimbabwe	Algeria; Azerbaijan; Bolivia; Denmark; Gabon; Guatemala; Iceland; Jamaica; Latvia; Morocco; Oman; Pakistan; Syrian Arab Republic; Trinidad and Tobago	Argentina; Finland; Iran, Islamic Rep.; Italy; Japan; Korea, Rep.; South Africa; Sweden
4th quartile	Afghanistan; Benin; Bhutan; Burkina Faso; Burundi; Comoros; Côte d'Ivoire; Eritrea; Gambia; Guinea-Bissau; Haiti; Kiribati; Lesotho; Malawi; Mauritania; Nepal; Rwanda; Samoa; Sierra Leone; Suriname; Swaziland; Togo; Tonga	Angola; Bangladesh; Bosnia and Herzegovina; El Salvador; Ethiopia; Kenya; Papua New Guinea; Paraguay; Senegal; Tajikistan; Yemen, Rep.	Bahrain; Ecuador; Greece; Kuwait; Lithuania; New Zealand; Philippines; Slovak Republic; Slovenia; Sri Lanka	Venezuela, RB

Vertical axis: FDI Attraction Index (High to Low, 1st quartile to 4th quartile)
Horizontal axis: FDI Potential Index (Low to High, 4th quartile to 1st quartile)

■ Above expectations   ■ In line with expectations   ▨ Below expectations

Source: UNCTAD World Investment Report 2012, http://unctad.org/en/Pages/DIAE/World%20Investment%20Report/Annex-Tables.aspx.

populous economies such as China, India, and Indonesia, which have successfully raised per capita FDI inflows. Bangladesh's per capita FDI stock is one of the lowest among comparators (see UNCTAD 2013 for more details).

The government and the private sector link low FDI inflows to the poor infrastructure and business environment. In the World Bank 2015 Doing Business database, Bangladesh ranks 173 of 189 economies in the Ease of Doing Business Index. Bangladesh ranks poorly under Getting Electricity, Enforcing Contracts, and Registering Property (185, 182, and 175, respectively). According to the World Bank's Investment Climate Assessment for Bangladesh, the top five investment climate constraints for metropolitan firms concerned electricity, political instability, governance, access to land, and access to finance. For nonmetropolitan firms, the top constraints were low demand for goods and services, rising inflation pressures, seasonal inaccessibility of roads, and the cost of finance. The private productive sector reports significant losses as a result of power scarcity. The issue is particularly detrimental to small and medium enterprises, which cannot afford generators. Manufacturing firms blame their low capacity utilization primarily on scarce electrical power.

Estimates put the cost of electricity shortages to Bangladesh at up to two percentage points of annual GDP. Private power producers are more efficient and cost-effective than state provision, which suffers from problems in governance, accountability, financial management, bad debt and collection rates, and inadequate physical capacity. Several recent initiatives have been promising: commercial losses have been reduced somewhat, financial strengthening and restructuring of power utilities is underway, and power supply reliability has improved, with some decrease in load shedding. FDI can actually play a critical role in physical infrastructure, including electricity, roads, and ports, as discussed in UNCTAD (2013). Bangladesh aims to engage with private investors, both nationals and foreigners, to help in its quest to develop its infrastructure. The current Five-Year Plan looks to private investment to substantially augment traditional public investment by utilizing the new public-private partnership policy adopted in 2010.[6]

Measures taken by the government to address this constraint have focused on term solutions, which raise costs and subsidies and add to fiscal vulnerabilities. The government has added 3,594 megawatts of capacity in the past four years (Ministry of Finance 2013). However, about 2,400 megawatts of this increase comes from government contracts with rental and quick rental plants (for terms of three to five years) that run on expensive (and government-subsidized) liquid fuel. Although this strategy has helped to reduce power shortages during summer and the irrigation season in the past three years, it has further increased the power sector's dependence on the budget for large subsidy payments to these private generators. Thus, the annual budgetary transfer to the power sector was around US$85 million per year during fiscal year (FY) 2007 to FY2009, US$140 million in FY2010, US$600 million in FY2011, and US$815 million in FY2012, the increase coinciding with the introduction of liquid fuel power plants. The annual budgetary transfer was expected to go down to about US$600 million in FY2013 because of tariff adjustments in phases since February 2011, but was not expected to reduce further unless short-term rental contracts were terminated and replaced by low-cost base load power plants. Several large, gas-fired or dual fuel power plants were awarded to the private sector including one large coal-fired plant (1,320 megawatts) based on imported coal, but they are yet to reach financial closure. It is critical for Bangladesh to implement sustainable solutions that are able to provide unsubsidized power at competitive prices.

Serviced land is another constraint for new or expanding entrepreneurs, including foreign investors. The cost, availability, and difficulty in procuring serviced land are cited as top issues. Land administration is divided between the Ministry of Law and the Ministry of Land, with little or no coordination. Municipal development bodies, such as the Rajdhani Unnayan Kartripakkha (RAJUK, Capital Development Authority), also play an important role. Procedures are manual, complex, and mired in red tape and delays. Property registration and titling procedures take as long as 425 days in Dhaka. Registration fees and stamp duties are some of the highest in the region. Land and building financing is limited for longer term commercial mortgages. Reforms of land registration and titling and of rules of usage have started; they include amendment of the Land Registration Act and undertaking the Demra (administrative subdivision in the capital Dhaka) pilot on land records computerization, which is intended for replication nationally. The digitization of 441,506 *khatians* and 4,089 *mouja* map sheets has been completed, covering 191 *moujas* under the Dhaka Metropolitan City Survey. It is expected that digitization of existing *mouja* maps and *khatians* in 55 districts will be completed by June 2014. The report on digital land zoning maps of 152 *upazilas* in 21 districts has been prepared to secure planned and effective use of land. The digital land zoning work in 40 other districts is progressing.[7] Promotion of private sector growth and the exigencies of food security are strong reasons for development of industrial and special economic zones. These zones will help balance and fulfill the land needs of industry and agriculture.

The government enacted the Economic Zones Act in August 2010, which aims to improve, among other things, the availability of serviced land for business enterprises.[8] Most important, the Act established an economic zones regime that is more flexible than the EPZ regime. The new regime allows the private sector to develop zones under a public-private partnership or 100 percent private model, with the eventual goal to bring all zones in the country under a single, streamlined organization. In the past, foreign companies setting up businesses inside the zones have been allowed to lease the land they use. Under the new regime, it will be possible for a foreign company to buy the land in a 100 percent private economic zone. In the new economic zones, leasing rates and utility prices will be established by the zone operators. This new, streamlined, and more comprehensible regime aims to be private sector–driven and investor friendly. It will reflect the best practices and learning from other zone regimes worldwide and will allow for investors to sell in the local market. Each new zone will be permitted to have

Strengthening Competitiveness in Bangladesh—Thematic Assessment
http://dx.doi.org/10.1596/978-1-4648-0898-2

three areas: an export processing area, a domestic processing area, and a non-processing area, improving the links between offshore and onshore companies.

With proper implementation of the new regime, economic zones could perform better in terms of job creation and attracting FDI. In FY2011, the eight EPZs created employment for more than 330,000 people, contributed to 28 percent of total exports, and attracted less than 28 percent of total FDI (box 8.2).[9] In addition, most EPZs (except for Uttara and Mongla, where location presents challenges for investors) are completely or nearly sold out. In comparator countries in the region, such as the Philippines, economic zones produced 85 percent of total exports and 65 percent of total FDI. With 103.3 million working-age people, Bangladesh has significant resources to improve zone performance.

Outside the economic zones, land-related information is scarce. Theoretically, foreign investors may obtain information on land availability from the Bangladesh Board of Investment (BOI), as well as from the land registry and cadastre. However, these two sources are not linked or coordinated to share data, although

---

Box 8.2 Benefits Offered to Foreign Investors in the Economic Zones

In addition to faster business start-up and streamlined procedures through a one-stop shop, the Government of Bangladesh is offering other incentives to attract foreign investors to economic zones, including the following:

- Customs duty advantages, including duty-free import of construction materials; duty-free import of machines, office equipment, spare parts, and so forth; and duty-free import and export of raw materials and finished goods. Customs clearance is offered at the factory site. Zone developers and operators will have the same advantages as companies located inside zones.
- Fiscal and financial incentives, including facilitating profit repatriation; allowing foreign investors to keep export proceeds in foreign currency accounts; setting up banking and offshore banking units in the zones; full repatriation of capital and dividends; relief from double taxation; exemption from dividend tax; accelerated depreciation on machinery or plant; allowing for the remittance of royalty, technical, and consultancy fees; and permitting nonresidents to open Non-Resident Foreign Currency Deposit accounts.
- Generalized System of Preferences facility (in export destinations in the European Union).
- Nonfinancial incentives, including 100 percent foreign ownership, most-favored-nation status, no ceiling on foreign and local investment, work permits issued directly by the Bangladesh Export Processing Zones Authority, and according residence to foreign workers.
- Investment guarantees, including operable Overseas Private Investment Corporation and Multilateral Investment Guarantee Agency schemes, and the Foreign Private Investment (Promotion and Protection) Act of 1980, which secures all foreign investment in Bangladesh.[a]

Note: These benefits are what the policy promises. Actual performance or time taken may vary from case to case (for example, time taken to repatriate profits).
a. For a complete list of incentives, see http://www.epzbangladesh.org.bd/bepza.php?id=IncentivesFac.

---

they are located in the same agency. In addition, the national land registry does not offer an inventory of public and private land plots available for greenfield FDI projects; nor does it centralize land registration data for the entire country and all city-, municipal-, or state-level registries. There is no land information system or geographic information system in Bangladesh. The procedures for leasing industrial land as well as the related transaction costs are the same for foreign- and domestically owned companies, as long as both are incorporated in Bangladesh. Before leasing public land in Dhaka, foreign companies may require approval from the BOI and Registrar of Joint Stock Companies (RJSC). Moreover, there are no restrictions on the amount of land that may be leased, and the maximum duration of lease of privately owned land is 99 years. Lease contracts offer the lessee the right to subdivide, sublease, or mortgage the leased land, or even use it as collateral. In sum, although lease rights in Bangladesh are strong, the scarcity of land continues to be a significant investment constraint.

Corruption is also a persistent problem and is frequently cited as a major constraint by investors (WEF 2012). It appears to be pervasive at all levels of government, resulting in increased costs and risks to investment. Bangladesh ranks 144 of 176 countries on the 2012 Corruption Perceptions Index,[10] with a score of 2.7, the lowest in the group of comparators. In addition, 85 percent of firms reported making informal payments to public officials, again the poorest record among the group of comparator countries.

Although Bangladesh's manufacturing labor force is competitive and has been growing fast, it reveals a low level of productivity. Despite light labor regulations, skill shortages and mismatches impair the efficiency of the labor market. Improving labor skills requires the strengthening of higher education and short-term vocational training measures. One promising initiative is the fully self-financed Institute of Fashion and Technology, established by the Bangladesh Garments Manufacturers and Exporters Association (BGMEA) to meet the training requirements of its industry. Furthermore, the government has supported a new initiative for building a National Vocational Skill Center. Weak innovation and low investment in technology constrain productivity enhancements in rural and urban areas. Innovation can be spurred by increasing domestic and foreign competition, as firms strive for better performance and market share. Interaction with foreign firms promotes technology and other spillovers.

A shortage of skilled workers is one of the often-cited constraints to industrialization and export growth in Bangladesh. The low level of literacy and years of schooling of the labor force make skill acquisition more difficult. About 37.6 percent of the population of the country remains illiterate and the years of schooling among the labor force averaged 4.8 years in 2010. As compared with many other Asian countries, Bangladesh has a low level of literacy. Moreover, the education level of workers is low compared with competing countries in the garments sector. Less schooling complicates the process of learning and skill acquisition.[11] (see the World Bank's 2013 education sector review, including the skills constraint.) Improvement in the literacy rate has largely contributed to Vietnam's success in the past decade. The number of people ages 15–24 years who did not complete primary school dropped from 25 percent in 1998 to 4 percent in 2010. By 2011, the literacy rate in Vietnam was about 93 percent, compared with 56 percent in Bangladesh.

Having easy access to foreign expertise can help compensate for low productivity and skill gaps, and can facilitate knowledge transfers and on-the-job professional and management training. There is an inherent connection between expediting foreigners' work permits and attracting more FDI. The issue of work permits for foreign skilled employees is specifically relevant to foreign companies that wish to bring in domestic directors, managers, and specialist staff to set up and operate foreign affiliates. According to the Bangladesh Export Processing Zones Authority (BEPZA), the number of foreign workers in EPZs grew about 8 percent per year between 2005 and 2011, reaching 1,575 in March 2011. Since garments account for about 90 percent of total exports from EPZs, it can be assumed that the sector accounts for the largest share of foreign workers. The BGMEA estimates that the garments sector as a whole employs about 17,000 foreign workers.[12] Anecdotal evidence confirms that there is indeed a growing number of supervisory and management workers from abroad, including from India, Korea, Pakistan, Sri Lanka, and Taiwan, China.

However, the process of obtaining a temporary work permit (TWP) for foreign professionals is relatively long in Bangladesh, officially taking seven to nine weeks (it often takes longer in practice), including obtaining an E-category visa.[13] No fast-track procedure is available. In most other South Asian economies, the average permit processing time is six weeks. One of the fastest approval processes is in Afghanistan, where a permit can be obtained within a week. Bangladesh only issues work permits for skilled foreigners; it does not allow permits for unskilled, non-Bangladeshi workers. The maximum duration of the initial TWP is two years, or up to five years with extensions. By contrast, some other South Asian economies allow unrestricted extensions of work permits.

Moreover, Bangladesh imposes quotas on skilled foreigners for domestic and foreign companies. The ratio of foreign to local employees in an industrial enterprise cannot exceed 1:20 at any time during regular production. The foreign-to-local ratio for employees in a commercial enterprise is 1:5. Other South Asian countries generally do not impose quotas on hiring skilled foreigners. However, India has two exceptions to the no-quota rule. The first exception applies to projects or contracts granted by Indian missions: in these cases, a maximum of 1 percent of the total persons employed can be foreign, highly skilled professionals, up to a maximum of 20 workers per project. The second exception applies to projects in the power and steel sector: a maximum of 1 percent of the total persons employed can be foreign, highly skilled professionals, with a maximum of 40 workers. If additional foreigners are required, clearance from the Indian government is needed. In Bangladesh, as in most other South Asian countries, there is no portability of TWPs. The TWP is linked to a single employer, not to a specific job category, industry, or geographic area. Skilled foreigners who want to change employers must reapply for a new work permit.

These constraints are not enough to explain why FDI has contributed so little to the Bangladeshi economy. Other low-income economies with smaller domestic markets and greater geographic isolation face similar constraints, but still have had better FDI inflows over the past decade. For example, Madagascar and Mozambique rank poorly on Transparency International's Corruption Perception Index[14] and the World Bank's Doing Business indicator for Getting Electricity,[15] but they overperform on UNCTAD's FDI Attraction indicator (UNCTAD 2012). Some emerging economies, such as Brazil and Indonesia, have similar overall Ease of Doing Business rankings as Bangladesh (130 and 128, respectively). Bangladesh is actually not taking advantage of its comparative advantages for foreign investors: an abundance of competitive labor, a large domestic market, and geographic proximity to the booming Asian market. It seems that there may be other factors at play that could help explain the poor FDI inflows into Bangladesh. For example, the Korean Export Processing Zone is still not fully operational 17 years after initiation because of bureaucratic impediments. Complexity in transferring land ownership to the investors and delay in getting clearance from the Department of Environment to develop the industrial plot have hampered its progress. More generally, an important question to elucidate is whether Bangladesh is actually open to FDI.

Is Bangladesh Really Open to FDI?

Bangladesh is often referred to as one of the most open economies in the region by international benchmarks. The World Bank's 2012 IAB Initiative states that of the 32 sectors for which data were collected, only the forestry sector exhibits ownership restriction (table 8.2). In the South Asia region, India and Sri Lanka impose the most restrictions on foreign ownership (figure 8.4). Most countries impose foreign equity restrictions in the media industries, such as television broadcasting and newspaper publishing. Sectors with the least foreign ownership restrictions include oil and gas, manufacturing (such as light manufacturing, food processing, and manufacturing of basic chemicals), electricity generation from renewable sources, wireless telecommunications, higher education, courier services, accommodation, waste management, and agriculture. Electricity transmission and distribution, freight rail transportation, and, to a lesser extent, water distribution are sectors that tend to be dominated by state-owned monopolies in the region. Other international publications and guides similarly convey a message of a welcoming stance toward FDI in Bangladesh (UNCTAD 2013).

However, analysis of the main elements of the investment framework points to a situation that is more complex. The investment framework is not as unequivocally open as general policy statements suggest. UNCTAD (2013) concludes that investors, foreign and national, operate in a challenging environment. They are confronted with major regulatory issues ranging from entry and establishment, taxation, access to skills and land, foreign exchange regulations, corruption, and public governance. Challenges in these specific areas are compounded

Strengthening Competitiveness in Bangladesh—Thematic Assessment
http://dx.doi.org/10.1596/978-1-4648-0898-2

Table 8.2 Maximum Shares of Foreign Equity Ownership Allowed in Various Sectors in South Asian Economies, 2012

percent

Sector subgroup	Afghanistan	Bangladesh	India	Indonesia	Nepal	Pakistan	Sri Lanka	Vietnam
Agriculture	100	100	100	95	100	100	100	100
Forestry	100	0	0	100	100	100	40	51
Mining	100	100	100	100	100	100	40	100
Oil and gas	100	100	100	95	100	100	100	100
Food processing	100	100	100	95	100	100	100	100
Manufacturing of basic chemicals	100	100	100	100	0	100	100	100
Light manufacturing	100	100	100	100	100	100	100	100
Electric power generation—biomass	100	100	100	95	100	100	49	100
Electric power generation—solar	100	100	100	100	100	100	49	100
Electric power generation—wind	100	100	100	100	100	100	49	100
Electric power transmission	49	100	100	95	0	100	0	0
Electric power distribution	49	100	100	95	0	100	49	0
Waste management and recycling	100	100	100	100	100	100	100	100
Water distribution	100	100	100	100	0	100	100	100
Freight rail transport	49	100	0	49	100	100	40	49
Freight transport by road	100	100	100	49	0	100	40	51
Internal waterways freight transport	100	100	100	49	100	100	40	49
International passenger air transport	100	100	49	49	100	49	49	49
Port operation	100	100	100	49	100	100	40	100
Courier activities	100	100	100	49	0	100	100	51
Accommodation services	100	100	100	100	100	100	100	100
Newspaper publishing	0	100	26	0	100	25	40	0
Television broadcasting	0	100	49	0	100	49	40	0
Fixed line telecoms infrastructure	49	100	74	49	100	100	100	49
Fixed line telecoms services	100	100	74	49	100	100	100	65
Wireless/mobile telecoms infrastructure	100	100	100	65	100	100	100	49
Wireless/mobile telecoms services	100	100	74	65	100	100	100	65
Banking	100	100	74	99	100	49	100	100
Life insurance	100	100	26	80	100	100	100	100
Health insurance	100	100	26	80	100	100	100	100
Professional services[a]	100	100	100	100	51	100	100	100
Higher education	100	100	100	0	100	100	100	100

Source: World Bank Group, Investing Across Borders survey 2012, http://iab.worldbank.org/.

a. Accounting, bookkeeping, and auditing services; tax consultancy.

Figure 8.4 Foreign Equity Restrictions in Bangladesh and South Asia, 2012

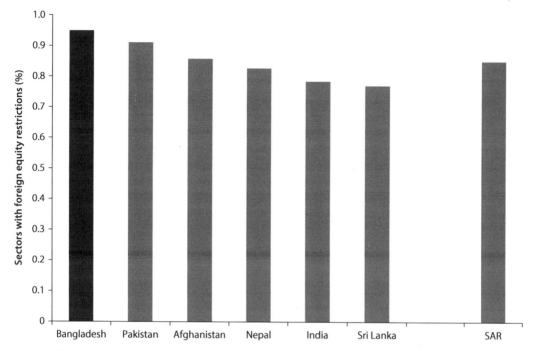

Source: World Bank Group, Investing Across Borders survey 2012, http://iab.worldbank.org/.
Note: The Investing Across Borders indicators measure statutory restrictions on foreign ownership of companies in 32 sectors. Industry coverage is not exhaustive, but the sectors covered capture most economic activity and account for a significant proportion of global gross domestic product and foreign direct investment flows. The index is a value from 0 to 1, with 1 = full foreign ownership allowed. SAR = South Asia region.

by a general level of complexity in the regulatory framework, a lack of clarity and transparency in regulations and procedures, and a complex institutional setup.

Moreover, non-equity barriers to FDI entry exist in multiple industries in Bangladesh. Several strategic sectors are dominated by state-owned enterprises operating as monopolies. Examples include transmission and distribution of electricity, freight rail transport, port operations, and fixed-line telecommunications infrastructure and services. Domestic companies have a considerable market share in the life and health insurance sectors, although these sectors do see modest foreign participation. While no foreign ownership restrictions appear to apply to the television broadcasting and newspaper publishing sectors, the data suggest that new entrants may experience difficulties in obtaining operating licenses.

FDI is managed by a complex set of laws and regulations under various authorities. They make up for the absence of a widely encompassing law on investment, entry, establishment, treatment, and protection of FDI.[16] The most important of these laws are the following:

- Foreign Private Investment Promotion and Protection Act (FPIPPA, 1980)
- Investment Board Act (1989)
- Bangladesh Export Processing Zones Authority Act (1980)

- Bangladesh Small and Cottage Industries Corporation Act (1957)
- Companies Act (1994)
- Private Export Processing Zones Act (1996)
- Acquisition and Requisition of Immovable Property Ordinance (1982)
- Economic Zones Act (2010).

Sector laws and regulations have an important bearing on the entry of FDI. For example, the scope and coverage of FPIPPA is limited, in contrast with many FDI-related laws in countries in the region and beyond. The entire act contains seven short substantive articles, covering mostly treatment, protection against expropriation, and repatriation of earnings and capital. FPIPPA remains vague and noncommittal when it comes to entry conditions and establishment procedures (UNCTAD 2013).

De facto entry into various sectors appears different from the scenario presented above in table 8.2. Discretionary and restrictive policies are found in Bangladesh's National Industrial Policy (1999, 2005, and 2010)—a source of FDI entry restrictions. The National Industrial Policy of 2010 establishes a list of 17 "controlled industries" in which the government sets maximum shares of foreign ownership and for which approval from the line ministry is required before registration with BOI, BEPZA, or the Bangladesh Small and Cottage Industries Corporation.[17] This list includes important sectors of the economy, such as banking and finance, insurance, power, natural gas and coal, large-scale infrastructure projects, telecommunications, and ports. New FDI in pharmaceuticals is not encouraged. The NIP prior to 2005 placed ready-made garments (RMGs) in the reserved list of exceptional industries where FDI was not encouraged. Although this provision on RMG has since disappeared, it may partly explain the low level of FDI in the sector, in spite of its economic significance and the importance of FDI flows in the industry in other LMICs (UNCTAD 2013).

Local business associations often publicly (via press articles) lobby the government to discourage FDI in garments, given the capacity of local entrepreneurs to invest more if infrastructure constraints were alleviated. In telecommunications, mobile telephony is dominated by foreign investors, with multinational companies owning a majority stake in the five privately owned operators, with the sixth one under full government ownership. Yet, foreign ownership is banned in important segments of the telecommunications sector. Regulatory and licensing guidelines by the Bangladesh Telecommunication Regulatory Commission, for example, mandate full national ownership for companies offering international gateway services, interconnection exchange services, and international Internet gateway services (UNCTAD 2013).

Some activities are left in a vacuum as they cannot get BOI support and are subject to relatively dispersed entry conditions under sector regulations. While foreign investment approval needs to be obtained from BOI to benefit from investment incentives such as capital repatriation and tax holidays, the mandate of BOI is restricted to industrial undertakings. These are defined to encompass the production and processing of goods as well as the provision of certain services as defined by the government. The services considered as "industries" are enumerated in NIP 2010 and include information technology–based activities, business process outsourcing, construction, tourism, telecommunications, transport, human resource development, and power generation. Several services, such as financial services, health, and education, are not covered. BOI approval is not required when opening a branch or liaison representative office of a foreign company that has applied to BOI for approval and registration.[18] Most countries in South Asia require some form of foreign investment approval or notification. In Sri Lanka and Nepal, obtaining it takes foreign companies 6 and 53 days, respectively, while India merely requires a declaration (table 8.3).

It takes about 45 days and 10 procedures to set up a foreign-owned subsidiary engaged in foreign trade in Bangladesh (figure 8.5). This is on par with the South Asia region. In addition to the procedures required of domestic companies, an authentication of the parent company's documentation abroad is required to file as a shareholder with the RJSC prior to incorporation. The paid-up capital of the company must be remitted in a local bank, and an encashment letter has to be issued. Moreover, the company is required to apply to the Chief Controller of Exports and Imports to obtain an Export Registration Certificate and Import Registration Certificate and to engage in international trade.

Procedures to set up a project inside an economic zone are faster. Projects in EPZs are regulated and registered separately by BEPZA. The focus of EPZs is

Table 8.3 Foreign Investment Approval or Notification Requirements in South Asia

Country	Mandatory foreign investment approval or declaration details	Time (days), when required
Afghanistan	Investments of more than US$3,000,000 are required to be approved by the High Commission on Investment.	3
Bangladesh	Foreign investment approval is only required to benefit from investment incentives or to establish a wholly foreign-owned branch/liaison office.	n.a.
India	Investment approvals are required for certain sectors. For manufacturing, FDI is permissible under the automatic route without prior approval from the government.	n.a.
Nepal	Foreign investors desiring to establish a wholly foreign-owned enterprise are required to apply for a foreign investment approval with the Department of Industry on a prescribed application form.	53
Pakistan	A foreign investment approval is not required unless for the establishment of a wholly foreign-owned branch/liaison office, which requires the Board of Investment's approval.	n.a.
Sri Lanka	Foreign investment approval should be obtained from the Sri Lankan Board of Investment, which can take anywhere between 3 and 10 business days.	6

Source: World Bank Group, Investing Across Borders database 2012, http://iab.worldbank.org/.
Note: FDI = foreign direct investment; n.a. = not applicable.

Figure 8.5 Setting Up a Foreign-Owned Subsidiary in Bangladesh and Comparators

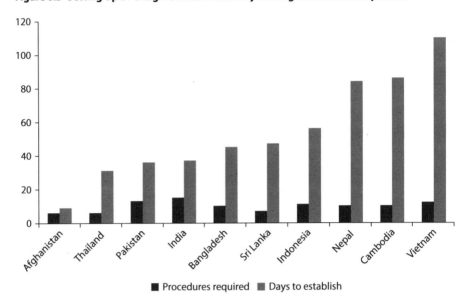

Procedures required ▪ Days to establish

Source: Investing across Borders database, http://iab.worldbank.org/.

nevertheless clearly on industrial export-oriented activities, as 100 percent of output (for a few, select industries, this percentage is somewhat lower) must be exported for a business to be eligible to invest in a zone. The establishment process inside EPZs requires more procedures than setting up a similar business outside the zones; however, it is faster. Once a company is established inside the zone, there is a one-year time limit within which it has to become fully operational.

Although the existing EPZs have been moderately successful in attracting FDI and creating jobs, the new economic zones regime has been designed to be a transformational tool in attracting FDI to Bangladesh. The Economic Zones Act, 2010, laid a foundation for the expansion of economic zones with more flexible rules, especially for allowing the private sector to develop zones and enabling zone companies to sell in the local market. Following the Filipino model, where economic zones currently account for 65 percent of all FDI, Bangladesh is striving to create 15 million jobs and increase its annual growth to 10 percent over the next 10 years. With technical support from the World Bank, the Government of Bangladesh has established a Jobs and Competitiveness Task Force with the mandate of converting 40,000 acres of land to economic zones to enable goals for job creation and growth. The Task Force is headed by the Prime Minister's Office and includes representatives from the Bangladesh Bank, Bangladesh Economic Zones Authority, BOI, and the Public-Private Partnership Office.

Uneven Playing Field for Multinational Firms

Foreign investors, particularly multinational firms from advanced economies, operate on an uneven playing field. The prevalence of corruption, discretionary government decisions instead of clear regulations and procedures, and weak enforcement of standards in the domestic market affect foreign investors asymmetrically. In addition, large domestic firms that are more likely to compete with foreign firms usually have their networks and connections that help them go through the bureaucratic maze and lobby for generous treatment.

Multinational firms often have to abide by strict anticorruption laws implemented in their home countries, as well as their own codes of conduct. For example, in 1998 the U.S. Congress and 33 other OECD countries took action against the bribery of foreign officials, essentially government officials, in an attempt to reduce corruption and money laundering through the global financial system. Corrupt political officials and those in high army offices were targeted with a view to preventing government officials from exploiting their positions to gain unfair commercial advantage. The U.S. Foreign Corrupt Practices Act continues to have a profound impact on the way U.S. firms undertake business at home and abroad. Any breach of the Foreign Corrupt Practices Act is taken as a serious offence. The penalties include being barred from tendering for U.S. government contracts, large fines, and, in some cases, criminal convictions for prosecuted company executives. Some of these convictions have resulted in jail time.[19]

Poor enforcement of standards is another a major concern for foreign investors. Sector analyses conducted in the context of this study and interviews with the private sector signal a recurrent problem with the limited capacity to enforce standards in Bangladesh. According to a number of foreign firms, this often provides an advantage to domestically owned firms that are willing to cut some corners in product quality, content, or weight. Even small infringements—say, of the product being 5 percent underweight—can translate to major profit differentials compared with foreign firms that are generally less likely to infringe rules and standards. In addition to posing potential hazards to the consumer, lack of enforcement of standards can reduce incentives for technology transfers and quality upgrading. The pharmaceutical industry is a case in point. Interviews with the private sector, national and multinational, indicate that the whole industry, including companies maintaining standards, suffers from the perception of noncompliance. Bangladesh's regulatory body, the Directorate General of Drug Administration, is severely understaffed. The Directorate General of Drug Administration lacks World Health Organization prequalification, and this favors domestic players that do not comply 100 percent with the quality standards. The lack of proper drug testing labs and the nonavailability of bio-equivalence study facilities increase the costs of manufacturing in and exporting from Bangladesh.

In the shipbuilding industry, smaller domestic vessels are often built without application of international (class) or national (Bangladesh's Domestic Vessel

Strengthening Competitiveness in Bangladesh—Thematic Assessment
http://dx.doi.org/10.1596/978-1-4648-0898-2

Code) standards.[20] This happens for several reasons. International classification is expensive and legally not required for inland waterway and coastal vessels. Furthermore, most yards do not have the skill to produce under class standards. These vessels do have to adhere to local standards, which are enacted and enforced by the government. However, the level of these technical rules and standards is relatively low (see Kathuria and Malouche 2016, chapter 1, on shipbuilding) and, in many cases, they are not enforced. According to government officials, only three surveyors were taking care of design approvals and supervision tasks for the entire domestic fleet in Bangladesh as of mid-2012. As a result, domestic nonclassed vessels are produced at lower cost and generally at lower quality levels. A number of accidents have led to large casualties in Bangladesh.

Similarly, multinationals are increasingly under intense scrutiny from their governments and consumers on labor, safety, and environmental standards. For example, the U.S. statutory authority for the Generalized System of Preferences program requires country beneficiaries to adhere to several criteria, including protection of specified labor rights and protection of intellectual property rights. European and American companies need to be careful; they usually choose to work with reputable suppliers that have a strong record of providing safe and healthy work environments and those who are meeting if not exceeding government standards throughout all aspects of their businesses.

However, the asymmetry in compliance between foreign and local firms is less of an issue since garments are sent to the export market, which generally demands such compliance. The unfortunate events of 2013 (most notably but not only the collapse of Rana Plaza that killed hundreds of workers) should serve to reduce this asymmetry further. As a result of these events, the government and major buyers in the European Union and the United States are moving quickly to adopt and enforce a much tougher set of compliance standards, dealing with labor issues as well as building and factory standards (see chapter 5, on standards, "Meeting the Quality Challenge: Technical Regulation, SPS Measures, and Quality Infrastructure").

Finally, FDI is not always welcomed by domestic firms, which is not unusual in a situation where large players are well entrenched in the market. But even garment firms, where the relevant market is exports, would prefer to direct FDI in the sector into certain segments. The BGMEA reportedly urged the Ministry of Commerce and BOI to impose restrictions on foreign investments in the RMG sector. Foreign investors from China, India, and elsewhere want to benefit from Bangladesh's zero-tariff duty with the European Union, agreed under Generalized System of Preferences rules that came into effect on January 1, 2011.[21] The association is concerned about increased FDI inflows into the sector that will hurt local factories through wage inflation, as foreign companies hire workers and pay them more, and the use of limited infrastructure, especially power and gas. According to Haque (2013), leadership in the Bangladesh Knitwear Manufacturers and Exporters Association reportedly complained that most Chinese entrepreneurs wanted to invest in the RMG sector, where local manufactures were strong enough. The Bangladesh Knitwear Manufacturers and Exporters Association apparently urged China's manufacturers to invest in high-end products like spinning, the woven textile segments, and the chemical industry, as Bangladesh spends billions of taka to import 70 percent of the required fabrics and 100 percent of raw materials.

International Payments and Investments

The ability to convert and transfer currency abroad is a crucial component of a country's investment and trade regime. Access to foreign exchange is necessary to pay for imports and being able to use export proceeds freely is an incentive for firms to engage in international business. The foreign exchange regime in a country is particularly important for foreign investors: the ability to freely convert local currency into foreign exchange and then to repatriate investment returns back home is a fundamental aspect of FDI.

Bangladesh maintains significant controls concerning its foreign exchange regime. The overarching law, the Foreign Exchange Regulation Act, was enacted in 1947. Although the law has been amended several times since then and comprehensive guidelines on its application and implementation have been introduced,[22] many underlying principles are out of date compared with the norms in most open economies today. For example, foreign exchange purchased by residents with local currency (taka) must generally be used for the initially stated purpose or be reconverted back into taka. In addition, although many cross-border business transactions are generally approved, the law states that "no person in or resident in Bangladesh shall … make any payment to or for the credit of any person resident outside Bangladesh"[23] unless exemption has been given, reflecting the restrictive underlying nature of the law. Modern day transactions such as Internet-based payments and receipts for purchases or services are allowed on a limited basis. Firms cannot invest abroad without an exhaustive approval process. A 2011 meeting of the International Chamber of Commerce Bangladesh called for significant reforms in Bangladesh's foreign exchange regulations. Business leaders identified capital controls preventing investment abroad by Bangladeshi entrepreneurs and restrictions on the convertibility of taka for business purposes as limiting beneficial trade and investment in the country (*Daily Star* 2011).

Although OECD countries generally have no controls at all on such flows and most LMICs do not require approvals, countries in South Asia tend to have relatively restrictive regimes for converting and transferring currency. Bangladesh's regime, however, appears to be on the upper end of the restrictive scale (see tables 8.4–8.6).

A generic problem is the scrutiny and approval process that is involved in most foreign exchange transactions, more so on the capital account. An official approval from BOI is required to bring a foreign loan into Bangladesh (table 8.4).[24] This involves a degree of discretion, and Bangladesh Bank is closely involved in the review of the foreign loan application. Approval is required from Bangladesh Bank to repatriate capital from a liquidated FDI project (except for companies that are listed on the stock exchange). Such approval requests must include audited financial statements and tax documentation. The amount of

Table 8.4 Controls and Restrictions on FDI-Related Capital Inflows and Outflows in South Asian Countries

Country	Inflows	Outflows	Description
Afghanistan	Open	Open	There are no legal restrictions on inward or outward FDI capital flows in Afghanistan, other than providing information for anti-money laundering purposes.
Bangladesh	Approval required	Approval required	Equity inflows may be made freely, but foreign loans require approval of the Board of Investment. Approval is also required for capital outflows from any company not listed on the stock exchange.
India	Restricted	Restricted	Equity inflows are subject to pricing guidelines for the issuance of shares. Foreign loans must be registered and must comply with term and rate requirements. Outflows of liquidated foreign investment require documentation; the sale of shares to an Indian resident must comply with securities pricing guidelines.
Nepal	Approval required	Approval required	Approval of the Department of Industries is required for equity and foreign loan inflows. Recommendation from the Department of Industries and approval from the central bank are required for FDI-related capital outflows.
Pakistan	Restricted	Restricted	Only notification is needed for equity inflows in manufacturing. Foreign loans must be documented and registered and comply with term requirements. Outflows require certification that the value is appropriate, after which notification to the central bank is needed.
Sri Lanka	Approval required	Restricted	Equity inflows require documentation and must be received via a particular type of account. Foreign loans require central bank approval. Outflows of liquidated foreign investments are allowed if made through the same account established for the inflow.

Source: World Bank Group, Converting and Transferring Currency survey 2012, http://iab.worldbank.org/.
Note: FDI = foreign direct investment.

foreign exchange approved to be purchased and transferred is calculated by Bangladesh Bank based on the net asset value of the company at the time of liquidation per the documentation provided.

Outward FDI from Bangladesh is especially restricted, being subject to close scrutiny. To date, only one local firm has been able to undertake outward FDI. This control limits Bangladeshi firms' ability to engage in international business and investment, and their flexibility to take unfettered decisions to enhance their growth and competitiveness.

The average time required in Bangladesh to make a dividend payment abroad is longer than in any other country in South Asia. Within South Asia, Nepal has an official approval requirement, estimated to take 15 days. In other countries, no approval or other procedures are required by law, although the internal processes of commercial banks to review the transfer request and any associated documents usually take a few days.

Although Bangladesh maintains fewer restrictions on current payments than on capital flows, many payments still have documentation requirements or are subject to quantitative limits (table 8.5). Interest and principal payments on foreign loans are automatically approved, as long as the initial loan was authorized by BOI. Similarly, dividend payments abroad may be made freely. Bangladesh Bank must be notified of each payment. Although these investment-related payments may be made freely by law, private sector respondents to the Investing Across Borders survey note that the notification requirement to Bangladesh Bank becomes an approval in practice, as authorized dealers seek the

Table 8.5 Restrictions on Foreign Exchange Payments Abroad in South Asian Countries

Country	Investment-related payments	Other payments	Description
Afghanistan	Open	Open	There are no legal restrictions on making interest payments, dividend payments, or other current payments abroad.
Bangladesh	Restricted	Restricted	Documentation of loan repayments and dividend payments is required to be submitted to the central bank, and such transfers must be consistently made through the same commercial bank. Documentation requirements and quantitative limits exist for other current payments.
India	Restricted	Restricted	Dividend payments require documentation and must be paid via a particular type of bank account. Interest payments may be paid without approval only if they comply with the initial loan terms. Documentation of import payments is necessary, and some quantitative limits exist for other current payments.
Nepal	Approval required	Approval required	Approval of the central bank is required for an initial dividend payment, for all loan payments, and for most other current payments unless the amount is less than some quantitative thresholds.
Pakistan	Restricted	Restricted	Documentation of dividend payments is needed, and must be made through the same authorized dealer. Loan repayments must comply exactly with the terms in the initial loan agreement. Documentation requirements or quantitative limits exist on other current payments.
Sri Lanka	Restricted	Documentation required	Dividend payments are allowed, if made through the same account established for the capital inflow. Loan repayments may be made as long as they comply exactly with the approved initial loan terms. Documentation is required to make any other current payments in foreign exchange.

Source: World Bank Group, Converting and Transferring Currency survey 2012, http://iab.worldbank.org/.

permission of Bangladesh Bank before converting and transferring foreign exchange abroad for such payments.

Bangladesh restricts residents' and firms' ability to hold bank accounts in foreign exchange. Certain types of foreign exchange accounts are permitted automatically, such as the Exporter's Retention Quota Accounts or a Resident Foreign Currency Account funded with foreign exchange brought in from visits abroad; but the latter type of account may not be credited with any foreign exchange earned through commercial activity. Opening foreign exchange accounts in Bangladesh for other purposes requires the approval of Bangladesh Bank, which is reported to take between 30 and 60 days. Foreign exchange bank accounts abroad are generally not allowed for firms, except under specific circumstances (such as temporarily to receive advance export payments). Bangladesh's restrictions on holding bank accounts in foreign currency are comparable to those in other South Asian countries, but stricter than those in other regions of the world.

Bangladesh restricts exporting firms' use of the foreign exchange they earn from their exports. Firms must repatriate all export earnings back to Bangladesh. They may keep up to 50 percent of these proceeds in foreign exchange in a specific type of bank account (known as an exporter's retention quota account), but the remaining foreign exchange must be converted into taka. All such export transactions must be carried out via a commercial bank that is an authorized dealer in Bangladesh. In the six countries covered by the survey in South Asia, only Pakistan imposes similar restrictions (table 8.6).

The authorities were preparing a strategy paper to review the Foreign Exchange Regulation Act (a September 2013 benchmark) and, in particular, to lay out a road map toward exchange control liberalization, assisted by International Monetary Fund (IMF) technical assistance. The objective of this reform is to facilitate foreign direct and portfolio investment (IMF 2013).

Table 8.6 Restrictions on Export Proceeds in South Asian Countries

Country	Restriction	Description
Afghanistan	No restriction	No restrictions.
Bangladesh	Repatriate and surrender	Repatriate full value of exported goods. Surrender at least 50 percent of export proceeds.
India	Repatriate	Repatriate full value of exported goods within 12 months. Repatriated foreign exchange must be kept in a particular type of bank account.
Nepal	Repatriate	All export proceeds must be repatriated. No surrender is required.
Pakistan	Repatriate and surrender	All export proceeds must be repatriated within 6 months, and immediately converted into local currency.
Sri Lanka	Restricted	Export proceeds may be kept in foreign currency abroad, but may not be used to acquire foreign capital assets.

Source: World Bank Group, Converting and Transferring Currency survey 2012, http://iab.worldbank.org/.
Note: Repatriation requires firms to transfer export proceeds received abroad back to the home country. Surrender requires the firms to convert the repatriated foreign exchange into local currency.

Policy Recommendations

The need for FDI in Bangladesh's future growth, diversification, and transition to middle-income country status is beyond debate. Transfers of skills and technology are likely to take place through business links with domestic enterprises, leading to industrial cluster development. In addition, FDI could play a greater role in developing directly and indirectly by triggering domestic investment in the country's infrastructure to further attract FDI. UNCTAD's Bangladesh Investment Policy Review (2013) elaborates on attracting FDI in physical infrastructure, including electricity, roads, and ports, following a specific request from the Government of Bangladesh.

Bangladesh has the potential to attract significantly higher levels of FDI in spite of the challenges it faces, but it has much work to do to turn that potential into reality. It can position itself as a competitive center for labor-intensive manufacturing and attract efficiency-seeking FDI. Its attractions include abundant labor supply; a mastery of large-scale, labor-intensive manufacturing in garments and to some extent footwear; a favorable location between two large and dynamic economies, India and China; as well as wide understanding of the English language. Preferential access to key consumer markets in high-income countries makes it an attractive platform for export-seeking FDI. Its entrepreneurial private sector is another important asset that could be exploited further with a business-enabling regulatory framework in place. In addition, if Bangladesh is able to stay on its current growth path, its market size could increase quickly and attract a wave of market-seeking FDI. However, to make good this potential, it would have to address some critical constraints to FDI, including the availability of serviced land and the asymmetry between local and foreign firms, and adopt a more welcoming and more proactive stance toward FDI.

Some institutional and regulatory changes would be needed to spur the contribution of FDI to Bangladesh's economic growth and job creation. Entry conditions are subject to general FDI as well as sector regulations, which lead to discretionary administrative procedures. BOI plays a minimal role in the overall FDI process. A more transparent law on investment should be adopted by parliament. And the dispersed administration of public land makes it difficult for Bangladesh to adequately manage its holdings. Although it is vital for local authorities to be involved in land management, a higher degree of coordination should be achieved at the national level to allocate public land to its most productive and essential use. This could be achieved through a coordination institution or body and the establishment of a public land database that would list all plots available for development by location, size, facilities, and other characteristics (UNCTAD 2013).

Bangladesh should adopt a more proactive and welcoming stance toward potential foreign investors, with BOI playing a key role to overcome Bangladesh's ambiguous attitude toward FDI. The strategy for attracting FDI in any host economy is to overcome imperfections and asymmetries in the provision of information about production possibilities. Foreign investors should get more administrative support early on when desiring to invest in Bangladesh, thereby reducing the hurdles and uncertainty they may face in a new environment. In place of cumbersome, highly discretionary screening of investment proposals, one-stop-shop investment promotion agencies ideally would be empowered to make the approval of investment projects rapid, automatic, and transparent. To foster interminisiterial coordination, BOI could house staff from the relevant ministries whose duties are to troubleshoot investor-ministry relations, with FDI approvals automatic if the ministry does not lodge a substantive objection within a (short) specified time period. In practice, the objective must be a genuine one-stop shop, not a one-more-stop shop (Moran 2006).

The asymmetry faced by foreign firms vis-à-vis local firms in Bangladesh is a more serious issue than might appear at first sight. This is a kind of "regulatory arbitrage" that local firms enjoy, and it will be an obstacle to attracting sustained, quality FDI. Addressing this will require an emphasis on non-discretion and a fair and thorough enforcement of standards, for example, such that foreign firms that enforce strict compliance and standards are not penalized.

BOI should arrange more high-level investment promotion missions to large, emerging economies, especially in Asia, including to China, India, and Japan. These missions should be preceded by preparatory missions to identify short-term FDI opportunities and requirements.[25] The cost of not seeking out investors may be high, as other competing countries, such as Cambodia and Vietnam, are aggressively pursuing Chinese and other Asian FDI. BOI missions could target the promotion of sectors in which FDI may play a more critical role, such as shipbuilding and bicycles (see Kathuria and Malouche 2016, chapters 1 and 2).

Foreign exchange transactions and FDI need a bolder approach on the part of Bangladesh Bank. Outward FDI is an essential part of the modern firm's kit and should be made easier. Making and receiving Internet-based payments should be allowed and current account transactions, such as dividends, interest payments, and so forth, could be speeded up with minimal hindrances. In general, the Foreign Exchange Regulations Act 1947 needs to be overhauled in keeping with the spirit of a modern economy. The government was preparing a strategy paper to review the Foreign Exchange Regulation Act (a September 2013 benchmark) and, in particular, to lay out a road map toward exchange control liberalization, assisted by IMF technical assistance. The objective of this reform is to facilitate foreign direct and portfolio investment (IMF 2013).

Notes

1. See http://iab.worldbank.org/.

2. A more detailed analysis of FDI performance in Bangladesh can be found in UNCTAD (2013).

3. FDI in the ready-made garments sector was restricted to EPZs until 2005 on the argument that Multi-Fiber Arrangement quotas were meant for Bangladeshi exporters.

Although that ban was lifted, in practice, the local RMG entrepreneurs' associations, the Bangladesh Garment Manufacturers and Exporters Association and the Bangladesh Knitwear Manufacturers and Exporters Association, which have considerable authority over export certification and registration procedures, create barriers to entry that virtually preclude FDI in the domestic RMG sector.

4. It is worth noting that half the growth in non-OECD FDI over this period is accounted for by China alone.

5. UNCTAD evaluates 177 countries in terms of their potential for FDI attraction. It takes into account market attractiveness (size, spending power, and growth potential), availability of low-cost labor and skills (unit labor cost, size of manufacturing sector), presence of natural resources, and presence of FDI-enabling infrastructure (UNCTAD 2012).

6. Infrastructure already benefits from strong technical and financial support from the multilateral banks and bilateral donors.

7. See Budget Speech 2013–14, http://www.mof.gov.bd/en/budget/13_14/budget _speech/speech_en.pdf.

8. This new act amends (a) the Bangladesh Export Processing Zones Authority (BEPZA) Act of 1980, which was promulgated by the government to attract investment in the government-owned and operated EPZs, and (b) the Private Export Processing Zones Authority Act of 1996, which allows for the separate establishment of *private* EPZs and established a separate authority—the Private EPZ Cell— to administer this separate regime. (The one private EPZ, Korean EPZ, faces stiff bureaucratic resistance that prevents it from really taking off.) To date, there are eight EPZs in Bangladesh (in Adamjee, Chittagong, Comilla, Dhaka, Ishwardi, Karnaphuli, Mongla, and Uttara), the one in Chittagong EPZ being the first zone established by BEPZA in 1983. Sixty percent of factories in these EPZs are fully foreign owned.

9. BEPZA's website (http://www.epzbangladesh.org.bd) reports a total investment level (domestic and foreign) of about US$313 million for FY2010/11, while the World Investment Report reports total FDI of US$1.13 billion for 2011. Thus, the total investment in EPZs was 28 percent of the total FDI in Bangladesh. BEPZA does not disaggregate the US$1.13 billion by domestic and foreign, but foreign investment is estimated as somewhat less than 28 percent of total investment.

10. The Corruption Perceptions Index ranks countries and territories based on how corrupt their public sector is perceived to be. http://www.transparency.org/research/cpi/.

11. An admittedly limited survey of 87 workers from 41 garment factories conducted in 2007 showed that a little over 50 percent of the workers had completed secondary education and less than 10 percent had gone beyond the tenth grade. About one-third of the workers had only primary education. The sample was drawn on the basis of proportional distribution of types of factories in the population (USAID 2007). See World Bank (2013) for more details.

12. See http://www.banglanews24.com/English/detailsnews.php?nssl=37953cab902d1f6 98bfb59b54d5e6369&nttl=2011040317348 (March 24, 2011).

13. The World Bank's Investing Across Borders Employing Skilled Expatriates survey measures the rules and practices for obtaining temporary work permits for foreign directors and specialist staff. It also assesses the ease of accessing information concerning work permits, the possibility for expediting procedures through an

official channel, restrictions concerning the composition of the Board of Directors of foreign companies, and limitations on spousal work permits. See http://iab .worldbank.org.

14. See http://www.transparency.org/research/cpi/.

15. See http://www.doingbusiness.org/data/exploretopics/getting-electricity.

16. As of July 2013, an investment policy has been drafted and circulated by the Government of Bangladesh, but not yet approved.

17. A short and standard list of "reserved industries" (weapons, nuclear power, security printing and mining, logging within reserved forests) is closed to any form of private investment for national security purposes.

18. Bangladesh is not party to the 1961 Hague Apostille Convention that facilitates the legalization requirements of foreign public documents between states that are party to the Convention. For companies, this is especially useful as it greatly facilitates the recognition of the parent companies' documents during the registration process in a new country. Currently, 103 states are party to the Hague Apostille Convention, including most OECD countries and countries in Europe and Central Asia. In South Asia, only India is a signatory, and the Indian government has yet to enact specific legislation in that regard.

19. Official statistics show that 400 American firms have collectively paid US$300 million in bribes and other questionable payments to foreign governments and political parties, including direct payments to the accounts of government officials in the mid-1970s. One of the organizations involved in such bribery was a major aerospace company. Executives at this company bribed foreign officials to favor their products not only in LMICs, but also in industrialized nations, including Italy, the Netherlands, and Japan. Scandals like these tested the public's confidence in the integrity of American businesses and, in 1977, the Foreign Corrupt Practices Act was signed into law. See www.fcpa.us.

20. Published in 2001 in accordance with Inland Shipping Ordinance, 1976.

21. "We want to keep the clothing sector reserved for the local entrepreneurs and we are lobbying for it," *Financial Express* quoted BGMEA vice president Siddiqur Rahman as saying. He claimed that FDI is unnecessary in the sector as it "is not capital-intensive." He also suggested that foreign investment should be toward the "backward linkage textiles industry to supply fabric to the woven and knitwear divisions." http://news.priyo.com/business/2011/06/18/local-investors-resent-fdi-flo-29095.html (June 18, 2011).

22. See http://www.bangladesh-bank.org/aboutus/regulationguideline/foreignexchange /fegv1cont.php.

23. Bangladesh Foreign Exchange Regulation Act, 5(1)(a), cited from http://www .bangladesh-bank.org/aboutus/regulationguideline/foreignexchange/fegv1cont.php on June 17, 2012.

24. The approval process from BOI to receive a foreign loan involves some degree of discretion. When the terms of the loan are considered, loans are more likely to be approved in business sectors being promoted by the government. The foreign exchange situation in Bangladesh is taken into account in the decision whether to grant the approval.

25. These missions will be supported by the Private Sector Development Support Project, financed by the World Bank (UNCTAD 2013).

References

Baldwin, R. 2012. "Trade and Industrialisation after Globalisation's 2nd Unbundling: How Building and Joining a Supply Chain Are Different and Why It Matters." NBER Working Paper 17716, National Bureau of Economic Research, Cambridge, MA.

Daily Star. 2011. "Call for Overhaul of Archaic Forex Law." March 6. http://www .thedailystar.net/news-detail-176550.

Farole, Thomas, and Deborah Winkler. 2014. *Harnessing FDI for Competitiveness: Local Spillovers and Global Value Chains in Sub-Saharan Africa.* Washington, DC: World Bank.

Gereffi, Gary, and Karina Fernandez-Stark. 2011. *Global Value Chain Analysis: A Primer.* Center on Globalization, Governance, and Competitiveness, Durham, NC: Duke University.

Haque, Moinul. 2013. "Businesses Not in Favour of FDI in Basic RMG Sector: Chinese FDI Encouraged in High-End Products." *New Age Online.* January 13. http://www .bd2day.net/english/newsdetail/detail/35/2345.

Hossain, Muhammad Amir. 2008. "Impact of Foreign Direct Investment on Bangladesh's Balance of Payments: Some Policy Implications." PN 0805, Bangladesh Bank, Dhaka, Bangladesh. https://www.bb.org.bd/pub/research/policynote/pn0805.pdf.

IMF (International Monetary Fund). 2013. "Bangladesh Second Review under the Three-Year Arrangement under the Extended Credit Facility and Request for Modification of Performance Criteria." http://www.imf.org/external/pubs/ft/scr/2013/cr13157.pdf.

Kafi, Md. Abdullahel, Mohammad Main Uddin, and M. Muzahidul Islam. 2007. "Foreign Direct Investment in Bangladesh: Problems and Prospects." *The Journal of Nepalese Business Studies* IV (December).

Kathuria, Sanjay, and Mariem Mezghenni Malouche, eds. 2016. *Attracting Investment in Bangladesh—Sectoral Analyses: A Diagnostic Trade Integration Study.* Directions in Development. Washington, DC: World Bank.

Milberg, W., and D. Winkler. 2013. *Outsourcing Economics: Global Value Chains in Capitalist Development.* New York: Cambridge University Press.

Ministry of Finance. 2013. *Bangladesh Economic Review.* Ministry of Finance, Government of Bangladesh. www.mof.gov.bd.

Moran, Theodore H. 2006. *Harnessing Foreign Direct Investment for Development: Policies for Developed and Developing Countries.* Washington, DC: Center for Global Development.

Nasrin, Shamima, Angathevar Baskaran, and Mammo Muchie. 2010. "Major Determinants and Hindrances of FDI Inflow in Bangladesh: Perceptions and Experiences of Foreign Investors and Policy Makers." GLOBELICS 8th International Conference. Kuala Lumpur, Malaysia, November 1–3, 2010.

OECD (Organisation for Economic Co-operation and Development). 2002. *Foreign Direct Investment for Development, Maximising Benefits, Minimising Costs, Review.* Paris: OECD.

Paus, E. A., and K. P. Gallagher. 2008. "Missing Links: Foreign Investment and Industrial Development in Costa Rica and Mexico." *Studies of Comparative International Development* 43: 53–80.

UNCTAD (United Nations Conference on Trade and Development). 2012. *World Investment Report: Towards a New Generation of Investment Policies.* Geneva, Switzerland: UNCTAD. http://unctad.org/en/PublicationsLibrary/wir2012_embargoed_en.pdf.

———. 2013. *UNCTAD 2013 Bangladesh Investment Policy Review.* Paris: UNCTAD.

USAID (United States Agency for International Development). 2007. "Gender and Trade Liberalization in Bangladesh: The Case of the Ready-Made Garments." Contract No. GEW-I-00-02-00018-00, Task Order No. 02, Washington, DC, USAID.

WEF (World Economic Forum). 2012. *The Global Competitiveness Report 2012–2013.* http://reports.weforum.org/global-competitiveness-report-2012-2013/#=.

World Bank. 2012. *Investing Across Borders.* Washington, DC: International Finance Corporation and World Bank.

———. 2013. *Seeding Fertile Ground: Education That Works for Bangladesh.* Bangladesh Education Sector Review Report 80613-BD. Washington, DC: World Bank. https://openknowledge.worldbank.org/bitstream/handle/10986/16768/806130ESW0BD0E00Box379859B00PUBLIC0.pdf.

———. 2014. *Doing Business 2014: Understanding Regulations for Small and Medium-Size Enterprises.* Washington, DC: World Bank.

———. 2015. *Doing Business 2015: Going beyond Efficiency.* Washington, DC: World Bank.

Environmental Benefits Statement

The World Bank Group is committed to reducing its environmental footprint. In support of this commitment, the Publishing and Knowledge Division leverages electronic publishing options and print-on-demand technology, which is located in regional hubs worldwide. Together, these initiatives enable print runs to be lowered and shipping distances decreased, resulting in reduced paper consumption, chemical use, greenhouse gas emissions, and waste.

The Publishing and Knowledge Division follows the recommended standards for paper use set by the Green Press Initiative. The majority of our books are printed on Forest Stewardship Council (FSC)–certified paper, with nearly all containing 50–100 percent recycled content. The recycled fiber in our book paper is either unbleached or bleached using totally chlorine-free (TCF), processed chlorine-free (PCF), or enhanced elemental chlorine-free (EECF) processes.

More information about the Bank's environmental philosophy can be found at http://www.worldbank.org/corporateresponsibility.